AF826802

Integrated Macro-Micro-Modelling Under Rational Expectations

Contributions to Economics

Christoph M. Schneider
Research and Development Management: From the Soviet Union to Russia
1994. ISBN 3-7908-0757-5

Lars Olof Persson/Ulf Wiberg
Microregional Fragmentation
1995. ISBN 3-7908-0855-5

Ernesto Felli/Furio C. Rosati/Giovanni Tria (Eds.)
The Service Sector: Productivity and Growth
1995. ISBN 3-7908-0875-X

Giovanni Galizzi/Luciano Venturini (Eds.)
Economics of Innovation: The Case of Food Industry
1996. ISBN 3-7908-0911-X

David T. Johnson
Poverty, Inequality and Social Welfare in Australia
1996. ISBN 3-7908-0942-X

Rongxing Guo
Border-Regional Economics
1996. ISBN 3-7908-0943-8

Oliver Fratzscher
The Political Economy of Trade Integration
1996. ISBN 3-7908-0945-4

Ulrich Landwehr
Industrial Mobility and Public Policy
1996. ISBN 3-7908-0949-7

Arnold Picot/Ekkehard Schlicht (Eds.)
Firms, Markets, and Contracts
1996. Corr. 2nd printing 1997
ISBN 3-7908-0947-0

Thorsten Wichmann
Agricultural Technical Progress and the Development of a Dual Economy
1997. ISBN 3-7908-0960-8

Ulrich Woitek
Business Cycles
1997. ISBN 3-7908-0997-7

Michael Carlberg
International Economic Growth
1997. ISBN 3-7908-0995-0

Massimo Filippini
Elements of the Swiss Market for Electricity
1997. ISBN 3-7908-0996-9

Frank Hoster/Heinz Welsch/Christoph Böhringer
CO_2 Abatement and Economic Structural Change in the European Internal Market
1997. ISBN 3-7908-1020-7

Christian M. Hafner
Nonlinear Time Series Analysis with Applications to Foreign Exchange Rate Volatility
1997. ISBN 3-7908-1041-X

Sardar M.N. Islam
Mathematical Economics of Multi-Level Optimisation
1998. ISBN 3-7908-1050-9

Sven-Morten Mentzel
Real Exchange Rate Movements
1998. ISBN 3-7908-1081-9

Lei Delsen/Eelke de Jong (Eds.)
The German and Dutch Economies
1998. ISBN 3-7908-1064-9

Mark Weder
Business Cycle Models with Indeterminacy
1998. ISBN 3-7908-1078-9

Tor Rødseth (Ed.)
Models for Multispecies Management
1998. ISBN 3-7908-1001-0

Michael Carlberg
Intertemporal Macroeconomics
1998. ISBN 3-7908-1096-7

continued on page 281

Michael Malakellis

Integrated Macro-Micro-Modelling Under Rational Expectations

With an Application to Tariff Reform in Australia

With 66 Figures
and 35 Tables

Physica-Verlag
A Springer-Verlag Company

Series Editors
Werner A. Müller
Martina Bihn

Author
Dr. Michael Malakellis
Tactical Global Management
Level 10 Waterfront Place
1 Eagle Street
Brisbane, QLD 4000
Australia

ISSN 1431-1933
ISBN 3-7908-1274-9 Physica-Verlag Heidelberg New York

Cataloging-in-Publication Data applied for
Die Deutsche Bibliothek – CIP-Einheitsaufnahme
Malakellis, Michael: Integrated macro-micro-modelling under rational expectations: with an application to tariff reform in Australia; with 35 tables / Michael Malakellis. – Heidelberg; New York: Physica-Verl., 2000
(Contributions to economics)
ISBN 3-7908-1274-9

Softcover-Design: Erich Kirchner, Heidelberg

SPIN 10755411 88/2202-5 4 3 2 1 0 – Printed on acid-free paper

This book is dedicated to Michelle and Sophie.

Preface

This monograph is concerned with the formulation and implementation of ORANI-INT, an intertemporal Computable General Equilibrium (CGE) model of the Australian economy. The aim is to bring together, in a balanced approach, theory and data for the purpose of developing a practical state-of-the-art tool for policy analysis. The modelling approach adopted is motivated by the recent trend in economy-wide modelling to combine the respective strengths of traditional CGE models and modern macroeconomic models. Traditional CGE models typically provide a dissagregate representation of the economy at a single point in time. Such models are useful for analysing issues involving the allocation of resources among the various agents identified at a particular point in time. Modern macroeconomic models, on the other hand, usually provide an aggregate representation of the economy over many points in time. Such models are useful for analysing issues involving the allocation of resources across time. A model that combines the strengths of static CGE models and modern macro-dynamic models is amenable to addressing a wide range of policy issues. To demonstrate this point ORANI-INT is used to analyse tariff reform.

The structure of this book is heavily influenced by my experiences at Monash University's Centre of Policy Studies/IMPACT Project (CoPS/IMPACT) as a student and as a Research Fellow. My interest in computable general equilibrium modelling was stimulated by a graduate course taught by Peter Dixon, Brian Parmenter, Alan Powell and Peter Wilcoxen at the University of Melbourne. From that course I emerged with three key ideas about economic modelling. First, formal economic models have much to contribute to government and business decision making. Second, CGE models have the potential to be powerful tools for applied economic analysis because they recognise that the economy is a system of interrelated agents. Third, decision-makers should ignore model projections that have not been thoroughly reconciled with the model's theoretical structure and database. A corollary of this idea is that a model's theoretical structure and database must be meticulously documented.

The above three ideas about economic modelling were reinforced by my experiences as a PhD student and Research Fellow at CoPS/IMPACT. I also quickly got the idea that the development and application of large-scale CGE models is very intensive in the use of a diverse range of highly skilled labour. At CoPS/IMPACT a team of about twenty people (about ten economists, three of whom are Professors, and several software developers, one of whom is a Professor of mathematics) is dedicated, directly or indirectly, to documenting, maintaining, enhancing and applying *MONASH*, a large-scale CGE model of the Australian economy. In writing this book I have been mindful of the fact that most applied economists do not have the luxury of working with a large team. Throughout the book I have tried to emphasise the advantages of drawing on the vast modelling infrastructure that is in the public domain and on using generic software that can be purchased at reasonable cost.

Although I have not formally divided the book up into parts, the chapters can be grouped under the headings: *theory*, *data*, *solution method* and *application*. ORANI-INT's theoretical structure is dealt with in chapters 1–3. The algorithm used to solve ORANI-INT is described in chapter 4. ORANI-INT's database is discussed in chapter 5. Finally, applications of ORANI-INT are presented in chapters 6 and 7.

To some readers the documentation of ORANI-INT's theoretical structure, database and solution algorithm will appear onerous. My aim is to provide the reader with all the information necessary to replicate the results presented in the book. Moreover, I have tried to back up the claim that the design principles underlying ORANI-INT and its solution algorithm are generic, and can be easily borrowed, by providing enough information for those wishing to do so. Where possible I have confined the finer details of the model to appendices.

Like any applied model ORANI-INT must be judged by the quality of its projections. Over one third of the book is devoted to analysing a range of simulations conducted with ORANI-INT. Some of these simulations are designed to highlight the key mechanisms in the model and some are designed to shed light on actual policy issues. In analysing the simulation results a large amount of effort is devoted to carefully reconciling ORANI-INT's projections with its theoretical structure and database. Whilst many readers will find the explanations of ORANI-INT's projections tedious, I am not aware of a better method for (a) providing evidence that the intended computations have been performed correctly and (b) bringing to the fore critical elements of the model's theoretical structure and database.

Whilst ORANI-INT and the applications reported in this book relate to the Australian economy, I anticipate that many of the topics covered will appeal to economists with little interest in the Australian economy or CGE models. For example, the solution algorithm described in chapter 4 is generic and should appeal to any modeller interested in solving models with rational expectations and/or explicit corner constraints. Similarly, the analysis of tariff reform presented in chapter 7 should appeal to any policy analyst interested in trade liberalisation issues.

Acknowledgements

This book is based on my doctoral dissertation read at the Centre of Policy Studies/IMPACT Project (CoPS/IMPACT) at Monash University. As a post-graduate student I was extremely fortunate for two related reasons. Firstly, I was given the opportunity of being part of the long tradition of graduate students that have, over the past three decades, studied computable general equilibrium modelling at the IMPACT Research Centre (previously at the University of Melbourne and now, combined with the Centre of Policy Studies, at Monash University). For this opportunity I thank Professor Alan Powell, who was the director of IMPACT when I commenced my candidature, and my then employer, the Industry Commission, which was also the principal sponsor of IMPACT. I am also grateful to Alan for his contribution as an associate supervisor. Alan's encouragement and assistance in subjecting my work to scrutiny via working papers, conferences and seminars has been invaluable. The second reason why I was especially fortunate is that Dr Mark Horridge, a former graduate student at IMPACT, was my supervisor. Mark's mastery of all aspects of computable general equilibrium modelling — theory, data and computing — made him an ideal teacher. He provided patient instruction on many aspects of the project and his generous inputs of time to discuss ideas and provide detailed comments on drafts of the dissertation were far greater than is expected of a supervisor. Mark was also very generous in sharing his ideas. He deserves most of the credit for the innovative features of the solution algorithm discussed in chapter 4. Mark came up with the idea of using homotopy parameters to convert a two-point-boundary-value problem into an initial value problem. He also came up with the idea behind the technique reported in chapter 4 for modelling corner constraints explicitly. I have learned much from Dr Horridge: as an applied economist and teacher, I will always aspire to his high standards.

As a graduate student at the CoPS/IMPACT I benefited greatly from interactions with other graduate students and with all members of staff. Several people deserve special thanks. Dr Matthew Peter was always prepared to discuss ideas and provide practical assistance. Professor Ken Pearson provided crucial technical support with the computational aspects of the project. Dr Tony Meagher provided most of the raw data as well as helpful advice. Professor Brian Parmenter and Professor Peter Dixon were extremely supportive and generous with their time. Professor Parmenter read drafts of several chapters and his detailed comments greatly improved my dissertation. Professor Dixon provided many valuable insights in the interpretation of results.

My doctoral dissertation also benefited from Dr Peter Wilcoxen's advice and assistance and from Dr Geoffrey Kingston's review of an early draft presented at the Perth 1991 Ph.D Conference in Economics and Business.

The elaboration of my dissertation into this monograph was completed mostly whilst I was a Research Fellow at CoPS/IMPACT under the directorship of Professor Peter Dixon. I am indebted to all my colleagues at CoPS/IMPACT for their support and encouragement and especially for generating an intellectually stimulating environment conducive to both state-of-the-art applied economic research and good fun. Peter Dixon's contribution to this book is outstanding. Without his support and encouragement this book would not have been written. He made the initial suggestion of converting the dissertation into a book and helped me put together a proposal. Peter also helped to greatly improve the book by suggesting the inclusion of chapter 7, which deals with tariff reform, and by providing extensive comments on various parts of the book. In mid-1997 when I decided to leave CoPS/IMPACT to chance my arm in the private sector the probability of finishing this book would have been next to zero if Peter had not generously allowed me to work exclusively on the manuscript in my last six weeks at CoPS/IMPACT. Apart from helping make this book a reality, I am also indebted to Peter Dixon at a more general level for teaching me the value of applied economic analysis and for greatly enhancing my ability to do such analysis.

Several other people made significant contributions to this book. Professor Adrian Pagan and Professor Jean Mercenier examined my doctoral dissertation and their detailed comments have helped improve this book. Professor Brian Parmenter provided detailed comments on drafts of chapter 7. Professor Warwick McKibbin provided comments on chapter 1. Dr Matthew Peter provided encouragement and support throughout the duration of the project as well as detailed comments on drafts of chapters 1 and 3. Finally, I am indebted to Dr Peter Higgs, the CEO of Tactical Global Management, my new employer. Since hiring me Peter has taken a keen interest in the book. His constant support and encouragement ensured that I remained committed to finishing the book. Peter also provided helpful comments on chapter 8.

MICHAEL MALAKELLIS

TACTICAL GLOBAL MANAGEMENT LTD

BRISBANE

JUNE 1999

Contents

PREFACE vii

ACKNOWLEDGMENTS ix

CHAPTER 1 INTRODUCTION: SCOPE AND PURPOSE 1

1.1 Introduction 1
1.2 State of the Art 3
1.2.1 Recursive CGE Models 4
1.2.2 Intertemporal CGE Models 5
1.3 Contributions of this Book 9
1.3.1 Drawing on Existing Modelling Infrastructure 18
1.3.2 Design of an Efficient and Transferable Solution Algorithm 18
1.3.3 The Implications of Alternative Expectations Assumptions 18
1.3.4 An Application to Tariff Reform 19
1.4 Organisation of the Remainder of this Book 19

CHAPTER 2 AN OVERVIEW OF ORANI-INT 21

2.1 Introduction 21
2.2 Nomenclature for Intertemporal Modelling 21
2.3 The Structure of ORANI-INT 23
2.4 Chapter Summary 25

CHAPTER 3 THE THEORETICAL STRUCTURE OF ORANI-INT 27

3.1 Introduction 27
3.1.1 Notational Conventions 28
3.1.2 Computational Issues and the Presentation of Equations 30
3.2 Industry Behaviour 30
3.2.1 Factor Demands 32
3.2.2 Demands for Composite Commodities and 'Other Cost' Tickets and the Supply of Output 34
3.2.3 Demands for Domestic and Foreign Commodities 34
3.3 Final Demands 35
3.3.1 Household Demands 35
3.3.2 Capital Creation 41
3.3.3 Government Demands 48
3.3.4 Foreign Demands 49
3.4 Zero Pure Profits Conditions 49
3.5 Market Clearing Conditions 52
3.6 Miscellaneous Equations 52
3.7 Chapter Summary 60

APPENDIX A3.1 THE LOG-LINEAR FORM OF THE ORANI-INT EQUATION SYSTEM 61

A3.1.1 Introduction 61

APPENDIX A3.2 THE INTERTEMPORAL BUDGET CONSTRAINT 91

A3.2.1 Introduction 91
A3.2.2 The Effects of Constraining the Growth of Net Foreign Liabilities 92

APPENDIX A3.3 ALTERNATIVE INVESTMENT SPECIFICATIONS 104

A3.3.1 Introduction 104
A3.3.2 Cost of Adjustment Models of Investment 104
A3.3.3 Time-to-build Models of Investment 108
A3.3.4 Concluding Remarks 109

APPENDIX A3.4 THE IMPLICATIONS OF THE IRREVERSIBILITY CONSTRAINT ON INVESTMENT 111

A3.4.1 Introduction 111
A3.4.2 Theoretical Implications 111
A3.4.3 Results from ORANI-INT 115

APPENDIX A3.5 A NOTE ON DIVISIA INDEXES 118

A3.5.1 Introduction 118
A3.5.2 The Differential Form of Divisia Indexes 118
A3.5.3 The Levels Form of Divisia Indexes 120
A3.5.4 Why Use Divisia Indexes? 122

CHAPTER 4 SOLUTION METHOD 124

4.1 Introduction 124
4.1.1 A Note on the Semantics Used in this Chapter 124
4.2 Alternative Solution Methods 125
4.2.1 Shooting Methods 126
4.2.2 Relaxation Methods 128
4.3 The ORANI-INT Solution Algorithm 128
4.3.1 The Euler Method 130
4.3.2 Newton-Raphson Method 138
4.3.3 The Hybrid Method 139
4.4 Modelling Sign Constraints 143
4.5 Chapter Summary 148

CHAPTER 5 GENERATING THE CONTROL PATH SOLUTION 149

5.1 Introduction 149
5.2 Constructing an Intertemporal Base Solution 150
5.3 The Control Scenarios 151
5.3.1 The Standard Closure 152
5.3.2 The BG Control Scenario 156
5.3.3 The CBG Control Scenario 157
5.4 Chapter Summary 166

APPENDIX A5.1 THE ORANI-13 DATABASE 167

A5.1 Introduction 167
A5.2 The PMH Database 167
A5.3 The ORANI-13 Database 170
A5.4 The ORANI-13A Database 177
A5.5 The ORANI-13B Database 177

CHAPTER 6 ORANI-INT'S SIMULATION PROPERTIES WITH AND WITHOUT FORWARD-LOOKING BEHAVIOUR 182

6.1 Introduction 182
6.2 An Overview of the Illustrative Experiments 182
6.3 Interpretation of Results 184
6.4 The Benchmark Experiment 184
6.4.1 Long-run Results 186
6.4.2 Results Coinciding With the Implementation of Shock 195
6.4.3 Results Over the Duration of the Shock 196
6.4.4 Pre-shock (Anticipation) Effects 196
6.5 The Investment Experiment 197
6.5.1 Long-run Results 197
6.5.2 Results Coinciding With the Implementation of Shock 200
6.5.3 Results Over the Duration of the Shock 201
6.5.4 Pre-shock (Anticipation) Effects 203
6.6 The Consumption Experiment 204
6.6.1 Long-run Results 207
6.6.2 Results Coinciding With the Commencement of the Shock 208
6.6.3 Results Over the Duration of the Shock 209
6.6.4 Pre-shock (Anticipation) Effects 209
6.7 The Full Intertemporal Experiment 212
6.8 The Surprise Experiment 216
6.9 Chapter Summary 220

CHAPTER 7 SHOULD TARIFF REDUCTIONS BE ANNOUNCED? 221

7.1 Introduction 221
7.2 Simulating the Tariff Reduction Strategies 222
7.2.1 Control Scenario 223
7.2.2 Choice of Exogenous Variables 223
7.2.3 Description of the Tariff Shocks 223
7.3. Simulation Results 224
7.3.1 Long-run Results 233
7.3.2 The Transition Paths 245
7.3.3 Structural Adjustment 250
7.4. Summary and Conclusions 252

CHAPTER 8 SUMMARY AND CONCLUSIONS 254

8.1 Introduction 254
8.2 Model Development 254
8.3 Applications 256
8.4 An Agenda for Future Research 257
8.4.1 Data and Parameters 257
8.4.2 Treatment of Expectations 258
8.4.3 Investment Technology 259
8.4.4 Greater Disaggregation 259
8.5 Final Comments 260

REFERENCES 261

AUTHOR INDEX 269

SUBJECT INDEX 271

LIST OF TABLES 277

LIST OF FIGURES 278

Chapter 1 Introduction: Scope and Purpose

1.1 Introduction

This monograph is concerned with the formulation and implementation of an intertemporal Computable General Equilibrium (CGE) model of the Australian economy. The aim is to bring together, in a balanced approach, theory and data for the purpose of developing a practical state-of-the-art tool for policy analysis. We demonstrate the model's potential with an application to tariff reform. Whilst the intertemporal CGE model and application presented in this book relate to the Australian economy, we anticipate that many of the topics dealt with will appeal to economists with little interest in the Australian economy or CGE models.

The modelling approach adopted is motivated by the recent trend in economy-wide modelling to combine the respective strengths of multi-sectoral CGE models and macroeconomic models. Until quite recently, economy-wide models with a predominantly macro focus were typically "...arbitrarily specified and as a result were frequently criticised as being 'ad hoc' " (Turnovsky, 1989). On the other hand, economy-wide models with a microeconomic focus that were derived from explicit optimisation problems, such as most CGE models, were criticised for lacking temporal detail.

The 'Lucas critique' and the perplexing stagflation phenomena of the 1970s influenced the emergence in the 1980s of economy-wide macro models that "...were based much more on intertemporal optimisation of representative agents in the economy" (*ibid*). Whilst the modern macroeconomics literature remains divided on key issues, including what causes economic fluctuations, there appears to be a general acceptance that macroeconomics should be based on microeconomic foundations.[1] Because of their rigorous microeconomic foundations, the macroeconomic models that have emerged from the "real" business cycle literature are natural candidates for reconciling traditional CGE models with macroeconomic models. However, many of the macroeconomic insights that have emerged from the "New Keynesian" literature, including the importance of imperfect competition, contracts and menu costs, have the potential to enhance the usefulness of intertemporal CGE models for analysing short-run

[1] See Mankiw (1990) for a review of the major streams of modern macroeconomic research how they have evolved.

structural adjustment issues and for generating short-to-medium term forecasts of the structure of the economy.

CGE models provide an analytical framework in which the economy is seen as a complete system of interdependent economic agents. The strength of CGE analysis is its potential to quantify the implications of sectoral interdependencies which are often crucial for understanding the effects of economic shocks on particular sectors and on the economy as a whole (see Parmenter, 1982). In analysing sectoral interdependence CGE models emphasise both direct and indirect sectoral linkages. Direct interactions may occur between users and producers *via* the demand and supply of goods and services. Indirect interactions arise mainly *via* economy-wide constraints such as limitations on the availability of factors of production. In either case, relative prices exert a crucial influence on the responses of economic agents.

Normally, CGE models are used as policy-analytic tools to compare two possible states of the economy at a particular point in time. The effect of an exogenous shock is assessed as the difference between the values of the endogenous variables in the unshocked (control) equilibrium and the value of these variables in the shocked (new) equilibrium, all other exogenous variables remaining at their control values. As with all comparative-static models, traditional CGE models are agnostic about the amount of calendar time that it takes to move from one equilibrium to another following some perturbation. Rather, timing is inferred from the degree of adjustment that factors of production are allowed in reaching a new 'equilibrium'. For short-run applications the point of interest is in the near future; it is usually assumed that at least one factor of production is exogenously fixed. Long-run applications focus on a point in time in the future that is distant enough for factors of production to respond fully to exogenous shocks.

Both short and long-run CGE applications capture only a single point of time and provide no information about how the economy evolves over time. For a wide range of policy issues the lack of temporal detail in traditional CGE models has not proved to be particularly limiting. CGE models have, for example, provided many important insights into taxation, trade, environmental and macroeconomic issues.

Whilst traditional CGE models are well suited to dealing with issues concerning the composition of the economy at a particular point in time, they are not so well suited to dealing with issues concerning the allocation of resources over time. Thus, for example, while comparative static CGE models are very useful for drawing attention to the sectoral implications and welfare effects of trade liberalisation policies, they do not offer much guidance on the timing of such policies. Guidance on policy timing and other issues involving resource allocation over time has typically been sought from intertemporal macroeconomic models.

Modern macroeconomic models that incorporate intertemporal optimising behaviour recognise explicitly that the behaviour of economic agents may be influenced by trade-offs between the present and the future. An intertemporal model provides the scope for enforcing intertemporal resource constraints on all agents (including governments) as well as allowing the consequences of expected future events to affect current decision making. However, since rather few macro models contain significant multi-sectoral detail, they are not very useful in the analysis of problems in which sectoral interdependencies are important.

The incorporation of intertemporal behaviour by economic agents into the CGE framework combines the strengths of the two modelling approaches. A CGE model that allows for intertemporal optimisation by some agents, and the imposition of economy-wide constraints that operate at all points in time is amenable to addressing a wide range of policy issues.

1.2 State of the Art

The origins of applied multi-sectoral economic analysis can be traced to Wassily Leontief. The open static input-output model developed by Leontief (1937) and its many derivatives continue to be used to analyse a wide range of issues. Whilst input-output models have proved to be useful tools for economic analysis they have some severe limitations (see Dixon and Parmenter, 1979). Attempts to overcome the main limitations of input-output models, particularly the passive role played by relative prices, led to the development of CGE modelling.

Johansen (1960) is credited with formulating and successfully implementing the first CGE model. Since the development of Johansen's multi-sectoral growth model (MSG) of Norway, CGE models have become standard tools for policy analysis. The widespread use of CGE models has been greatly aided by the development of generic, user-friendly software for solving them.

The popularity of CGE analysis is reflected by its extensive literature: surveys are provided by Shoven and Whalley (1984), Pereira and Shoven (1988), Robinson (1989, 1991), Bergman (1990) and Dixon and Parmenter (1997). Whilst the reviews by Pereira and Shoven (1988) and Dixon and Parmenter (1997) deal with multi-period CGE models, dynamic aspects of CGE modelling receive very little attention in the other surveys. Below, we review a representative selection of multi-period CGE models. Many of the models that we review are of historical interest only. We give special emphasis to models incorporating the most recent developments in dynamic CGE modelling and for which documentation is available. A distinction is made between recursive and intertemporal models. The agents in recursive models do not require information about the future to make current decisions. Such models are consistent with both static and backward-looking (adaptive) expectations and may be solved period by period. Leading examples of recursive CGE models are discussed in section 1.2.1. In intertemporal models, on the other hand, current decisions by agents depend upon information about the future. They cannot, therefore, be solved one period at a time. Typically, agents in intertemporal models have expectations that are rational and certain (i.e., they have perfect foresight). A selection of intertemporal CGE models is described in section 1.2.2. A table that compares our model with four leading intertemporal CGE models is included in section 1.2.3.

1.2.1 Recursive CGE Models

One of the earliest attempts to incorporate time explicitly in a CGE model was made by Hudson and Jorgenson (1974). This model, used to quantify the impacts of energy policies on US growth, also represents one of the first attempts to integrate a CGE and macroeconomic model. The Hudson-Jorgenson model consists of a nine sector, static CGE model coupled to a highly aggregated (five behavioural equations) macro-econometric growth model. The growth model provides forecasts of aggregate consumption, investment, government expenditure and exports to the CGE model. Recursive dynamics are introduced into the model via capital and savings accounting identities as well as via lags in the consumption and leisure demand functions.

The latest version of Johansen's (1960) CGE model of the Norwegian economy, MSG-4 (documented by Longva *et. al.*, 1985), is also recursively dynamic. Like its predecessors, the structural equations of MSG-4 are expressed in log-linear form. The model is used to analyse the macroeconomic and sectoral prospects of the Norwegian economy. It distinguishes 32 sectors that produce 42 commodities and is specifically designed to address issues related to the interaction between economic growth and energy demands and supplies. The dynamics in this model are confined to the accounting relationship between investment and capital stock. Either aggregate capital stock or the economy-wide rate of return is held constant. The model is calibrated to coincide with actual data for a particular year (or period). Since this data usually reflects the economy in long-run disequilibrium, the calibration exercise involves manipulating exogenous demand variables, sector specific rates of technical change and econometrically estimated "adjustment parameters". These adjustment parameters are supposed to reflect short-run phenomena such as capacity utilisation rates, non-competitive price setting behaviour and climatic conditions (which have important implications for energy use). The model may be steered through time from the initial disequilibrium towards a previously calculated long-run equilibrium by normalising parameters and exogenous growth rates.

The GEMTAP (General-Equilibrium-Model Taxation Package) model developed for tax policy analysis by Ballard, Fullerton, Shoven and Whalley (1985) is also recursive; households make savings decisions on the basis of static expectations about future rates of return to capital. Single period equilibria are linked via an accumulation relation between savings and capital stocks. GEMTAP incorporates a very detailed treatment of taxes and disaggregates the household sector into 12 consumer groups that differ in endowments and preferences. The model also distinguishes 19 productive sectors and 19 commodities (of which 16 are available to consumers).

The final two models discussed in this section, ORANI-F and MONASH, are of the Australian economy. ORANI-F (documented in Horridge *et al*, 1993) is a forecasting version of its predecessor, ORANI (described in Dixon, Parmenter, Sutton and Vincent, 1982). ORANI and ORANI-F share many common features. Both models are very large. They identify 112 sectors producing 114 commodities. One representative household is modelled and labour is disaggregated into 10 occupational categories. In the spirit of Johansen's MSG model, the structural equations of ORANI and ORANI-F are expressed in log-linear (percentage change) form. Both models relate to a single-period only. However, the length in calendar time of that single period is implicit in ORANI but explicit in ORANI-F. The latter model keeps track of stocks and annual flows via the specification of accumulation relations between sector-specific investment and capital stocks, between budget deficits and government debt, and between trade deficits and foreign debt.

MONASH is a descendant of ORANI and ORANI-F (see Dixon and Rimmer, 1998a). In its standard form MONASH is capable of generating annual time paths for its variables. Recursive dynamics are provided by accumulation relationships that link annual equilibria over time and by partial adjustment mechanisms in the specification of sectoral investment and the trade-off between wages and employment.[2] MONASH contains a great deal more regional, occupational and commodity detail than its predecessors. A key novel feature of the MONASH model is that it can be used to update input-output databases to reflect the latest available macro and sectoral information about the economy.

1.2.2 Intertemporal CGE Models

Among the earliest efforts at intertemporal CGE modelling[3] are the multi-period programming models applied to developing countries in the 1970's, Eckhaus and Parikh (1968) describe a range of such models for the Indian economy. These were extended by Manne and Weiskoph (1970) and similar models were developed for Turkey (Blitzer, Cetin and Manne, 1970) and Mexico (Manne, 1973).

An interesting intertemporal CGE model of the programming genre is Manne's (1977) ETA-Macro model. This model was designed to address energy issues and consisted of two sub-models—ETA (Energy Technology Assessment), a detailed activity analysis model of the US energy sector and Macro, an aggregation of the rest of the economy into a single non-energy sector. This work has recently been extended into a multi-country framework by Manne (1991). The world model, called Global 2100, has been used to analyse CO_2-energy-economy interactions.

---

2 Several special-purpose versions of MONASH have been developed to explore alternative dynamic specifications. For example, Dixon and Malakellis (1996) developed a version of the model in which sectoral investment behaviour was based on intertemporal optimising behaviour and model-consistent expectations. Another approach explored with MONASH involves borrowing macro-dynamics from a macroeconometric model. Malakellis and Dixon (1994) experimented with interfacing MONASH with MM, a New-Keynesian style macroeconometric model that allows for rational expectations in financial markets (see Powell and Murphy, 1997). Dixon, Malakellis, McDonald and Meagher (1996) also experimented with interfacing MONASH with TRYM, a macro model similar to MM (see Commonwealth Treasury, 1996).

3 The relationship between programming models and CGE models is discussed in Dixon (1975).

Global 2100 distinguishes five geographical regions and an ETA-Macro type model is specified for each. Projections from this model cover 10-year time intervals from 2000 to 2100.

There are many problems associated with the programming approach to CGE modelling (see, for example, Taylor, 1975). Recognition of these problems influenced the trend towards Johansen's (1960) approach of specifying a CGE model as a set of explicit relationships characterising a competitive equilibrium (rather than as a programming problem, the solution of which is a competitive equilibrium). The Johansen approach is now the dominant method of specifying both static and multi-period CGE models. Early examples of this approach to specifying intertemporal CGE models are the 12 sector, 10 period model of the Turkish economy developed by Dervis (1975) and the 24 sector, 5 period model of the Australian economy developed by Meagher (1978). Recently however, there have been some notable exceptions to this trend. Apart from Global 2100 which is discussed above, the programming approach is used by Blitzer and Eckhaus (1986) to build a 9 sector, 6 period model of the Mexican economy; by Blitzer *et al* (1994) to build a 10 sector, 5 period model for Egypt; and by Dixon (1990) to construct a 50 period CGE model for the analysis of water utility pricing policies in Australia.

Intertemporal CGE models have become very popular for analysing tax policy issues. Pereira and Shoven (1988) survey some of these models. Most of the tax models are highly aggregated. Summers (1981) uses a intertemporal CGE model with one productive sector to analyse the steady-state effects of capital taxes in the US. Dynamics are modelled via an overlapping generations (OLG) life-cycle model of savings. Summers does not use the model to trace out the transition path of the economy from the initial steady state to the new steady state.

Transitional as well as steady-state effects of alternative taxation structures are examined by Auerbach and Kotlikoff (1983). Like Summers, they embed an OLG life-cycle model of consumption into an aggregated CGE model. The model identifies 55 cohorts of households and a single productive sector. The government sector is explicitly modelled with the present value of government expenditures required to equal the present value of government revenues. This model was extended by Auerbach, Kotlikoff and Skinner (1983) to endogenise the supply of labour and the date of retirement. A further refinement (see Auerbach and Kotlikoff, 1987) allowed for forward-looking investment behaviour by the representative producer. Investment decisions are made to maximise the present value of the firm subject to adjustment costs.

A two-sector (corporate and non-corporate) intertemporal CGE model is used by Bovenberg (1988) to analyse the effects of differential taxation of capital income. Savings decisions by the representative household and investment decisions by the two productive sectors are forward-looking. The investment process is subject to adjustment costs. In Bovenberg's model the structural equations appear in log-linear form. In the intertemporal framework, this involves log-linearising the static equations (as in MSG-4 and ORANI) as well as the differential equations. A similar, but slightly disaggregated (5 productive sectors), model is used by Goulder and Summers (1989) to analyse the incidence and allocative effects of tax changes.

The impacts of US tax policy on the efficiency of capital allocation are examined by Jorgenson and Yun (1986) using a CGE model with a single productive sector and a forward-looking, infinitely-lived representative consumer. The innovations in this study do not relate to the type of behaviour modelled, but rather, to the method of estimating the unknown parameters that characterise technology and preferences. The usual approach adopted by CGE modellers is to infer the values of these unknown parameters by reference to a single data point (i.e., the calibration method). In contrast, Jorgenson and Yun estimate these parameters econometrically.

Ballard and Goulder (1985) develop a more disaggregated tax model; they elaborate GEMTAP to include a forward-looking, infinitely-lived representative household. They use the model to examine the impacts of a consumption tax in the US under different specifications of the degree of foresight of the representative household. In Ballard and Goulder (1987) this model was extended into a 55-cohort OLG framework.

Intertemporal CGE models that are not focussed primarily on tax policy analysis are typically less aggregated. The intertemporal CGE model used by Jorgenson and Wilcoxen (1990) to analyse the impacts of US environmental regulations identifies 35 productive sectors. A single capital stock that is perfectly malleable and mobile among the sectors is assumed and the investment decisions made by producers are forward-looking. There are no adjustment costs in the investment process but the total supply of capital in each period is fixed by past investments. Households are also forward-looking with full consumption (i.e., goods and leisure) allocated across time by an intertemporal utility-maximising representative household. In each period, full consumption is allocated between goods and leisure to determine aggregate consumption and savings and the supply of labour. Both the government budget deficit and current account balance are exogenous. In keeping with the approach of Jorgenson and Yun, the parameters of the model are estimated econometrically.

Typically, the intertemporal control solution (or intertemporal benchmark equilibrium) of an intertemporal CGE model is constructed to exhibit steady-state growth. An innovative aspect of the Jorgenson-Wilcoxen model is that the intertemporal control solution exhibits steady-state growth in the long run only. This feature is shared by the model built by Mercenier and Sampaio de Souza (1994) to examine the impacts of alternative growth strategies for Brazil. The Mercenier-Sampaio de Souza model includes six productive sectors, each of which constructs its own capital goods. Investment decisions are forward-looking and subject to sector-specific adjustment costs. Labour is mobile between sectors but fixed in aggregate. A representative intertemporal utility-maximising household allocates consumption across time. Government expenditure is exogenous and an intertemporal budget constraint requires the government deficit to be eliminated gradually in the first 5 periods of a 25 period horizon. Borrowing from overseas is restricted by the requirement that the present value of trade surpluses compensates for initial indebtedness.

Bovenberg and Goulder (1991) constructed a two region (US and the rest of the world) intertemporal CGE model which they used to analyse a range of issues; the impacts of savings and investment-promoting schemes (Goulder and Eichengreen, 1989), the effects of taxing foreign-owned capital and trade liberalisation issues (Eichengreen and Goulder, 1991 and Goulder and Eichengreen, 1992). The model identifies 10 domestic industries producing 10 commodities and a single foreign industry producing 10 commodities. Labour is mobile between sectors but supply is fixed in aggregate. Investment decisions are forward-looking and a single type of capital is produced. The mobility of capital between sectors is limited by sector-specific adjustment costs. Consumption decisions are also forward-looking; a representative household maximises intertemporal utility subject to a lifetime budget constraint. An innovative feature of this model is that agents choose between domestic and foreign assets in their wealth portfolio on the basis of relative rates of return.

A common feature of the final two models that we examine in this section, G-Cubed and MM2, is that they evolved from macro-dynamic models. G-Cubed is a multi-region intertemporal CGE model developed by McKibbin and Wilcoxen (1992, 1998) to analyse global warming issues. G-Cubed is based on two existing models: the first, discussed above, is the Jorgenson-Wilcoxen model and, the second, is MSG2 (McKibbin-Sachs-Global), an aggregated intertemporal CGE model of the world economy developed by McKibbin and Sachs (1991). The macroeconomic features of MSG2 are combined with the sectoral detail of the Jorgenson-Wilcoxen model to produce a model potentially capable of addressing issues in which both sectoral and macroeconomic effects are important.

G-Cubed divides the world economy into 8 regions: each region has 12 productive sectors and a representative household. Consumption and investment decisions are based partly on forward-looking behaviour and partly on backward-looking behaviour. A portion of consumption is determined by current income (interpreted as liquidity-constrained behaviour). Similarly, a portion of investment in each sector is determined by current profits (interpreted as firms constrained to financing investment expenditures out of retained earnings because they are unable to borrow and lend). A single type of capital is modelled and its mobility between sectors is constrained by sector-specific adjustment costs. Government expenditure in each region is assumed to be exogenous and constant in all periods. Asset markets in the OECD regions are assumed to be perfectly integrated. In the non-OECD countries, exchange rates are pegged to the US dollar and their borrowings from the rest of the world are constrained. In G-Cubed money must be used in transactions. The demand for real money balances is modelled as a function of GDP and short-term nominal interest rates.

MM2 is described as a "fully integrated macro-CGE" model of Australia (Powell and Murphy, 1997). MM2 evolved from MM a quarterly macroeconometric model. Five key features of MM2 that are carried over from MM are: (i) it is a quarterly model; (ii) the short run is characterised by sticky prices and quantities; (iii) agents in financial markets have perfect foresight; (iv) agents in the real economy are backward looking; and (v) the model converges to a long run that is consistent with a neo-classical balanced growth path. The key difference between MM and MM2 is that the former contains one productive sector whilst the latter contains eighteen. Demands for employment, investment and imports are determined at the industry level, as are supplies to foreigners and to domestic agents.

1.3 Contributions of this Book

The model presented in this book shares many of the features incorporated in the models surveyed in the previous section. However, the main source of inspiration is the stylised intertemporal CGE model of the Australian economy described by Dixon and Parmenter (1990). The aim of this stylised model was to outline the theoretical structure of an intertemporal version of ORANI. We go one step further by operationalising an intertemporal CGE model that is based on ORANI. The ancestry of our model is reflected in its nickname, ORANI-INT (INTertemporal).

To place ORANI-INT in the intertemporal CGE literature we list its key features in table 1.1 alongside those of four models discussed above in section 1.2.2. The four models chosen for the comparison are those described by Mercenier and Sampaio de Souza (1994), Bovenberg and Goulder (1991), Jorgenson and Wilcoxen (1993), and McKibbin and Wilcoxen (1998). These models are chosen because they represent the latest developments in the class of models to which ORANI-INT belongs. Using the four models listed in table 1.1 (hereafter referred to as M-S, B-G, J-W and M-W respectively) as reference points, the key identifying features of ORANI-INT can be summarised as follows:

- like M-S and J-W it represents a single country with open economy features;
- like M-S each sector produces its own capital using sector-specific technology;
- like J-W investment decisions are driven by forward-looking rates of return;
- like J-W we use a time-to-build investment specification that does not incorporate convex adjustment costs;
- unlike any of the four models sectoral investment decisions are irreversible;
- like all four models an infinitely lived representative household allocates expenditures across time to maximise intertemporal utility;
- like M-S and J-W emphasis is placed on the real side of the economy with financial markets accommodating;
- like M-S, B-G and M-W labour supply decisions are not determined by the solution of the households' intertemporal utility maximisation problem;
- like M-S and M-W the government deficit is endogenous;
- unlike any of the four models the budget deficit is determined residually (implying Ricardian equivalence);

Table 1.1: Comparison of ORANI-INT with Four State-Of-The-Art Models

Model[(a)]	Feature
	1. Country coverage
M–S(1)	Brazil.
B–G(1)	US and RoW (rest of world).
J–W(1)	US.
M–W(1)	US, Japan, Australia, Other OECD, China, LDCs, OPEC and Eastern Europe and the former Soviet Union.
O-I(1)	Australia.
	2. Time Horizon
M–S(2)	25 periods, 4 years apart.
B–G(2)	30 periods, 1 year apart.
J–W(2)	Annual results reported for 1973–2020. Model solved to 2100.
M–W(2)	Annual results reported for 1990–2020. Model solved to 2100.
O-I(2)	30 periods, 1 year apart.
	3. Specification of Household Behaviour
M–S(3)	*Disaggregation* Single representative infinitely-lived household. *Atemporal behaviour* **Objective**: Maximise a two-tiered instantaneous utility function. At the top level, utility is a CES aggregate of 6 composite goods. At the second level, each composite good is a CES combination of domestic and imported goods. **Constraint**: Aggregate expenditure fixed and all prices exogenous. *Intertemporal behaviour* **Objective**: Maximise intertemporal utility function, which is a CES aggregate of total consumption in each period. **Constraint**: Intertemporal budget constraint. **Expectations**: Model consistent.
B–G(3)	*Disaggregation* Single representative infinitely-lived household. *Atemporal behaviour* **Objective**: Maximise a four-tiered instantaneous utility function. At the top level, utility is a Cobb-Douglas (C-D) aggregate of total consumption in period t and a portfolio preference index. At the second level, total consumption is a C-D combination of 17 composite goods and the portfolio preference index is a CES combination of share of portfolio devoted to domestic and foreign assets. At the next level composite goods are CES aggregates of domestic and imported goods. At lowest level, the 17 domestic goods are Leontief aggregates of the 10 domestic outputs. The same applies to imported goods. **Constraint**: Aggregate expenditure given and all prices exogenous. *Intertemporal behaviour* **Objective**: Maximise intertemporal utility function, which is a CES aggregate of total consumption in each period. **Constraint**: Intertemporal budget constraint. **Expectations**: Model consistent.

... continued

Table 1.1 (cont.): Comparison of ORANI-INT with Four State-Of-The-Art Models

Model	Feature
J–W(3)	*Disaggregation* Static consumption decisions are made by 672 types of households. Intertemporal decisions are made by a representative infinitely-lived household. *Atemporal behaviour* **Objective**: Maximise a 5-tiered instantaneous utility function. Substitution at all levels of the tier structure are characterised by parameters that are estimated econometrically using translog functional forms. At the top level households choose between leisure and expenditure. Second, expenditure is allocated among 5 aggregate commodities (e.g., food, energy and etc). Third, each aggregate commodity is made up of labour and capital and 15 sub-aggregate goods. At the next level the 15 sub-aggregate goods are functions of 35 composite goods. Each composite good is an aggregate of domestic and imported goods. **Constraint**: Aggregate expenditure fixed and all prices exogenous. *Intertemporal behaviour* **Objective**: Maximise intertemporal utility function, which is a Cobb-Douglas aggregate of full consumption (i.e., goods and leisure) in each period. **Constraint**: Intertemporal wealth constraint (includes imputed value of leisure). **Expectations**: Model consistent.
M–W(3)	*Disaggregation* Single representative infinitely-lived household. *Atemporal behaviour* **Objective**: Maximise a 4-tiered instantaneous utility function. At the top level, utility is a C-D aggregate of capital services, labour, energy and materials. At the second level: (i) capital services is a Leontief function of household capital; (ii) the energy bundle is a CES aggregate of 5 composite energy commodities; and (iii) the materials bundle is a CES aggregate of 7 composite non-energy commodities. At the third level the 5 composite energy commodities and the 7 composite non-energy commodities are CES aggregates of domestic commodities and composite foreign commodities. At the lowest level, the foreign composite is a C-D aggregation of commodities of the same category from the 7 other regions. **Constraint**: Aggregate expenditure fixed and all prices exogenous. *Intertemporal behaviour* Households are confronted by two intertemporal problems. Firstly, how to allocate aggregate consumption over time. Secondly, how much to invest in household capital. **1. Objective**: Maximise intertemporal utility function, which is the sum of the logs of private and government consumption in each period. **Constraint**: Intertemporal wealth constraint. **Implementation**: The consumption function implemented is a weighted sum of the forward-looking behaviour implied by the solution of the above intertemporal optimisation problem and of *ad hoc* backward-looking behaviour (i.e., a constant portion of real after-tax current income is consumed). The weight assigned to forward-looking behaviour in the consumption function is 0.3. **2. Objective**: Maximise the present value of future household capital services flows. **Constraint**: Capital services are the rental rate times the stock of household capital and the accumulation of this capital is subject to convex adjustment costs.

... continued

Table 1.1 (cont.): Comparison of ORANI-INT with Four State-Of-The-Art Models

Model	Feature
O-I(3)	*Disaggregation* Single representative infinitely-lived household. *Atemporal behaviour* **Objective**: Maximise a two-tiered instantaneous utility function. At the top level, utility is a Stone-Geary aggregate of 13 composite goods. At the next level composite goods are CES aggregates of domestic and imported goods. **Constraint**: Aggregate expenditure fixed and all prices exogenous. *Intertemporal behaviour* **Objective**: Maximise intertemporal utility function, which is a Stone-Geary aggregate of total consumption in each period. **Constraint**: Intertemporal budget constraint. **Expectations**: Model consistent.
	4. Production Structure
M–S(4)	*Disaggregation* Six single-product sectors. *Atemporal behaviour* **Objective**: Choose output level and mix of inputs to maximise current period profits. **Constraint**: Capital stock and prices given; 2-tiered production technology. At top level, Leontief between value added and intermediate inputs of composite goods. At next level, value added is a CES aggregate of labour and capital and composite goods are CES aggregates of domestic and imported goods. *Intertemporal behaviour* **Objective**: Choose path of investment to maximise the present value of future dividend payments to shareholders. **Constraint**: Future prices given; the accumulation of capital is subject to an explicit 1-year gestation lag and to quadratic adjustment costs. **Expectations**: Model consistent.
B–G(4)	*Disaggregation* Ten single-product sectors. *Atemporal behaviour* **Objective**: Choose output level and mix of inputs to maximise current period profits. **Constraint**: Capital stock and prices given; 3-tiered production technology. At the top level, value-added and intermediate inputs of composite goods are combined in fixed proportions. At the next level, value-added is a CES aggregate of labour and capital and composite good i is a CES aggregate of domestic and imported good i.. Domestic good i is in turn a Leontief aggregate of the 10 domestic sectoral outputs. Similarly, imported good i is a Leontief aggregate of the 10 foreign sectoral outputs. *Intertemporal behaviour* **Objective**: Choose path of investment to maximise the present value of future dividend payments to shareholders. **Constraint**: Future prices given; the accumulation of capital is subject to quadratic adjustment costs; the debt-to-capital ratio is fixed; dividend payments are a constant fraction of after-tax profits. The investment technology in each sector is an identical Leontief aggregate of the 17 composite commodities. **Expectations**: Model consistent.

... continued

Table 1.1 (cont.): Comparison of ORANI-INT with Four State-Of-The-Art Models

Model	Feature
J–W(4)	<u>*Disaggregation*</u> 35 multi-product sectors. <u>*Atemporal behaviour*</u> **Objective**: Choose output level and mix of inputs to maximise current period profits. **Constraint**: Capital stock and prices given; 5-tiered production technology. Parameters at all levels are estimated econometrically. At the top level firms choose their output mix. The 35 domestic outputs are treated as imperfect substitutes. Second, the input mix is allocated between capital, labour, an energy aggregate and a materials aggregate. Third, the energy aggregate is made up of five composite commodities and the materials aggregate is made up of 10 sub-aggregate goods. Fourth, the sub-aggregate goods are made up of 30 composite goods. Finally, each composite good is an aggregate of domestic and imported goods. <u>*Intertemporal behaviour*</u> **Objective**: Choose path of investment to minimise the present value of the stream of future costs. **Constraint**: Future prices given; the accumulation of capital is subject to an implicit 1-year gestation lag; the path of output is given. There is a single capital good which is perfectly malleable and mobile among sectors. A multi-tiered technology, similar to that described above for current production, is used to produce the capital good. **Expectations**: Model consistent.
M–W(4)	<u>*Disaggregation*</u> 12 single-product sectors that supply commodities for current production and for final usage other than investment. Two other sectors produce capital goods for firms and households. <u>*Atemporal behaviour*</u> **Objective**: Choose output level and mix of inputs to maximise current period profits. **Constraint**: Capital stock and prices given; 4-tiered production technology. At the top level, output is a CES function of capital, labour, energy and materials. At the second level: (i) the energy bundle is a CES aggregate of 5 composite energy commodities; and (ii) the materials bundle is a CES aggregate of 7 composite non-energy commodities. At the third level the 5 composite energy commodities and the 7 composite non-energy commodities are CES aggregates of domestic commodities and composite foreign commodities. At the lowest level, the foreign composite is a C-D aggregation of commodities of the same category from the 7 other regions. <u>*Intertemporal behaviour*</u> **Objective**: Choose the path of investment to maximise the market value of the firm. **Constraint**: The accumulation of capital is subject to quadratic adjustment costs. Capital is created using an investment good produced by a special sector. Sector specificity of capital stock is determined by the value of the adjustment cost parameter. **Implementation**: For each sector the investment demand function implemented is a weighted sum of the forward-looking behaviour implied by the solution of the above intertemporal optimisation problem and of *ad hoc* backward-looking behaviour (i.e., a constant portion of investment is funded out of current period profits). The weight assigned to forward-looking behaviour in each investment function is 0.3.

... continued

Table 1.1 (cont.): Comparison of ORANI-INT with Four State-Of-The-Art Models

Model	Feature
O-I(4)	*Disaggregation* Thirteen single-product sectors. *Atemporal behaviour* **Objective**: Choose output level and mix of inputs to maximise current period profits. **Constraint**: Capital stock and prices given; 2-tiered production technology. At top level, Leontief between value added and intermediate inputs of composite goods. At next level, value added is a CES aggregate of labour, capital and land and, composite goods are CES aggregates of 13 domestic and 13 imported goods. *Intertemporal behaviour* **Objective**: Choose path of investment to minimise the present value of costs. **Constraint**: Future prices given; accumulation of capital subject to a 1-year gestation lag; path of output given. Investment decisions are irreversible and capital-creation technology is sector-specific. Capital goods are Leontief aggregates of composite commodities. **Expectations**: Model consistent.
	5. Specification of the labour market
M–S(5)	**Supply**: Labour inputs are homogeneous. The aggregate supply of labour is typically exogenous but short-run real wage rigidities can be imposed. **Demand**: The nominal wage is uniform across sectors. It adjusts to clear the labour market. Each sector hires labour up to the point where the nominal wage is equal to the value of the marginal product of labour.
B–G(5)	**Supply**: Labour inputs are homogeneous in each region. The aggregate supply of labour in each region is exogenous. **Demand**: The nominal wage is uniform across domestic sectors. It adjusts to clear the domestic labour market. Each sector hires labour up to the point where the nominal wage is equal to the value of the marginal product of labour.
J–W(5)	**Supply**: Determined endogenously as part of the solution to the representative households' intertemporal utility maximisation problem. **Demand**: Labour is perfectly mobile. The market-clearing nominal wage is uniform across sectors. Each sector hires labour up to the point where the nominal wage is equal to the value of the marginal product of labour.
M–W(5)	**Supply**: Labour inputs are homogeneous in each region. The nominal wage in each region is uniform across sectors. In the short run the supply of labour is determined by institutional nominal wage-setting behaviour. In the long run the supply of labour is exogenous. **Demand**: The nominal wage is assumed to be sticky. It is a function of current and expected inflation and on labour demand relative to labour supply. Each sector hires labour up to the point where the nominal wage is equal to the value of the marginal product of labour.
O-I(5)	**Supply**: Labour inputs are homogeneous. The aggregate supply of labour is exogenous. **Demand**: The nominal wage is uniform across sectors. It adjusts to clear the labour market. Each sector hires labour up to the point where the nominal wage is equal to the value of the marginal product of labour.

... continued

Table 1.1 (cont.): Comparison of ORANI-INT with Four State-Of-The-Art Models

Model	Feature
	6. Government Behaviour
M–S(6)	**Constraint**: Present value of government current expenditures are equal to present value of tax revenues. In the first period real government consumption is fixed and the deficit is a residual. In the next four periods the deficit (surplus) is eliminated. The budget is balanced thereafter. Government infrastructure expenditure is financed by long-term bonds. The present value of interest repayments is equal to present value of implicit rentals to infrastructure. **Expenditures**: Transfers to households, consumption of domestic goods only and interest payments on debt. **Revenues**: Income taxes and indirect taxes (including tariffs and export subsidies).
B–G(6)	**Constraint**: Real government expenditure is exogenous and increases at the steady-state growth rate. The budget is balanced in each period through lump-sum adjustments to income taxes. **Expenditures**: Transfers to households and consumption of goods represent fixed share of overall spending. Composition of government consumption is exogenous. **Revenues**: All major US taxes modelled.
J–W(6)	**Constraint**: Budget deficit is specified exogenously in each period. **Expenditures**: Transfers and interest paid to domestic and foreign households. Consumption of goods in fixed proportion. **Revenues**: Indirect taxes, income taxes, capital income of government firms and non-tax receipts.
M–W(6)	**Constraint**: Real government spending is exogenous. A lump sum tax is levied in each period equal to interest payments on outstanding government debt. **Expenditures**: Goods and services, interest payments, investment tax credits and transfers to households. **Revenues**: Sales, corporate and personal taxes and debt issuance.
O-I(6)	**Constraint**: Real government expenditure is exogenous and increases at the steady-state growth rate. **Expenditures**: Consumption of goods and services is explicit. The composition of consumption is exogenous. Other expenditures are implicit. **Revenues**: Indirect taxes on all activities are explicit, other revenues are implicit.
	7. Specification of financial markets
M–S(7)	**Assets**: Domestic equities, government bonds and foreign assets. **Returns**: Arbitrage ensures that rates of return on all assets are continually equalised. **Risk premia**: On domestic equities.
B–G(7)	**Assets**: Domestic and foreign equities that are imperfect substitutes. **Returns**: Average portfolio returns to domestic and foreign residents may vary in the short-run only. **Risk premia**: Implicit on domestic and foreign equities.
J–W(7)	**Assets**: Domestic and foreign equities and bonds, which are perfect substitutes. **Returns**: Rate of return on all assets is the same. **Risk premia**: Implicit on equities and domestic bonds..

... continued

Table 1.1 (cont.): Comparison of ORANI-INT with Four State-Of-The-Art Models

Model	Feature
M–W(7)	The treatment of financial markets differs across regions. Below we confine our comments to the specification of financial markets in the OECD countries. **Assets**: Domestic and foreign bonds and equities, which are perfect substitutes. Money enters the model through a transactions constraint. The supply of money is exogenous. **Returns**: Arbitrage ensure that risk-adjusted expected returns are equalised across all assets. Adjustment costs allow returns on equities to diverge from returns on bonds in the short term. **Risk premia**: Allowed for on all assets.
O-I(7)	**Assets**: Domestic and foreign equities and bonds, which are perfect substitutes. **Returns**: Risk-adjusted expected returns are equalised beyond year 1. **Risk premia**: On domestic equities.
	8. Specification of the external sector
M–S(8)	**Constraint**: Present value of future trade surpluses compensate for initial indebtedness. **Imports**: Domestic and foreign goods are imperfect substitutes. **Exports**: Depend on competitiveness and exogenous foreign activity.
B–G(8)	**Constraint**: Balance of payments equilibrium; with savings and portfolio decisions by domestic and foreign households determining the supply of loanable funds (i.e., current account deficit). **Imports**: Domestic and foreign goods are imperfect substitutes. **Exports**: Depend on competitiveness and foreign activity levels.
J–W(8)	**Constraint**: Current account is exogenous. **Imports**: Domestic and foreign goods are imperfect substitutes. **Exports**: Depend on competitiveness and exogenous foreign income.
M–W(8)	**Constraint**: Balance of payments equilibrium; with savings and portfolio decisions by domestic and foreign households determining the supply of loanable funds (i.e., current account deficit). **Imports**: Domestic and foreign goods are imperfect substitutes. **Exports**: Depend on competitiveness and on endogenous foreign activity.
O-I(8)	**Constraint**: Supply of loanable funds is infinite at exogenous world rate of interest. The present value of the stream of future current account deficits is constrained by the requirement that the ratio of foreign debt to GDP is stable in the terminal period. **Imports**: Domestic and foreign goods are imperfect substitutes. **Exports**: Depend on competitiveness and exogenous foreign activity.
	9. Implementation
M–S(9)	**Control Solution**: Base year (1980) replication. The intertemporal shadow price of capital is reconciled with base year investment and assumed costs of adjustment by including a sector-specific slack variable. The slack variable is assumed to capture, among other things, risk premia. Base year household savings are reconciled with intertemporal optimising behaviour by adjusting export demands (i.e., supply of foreign savings). **Parameters**: Calibration supplemented with values for the free parameters inferred from the econometric literature. **Solution Technique**: MINOS (linear programming).

... continued

Table 1.1 (cont.): Comparison of ORANI-INT with Four State-Of-The-Art Models

Model	Feature
B–G(9)	**Control Solution**: Steady-state growth for US and RoW. The model incorporates non-neutralities of the tax system with respect to inflation. The steady-state inflation rate is specified exogenously. **Parameters**: Calibration supplemented with values for the free parameters inferred the econometric literature. **Solution Technique**: Variant of Fair-Taylor method.
J–W(9)	**Control Solution**: Converges towards steady-state growth. The model incorporates non-neutralities in financing the government deficit with respect to inflation. The steady-state inflation rate is exogenous. **Parameters**: Estimated econometrically **Solution Technique**: Variant of Fair-Taylor method.
M–W(9)	**Control Solution**: Converges to balanced growth. Base year (1990) replication is achieved by adding a slack variable to each of the model's costate equations. These slack variables are then held constant at their base year values. **Parameters**: Mixture of calibration and econometric estimation. **Solution Technique**: First-order approximations derived using a dynamic programming approach.
O-I(9)	**Control Solution**: Based on 1980-81 input-output data. Control solution can be characterised by either (i) balanced growth in all periods or (ii) unbalanced growth initially converging asymptotically towards balanced growth. **Parameters**: Calibration supplemented with econometric estimates of the free parameters. **Solution Technique**: Variant of Euler method.

(a) The model identifiers M-S, B-G, J-W and M-W refer to the models reported in: Mercenier and Sampaio de Souza (1994), Bovenberg and Goulder (1991), Jorgenson and Wilcoxen (1993) and McKibbin and Wilcoxen (1998). ORANI-INT is identified as O-I. The table is divided into 9 sections. Appended to each model identifier is a bracketed number that indicates the section to which the description in the adjacent column belongs.

- like B-G and M-W the current account balance is endogenous; and
- like M-S and B-G most parameters in the model are estimated using calibration, rather than econometric, techniques.

The above list of features indicates that ORANI-INT's theoretical structure contains few novel features. The primary contribution of this monograph is practical: it details the development of an intertemporal CGE model of the Australian economy and presents an application of the model to the analysis of a topical policy issue. In so doing we confronted several methodological and empirical issues. We anticipate that our experiences in dealing with these issues will prove useful to economic modellers generally (not necessarily CGE modellers) and to policy-makers. In the following four sub-sections we briefly describe the main issues dealt with in this monograph.

1.3.1 Drawing on Existing Modelling Infrastructure

In developing ORANI-INT we demonstrate how the many years of research effort embodied in existing modelling infrastructure need not be discarded when developing a state-of-the-art multi-sectoral model. There are many CGE models used throughout the world but most of these are either static or have minimal dynamics. The methodology presented in this monograph shows how a static CGE model can be easily embedded in a dynamic framework that allows for rational expectations. Typically, static CGE models are rich in structural detail. Our approach is to embed a static CGE model in an intertemporal framework without compromising significantly on the structural detail. Such a model has the potential to deal with a wide range of issues concerning the allocation of resource both at a particular point in time and over time.

1.3.2 Design of an Efficient and Transferable Solution Algorithm

In a survey on the formulation and solution of CGE models, Manne (1985) highlights the trade-off that CGE modellers must face between model size and empirical relevance on the one hand, and computation and interpretation of results on the other. One of the challenges of constructing ORANI-INT was to keep it computationally tractable without compromising significantly on the type and degree of economic detail modelled. The method that we develop to solve ORANI-INT has the potential to handle very large and complex models efficiently. Specifically, there is no need to restrict the number of costate variables (e.g., by assuming that capital stocks are homogeneous) nor to assume that the solution will always be interior.

The solution algorithm that we use is portable, efficient and flexible. The algorithm is independent of the model's structure; hence, it can be used to solve a wide range of models, including macroeconomic models, CGE models and partial equilibrium models. The modeller is provided with the capacity to routinely change: (a) any aspect of the model's theoretical structure; (b) any part of the database; and (c) the partitioning of variables between the exogenous and endogenous categories. Moreover, because the algorithm is implemented using commercially available software it is readily accessible to other modellers who do not have the resources to tailor their own algorithms.

1.3.3 The Implications of Alternative Expectations Assumptions

The treatment of expectations in economic models is a controversial issue. Statistical tests of alternative expectations formation hypotheses have not proved to be decisive. In the absence of robust statistical evidence it is necessary to appeal to other criteria to justify the expectations formation hypothesis adopted. A compelling case for assuming that agents form model-consistent expectations has been made in the theoretical literature that has its roots in the works of Lucas

(1972 and 1976), Sargent and Wallace (1975) and Fischer (1977). Whilst a detailed assessment of alternative expectations hypotheses is beyond the scope of this book, we do explore some of these alternatives using ORANI-INT. The realism of a particular expectations hypothesis can be assessed, at least partially, by the plausibility of the behaviour that it implies. Our approach is to compare the simulation properties of ORANI-INT under static and model-consistent expectations. First we establish a benchmark experiment in which all agents are endowed with static expectations. The results of the benchmark experiment are then used to contrast the implications of jointly and separately introducing model-consistent consumption and investment behaviour. As part of this exercise we show how announcement effects can be analysed when expectations are model consistent.

1.3.4 An Application to Tariff Reform

With many countries moving towards freer trade the application of ORANI-INT to the issue of tariff reform is topical. CGE models have made a large contribution to the analysis of tariff reform. For example, they have been used to identify the agents that win or lose from changes in industry protection. The international literature dealing with the qualitative and quantitative effects of tariff reform is vast. However, one aspect of tariff reform that has not been addressed adequately by applied economists relates to the timing issues associated with such policies, including adjustment paths and announcement effects. We demonstrate how a model like ORANI-INT can be used to analyse the impacts of alternative tariff reform strategies on the allocation of resources over time. Australia is an ideal case study because it has experimented with announced and unannounced tariff reforms in recent history.

1.4 Organisation of the Remainder of this Book

The remainder of this monograph is organised into seven chapters. In the next two chapters we describe the theoretical structure of ORANI-INT. Chapter 2 contains an overview of ORANI-INT as well as an outline of the nomenclature that used throughout the monograph. In chapter 2 we make a distinction between the atemporal and intertemporal parts of ORANI-INT and establish the relationship between ORANI and the atemporal core of ORANI-INT. The theoretical structure of ORANI-INT is described in detail in chapter 3.

In chapter 4 we describe the method used to compute solutions for ORANI-INT. The solution procedure that we use is based on a hybrid of the Euler and Newton-Raphson methods. The ORANI-INT solution method allows us to compute accurate solutions quickly and provides maximum scope for model modifications. The method also accommodates nonnegativity constraints, which are explicit in the ORANI-INT investment specification.

The ORANI-INT database is described in chapter 5. Most of the data that we use is borrowed from the ORANI data files. A requirement of the ORANI-INT solution method is that we start our computations from an existing intertemporal solution to the model. We explain how an intertemporal solution is generated from the single period input-output data used by ORANI. Two such intertemporal solutions, which we call control path solutions, are reported. One of the control path solutions exhibits balanced growth in all periods. The other control path solution converges to, but does not start from, balanced growth. These control path solutions are used as starting points for the computations reported in chapters 6 and 7.

The results of five illustrative experiments, which have in common a permanent expansion in government expenditure, are reported in chapter 6. These experiments are designed primarily to highlight the properties of ORANI-INT rather than to address any actual policy issues. The effects of this policy shock are examined both with and without forward-looking behaviour. Also, the effects of announcing such a policy in advance of its implementation are compared to the case where the shock is implemented without warning.

In chapter 7 we demonstrate the potential of ORANI-INT for policy analysis by using the model to assess the macroeconomic and sectoral implications of three alternative tariff reform strategies. The three reform strategies that we examine are: (a) an unannounced reduction in tariffs; (b) an announced reduction in tariffs that is implemented in one hit; and (c) an announced program of phased tariff reductions.

Chapter 8 contains a summary of the main achievements: these are divided into four areas; theory, data, computation and applications. Before providing some concluding remarks we also suggest an agenda for future research.

Chapter 2 An Overview of ORANI-INT

2.1 Introduction

The purpose of this chapter is to provide an overview of the theoretical structure of ORANI-INT and to set out the nomenclature that is used in the remainder of the monograph. The relationship between ORANI-INT and ORANI is made clear and the sources of intertemporal behaviour identified. A distinction is made between the static and dynamic equations in ORANI-INT. Static equations relate variables in a particular period while dynamic equations relate variables in different, often adjacent, time periods. The equations of the model are discussed in detail in chapter 3.

2.2 Nomenclature for Intertemporal Modelling

The nomenclature used in this study is set out in table 2.1. The model interrelates the values of a set of variables V at successive time points t=0, 1, 2, ..., T. The time points correspond to particular calendar dates and are separated by intervals of time (measured in years) L_t, where L_t is the number of years between time points t and t+1. Variables with subscript t=0 refer to the most recent date for which historical data is available. All such variables are therefore predetermined.

In ORANI-INT agents can make and implement decisions at the chosen set of time points only. The information set, upon which agents make decisions, is assumed to be revised instantaneously at each time point. Thus, new information has no effect on behaviour in the preceding interval.

Each variable V can be mapped to a time point or to an interval. A stock variable V_t is the level of the relevant stock at the instant t (e.g., midnight on June 30th 1996). In the case of a flow variable, V_t is the flow in the financial year containing time point t. If annual data is used and the interval [t, t+1) is greater than 1 year, it is necessary to postulate some growth rule governing those flows which are accumulated to form stocks (e.g., investment). One option is to assume that the flow observed in the year containing time point t is the average annual flow rate during the interval [t, t+1), a period of L_t years. This option would be a valid approximation where L_t is relatively small. For longer time intervals, a more elaborate growth rule may be necessary.

Table 2.1: Notational Conventions

Timepoint t	Interval length[(a)] L_t	Relative time S_t	Level of variable V	Change in variable v	Calendar date CD	Data year DY
0		0	V_0	0	1996	1995-96
	$L_0=1$					
1		1	V_1	v_1	1997	1996-97
	$L_1=1$					
2		2	V_2	v_2	1998	1998-99
	$L_2=2$					
3		4	V_3	v_3	2000	1999-00
	$L_3=2$					
4		6	V_4	v_4	2002	2001-02
	$L_4=5$					
5		11	V_5	v_5	2007	2006-07
⋮	⋮	⋮	⋮	⋮	⋮	⋮
T-1						
	$L_{T-1}=S_T-S_{T-1}$					
T		$S_T=N$	V_T	v_T	1996+N	(CD-1)-CD

(a) The values shown here for L_t are chosen purely to illustrate that L_t is a varying function of t.

In the current version of ORANI-INT we have assumed that $L_t=1$ for all t. However, our nomenclature is designed to accommodate a more general specification of interval lengths. The size of ORANI-INT is a function of the number of time points identified and allowing for interval lengths greater than 1 year has important efficiency implications for the computation of the model. In future implementations of ORANI-INT we intend to experiment with variable interval lengths.

Several authors, including Wilcoxen (1985) and Mercenier and Michel (1994a), have explored the potential of unequal interval lengths. We anticipate that with variable interval lengths the number of years over which ORANI-INT is solved may be quite large (say 50 years or more), while the number of time points identified may be significantly less. Strategic location of the time points will ensure that time aggregation errors will be minimised. For instance, time points may be densely concentrated where the dynamic variables of the model are expected to change significantly (or where there is a particular interest from a policy viewpoint). Conversely, where the dynamic variables are expected to change more slowly (or where policy interest is less pronounced — perhaps far into the future) the time points may be more sparsely concentrated.

2.3 The Structure of ORANI-INT

ORANI-INT consists of a system of optimality conditions and definitional equations. The optimality conditions characterise the behaviour of households and producers in competitive markets and are derived from the solutions of a series of constrained optimisation problems. Some of the optimisation problems faced by the agents are intertemporal and some are static. In the former problems, the values of choice variables in a particular period are conditional upon the values of variables in the future. In static optimisation problems, on the other hand, the values of choice variables in a particular period are conditional upon the values of other variables in the same period only.

A stylised model of household behaviour may represent the two types of problems. The household is confronted by two basic problems: firstly, how much to spend in each period and secondly, how to allocate expenditure in each period among different commodities. Assuming that utility is additively separable in time, the former problem is intertemporal and the latter static. Similarly, producers may face both static and intertemporal optimisation problems. Typically, for example, investment decisions are assumed to be intertemporal in nature whilst labour hiring decisions are treated as static.

Single period CGE models contain optimality conditions derived from the solutions of static optimisation problems. Variables such as investment and aggregate household expenditure, which are dependent on expectations of future outcomes, are usually specified as exogenous to the static CGE model. Alternatively, such variables are endogenised in an *ad hoc* manner. This approach ensures that inter-sectoral resource allocations are optimal in each period but it does not ensure that inter-period resource allocations are optimal. To overcome this problem the values of variables that are dependent on expectations of future outcomes must be derived from the solutions of intertemporal optimisation problems.

The core of ORANI-INT consists of a sequence of T identical single-period CGE sub-models, each of which represents the economy at a different point in time. Sectoral investment and aggregate household consumption are exogenous to each of these single-period CGE sub-models. Overlaid on this structure are sub-models of sectoral investment and aggregate household expenditure that are based on intertemporal optimising behaviour. Amongst other things, commodity prices and factor returns are exogenous to the intertemporal sub-models at each point in time. Solving the static sub-models simultaneously with the intertemporal sub-models yields a sequence of T intertemporally efficient equilibria. That is, resources are allocated optimally at each point in time as well as through time.

Rather than building ORANI-INT from scratch we have adopted an approach that makes maximum use of existing modelling infrastructure. Australia has a strong tradition of CGE modelling dating back to the mid 1970s.[1] Much of this

---

1 For details about CGE modelling in Australia and its influence on policy reform see Powell and Snape (1993).

modelling effort is embodied in ORANI, a static CGE model (see Dixon, Parmenter, Sutton and Vincent, 1982), which continues to be maintained and developed by teams of economists in academia and in government agencies. Given our reluctance to discard the research effort embodied in existing modelling infrastructure, the standard version of ORANI [as described in Dixon, Parmenter, Sutton and Vincent, (1982) and extended in Codsi, Horridge and Pearson (1988)] stands out as the obvious model to use in generating the sequence of T identical single-period CGE sub-models which forms the core of ORANI-INT. However, the standard version of ORANI is very large[2] and quite demanding on computing resources. This size factor becomes an important consideration in developing ORANI-INT because the chosen single-period CGE sub-model must be replicated T times.[3] For development purposes, therefore, it is preferable to use a less cumbersome version of ORANI that is still capable of producing realistic empirical results. Accordingly, we use ORANI-13, a modified version of standard ORANI, as our single-period CGE sub-model. There are five key differences between the standard version of ORANI and ORANI-13. They are:

1. ORANI-13 has 13 single product industries while ORANI has 113 industries, several of which produce more than one product;
2. ORANI-13 recognises one type of labour only whereas ORANI recognises eight occupational groups;
3. ORANI-13 treats demands for margins as if they were direct demands[4] while in ORANI the demand for a margin is assumed to be proportional to the direct demand for the good or service to which it applies;
4. compared to ORANI the range of technical/taste change variables in ORANI-13 is limited;[5]and
5. The equations that govern the behaviour of investors in ORANI are not included in ORANI-13.[6]

---

2 As specified in Dixon, Parmenter, Sutton and Vincent (1982) ORANI consists of several million equations. However, in practical applications of ORANI the number of equations implemented is about one million. To make the computation of ORANI manageable, the model-user must condense the equation system by instructing the software to substitute out specified variables with specified equations (see Codsi and Pearson, 1988). The condensed system contains about 10,000 equations.

3 The simulations reported in chapters 6 and 7 are based on an implementation of ORANI-INT where T equals 30. We have also implemented the model with different values of T (i.e., 20 and 40) to test its sensitivity to the length of the time horizon.

4 By direct demands we mean demands for goods and services by producers (i.e., intermediate inputs) and by final users (i.e., investors, consumers and governments). Margins are services (e.g., transport, retail trade, communications etc.) that are used to facilitate the transfer of commodities from their sources to their users.

5 Every commodity and factor flow in ORANI has a technical/taste change variable associated with it. In most applications of the model, however, these variables are all exogenous and not shocked.

6 Specifically, equations 19.7, 19.8 and 19.9 in Dixon, Parmenter, Sutton and Vincent (1982) are not included in ORANI-13.

The ORANI-INT structure is presented schematically in figure 2.1. ORANI-13 is replicated T times, where T is the length of our time horizon in years, by indexing all the variables in the model with respect to time. Sectoral investment and aggregate household expenditure are exogenous in ORANI-13. The sequence of ORANI-13 models accounts for the bulk of the equations in ORANI-INT. The equations within each of these sub-models are static since they relate variables in a single time period only. The remaining equations are dynamic; they express relationships among variables at different points in time. The purpose of the dynamic equations is to link the sequence of ORANI-13 sub-models across time. These links are provided by accumulation relations between stocks and flows and by intertemporal optimising behaviour on the part of investors and households. Implicit in the specification of the model is the assumption that agents have model consistent expectations.

As indicated by the directions of the arrows in figure 2.1 the ORANI-13 sub-models are linked through time via both forward and backward linkages. For investment, the backward linkages are provided by the capital accumulation equations whilst the forward linkages are provided by the specification of forward-looking rates of return. Similarly, consumption in each period is linked (forward) to future prices and income while current debt is linked (backwards) to past saving. In ORANI-INT only one representative household is modelled and capital is assumed to be sector-specific. This means that the model incorporates 14 independent types of forward-looking behaviour. Of these, 13 relate to the planning of sectoral investment whilst the other relates to the planning of aggregate consumption. There are also 14 accumulation identities modelled; again, 13 of these relate to the accumulation of sectoral capital stocks and the final one relates to the accumulation of foreign debt.

Two sets of boundary conditions complete the model. The initial conditions reflect the state of the economy as described by the latest available data whilst the terminal conditions reflect assumptions about the long-run tendencies of the economy.

2.4 Chapter Summary

The main purpose of this chapter was to provide the reader with a brief overview of the structure of ORANI-INT. The overview should help the reader keep in perspective the details of the model's theoretical structure presented in the next chapter. This chapter also made clear that the atemporal core of ORANI-INT is borrowed from a modified version of ORANI. The design principles underlying ORANI-INT are generic. Any conventional static CGE model can be easily embedded in an intertemporal framework.

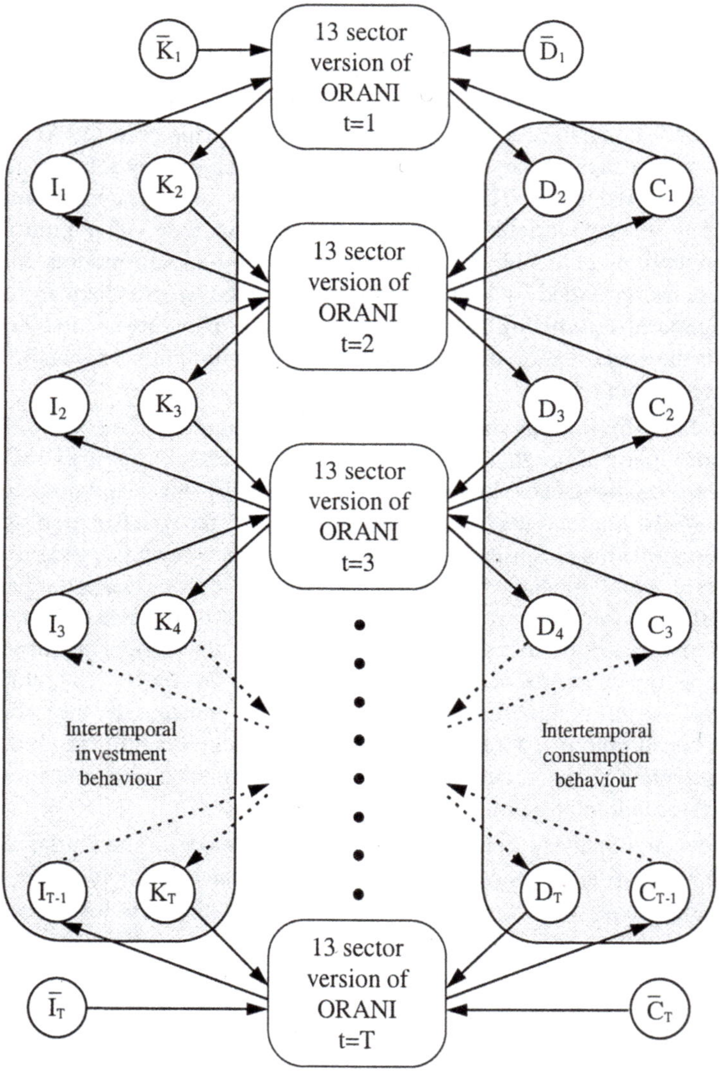

Key:	I_t	t=1,2, ...,T-1	Investment in year t depends on future returns.
	K_t	t=2, ...,T	Capital stock in year t depends on past investments.
	$\bar{K}_1$		Exogenous capital stock in year 1 (initial condition).
	$\bar{I}_T$		Exogenous investment in year T (terminal condition).
	C_t	t=1,2, ...,T-1	Consumption in year t depends on future prices and income.
	D_t	t=2, ...,T	Debt in year t depends on past savings behaviour.
	$\bar{D}_1$		Exogenous stock of debt in year 1 (initial condition).
	$\bar{C}_T$		Exogenous consumption in year T (terminal condition).

Figure 2.1: Schematic Representation of ORANI-INT

Chapter 3 The Theoretical Structure of ORANI-INT

3.1 Introduction

Five types of agents are recognised in ORANI-INT: producers, consumers, investors, governments and foreigners. Producers are grouped into 13 industrial sectors. Each of these sectors produces a single commodity. For each domestic commodity there is assumed to be an imperfect foreign substitute. The 26 commodities are used by the domestic agents (i.e., producers, consumers, investors and governments). A representative foreign agent uses the 13 domestically produced commodities. As well as intermediate inputs, producers use three primary factors (agricultural land, labour and sector-specific capital) and inputs of 'other cost' tickets (which cover miscellaneous industry expenses). Capital is industry-specific and is created by the using industry. Investors can allocate their funds across 15 types of perfectly substitutable assets. These include shares in the 13 industries and foreign and domestic bonds. Zero pure profits are assumed in all activities with taxes on commodity flows putting wedges between basic prices (i.e., the price received by producers before commodity taxes) and purchasers' prices (i.e., the tax inclusive prices).

The demand and supply of most commodities is determined by the optimising behaviour of producers, investors and consumers in the context of competitive markets. Investors and consumers are forward-looking and their expectations are model-consistent. Government demands for commodities are assumed to be exogenous while demands by foreigners are specified in an ad hoc manner. The demands for factors and the supply of capital are also derived from optimising behaviour and competitive market assumptions. The supplies of labour and agricultural land can be specified exogenously or they can be determined by their demands.

In the remainder of this chapter we derive the ORANI-INT equation system. The description of many of the atemporal equations in ORANI-INT draws on the description of ORANI contained in Dixon, Parmenter, Sutton and Vincent (1982) and in Codsi, Horridge and Pearson (1988).[1] To structure the discussion we have partitioned the equations into the following five categories:

---

[1] While the description of the theoretical structure of ORANI -INT in this chapter is self-contained, further details about the atemporal parts of the model can be found in these two

1. those describing producers demands for commodity inputs and for variable primary factors;
2. those describing final demands for commodities by consumers, investors, governments, exporters, and importers;
3. those relating the demands and supplies of commodities and primary factors;
4. those relating prices to costs in all activities; and
5. those that define a range of macroeconomic aggregates.

Each of these five categories of equations is described in turn in the next five sections (i.e., 3.2 - 3.6). However, before turning to the equations we make two digressions. The notation employed in describing the equations in ORANI-INT is necessarily tedious. In some cases we need to use four subscripts and a superscript to distinguish a variable. In sub-section 3.1.1 we set out the main notational conventions that we follow in this chapter. The second digression, presented in sub-section 3.1.2, explains how the equations derived in this chapter are represented in the software that we use to solve ORANI-INT.

3.1.1 Notational Conventions

In describing the equations of the model we will explain each new piece of notation as it is introduced. In this sub-section we provide a brief description of our notation. This description is not meant to be exhaustive. Rather, our aim is to help the reader come to grips with the notation by describing those parts of it that are generic.

The variables and parameters in the model are denoted by a symbol that is usually accompanied by a superscript and one or more subscripts. Several symbols are reserved for describing particular classes of variables. These are as follows:

X ⇔ demands for commodities, primary factors and 'other cost' tickets;

Z ⇔ supplies of commodities, primary factors and 'other cost' tickets;

P ⇔ prices of commodities, primary factors and 'other cost' tickets;

A ⇔ technical or taste change;

V ⇔ indirect tax revenues;

τ ⇔ ad valorem tax rate; and

T ⇔ power of tax (i.e., $1 + \tau$).

To indicate the agent or primary factor to which the above variables apply we use superscripts. To avoid confusion with exponents the superscripts are put in brackets. We use the following superscripted numbers to differentiate agents:

(1) ⇔ producers;

references. Dixon, Parmenter, Sutton and Vincent (1982) describe in detail the theoretical structure of ORANI. A faithful computer implementation of this model is described in Codsi, Horridge and Pearson (1988). A range of accounting equations defining macroeconomic variables was added to the computer implementation of the model for reporting purposes.

(2) ⇔ capital creators;
(3) ⇔ households;
(4) ⇔ exporters;
(5) ⇔ government; and
(6) ⇔ importers.

Primary factors and 'other cost' tickets are distinguished by the following superscripts:

(F) ⇔ primary factor composite (i.e., a CES aggregate of labour, capital and agricultural land);
(L) ⇔ labour;
(K) ⇔ capital;
(N) ⇔ agricultural land; and
(O) ⇔ 'other cost' tickets.

We also use superscripts, (R) and (Π), to distinguish real macroeconomic variables from their price counterparts.

To identify commodity type, commodity source, industrial sector, and years we use the following subscripts:

i ⇔ commodity type, range 1 to 13;
s ⇔ commodity source, s=d denotes domestic source, s=f denotes foreign source, and s=• denotes a CES aggregate of a domestic and foreign good;
j ⇔ industrial sector, range 1 to 13; and
t ⇔ year, range for most variables is 1 to T but for some variables 0 and T+1 is relevant.

While not all variables carry all four subscripts, those that are carried appear in the order listed above.

To demonstrate how our notation scheme works we offer several examples:

$X^{(K)}_{j,t}$ ⇔ demand for capital by sector j in year t;
$X^{(2)}_{i,s,j,t}$ ⇔ demand by capital creators in sector j for commodity i from source s in year t;
$Z^{(1)}_{j,t}$ ⇔ supply of output by sector j in year t;
$P^{(L)}_{j,t}$ ⇔ price of labour to sector j in year t;
$P^{(1)}_{i,s,j,t}$ ⇔ price to producers in sector j for commodity i from source s in year t;
$C^{(R)}_{t}$ ⇔ aggregate real household consumption in year t;
$C^{(\Pi)}_{t}$ ⇔ price deflator for aggregate household consumption in year t;
$X^{(5)}_{i,\bullet,t}$ ⇔ demand by government for composite (domestic and foreign) commodity i in year t;
$T^{(3)}_{i,d,t}$ ⇔ power of the tax on domestically produced commodity i used by households in year t; and
$T^{(2)}_{i,f,j,t}$ ⇔ power of the tax on foreign-sourced commodity i used by capital creators in sector j in year t.

3.1.2 Computational Issues and the Presentation of Equations

In chapter 4 we describe the method by which ORANI-INT is solved. Whilst the software that we use allows us to implement ORANI-INT's structural equations directly in their non-linear form, we choose instead to implement the structural equations in their log-linear form. This choice is of no consequence to the solutions that we obtain. However, as will be explained in chapter 4, we find the linearised equations convenient for three main reasons: first, they are easier to calibrate; second, for many equations we find the linear form easier to interpret than the non-linear form; and third, it is easier to devise back-of-the-envelope calculations with the linearised equations. This last advantage is important because back-of-the-envelope calculations provide a means for checking that the model has been implemented correctly and also because such calculations can be used to bring to the fore the critical elements of the model's theory and data base underlying the results of a particular experiment. In explaining the results of the illustrative simulations presented in chapters 6 and 7 we make liberal use of back-of-the-envelope calculations.

In this chapter we present the ORANI-INT equation system in both its non-linear and linear forms. The model's equations are derived in their non-linear form in sections 3.2 - 3.6. In appendix 3.1 we present the linearised equation system in a table. The linearised equations listed in this table are mapped to their non-linear counterparts derived in sections 3.2 - 3.6.

3.2 Industry Behaviour

ORANI-INT recognises 13 industrial sectors. Each of these sectors produces a unique commodity output and a unique capital good. The capital formation process is assumed to be sector-specific so that the representative agent in each sector must make current production decisions as well as investment decisions. In each period the representative producer/investor (hereafter referred to simply as the producer) takes all prices as given and decides simultaneously how much to invest, how much to produce and what inputs to use. For convenience we have divided the producer's decision problem into an atemporal part and an intertemporal part. In this section we deal with the producer's atemporal problem which involves choosing for each year the optimal output level and the optimal usage of inputs other than capital. The producer's intertemporal problem is to choose the optimal time paths of investment and capital stock. The intertemporal problem is dealt with in section 3.3.2.

The production technology assumed in ORANI-INT is represented schematically in figure 3.1. The ovals in the figure indicate the form of the functional relationship between the variables contained in the boxes. The production function is nested and has two tiers. Constant returns to scale are assumed at both levels of the production function. At the top level the production function is assumed to be Leontief (i.e., inputs are used in fixed proportions). In year t industry j uses intermediate inputs of composite commodity i, $X^{(1)}_{i,\bullet j,t}$, in fixed proportion with: intermediate inputs of composite commodity k, $X^{(1)}_{k,\bullet j,t}$ k≠i; a composite primary factor input, $X^{(F)}_{j,t}$; and 'other cost' tickets, $X^{(O)}_{j,t}$. At the bottom level of the nest the composite commodities are defined by a CES aggregate that allows producers to respond to changes in the relative prices of domestic and foreign goods of the same input-output category by substituting between $X^{(1)}_{i,d,t}$, domestically sourced commodity i, and $X^{(1)}_{i,f,t}$, foreign sourced commodity i. Composite primary factor inputs are defined by a CES aggregate that allows producers to respond to changes in the relative prices of factors by substituting between $X^{(N)}_{j,t}$, agricultural land, $X^{(K)}_{j,t}$, fixed capital, and $X^{(L)}_{j,t}$, labour.

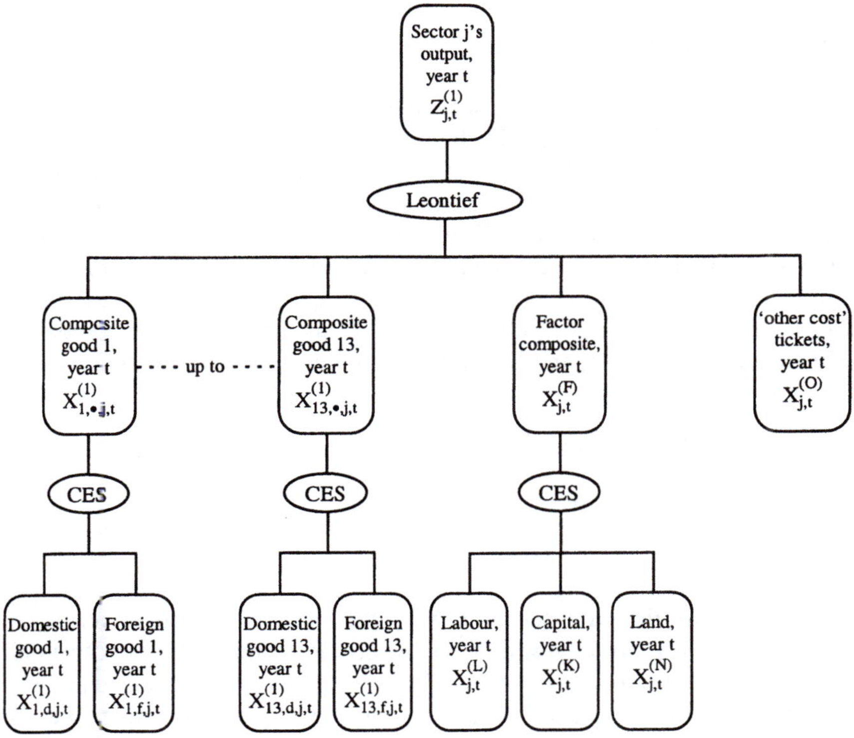

Figure 3.1: Specification of Production Technology

The production technology assumed in ORANI-INT allows us to treat the producer's atemporal optimisation problem in three parts. The separability assumed between the two tiers of the production function allows us to derive the input demand equations for the 13 domestic and 13 foreign commodities and for labour and agricultural land independently of the input demand equations for 'other cost' tickets, the factor composite and the 13 composite commodities. In addition, because the top level of the production function has the Leontief form the demand equations for commodity inputs can be derived separately from the factor demand equations.

In the next sub-section we explain how the demand for the factor composite and the demands for labour and agricultural land can be derived from the solution to a profit maximisation problem. In sub-section 3.2.2 we deal with the upper level of the production function. At this level the production function is assumed to be Leontief and, with the demand for the factor composite already determined, the demands for composite commodities and 'other cost' tickets and the supply of output, $Z^{(1)}_{j,t}$, can also be determined. The input demands for the 13 domestic and 13 foreign commodities are dealt with in sub-section 3.2.3.

3.2.1 Factor Demands

In each period the representative producer in each sector takes as given all prices and the *effective* stock of capital. In this context the term *effective* is used to indicate that a variable, in this case the capital stock, has been adjusted for technical change. Below we will use a superscript * to distinguish such variables. For example, $X^{(K^*)}_{j,t}$ is the demand for effective units of capital. As will be explained in section 3.3.2 the stock of capital available in the current period is assumed to be a function of past investments only. Under these conditions the representative producer in sector j chooses $X^{(F^*)}_{j,t}$, effective units of the primary factor composite, $X^{(L^*)}_{j,t}$, effective units of labour, and $X^{(N^*)}_{j,t}$, effective units of agricultural land, in each year to maximise profits in year t,

$$\Xi_{j,t} = P^{(F^*)}_{j,t} X^{(F^*)}_{j,t} - P^{(L^*)}_{j,t} X^{(L^*)}_{j,t} - P^{(N^*)}_{j,t} X^{(N^*)}_{j,t}. \qquad j = 1, ..., 13, t = 1, ..., T \qquad (3.2.1)$$

The production technology, given by

$$X^{(F^*)}_{j,t} = CES(X^{(L^*)}_{j,t}, X^{(K^*)}_{j,t}, X^{(N^*)}_{j,t}), \qquad j = 1, ..., 13, t = 1, ..., T \qquad (3.2.2)$$

is taken as given by the producer as is $X^{(K^*)}_{j,t}$, the stock of capital in year t. In equation (3.2.1) $\Xi_{j,t}$ is profit in year t, $P^{(L^*)}_{j,t}$ is the cost to sector j of an effective unit of labour, $P^{(N^*)}_{j,t}$ is the cost to sector j of an effective unit of agricultural land and $P^{(F^*)}_{j,t}$ is the price to sector j of the factor composite per effective unit of output. We use the notation CES( ) in equation (3.2.2) to denote a constant elasticity of substitution function, the arguments of which are enclosed in the brackets. The effective units of $X^{(F)}_{j,t}$, $X^{(K)}_{j,t}$, $X^{(L)}_{j,t}$ and $X^{(N)}_{j,t}$ and the corresponding effective prices are defined as follows:

$$X^{(F^*)}_{j,t} = \frac{X^{(F)}_{j,t}}{A^{(F)}_{j,t}}; \; X^{(K^*)}_{j,t} = \frac{X^{(K)}_{j,t}}{A^{(K)}_{j,t}}; \; X^{(L^*)}_{j,t} = \frac{X^{(L)}_{j,t}}{A^{(L)}_{j,t}}; \; X^{(N^*)}_{j,t} = \frac{X^{(N)}_{j,t}}{A^{(N)}_{j,t}};$$

$$P^{(F^*)}_{j,t} = P^{(F)}_{j,t} A^{(F)}_{j,t}; \; P^{(K^*)}_{j,t} = P^{(K)}_{j,t} A^{(K)}_{j,t}; \; P^{(L^*)}_{j,t} = P^{(L)}_{j,t} A^{(L)}_{j,t}; \text{ and } P^{(N^*)}_{j,t} = P^{(N)}_{j,t} A^{(N)}_{j,t}$$

The variables $A_{j,t}^{(F)}$, $A_{j,t}^{(K)}$, $A_{j,t}^{(L)}$ and $A_{j,t}^{(N)}$ denote, respectively, all-primary-factor technical change, capital-saving technical change, labour-saving technical change and agricultural-land-saving technical change.

Using the method of Lagrange multipliers we can solve the above optimisation problem and derive the following demand equations for labour, agricultural land and for the factor composite:

$$X_{j,t}^{(L*)} = X_{j,t}^{(F*)} \zeta_{j,t}^{(L)1/(1+\mu)} \left\{ \frac{P_{j,t}^{(L*)}}{P_{j,t}^{(F*)}} \right\}^{\frac{-1}{1+\mu}}; \qquad j = 1, \ldots, 13, t = 1, \ldots, T \qquad (3.2.3)$$

$$X_{j,t}^{(N*)} = X_{j,t}^{(F*)} \zeta_{j,t}^{(N)1/(1+\mu)} \left\{ \frac{P_{j,t}^{(N*)}}{P_{j,t}^{(F*)}} \right\}^{\frac{-1}{1+\mu}}; \qquad j = 1, \ldots, 13, t = 1, \ldots, T \qquad (3.2.4)$$

$$X_{j,t}^{(F*)} = X_{j,t}^{(K*)} \zeta_{j,t}^{(K)-1/\mu} \left[1 - \zeta_{j,t}^{(L)1/(1+\mu)} \left\{ \frac{P_{j,t}^{(L*)}}{P_{j,t}^{(F*)}} \right\}^{\frac{\mu}{1+\mu}} - \zeta_{j,t}^{(N)1/(1+\mu)} \left\{ \frac{P_{j,t}^{(N*)}}{P_{j,t}^{(F*)}} \right\}^{\frac{\mu}{1+\mu}} \right]^{\frac{1}{\mu}}.$$

$$j = 1, \ldots, 13, t = 1, \ldots, T \qquad (3.2.5)$$

In equations (3.2.3) - (3.2.5) ζ and μ are parameters that have the following properties: $-1 < \mu \neq 0$; $\zeta_{j,t}^{(L)}, \zeta_{j,t}^{(K)}, \zeta_{j,t}^{(N)} > 0$; and $\zeta_{j,t}^{(L)} + \zeta_{j,t}^{(K)} + \zeta_{j,t}^{(N)} = 1$.

Pure profits accruing to the users of primary factors are assumed to be zero. Thus, the revenue generated by the primary factors is equal to the cost of using them. That is:

$$P_{j,t}^{(F*)} X_{j,t}^{(F*)} = P_{j,t}^{(K*)} X_{j,t}^{(K*)} + P_{j,t}^{(L*)} X_{j,t}^{(L*)} + P_{j,t}^{(N*)} X_{j,t}^{(N*)} \qquad j = 1, \ldots, 13, t = 1, \ldots, T \qquad (3.2.6)$$

The only new variable introduced in equation (3.2.6) is $P_{j,t}^{(K*)}$, the rental price of an effective unit of capital specific to sector j. Substituting equations (3.2.3) - (3.2.5) into the zero pure profits condition (3.2.6) and solving for the price of the factor composite, $P_{j,t}^{(F*)}$, we obtain the unit cost function that is dual to the CES production function (3.2.2). That is:

$$P_{j,t}^{(F*)} = \left\{ \zeta_{j,t}^{(L)1/(1+\mu)} P_{j,t}^{(L*)\mu/(1+\mu)} + \zeta_{j,t}^{(K)1/(1+\mu)} P_{j,t}^{(K*)\mu/(1+\mu)} + \zeta_{j,t}^{(N)1/(1+\mu)} P_{j,t}^{(N*)\mu/(1+\mu)} \right\}^{\frac{1+\mu}{\mu}}.$$

$$j = 1, \ldots, 13, t = 1, \ldots, T \qquad (3.2.7)$$

Rearranging the unit cost function we can obtain an expression for the term in square brackets in equation (3.2.5) that relates the price of capital to the price of the factor composite as follows:

$$\left[1 - \zeta_{j,t}^{(L)1/(1+\mu)} \left\{ \frac{P_{j,t}^{(L*)}}{P_{j,t}^{(F*)}} \right\}^{\frac{\mu}{1+\mu}} - \zeta_{j,t}^{(N)1/(1+\mu)} \left\{ \frac{P_{j,t}^{(N*)}}{P_{j,t}^{(F*)}} \right\}^{\frac{\mu}{1+\mu}} \right] = \zeta_{j,t}^{(K)1/(1+\mu)} \left\{ \frac{P_{j,t}^{(K*)}}{P_{j,t}^{(F*)}} \right\}^{\frac{\mu}{1+\mu}}.$$

$$j = 1, \ldots, 13, t = 1, \ldots, T \qquad (3.2.8)$$

Substituting equation (3.2.8) into equation (3.2.5) and rearranging we obtain a demand function for capital that has the same form as the demand functions for labour and agricultural land (i.e., equations (3.2.3) and (3.2.4)). That is:

$$X_{j,t}^{(K*)} = X_{j,t}^{(F*)} \zeta_{j,t}^{(K)1/(1+\mu)} \left\{ \frac{P_{j,t}^{(K*)}}{P_{j,t}^{(F*)}} \right\}^{\frac{-1}{1+\mu}}. \qquad j = 1, ..., 13,\ t = 1, ..., T \qquad (3.2.9)$$

3.2.2 Demands for Composite Commodities and 'Other Cost' Tickets and the Supply of Output

Having worked out the profit maximising input of the factor composite in the previous sub-section we can now derive the profit maximising output level. Since the top tier of the nested production function has the Leontief form we can express sector j's output in year t, $Z_{j,t}^{(1)}$, as follows:

$$Z_{j,t}^{(1)} = \mathrm{Min}\left\{ \frac{X_{1,\bullet,j,t}^{(1)}}{A_{1,\bullet,j,t}^{(1)}}, \ldots, \frac{X_{13,\bullet,j,t}^{(1)}}{A_{13,\bullet,j,t}^{(1)}} ; \frac{X_{j,t}^{(F)}}{A_{j,t}^{(F)}} ; \frac{X_{j,t}^{(O)}}{A_{j,t}^{(O)}} \right\}. \qquad j = 1, ..., 13,\ t = 1, ..., T \qquad (3.2.10)$$

The A terms in equation (3.2.10) are positive parameters. Using the expression for $X_{j,t}^{(F*)}$ derived in equation (3.2.5), the profit maximising output level is:

$$Z_{j,t}^{(1)} = X_{j,t}^{(K*)} \zeta_{j,t}^{(K)-1/\mu} \left[1 - \zeta_{j,t}^{(L)1/(1+\mu)} \left\{ \frac{P_{j,t}^{(L*)}}{P_{j,t}^{(F*)}} \right\}^{\frac{\mu}{1+\mu}} - \zeta_{j,t}^{(N)1/(1+\mu)} \left\{ \frac{P_{j,t}^{(N*)}}{P_{j,t}^{(F*)}} \right\}^{\frac{\mu}{1+\mu}} \right]^{\frac{1}{\mu}}.$$

$$j = 1, ..., 13,\ t = 1, ..., T \qquad (3.2.11)$$

The demand equations for inputs of the 13 composite commodities and 'other cost' tickets have the following form:

$$X_{i,\bullet,j,t}^{(1)} = Z_{j,t}^{(1)} A_{i,\bullet,j,t}^{(1)}. \qquad i = 1, ..., 13,\ j = 1, ..., 13,\ t = 1, ..., T \qquad (3.2.12)$$

$$X_{j,t}^{(O)} = Z_{j,t}^{(1)} A_{j,t}^{(O)}. \qquad j = 1, ..., 13,\ t = 1, ..., T \qquad (3.2.13)$$

Since the profit maximising output level is known from equation (3.2.9), the profit maximising inputs of the 13 composite commodities and 'other cost' tickets can be derived from equations (3.2.12) and (3.2.13).

3.2.3 Demands for Domestic and Foreign Commodities

The representative producer in sector j takes as given all prices and the usage of composite commodity i in year t and chooses $X_{i,s,j,t}^{(1)}$, inputs of commodity i from source s in year t, to minimise

$$P^{(1)}_{i,\bullet,j,t}\, X^{(1)}_{i,\bullet,j,t} = P^{(1)}_{i,d,j,t}\, X^{(1)}_{i,d,j,t} + P^{(1)}_{i,f,j,t}\, X^{(1)}_{i,f,j,t}, \quad i = 1, \ldots, 13, j = 1, \ldots, 13, t = 1, \ldots, T \qquad (3.2.14)$$

the cost to industry j of composite commodity i in year t, subject to the constraint that

$$X^{(1)}_{i,\bullet,j,t} = \text{CES}(X^{(1)}_{i,d,j,t}, X^{(1)}_{i,f,j,t}). \quad i = 1, \ldots, 13, j = 1, \ldots, 13, t = 1, \ldots, T \qquad (3.2.15)$$

In equation (3.2.14) the Ps denote the prices paid by the producers in sector j for the corresponding Xs. Following Armington (1969, 1970) the CES specification of composite commodities implies that domestic and foreign commodities of the same input-output classification are imperfect substitutes.

From the solution to the above cost minimisation problem we can derive input demand equations that have the following form:

$$X^{(1)}_{i,s,j,t} = X^{(1)}_{i,\bullet,j,t} \varsigma^{1/(1+\nu)}_{i,s,j,t} P^{(1)-1/(1+\nu)}_{i,s,j,t} \left\{ \sum_k \varsigma^{1/(1+\nu)}_{i,k,j,t} P^{(1)\nu/(1+\nu)}_{i,k,j,t} \right\}^{\frac{1}{\nu}};$$

$$i = 1, \ldots, 13, s = d,f, k = d,f, t = 1, \ldots, T \qquad (3.2.16)$$

where ς and ν are parameters (with $-1 < \nu \neq 0$; $\varsigma_{i,k,j,t} > 0$; and $\sum_i \varsigma_{i,k,j,t} = 1$). The prices of the composite commodities are given by the unit cost functions that are dual to the CES production functions (3.2.15). That is:

$$P^{(1)}_{i,\bullet,j,t} = \left\{ \sum_s \varsigma^{1/(1+\nu)}_{i,s,j,t} P^{(1)\nu/(1+\nu)}_{i,s,j,t} \right\}^{\frac{1+\nu}{\nu}}$$

$$i = 1, \ldots, 13, s = d,f, j = 1, \ldots, 13, t = 1, \ldots, T \qquad (3.2.17)$$

3.3 Final Demands

In ORANI-INT four sources of final demand are identified for the 13 domestically produced commodities and their foreign substitutes. These are demands by households, capital creators, governments and foreigners. In the following four sub-sections we describe the commodity demand equations for each of these four agents.

3.3.1 Household Demands

The forward-looking consumption model implemented in ORANI-INT is a discrete time elaboration of Lluch's (1973) Extended Linear Expenditure System (ELES). We make three key assumptions about the behaviour of households. Firstly, we assume that the behaviour of all households in the economy is identical. This assumption allows us to deal with the household sector as if it were a single aggregative agent. To differentiate the representative household from the household sector we identify variables that refer to the former by marking them with tildes. For example, $\tilde{U}$ is the level of utility derived by the representative household while U is the level of utility derived by the household sector. Since all households are identical it follows that $U = Q\tilde{U}$, where Q is the number of households. Secondly, we avoid tackling inter-generational transfer issues (e.g., bequests) by assuming that households are infinitely lived. Thirdly, we assume that households have model-consistent expectations.

The representative household takes as given all prices and its lifetime income and allocates its expenditure across commodities and across time to maximise its intertemporal utility. The specification of the household's intertemporal utility function is represented schematically in figure 3.2. The ovals in the figure indicate the form of the functional relationship between the variables contained in the boxes. The utility function is nested with three tiers. At the top tier of the nest, intertemporal utility is the discounted sum of the single-period utility functions. At the second tier, utility in each year is a Stone-Geary (or Klein-Rubin) function of the above-subsistence quantities of composite commodities consumed. The total quantity of composite commodity i consumed is denoted $\tilde{X}^{(3)}_{i,\bullet,t}$ and the subsistence quantity of composite commodity i consumed is denoted by the parameter $\tilde{\gamma}^{(3)}_{i,\bullet}$. Thus, the above-subsistence consumption of composite commodity i is $[\tilde{X}^{(3)}_{i,\bullet,t} - \tilde{\gamma}^{(3)}_{i,\bullet}]$. At the bottom level of the nest the composite commodities are defined by a CES aggregate that allows households to respond to changes in the relative prices of domestic and foreign goods of the same input-output category by substituting between $\tilde{X}^{(3)}_{i,d,t}$, domestically sourced commodity i, and $\tilde{X}^{(3)}_{i,f,t}$, foreign sourced commodity i.

The separability of the intertemporal utility function allows us to treat the household's optimisation problem as three sub-problems, corresponding to the three tiers of the utility function depicted in figure 3.2. We derive the equations in ORANI-INT that relate to household behaviour from the solutions to these three sub-problems. Working up from the bottom level of the utility structure shown in figure 3.2 we derive equations which show how the household allocates its expenditure across: the 13 domestic and 13 foreign commodities; the 13 composite commodities; and time.

Allocation of Expenditure Across Domestic and Foreign Commodities

At the bottom level of the nested utility function the household takes as given all prices and $\tilde{X}^{(3)}_{i,\bullet,t}$, the quantity of composite commodity i in year t. The quantity of $\tilde{X}^{(3)}_{i,s,t}$, commodity i from source s in year t, is chosen to minimise

$$P^{(3)}_{i,\bullet,t}\tilde{X}^{(3)}_{i,\bullet,t} = P^{(3)}_{i,d,t}\tilde{X}^{(3)}_{i,d,t} + P^{(3)}_{i,f,t}\tilde{X}^{(3)}_{i,f,t}\,, \qquad i = 1, \ldots, 13,\ t = 1, \ldots, T \qquad (3.3.1)$$

the cost of composite commodity i in year t, subject to the constraint that

$$\tilde{X}^{(3)}_{i,s,t} = \mathrm{CES}(\, \tilde{X}^{(3)}_{i,d,t}\,, \tilde{X}^{(3)}_{i,f,t}\,)\,. \qquad i = 1, \ldots, 13,\ t = 1, \ldots, T \qquad (3.3.2)$$

In equation (3.3.1) the Ps denote the prices paid by the household for the corresponding Xs. Again we follow Armington (1969, 1970) in assuming that domestic and foreign commodities of the same input-output classification are imperfect substitutes.

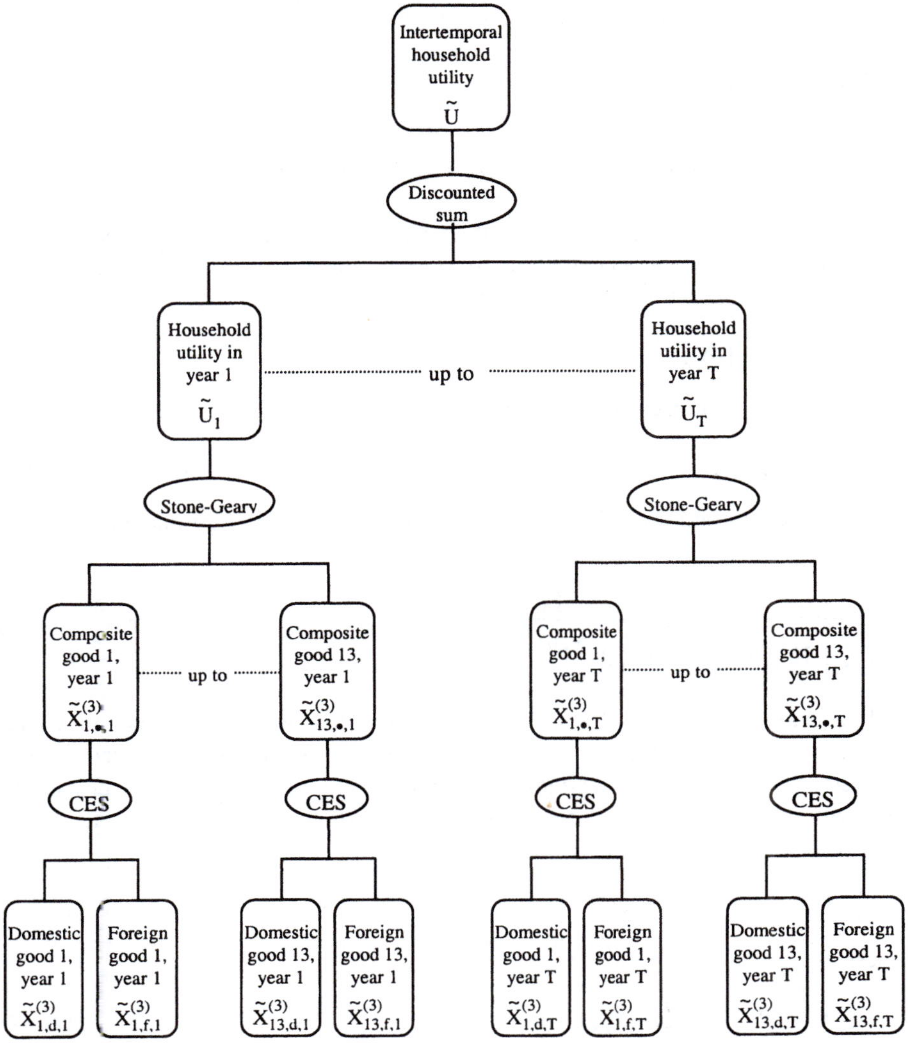

Figure 3.2: Specification of Household Utility

Using the method of Lagrange multipliers we can derive a solution to the above optimisation problem in which the demand equations have the following form:

$$\tilde{X}^{(3)}_{i,s,t} = \tilde{X}^{(3)}_{i,\bullet,t}\, \xi_{i,s,t}^{1/(1+\varepsilon)} P_{i,s,t}^{(3)-1/(1+\varepsilon)} \left\{ \sum_{k} \xi_{i,k,t}^{1/(1+\varepsilon)} P_{i,k,t}^{(3)\varepsilon/(1+\varepsilon)} \right\}^{\frac{1}{\varepsilon}} .$$

$$i = 1, \ldots, 13;\ s = d,f;\ k = d,f;\ t = 1, \ldots, T \qquad (3.3.3)$$

In equation (3.3.3) ξ and ε are parameters (with $-1 < \varepsilon \neq 0$; $\xi_{i,k,t} > 0$; and $\sum_i \xi_{i,k,t} = 1$). The price of the composite commodity is given by the unit cost function that is dual to the CES production function (3.3.2). That is:

$$P^{(3)}_{i,\bullet,t} = \left\{ \sum_s \xi^{1/(1+\varepsilon)}_{i,s,t} P^{(3)\varepsilon/(1+\varepsilon)}_{i,s,t} \right\}^{\frac{(1+\varepsilon)}{\varepsilon}} . \qquad i = 1, ..., 13;\ s = d,f;\ t = 1, ..., T \qquad (3.3.4)$$

Allocation of Expenditure Across Composite Commodities

At the second level of the nested utility function the household takes as given all prices and $\tilde{C}_t$, its total expenditure in year t. The quantity of $\tilde{X}^{(3)}_{i,\bullet,t}$, composite commodity i in year t, is chosen to maximise

$$\tilde{U}_t = \sum_{i=1}^{13} \beta_i \ln [\, \tilde{X}^{(3)}_{i,\bullet,t} - \tilde{\gamma}_{i,\bullet}] , \qquad t = 1, ..., T \qquad (3.3.5)$$

utility[2] in year t, subject to the constraint

$$\tilde{C}_t = \sum_{i=1}^{13} P^{(3)}_{i,\bullet,t} \tilde{X}^{(3)}_{i,\bullet,t} . \qquad t = 1, ..., T \qquad (3.3.6)$$

The first order conditions derived from the solution to this optimisation problem are:

$$\frac{\beta_i}{P^{(3)}_{i,\bullet,t}[\, \tilde{X}^{(3)}_{i,\bullet,t} - \tilde{\gamma}_{i,\bullet}]} = \frac{\beta_k}{P^{(3)}_{k,\bullet,t}[\, \tilde{X}^{(3)}_{k,\bullet,t} - \tilde{\gamma}_{k,\bullet}]} \qquad i,k = 1, ..., 13;\ i \neq k;\ t = 1, ..., T \qquad (3.3.7)$$

and the budget constraint (3.3.6). We assume that the sum of the β_is is one. Under this assumption summing equation (3.3.7) over k gives a demand system that is consistent with the Linear Expenditure System (LES) where the above-subsistence expenditure on composite commodity i is a constant share of $\tilde{C}^{(a)}_t$, total above-subsistence expenditure. That is:

$$P^{(3)}_{i,\bullet,t}[\, \tilde{X}^{(3)}_{i,\bullet,t} - \tilde{\gamma}_{i,\bullet}] = \beta_i\, \tilde{C}^{(a)}_t \qquad i = 1, ..., 13;\ t = 1, ..., T \qquad (3.3.8)$$

where,

$$\tilde{C}^{(a)}_t = \sum_{k=1}^{13} P^{(3)}_{k,\bullet,t}[\, \tilde{X}^{(3)}_{k,\bullet,t} - \tilde{\gamma}_{k,\bullet}] . \qquad t = 1, ..., T \qquad (3.3.9)$$

We can obtain an expression for total expenditure on composite commodity i in year t by re-arranging equation (3.3.8) as follows:

$$P^{(3)}_{i,\bullet,t} \tilde{X}^{(3)}_{i,\bullet,t} = \beta_i\, \tilde{C}^{(a)}_t + P^{(3)}_{i,\bullet,t} \tilde{\gamma}^{(3)}_{i,\bullet} \qquad i = 1, ..., 13;\ t = 1, ..., T \qquad (3.3.10)$$

Because of the particular normalisation that we have chosen for the βs in the utility function (i.e., they sum to one), we can interpret $\tilde{U}_t$ as real *above-*

---

[2] Household preferences are defined over consumption only. We do not attempt to model labour supply because the necessary parameter values are unavailable. The expenditure and price elasticities that we use are taken from the ORANI parameter files and these do not support the disaggregation of preferences over consumption and leisure.

subsistence consumption in year t, say $\tilde{C}_t^{(R,a)}$. The following deflator for *above-subsistence* expenditure, $\tilde{C}_t^{(\Pi,a)}$, is derived from the above-subsistence unit expenditure function that is dual to the Stone-Geary utility function:

$$C_t^{(\Pi,a)} = \prod_{i=1}^{13} \left\{ \frac{P_{i,\bullet,t}^{(3)}}{\beta_i} \right\}^{\beta_i} . \qquad t = 1, \ldots, T \qquad (3.3.11)$$

Allocation of Expenditure Across Time

At the top level of the utility nest the problem for the household is to choose $\tilde{C}_t^{(a)}$, total above-subsistence expenditure in year t, to maximise intertemporal utility,[3]

$$\tilde{U} = \sum_{t=1}^{T} \tilde{U}_t (1 + \rho)^{-t} , \qquad (3.3.12)$$

subject to the following budget constraint:

$$\tilde{\Omega} = \sum_{t=1}^{T} \left\{ \frac{\tilde{C}_t}{\prod_{u=0}^{t-1} [1 + B_{d,t}]} \right\} . \qquad (3.3.13)$$

The parameter ρ in equation (3.3.12) is the pure time preference rate. The household takes as given all prices as well as, $B_{d,t}$, the nominal safe domestic bond rate, and $\tilde{\Omega}$, the present value of the expected stream of disposable income. Whilst the budget constraint is expressed in terms of total expenditure rather than total above-subsistence expenditure (the choice variable) we can deduce from equations (3.3.6) and (3.3.9) a straightforward relationship between the two expenditure concepts. That is:

$$\tilde{C}_t = \tilde{C}_t^{(a)} + \sum_{i=1}^{13} P_{i,\bullet,t}^{(3)} \tilde{\gamma}_{i,\bullet}^{(3)} \qquad t = 1, \ldots, T \qquad (3.3.14)$$

To solve the above optimisation problem it is convenient to use the indirect form of the single-period utility function. Rearranging equation (3.3.8) we can obtain an expression in which the above-subsistence quantity of composite commodity i consumed in year t is a function of its price and total above-subsistence consumption in year t. That is:

$$[\tilde{X}_{i,\bullet,t}^{(3)} - \tilde{\gamma}_{i,\bullet}] = \frac{\beta_i \tilde{C}_t^{(a)}}{P_{i,\bullet,t}^{(3)}} . \qquad i = 1, \ldots, 13; t = 1, \ldots, T \qquad (3.3.15)$$

The indirect form of the single-period utility function (3.3.5) can therefore be written as:

[3] Note that $\tilde{U}_t$ has dimensions utils per unit time period as seen during that time period, while $\tilde{U}$ is measured in utils as seen at t=0.

$$\tilde{U}_t = \sum_{i=1}^{13} \beta_i \ln\left[\frac{\beta_i \tilde{C}_t^{(a)}}{P_{i,\bullet,t}^{(3)}}\right]. \qquad t = 1, ..., T \qquad (3.3.16)$$

Again we can use the method of Lagrange multipliers to derive a solution to the household's intertemporal optimisation problem. The first-order conditions that characterise the solution to this problem are:

$$\frac{\partial \tilde{U}_{t+1}/\partial \tilde{C}_{t+1}^{(a)}}{\partial \tilde{U}_t/\partial \tilde{C}_t^{(a)}} = \frac{\tilde{C}_t^{(a)}}{\tilde{C}_{t+1}^{(a)}} = \left[\frac{1+\rho}{1+B_{d,t}}\right]; \qquad t = 1, ..., T-1 \qquad (3.3.17)$$

and the budget constraint (3.3.13). Since expectations are assumed to be model consistent, the household's expectations about future prices and quantities are realised. The optimising household allocates its budget across time to equalise the marginal utility of consumption across time. Equation (3.3.17) implies that the path of nominal above-subsistence consumption will be rising (falling) over time if the nominal bond rate is greater (smaller) than the time preference rate.

Although the representative household takes, $\tilde{\Omega}$, the present value of its stream of disposable income as given, Ω, the present value of the *aggregate* income stream ($\Omega = Q\tilde{\Omega}$), is endogenous to the economy as a whole. Its value is determined indirectly by an economy-wide budget constraint. The economy-wide budget constraint is enforced by a terminal condition that requires the ratio of net foreign liabilities (i.e., national debt) to GDP to stabilise by the end of the planning period. That is:

$$\frac{D_t}{GDP_t} = \frac{D_{t+1}}{GDP_{t+1}}, \qquad t = T-1 \qquad (3.3.18)$$

where D is the nominal Australian dollar value of net foreign liabilities. For simplicity we assume that foreign interests in Australia (or *vice versa*) are held as debt rather than equity and that net foreign liabilities are denominated in foreign currency. Under these assumptions net foreign liabilities accumulate as follows:

$$\frac{D_t}{\Phi_t} = \frac{1}{\Phi_{t-1}}\left\{D_{t-1}[1 + B_{f,t-1}] - (E_t - M_t) + S_t\right\}, \qquad t = 1, ..., T \qquad (3.3.19)$$

where Φ is the nominal exchange rate (\$Australian/\$Foreign); $B_{f,t}$ is the nominal safe foreign bond rate; E and M are the domestic currency values of exports and imports; and S represents unrequited transfers. Implicit in equation (3.3.19) is the idea that net foreign liabilities can be accumulated actively or passively. Active accumulation occurs when trade deficits or unrequited transfers (e.g., foreign aid) add to the stock of net foreign liabilities. Passive accumulation occurs when interest on existing net foreign liabilities is added to the stock of net foreign liabilities in the next year or when exchange rate movements cause existing liabilities to be re-valued.

In appendix 3.2 we explain how the debt constraint (3.3.18) is sufficient to tie down the value of Ω. A brief sketch of the explanation is as follows. Factor incomes are constrained over the planning horizon because either the quantity or price of each factor in each year is exogenous. These factor incomes are absorbed by domestic agents (consumers, investors and governments) and by foreign agents (through the trade balance). The path of government expenditure is exogenous while the path of investment expenditure is linked to capital growth (which is constrained). Thus, in each year any resources not absorbed by the government or by capital creators must be consumed or absorbed by foreigners. Net borrowings from the foreign sector occur through the trade balance and the constraint on the growth of net foreign liabilities in the terminal year determines the discounted sum of the trade balances over the planning horizon. This leaves Ω to be determined as a residual.

In our implementation of ORANI-INT we find it convenient to modify equations (3.3.17) and (3.3.18) slightly as follows:

$$\frac{\tilde{C}_t^{(a)}}{\tilde{C}_{t+1}^{(a)}} = \left[\frac{1+\rho}{1+B_{d,t}}\right] F_t^{(3)} \text{ ;and} \qquad t = 1, \ldots, T\text{-}1 \qquad (3.3.17a)$$

$$\frac{D_t}{GDP_t} = \frac{D_{t+1}}{GDP_{t+1}} F_t^{(3)}\,, \qquad t = T\text{-}1 \qquad (3.3.18a)$$

The variable $F_t^{(3)}$ is a shifter that is usually exogenous and assigned the value of 1. It is included in the model to provide us with the flexibility to switch equations (3.3.17a) and (3.3.18a) off by changing the closure of the model at run time. For example, in chapter 6 we exploit this flexibility to test alternative specifications of household behaviour.

3.3.2 Capital Creation

Investment in physical capital is done by producers and involves the construction of a sector-specific asset that yields a stream of capital services. Producers make two investment-related decisions: first, they choose the optimal level of capital creation in each period; and second, they choose the optimal mix of inputs to construct their capital. We deal with these two decisions in turn.

Optimal Level of Capital Creation in Each Period

Financial markets are assumed to be perfectly competitive—agents can borrow and lend as much as they like at the safe domestic bond rate, $B_{d,t}$. Thus, whether investment in physical capital is financed from retained earnings or borrowings is of no consequence. We assume that, in the long run, arbitrage will ensure that risk adjusted sectoral rates of return are equal to $B_{d,t}$. In the short run, which we define as the period over which the path of capital stocks cannot be adjusted, sectoral rates of return are allowed to adjust to clear the capital markets. As will be explained below we assume that the capital creation process is characterised by a 1-year gestation lag. Since the stock of productive capital available in the current year depends on past investments, the short run in ORANI-INT is as long as the gestation lag and begins at the start of the planning period.

Our assumptions about capital markets are captured by the following arbitrage condition:

$$\Psi_{j,t} = B_{d,t} + H_{j,t} + F^{(2)}_{j,t} . \qquad j=1, ..., J, t=1, ..., T \qquad (3.3.20)$$

The new variables introduced in equation (3.3.20) are: $\Psi_{j,t}$, the sector-specific rate of return; $H_{j,t}$, the sector-specific risk premium;[4] and $F^{(2)}_{j,t}$, a slack variable. The purpose of the slack variable is to provide us with the option of not enforcing the arbitrage condition. To enforce the arbitrage condition we treat $F^{(2)}_{j,t}$ as an exogenous variable and set it to zero. In cases where we consider the arbitrage condition to be inappropriate we allow $F^{(2)}_{j,t}$ to be endogenous.[5]

The representative producer in the jth sector takes the time paths of all prices, including $B_{d,t}$, as given. The choice variables in the producer's intertemporal optimisation problem are $Z^{(K)}_{j,t}$, the supply of sector-specific capital in year t, for t=2, ...,T and $Y_{j,t}$, gross investment in year t, for t=1, ...,T-1. In choosing the paths of $Z^{(K)}_{j,t}$ and $Y_{j,t}$ the producer maximises χ, the risk-adjusted present value of the expected future stream of profits accruing from the ownership of capital, given by:

$$\chi_j = \sum_{t=1}^{T} \left\{ \frac{P^{(K)}_{j,t} Z^{(K)}_{j,t} - P^{(Y)}_{j,t} Y_{j,t}}{\prod_{u=0}^{t-1} [1 + \Psi_{j,u}]} \right\} \qquad j = 1, ..., 13 \qquad (3.3.21)$$

where $P^{(Y)}_{j,t}$ is the price of a unit of investment. The constraints faced by the producer are:

$$Z^{(K)}_{j,t+1} = Z^{(K)}_{j,t}[1 - \delta_j] + N_{j,t} ; \qquad j = 1, ..., 13, t = 1, ..., T \qquad (3.3.22)$$

$$N_{j,t} = Y_{j,t} ; \qquad j = 1, ..., 13, t = 1, ..., T \qquad (3.3.23)$$

$$Y_{j,t} \geq 0 ; \qquad j = 1, ..., 13, t = 1, ..., T \qquad (3.3.24)$$

$$Z^{(K)}_{j,1} = \hat{Z}^{(K)}_{j,1} ; \text{ and} \qquad j = 1, ..., 13 \qquad (3.3.25)$$

$$Z^{(K)}_{j,T+1} = \hat{Z}^{(K)}_{j,T+1} . \qquad j = 1, ..., 13 \qquad (3.3.26)$$

Apart from the non-negativity constraint on investment, (3.3.24), all other constraints are assumed to hold as equalities. The non-negativity constraint on sectoral investment reflects our assumption that investment decisions are

---

4 We assume that this risk premium reflects undiversifiable risk.

5 As will be explained in chapter 5 we consider the arbitrage condition to be inappropriate for sectors whose activities are dominated by the government. We treat the path of capital stock in these sectors as exogenous and allow the path of $F^{(2)}_{j,t}$ to be endogenous.

irreversible; capital is sector specific and cannot be transferred to other sectors. Because investment decisions are irreversible, the representative producer must consider the profitability of capital for its entire life.

Equation (3.3.22) is the accumulation relationship between capital stocks and investment. In this formulation the productivity of a unit of capital is assumed to be independent of its age. However, a constant proportion, δ, of each sector's capital stock is lost each year. In contrast to most intertemporal CGE models, our investment technology does not incorporate convex adjustment costs. Our model of investment is a special case of the time-to-build models (see, for example, Kydland and Prescott (1982) and Dixon (1990)) in which the gestation lag is one year.[6] This assumption is reflected in equation (3.3.23) which describes how $N_{j,t}$, the increment to sector j's capital stock in year t, is determined. With a one year gestation lag, the additional productive capital available at the start of period t+1 is equal to the investment undertaken in period t. We write the accounting relationship (3.3.22) and the technological relationship (3.3.23) separately to emphasise that the two are conceptually distinct. In a more general specification, some of the investment undertaken in period t might relate to capital stock that will come on stream several periods hence.

Equation (3.3.25) is the initial condition relating to capital stocks. The stock of capital available for use in the first period of the plan is exogenous because it depends on investment decisions taken in the past. Finally, equation (3.3.26) indicates that terminal period capital stocks are exogenous. To indicate that capital stocks are exogenous in the first and last periods we use the hat symbol (i.e., ^).

To solve the producer's intertemporal optimisation problem we use the method of Lagrange multipliers. We form the Lagrangian function by combining the firm's objective function given by equation (3.3.21) with the constraints (3.3.22)—(3.3.26). To simplify the problem we use equation (3.3.23) to substitute $N_{j,t}$ out of the capital accumulation constraint. The resulting Lagrangian function is expressed as follows:

$$\mathcal{L}_j = \sum_{t=1}^{T} \left\{ \frac{P^{(K)}_{j,t} Z^{(K)}_{j,t} - P^{(Y)}_{j,t} Y_{j,t}}{\prod_{u=0}^{t-1} [1 + \Psi_{j,u}]} + \Lambda_{j,t} \left[Z^{(K)}_{j,t+1} - Z^{(K)}_{j,t} [1 - \delta_j] - Y_{j,t} \right] \right\}$$

$$j = 1, \ldots, 13 \qquad (3.3.27)$$

where $\Lambda_{j\,t}$ is a Lagrange multiplier. The solution to the producer's optimisation problem is given by the following first order conditions:

$$\frac{\partial \mathcal{L}_j}{\partial Y_{j,t}} = - P^{(Y)}_{j,t} \prod_{u=0}^{t-1} \left[1 + \Psi_{j,u} \right]^{-1} - \Lambda_{j,t} \geq 0;$$

6 In appendix 3.3 we explain that the specification of investment in modern CGE models is usually based on the adjustment cost model of investment. We also explain the sense in which the investment specification in ORANI-INT is a special case of the time-to-build investment model and our reasons for adopting this approach.

$$Y_{j,t} \geq 0 \; ; \qquad Y_{j,t}\frac{\partial \mathcal{L}_j}{\partial Y_{j,t}} = 0; \qquad j = 1, ..., 13, t = 1, ..., T \qquad (3.3.28)$$

$$\frac{\partial \mathcal{L}_j}{\partial Z^{(K)}_{j,t}} = P^{(K)}_{j,t} \prod_{u=0}^{t-1} \left[1 + \Psi_{j,u}\right]^{-1} + \Lambda_{j,t-1} - \Lambda_{j,t}[1 - \delta_j] \; ; \quad j = 1, ..., 13, t = 2, ..., T \qquad (3.3.29)$$

and

$$\frac{\partial \mathcal{L}_j}{\partial \Lambda_{j,t}} = Z^{(K)}_{j,t+1} - Z^{(K)}_{j,t}[1 - \delta_j] - Y_{j,t} = 0. \qquad j = 1, ..., 13, t = 1, ..., T \qquad (3.3.30)$$

Condition (3.3.28) implies that either (i) the marginal condition on investment holds as an equality and investment is nonnegative, or (ii) the marginal condition holds as an inequality and investment is zero. It is convenient to transform the marginal condition on investment into an equality as follows:

$$-P^{(Y)}_{j,t} \prod_{u=0}^{t-1} \left[1 + \Psi_{j,u}\right]^{-1} - \Lambda_{j,t} - \Gamma_{j,t} = 0 \qquad j = 1, ..., 13, t = 1, ..., T \qquad (3.3.31)$$

where $\Gamma_{j,t}$ is a slack variable. Since $\Gamma_{j,t} = \partial \mathcal{L}_j/\partial Y_{j,t}$, $\Gamma_{j,t} = 0$ when $Y_{j,t} \geq 0$. Conversely, when $\Gamma_{j,t} > 0$, $Y_{j,t} = 0$. Equation (3.3.31) can be rearranged to obtain the following expressions for the Lagrange multipliers:

$$\Lambda_{j,t} = -P^{(Y)}_{j,t} \prod_{u=0}^{t-1} \left[1 + \Psi_{j,u}\right]^{-1} - \Gamma_{j,t} \,. \qquad j = 1, ..., 13, t = 1, ..., T \qquad (3.3.32)$$

The equilibrium conditions for sectoral capital stocks can be derived by substituting equation (3.3.32) into equation (3.3.29). Rearranging the resultant expression we obtain:

$$P^{(K)}_{j,t} = \left[1 + \Psi_{j,t-1}\right] P^{(A)}_{j,t-1} - \left[1 - \delta_j\right] P^{(A)}_{j,t} \,, \qquad j = 1, ..., 13, t = 2, ..., T \qquad (3.3.33)$$

where

$$P^{(A)}_{j,t} = P^{(Y)}_{j,t} + F^{(Y)}_{j,t} \,, \text{ and } F^{(Y)}_{j,t} = \Gamma_{j,t} \prod_{u=0}^{t-1} \left[1 + \Psi_{j,u}\right]^{-1}.$$

To interpret equation (3.3.33) we establish first that $P^{(K)}_{j,t}$ is the marginal revenue product of capital. The marginal product of capital can be derived from the production function (3.2.2) as follows:

$$\frac{\partial X^{(F)}_{j,t}}{\partial X^{(K)}_{j,t}} = \zeta^{(K)}_{j,t} \left\{\frac{X^{(F)}_{j,t}}{X^{(K)}_{j,t}}\right\}^{1+\mu} \left\{\frac{A^{(K)}_{j,t}}{A^{(F)}_{j,t}}\right\}^{\mu} . \qquad j = 1, ..., 13, t = 1, ..., T \qquad (3.3.34)$$

Solving the capital demand function (3.2.9) for $P^{(K)}_{j,t}$ gives:

$$P^{(K)}_{j,t} = P^{(F)}_{j,t}\zeta^{(K)}_{j,t}\left\{\frac{X^{(F)}_{j,t}}{X^{(K)}_{j,t}}\right\}^{1+\mu}\left\{\frac{A^{(K)}_{j,t}}{A^{(F)}_{j,t}}\right\}^{\mu}. \qquad j = 1, ..., 13, t = 1, ..., T \qquad (3.3.35)$$

We can show that $P^{(K)}_{j,t}$ is equal to the marginal revenue product of capital by substituting equation (3.5.34) into (3.3.35) as follows:

$$P^{(K)}_{j,t} = P^{(F)}_{j,t}\frac{\partial X^{(F)}_{j,t}}{\partial X^{(K)}_{j,t}}. \qquad j = 1, ..., 13, t = 1, ..., T \qquad (3.3.36)$$

From equilibrium condition (3.3.33) we can deduce that the marginal revenue product of capital, $P^{(K)}_{j,t}$, is the imputed rental cost of an asset that yields a unit of capital services. That is, it is the price that a producer would, if they were able, pay to hire an asset that yielded a unit of capital services. In the case where the nonnegativity constraints on investment are never binding (i.e., $F^{(Y)}_{j,t} = 0$) producers would be indifferent between owning or renting their capital. Under these circumstances, equation (3.3.33) can be simplified and rearranged as follows:

$$P^{(K)}_{j,t} = \Psi_{j,t-1}P^{(Y)}_{j,t-1} + \delta_j P^{(Y)}_{j,t} - \left(P^{(Y)}_{j,t} - P^{(Y)}_{j,t-1}\right), \qquad j = 1, ..., 13, t = 2, ..., T \qquad (3.3.37)$$

Equation (3.3.37) implies that in equilibrium the stock of capital held by the firm will be such that the marginal revenue product of capital is equal to the marginal cost of capital. The marginal cost of a unit of capital services in period t is given by the RHS of equation (3.3.37). The first term, $\Psi_{d,t-1}P^{(Y)}_{j,t-1}$, is the opportunity cost of funds tied up in the ownership of the capital services producing asset. The opportunity cost component is calculated on the basis that investment costs are incurred in period t-1 for capital which comes on stream in period t. The second term, $\delta_j P^{(Y)}_{j,t-1}$, is the depreciation cost associated with the usage of the capital for one period. The final term in brackets on the RHS of equation (3.3.37) captures capital gains/losses.

When the nonnegativity constraints on investment are binding, the imputed rental value of capital diverges from the cost of owning and using it. The variable $F^{(Y)}_{j,t}$ captures the difference between the cost of constructing a unit of capital in period t (i.e., $P^{(Y)}_{j,t}$) and the implicit market valuation of that unit of capital in period t. The implicit market valuation of capital is the price that a firm would, if it were allowed, buy or sell a unit of capital. Whether the imputed rental value of capital is greater or smaller than the cost of owning and using it depends on the relative size of $F^{(Y)}_{j,t}$ in adjacent periods. We discuss this and the behavioural implications of the nonnegativity constraints more fully in appendix 3.4.

Equilibrium condition (3.3.33) provides the path of $P^{(K)}_{j,t}$ for t = 2, ...,T. In the first period of the plan the stock of capital is exogenous because it depends on past investment decisions. We do not assume that past investment decisions were intertemporally optimal. Hence, $P^{(K)}_{j,t}$ in period 1 is not obtained from equilibrium condition (3.3.33). In the model the rental price of capital in period 1 is determined as a residual and is consistent with the assumption that the demand and supply of capital are equal.

The producer's optimisation problem is specified over a finite time horizon and the equilibrium conditions that we derive from it cannot determine the values of variables beyond the arbitrarily chosen terminal period. In our model investment in period T, the terminal period, depends on demands for capital in the future. Therefore, since the equilibrium conditions derived from the optimisation problem cannot determine jointly the values of $Z^{(K)}_{j,T+1}$ and $Y_{j,T}$ the values of one of these vector variables must be specified exogenously. We choose to specify the values of $Z^{(K)}_{j,T+1}$ by exogenising the growth in capital stocks between years T and T+1. Because we do not know in advance what $Z^{(K)}_{j,T}$ will be, we include an equation in the model that automates this procedure. That is, we implement equations of the form:

$$\frac{Z^{(K)}_{j,t+1}}{Z^{(K)}_{j,t}} = F^{(K)}_{j,t} . \qquad j = 1, ..., 13, t = T \qquad (3.3.38)$$

The variable $F^{(K)}_{j,T}$ is the exogenous rate of growth of capital stocks in the terminal period. Note that equation (3.3.38) is not part of the producer's optimisation problem. In formulating their optimal investment plan, producers simply take $Z^{(K)}_{j,T+1}$ to be exogenous. Equation (3.3.38) is a device that we use to provide a value for this variable. Since sectoral capital growth rates between years T and T+1 are assumed to be exogenous in equation (3.3.38), the values that we obtain for $Z^{(K)}_{j,T+1}$ will be good approximations to the values that $Z^{(K)}_{j,T+1}$ would adopt in a plan lasting $T^* > T$ periods only if the capital stock growth paths have converged to the exogenous rate of growth, $F^{(K)}_{j,T}$, by period T. In ORANI-INT we ensure that the growth paths of sectoral capital stocks converge to this exogenous rate of growth by choosing the value of T large enough.

In our implementation of ORANI-INT we find it convenient to modify equation (3.3.33) as follows:

$$\left[1 + \Psi_{j,t-1}\right] = \frac{P^{(K)}_{j,t}}{P^{(A)}_{j,t-1}} + \left[1 - \delta_j\right] K^{(A)}_{j,t} , \qquad j = 1, ..., 13, t = 2, ..., T \qquad (3.3.33a)$$

where,

$$K^{(A)}_{j,t} = \frac{P^{(A)}_{j,t}}{P^{(A)}_{j,t-1}} F^{(A)}_{j,t} , \qquad j = 1, ..., 13, t = 2, ..., T \qquad (3.3.33b)$$

The variable $K^{(A)}_t$ denotes capital gains and $F^{(A)}_t$ is a shifter that is usually exogenous and assigned the value of 1. This shifter provides us with the flexibility to impose static expectations in the investment specification by changing the closure of the model at run time. In chapter 6 we exploit this flexibility to test alternative specifications of investment behaviour.

Optimal Mix of Inputs for the Production of Physical Capital

As mentioned above capital is assumed to be sector-specific and its composition varies across industries. The technology for assembling units of capital in ORANI-INT is represented schematically in figure 3.3. A unit of fixed capital for use in industry j is constructed according to a two-tiered technology. At the top level sector j creates units of capital by combining inputs of produced (i.e., non-primary) composite goods according to a Leontief production function (i.e., inputs of composite goods are used in fixed proportions). That is:

$$Y_{j,t} = \mathrm{Min}\left\{\frac{X^{(2)}_{1,\bullet,j,t}}{A^{(2)}_{1,\bullet,j,t}}, \ldots, \frac{X^{(2)}_{13,\bullet,j,t}}{A^{(2)}_{13,\bullet,j,t}}\right\}; \qquad j = 1, \ldots, 13, t = 1, \ldots, T \qquad (3.3.39)$$

where $X^{(2)}_{i,\bullet,j,t}$ is the demand for composite good i by sector j for the purpose of creating capital in year t and the A terms are positive parameters. At the next level, composite good i is assembled from domestically produced and imported good i according to a CES (Armington) production function:

$$X^{(2)}_{i,\bullet,j,t} = \mathrm{CES}(X^{(2)}_{i,d,j,t}, X^{(2)}_{i,f,j,t}). \qquad i = 1, \ldots, 13, j = 1, \ldots, 13, t = 1, \ldots, T \qquad (3.3.40)$$

The representative capital creator in sector j takes as given all prices and chooses $X^{(2)}_{i,s,j,t}$, inputs of good i from source s for the purpose of capital creation in sector j in year t, to minimise $P^{(Y)}_{j,t}Y_{j,t}$, investment costs in year t, subject to the capital creation technology given by equations (3.3.39) and (3.3.40). Sector j's investment costs in year t are given by:

$$P^{(Y)}_{j,t}Y_{j,t} = \sum_{i=1}^{13}\left\{P^{(2)}_{i,d,j,t}X^{(2)}_{i,d,j,t} + P^{(2)}_{i,f,j,t}X^{(2)}_{i,f,j,t}\right\}. \qquad j = 1, \ldots, 13, t = 1, \ldots, T \qquad (3.3.41)$$

In equation (3.3.41) the Ps denote the prices paid by capital creators in sector j for the corresponding Xs. The solution to this cost minimisation problem yields the following input demand equations:

$$X^{(2)}_{i,s,j,t} = Y_{j,t}A^{(2)}_{i,\bullet,j,t}\vartheta^{1/(1+\upsilon)}_{i,s,j,t}P^{(2)-1/(1+\upsilon)}_{i,s,j,t}\left\{\sum_k \vartheta^{1/(1+\upsilon)}_{i,k,j,t}P^{(2)\upsilon/(1+\upsilon)}_{i,k,j,t}\right\}^{\frac{1}{\upsilon}};$$

$$i = 1, \ldots, 13, s = d,f, k = d,f, t = 1, \ldots, T \qquad (3.3.42)$$

where ϑ and υ are parameters (with $-1 < \upsilon \neq 0$; $\vartheta_{i,k,j,t} > 0$; and $\Sigma_i\vartheta_{i,k,j,t} = 1$). Note that $Y_{j,t}$ has already been determined from the solution to the producer's intertemporal optimisation problem.

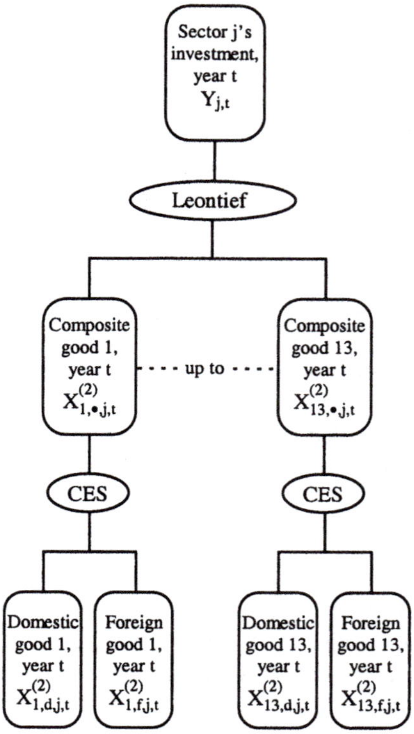

Figure 3.3: Technology for Creating Capital

3.3.3 Government Demands

There is no formal theory explaining government demands in ORANI-INT. The default setting in the model is for the level and composition of real government expenditure to be exogenous. Some flexibility in the composition of government expenditure is provided by the following equation:

$$\frac{X^{(5)}_{i,s,t}}{C^{(R)}_t} = F^{(5)}_{i,s,t}\, F^{(5)}_t, \qquad i = 1, \ldots, 13;\ s = d,f;\ t = 1, \ldots, T \qquad (3.3.43)$$

where $F^{(5)}_{i,s,t}$ is a shift variable that determines the composition of government demands and $F^{(5)}_t$ is a shift variable that allows for uniform changes in the ratio of the government's demand for commodity i from source s in year t to $C^{(R)}_t$, aggregate real household consumption.

3.3.4 Foreign Demands

We model export demands by specifying an inverse relationship between $X_{i,t}^{(4)}$, the quantity of Australian commodity i demanded by foreigners, and $P_{i,t}^{(E)}$, the f.o.b foreign currency price of that commodity. Specifically, we assume that:

$$X_{i,t}^{(4)} = F_{i,t}^{(4q)} \left\{ \frac{P_{i,t}^{(E)}}{F_{i,t}^{(4p)}} \right\}^{\eta_i} ; \qquad i = 1, \ldots, 13 \quad t = 1, \ldots, T \qquad (3.3.44)$$

where η_i is a negative parameter (the foreign demand elasticity) and the slack variables $F_{i,t}^{(4q)}$ and $F_{i,t}^{(4p)}$ are included to allow for horizontal (quantity) and vertical (price) shifts in the export demand functions.

Following the treatment of exports in ORANI we divide the commodities in ORANI-INT into two groups. The first group contains the traditional export commodities (i.e., *Agriculture*, *Mining* and *Manufacturing*) which account for about 80 percent of total exports. The second group contains the remaining commodities, which are classified as non-traditional exports.[7] For the non-traditional exports we adopt the small country assumption (i.e., the foreign elasticity of demand is high). In contrast, we assume that the foreign currency prices of the traditional exports can be influenced by Australian exporters (i.e., the foreign elasticities of demand are lower).[8]

3.4 Zero Pure Profits Conditions

Underpinning the specification of the price system in ORANI-INT are two key assumptions: first, there are no pure profits in production, capital creation, importing or exporting (i.e., prices are set to just cover costs in all activities including a, possibly imputed, return on capital and land); and second, basic prices are uniform across users and producing industries – differences across users in purchasers' prices are accounted for entirely by sales taxes. Below we describe the relationships between unit prices and unit costs in production, capital creation, importing and exporting. We then turn to the relationships between basic prices and purchasers' prices.

---

7 While some of the commodities in ORANI-INT are not exported (e.g., *Construction* and *Ownership of Dwellings*) we find it convenient to define export demand functions for such commodities [n.b., equation (3.3.44) applies to all commodities rather than to a subset] and to arbitrarily treat them as non-traditional exports. This treatment of non-exportables does not have any effect on the model's results.

8 The export demand elasticities are set at -20 for the non-traditional exports. For the traditional exports the export demand elasticities are set at: -7.2 for *Agriculture*; -13.4 for *Mining*; and -6.9 for *Manufacturing*.

Relationship Between Unit Prices and Unit Costs in Production

Under the two assumptions of no pure profits in production and uniformity of basic prices across producers we can relate $P^{(Z)}_{j,t}Z_{j,t}$, the value of sector j's output in year t at basic prices, to the cost of inputs as follows:

$$P^{(Z)}_{j,t}Z_{j,t} = P^{(F)}_{j,t}X^{(F)}_{j,t} + P^{(O)}_{j,t}X^{(O)}_{j,t} + \sum_{i=1}^{13} P^{(1)}_{i,\bullet,j,t}X^{(1)}_{i,\bullet,j,t} \cdot \qquad j = 1, ..., 13, t = 1, ..., T \qquad (3.4.1)$$

Because we have assumed constant returns to scale in production, unit prices and unit costs are independent of the level of output. That is, we can express equation (3.4.1) in terms of prices only. As explained in sub-section 3.2.2, sector j uses inputs of $X^{(F)}_{j,t}$, $X^{(O)}_{j,t}$ and $X^{(1)}_{i,\bullet,j,t}$, i=1, ..., 13, in fixed proportions to its output. Thus, all the quantity terms on the RHS of equation (3.4.1) can be re-written as functions of $Z_{j,t}$. From equation (3.2.10) we can deduce that:

$$X^{(F)}_{j,t} = Z^{(1)}_{j,t}A^{(F)}_{j,t} . \qquad j = 1, ..., 13, t = 1, ..., T \qquad (3.4.2)$$

Similar expressions for $X^{(1)}_{i,\bullet,j,t}$ and $X^{(O)}_{j,t}$ are given by equations (3.2.12) and (3.2.13). Substituting equations (3.2.12), (3.2.13) and (3.4.2) into equation (3.4.1) and making the appropriate cancellations yields the following relationship between unit prices and unit costs:

$$P^{(Z)}_{j,t} = P^{(F)}_{j,t}A^{(F)}_{j,t} + P^{(O)}_{j,t}A^{(O)}_{j,t} + \sum_{i=1}^{13} P^{(1)}_{i,\bullet,j,t}A^{(1)}_{i,\bullet,j,t} ; \qquad j = 1, ..., 13, t = 1, ..., T \qquad (3.4.3)$$

where $P^{(F)}_{j,t}$ and $P^{(1)}_{i,\bullet,j,t}$ are defined by equations (3.2.7) and (3.2.15). Since each sector produces a single commodity, the basic price of domestically produced commodity i, $P^{(Z)}_{i,d,t}$, can be expressed as:

$$P^{(Z)}_{i,d,t} = P^{(Z)}_{j,t} \qquad j,i = 1, ..., 13, i=j, t = 1, ..., T \qquad (3.4.4)$$

Relationship Between Unit Prices and Unit Costs in Capital Creation

The relationship between unit prices and unit costs for capital creation can be derived by using equation (3.3.42) to eliminate the quantity terms in the zero pure profits condition for capital creation given by equation (3.3.41). After making appropriate cancellations we obtain:

$$P^{(Y)}_{j,t} = \sum_{i=1}^{13} A^{(2)}_{i,\bullet,j,t} \left\{ \sum_{s} \vartheta^{1/(1+\upsilon)}_{i,s,j,t} P^{(2)\upsilon/(1+\upsilon)}_{i,s,j,t} \right\}^{\frac{1+\upsilon}{\upsilon}} . \qquad j = 1, ..., 13; s = d,f; t = 1, ..., T \qquad (3.4.5)$$

Relationship Between Unit Prices and Unit Costs in Exporting

The f.o.b foreign currency price of a unit of export good i, $P^{(E)}_{i,t}$, is related to the unit price of domestic good i, $P^{(Z)}_{i,d,t}$, as follows:

$$P^{(E)}_{i,t}\Phi_t = P^{(Z)}_{i,d,t}T^{(4)}_{i,t} . \qquad i = 1, ..., 13\ t = 1, ..., T \qquad (3.4.6)$$

In equation (3.4.6) Φ_t is the nominal exchange rate ($Australian/$Foreign) in year t and $T^{(4)}_{i,t}$ is the power of the tax/subsidy (i.e., one plus the rate of tax/subsidy) on export good i in year t.

Relationship Between Unit Prices and Unit Costs in Importing

The basic price of imported good i (i.e., the price received by Australian importers), $P^{(Z)}_{i,f,t}$, is related to $P^{(M)}_{i,t}$, the c.i.f foreign currency price of imported good i as follows:

$$P^{(Z)}_{i,f,t} = P^{(M)}_{i,t}\Phi_t T^{(6)}_{i,t}, \qquad i = 1, ..., 13\ t = 1, ..., T \qquad (3.4.7)$$

where $T^{(6)}_{i,t}$ is the power of the tariff on imported good i in year t.

Relationship Between Basic Prices and Purchasers' Prices

In ORANI-INT commodities are used by four groups of domestic agents: producers; capital creators; households; and governments. For each of these four user groups the cost of good i from source s is equal to the basic price of that good plus a user-specific sales tax. Thus, the purchasers' prices for the four user groups defined as follows:

$$P^{(1)}_{i,s,j,t} = P^{(Z)}_{i,s,t}T^{(1)}_{i,s,j,t}; \qquad i,j = 1, ..., 13;\ s = d,f;\ t = 1, ..., T \qquad (3.4.8)$$

$$P^{(2)}_{i,s,j,t} = P^{(Z)}_{i,s,t}T^{(2)}_{i,s,j,t}; \qquad i,j = 1, ..., 13;\ s = d,f;\ t = 1, ..., T \qquad (3.4.9)$$

$$P^{(3)}_{i,s,t} = P^{(Z)}_{i,s,t}T^{(3)}_{i,s,t}; \qquad i = 1, ..., 13;\ s = d,f;\ t = 1, ..., T \qquad (3.4.10)$$

and

$$P^{(5)}_{i,s,t} = P^{(Z)}_{i,s,t}T^{(5)}_{i,s,t}. \qquad i = 1, ..., 13;\ s = d,f;\ t = 1, ..., T \qquad (3.4.11)$$

In equations (3.4.8) - (3.4.11) the Ts are powers of taxes/subsidies and the LHS Ps are purchasers' prices. Recall that the superscripts (1), (2), (3) and (5) refer to producers, capital creators, households and governments respectively. For example, $T^{(2)}_{i,s,j,t}$ is the power of the tax/subsidy on good i from source s in year t purchased by capital creators in sector j.

Relationship Between the Domestic and Foreign Interest Rates

In the model we identify domestic and foreign interest rates. We assume that uncovered interest parity holds so that the relationship between the domestic and foreign interest rates can be expressed as follows:

$$[1 + B_{d,t}] = \frac{\Phi_{t+1}}{\Phi_t}[1 + B_{f,t}]. \qquad t = 1, 2, ..., T \qquad (3.4.12)$$

Relationship Between the Price of Labour Across Sectors

Labour inputs are assumed to be homogeneous and perfectly mobile across sectors. This means that the price of labour will be uniform across sectors. That is:

$$W_t^{(\Pi)} = P_{j,t}^{(L)}. \qquad t = 1, 2, ..., T \qquad (3.4.13)$$

In equation (3.4.13) $W_t^{(\Pi)}$ is the unit price of labour to all sectors in year t.

3.5 Market Clearing Conditions

The market clearing equations ensure that demand equals supply for domestically produced commodities and for primary factors. Total demand for domestically produced commodity i comprises demands for that commodity by producers, capital creators, governments and foreigners. Thus, the market clearing equations for domestic commodities are:

$$Z_{i,t}^{(1)} = \sum_{j=1}^{13} X_{i,d,j,t}^{(1)} + \sum_{j=1}^{13} X_{i,d,j,t}^{(2)} + X_{i,d,t}^{(3)} + X_{i,t}^{(4)} + X_{i,d,t}^{(5)}. \qquad i = 1, ..., 13 \; t = 1, ..., T \qquad (3.5.1)$$

The market clearing conditions for the primary factors capital, labour and agricultural land are:

$$Z_{j,t}^{(K)} = X_{j,t}^{(K)}; \qquad j = 1, ..., 13 \; t = 1, ..., T \qquad (3.5.2)$$

$$L_t = W_t^{(R)}; \qquad j = 1, ..., 13 \; t = 1, ..., T \qquad (3.5.3)$$

$$W_t^{(R)} = \sum_{j=1}^{13} X_{j,t}^{(L)}; \qquad j = 1, ..., 13 \; t = 1, ..., T \qquad (3.5.4)$$

and

$$Z_{j,t}^{(N)} = X_{j,t}^{(N)}. \qquad j = 1, ..., 13 \; t = 1, ..., T \qquad (3.5.5)$$

The new variables introduced in equations (3.5.1) and (3.5.4) are: L_t, aggregate labour supply; $W_t^{(R)}$ aggregate demand for labour; and $Z_{j,t}^{(N)}$, the supply of agricultural land to sector j. The absence of a j subscripts on L_t and $W_t^{(R)}$ indicates that labour is assumed to be homogeneous.

3.6 Miscellaneous Equations

The final category of equations consists mainly of accounting relationships that serve to define key price and quantity aggregates. Also included in this category are equations that provide the model-user with the option of indexing $P_{j,t}^{(O)}$, the price of 'other cost' tickets to sector j, to the consumer price index. The degree of indexation is user specified.

Macroeconomic Variables

We define nominal GDP from both the expenditure and income sides of the National Accounts. From the expenditure side, GDPE is the sum of: C, aggregate private consumption; I, aggregate investment; G, government expenditure; and BoT, the trade balance. That is:

$$GDPE_t = C_t + I_t + G_t + BoT_t \qquad t = 1, ..., T \qquad (3.6.1)$$

In turn, C, I and G are aggregations of previously defined variables:

$$C_t = \sum_{i=1}^{13} P^{(3)}_{i,\bullet,t} X^{(3)}_{i,\bullet,t} \qquad t = 1, ..., T \qquad (3.6.2)$$

$$I_t = \sum_{j=1}^{13} P^{(Y)}_{j,t} Y_{j,t} \qquad t = 1, ..., T \qquad (3.6.3)$$

$$G_t = \sum_{i=1}^{13} \left\{ P^{(5)}_{i,d,t} X^{(5)}_{i,d,t} + P^{(5)}_{i,f,t} X^{(5)}_{i,f,t} \right\} \qquad t = 1, ..., T \qquad (3.6.4)$$

The trade balance is defined in domestic currency units and is the difference between E, aggregate exports, and M, aggregate imports:

$$BoT_t = E_t - M_t \qquad t = 1, ..., T \qquad (3.6.5)$$

Aggregate exports and imports are defined as follows:

$$E_t = \frac{1}{\Phi_t} \sum_{i=1}^{13} P^{(E)}_{i,t} X^{(4)}_{i,t} \qquad t = 1, ..., T \qquad (3.6.6)$$

$$M_t = \frac{1}{\Phi_t} \sum_{i=1}^{13} P^{(M)}_{i,t} X^{(M)}_{i,t} \qquad t = 1, ..., T \qquad (3.6.7)$$

where $X^{(M)}_{i,t}$, which has not been previously defined, is the quantity of imported good i used by: producers; investors; households; and government. That is,

$$X^{(M)}_{i,t} = \sum_{j=1}^{13} X^{(1)}_{i,f,j,t} + \sum_{j=1}^{13} X^{(2)}_{i,f,j,t} + X^{(3)}_{i,f,t} + X^{(5)}_{i,f,t} \qquad i = 1, ..., 13 \; t = 1, ..., T \qquad (3.6.8)$$

From the income side of the National Accounts GDPI is defined as the sum of GDPFC, GDP at factor cost (or value-added), and NIT, net indirect taxes:

$$GDPI_t = GDPFC_t + NIT_t \qquad t = 1, ..., T \qquad (3.6.9)$$

GDP at factor cost is the sum of factor payments:

$$GDPFC_t = W_t + K_t + N_t \qquad t = 1, ..., T \qquad (3.6.10)$$

where W, K and N denote payments to labour, capital and agricultural land. Net indirect taxes are the sum of O, 'other cost' tickets (mainly production taxes), and V, net indirect taxes on commodity flows:

$$NIT_t = O_t + V_t \qquad t = 1, ..., T \qquad (3.6.11)$$

Payments to labour, capital and agricultural land are measured as follows:

$$W_t = \sum_{j=1}^{13} P_{j,t}^{(L)} X_{j,t}^{(L)} ; \qquad t = 1, ..., T \qquad (3.6.12)$$

$$K_t = \sum_{j=1}^{13} P_{j,t}^{(K)} X_{j,t}^{(K)} ; \qquad t = 1, ..., T \qquad (3.6.13)$$

$$N_t = \sum_{j=1}^{13} P_{j,t}^{(N)} X_{j,t}^{(N)} . \qquad t = 1, ..., T \qquad (3.6.14)$$

Aggregate payments for 'other cost' tickets are given by:

$$O_t = \sum_{j=1}^{13} P_{j,t}^{(O)} X_{j,t}^{(O)} . \qquad t = 1, ..., T \qquad (3.6.15)$$

Net indirect tax revenue is the sum of net indirect tax revenues collected from: sales of domestic and foreign goods to producers, capital creators, households and government. That is,

$$V_t = V_t^{(1)} + V_t^{(2)} + V_t^{(3)} + V_t^{(4)} + V_t^{(5)} + V_t^{(6)}; \qquad t = 1, ..., T \qquad (3.6.16)$$

where:

$$V_t^{(1)} = \sum_{i=1}^{13} \sum_{j=1}^{13} \left\{ P_{i,d,t}^{(Z)} X_{i,d,j,t}^{(1)} [T_{i,d,j,t}^{(1)} - 1] + P_{i,f,t}^{(Z)} X_{i,f,j,t}^{(1)} [T_{i,f,j,t}^{(1)} - 1] \right\}; \qquad t = 1, ..., T \qquad (3.6.17)$$

$$V_t^{(2)} = \sum_{i=1}^{13} \sum_{j=1}^{13} \left\{ P_{i,d,t}^{(Z)} X_{i,d,j,t}^{(2)} [T_{i,d,j,t}^{(2)} - 1] + P_{i,f,t}^{(Z)} X_{i,f,j,t}^{(2)} [T_{i,f,j,t}^{(2)} - 1] \right\}; \qquad t = 1, ..., T \qquad (3.6.18)$$

$$V_t^{(3)} = \sum_{i=1}^{13} \left\{ P_{i,d,t}^{(Z)} X_{i,d,t}^{(3)} [T_{i,d,t}^{(3)} - 1] + P_{i,f,t}^{(Z)} X_{i,f,t}^{(3)} [T_{i,f,t}^{(3)} - 1] \right\}; \qquad t = 1, ..., T \qquad (3.6.19)$$

$$V_t^{(4)} = \sum_{i=1}^{13} P_{i,d,t}^{(Z)} X_{i,t}^{(4)} [T_{i,t}^{(4)} - 1]; \qquad t = 1, ..., T \qquad (3.6.20)$$

$$V_t^{(5)} = \sum_{i=1}^{13} \left\{ P_{i,d,t}^{(Z)} X_{i,d,t}^{(5)} [T_{i,d,t}^{(5)} - 1] + P_{i,f,t}^{(Z)} X_{i,f,t}^{(5)} [T_{i,f,t}^{(5)} - 1] \right\}; \qquad t = 1, ..., T \qquad (3.6.21)$$

and

$$V_t^{(6)} = \sum_{i=1}^{13} P_{i,t}^{(M)} X_{i,t}^{(M)} \Phi_t [T_{i,t}^{(6)} - 1] . \qquad t = 1, ..., T \qquad (3.6.22)$$

Each of the nominal macroeconomic variables described above is decomposed into a quantity and a price index. There is no theoretically correct way of decomposing value indexes such as nominal consumption into price and quantity indexes. In ORANI-INT we use Divisia indexes to decompose value indexes into price and quantity components.[9] For example, we decompose aggregate nominal consumption into real aggregate consumption and a consumption deflator. We denote quantity indexes with the superscript (R) and price indexes with the superscript (Π). For example, $C_t^{(R)}$ and $C_t^{(\Pi)}$ denote real aggregate private consumption and the consumption price deflator respectively. A Divisia index of

9 See Vogt (1978) and Samuelson and Swamy (1974) for a general discussion about the properties of Divisia indexes.

the quantities X_i, i=1, ...,N, can be loosely interpreted as some average of a Laspeyres and Paasche index of those quantities. A Divisia index can also be interpreted as a chained Laspeyres index. In appendix 3.5 we briefly discuss the use of Divisia indexes in ORANI-INT. In the appendix we explain that computational convenience is the key reason for using Divisia indexes rather than Laspeyres or Paasche indexes in ORANI-INT.

The Divisia price and quantity indexes in ORANI-INT are based on complicated path-dependent line integrals. Below we present the ORANI-INT Divisia indexes in their general, rather than specific, forms. The real counterparts of the expenditure aggregates appearing in equation (3.6.1) are represented as follows:

$$C_t^{(R)} = \text{Divisia}\left(\boldsymbol{X}_t^{(3)}, \boldsymbol{S}_t^{(3)}, \text{Þ}_t \right); \qquad t = 1, ..., T \qquad (3.6.23)$$

$$I_t^{(R)} = \text{Divisia}\left(\boldsymbol{X}_t^{(2)}, \boldsymbol{S}_t^{(2)}, \text{Þ}_t \right); \qquad t = 1, ..., T \qquad (3.6.24)$$

$$G_t^{(R)} = \text{Divisia}\left(\boldsymbol{X}_t^{(5)}, \boldsymbol{S}_t^{(5)}, \text{Þ}_t \right); \qquad t = 1, ..., T \qquad (3.6.25)$$

$$E_t^{(R)} = \text{Divisia}\left(\boldsymbol{X}_t^{(4)}, \boldsymbol{S}_t^{(4)}, \text{Þ}_t \right); \text{ and} \qquad t = 1, ..., T \qquad (3.6.26)$$

$$M_t^{(R)} = \text{Divisia}\left(\boldsymbol{X}_t^{(M)}, \boldsymbol{S}_t^{(M)}, \text{Þ}_t \right). \qquad t = 1, ..., T \qquad (3.6.27)$$

In equations (3.6.23) — (3.6.27) the ***X***s are vectors of quantities and the ***S***s are vectors of shares (or weights). For example:

$$\boldsymbol{X}_t^{(2)} = \{X_{i,s,j,t}^{(2)} \mid i=1,2,...,13;\ s=d,f;\ j=1,2,...,13\};$$

$$\boldsymbol{X}_t^{(3)} = \{X_{i,s,t}^{(3)} \mid i=1,2,...,13;\ s=d,f\};$$

$$\boldsymbol{S}_t^{(4)} = \{(P_{i,t}^{(E)} X_{i,t}^{(4)})/E_t \mid i=1,2,...,13\}; \text{ and}$$

$$\boldsymbol{S}_t^{(5)} = \{(P_{i,s,t}^{(5)} X_{i,s,t}^{(5)})/G_t \mid i=1,2,...,13;\ s=d,f\} .$$

The variable Þ_t in equations (3.6.23) - (3.6.27) is used to indicate that the Divisia indexes in ORANI-INT are path dependent.

The price deflators associated with the expenditure aggregates appearing in equation (3.6.1) have similar forms to the quantity indexes. The vectors of quantities (i.e., the ***X***s) appearing in the quantity indexes are replaced by vectors of prices (denoted by ***Ps***) in the price indexes. Thus, the price indexes corresponding to the quantity indexes defined by equations (3.6.23) — (3.6.27) can be represented as follows:

$$C_t^{(\Pi)} = \text{Divisia}\left(\boldsymbol{P}_t^{(3)}, \boldsymbol{S}_t^{(3)}, \text{Þ}_t \right); \qquad t = 1, ..., T \qquad (3.6.28)$$

$$I_t^{(\Pi)} = \text{Divisia}\left(\boldsymbol{P}_t^{(2)}, \boldsymbol{S}_t^{(2)}, \text{Þ}_t \right); \qquad t = 1, ..., T \qquad (3.6.29)$$

$$G_t^{(\Pi)} = \text{Divisia}\left(\boldsymbol{P}_t^{(5)}, \boldsymbol{S}_t^{(5)}, \text{Þ}_t \right); \qquad t = 1, ..., T \qquad (3.6.30)$$

$$E_t^{(\Pi)} = \text{Divisia}\left(\boldsymbol{P}_t^{(4)}, \boldsymbol{S}_t^{(4)}, \text{Þ}_t \right); \text{ and} \qquad t = 1, ..., T \qquad (3.6.31)$$

$$M_t^{(\Pi)} = \text{Divisia}\left(\boldsymbol{P}_t^{(M)}, \boldsymbol{S}_t^{(M)}, \text{Þ}_t \right). \qquad t = 1, ..., T \qquad (3.6.32)$$

The aggregates appearing in the GDP identity defined from the income side of the national accounts are also decomposed into price and quantity indexes. Note that it is not necessary to define an index of aggregate employment. We have assumed that labour is homogeneous and perfectly mobile. Under these conditions the price of labour is the same to all industries. There is no need to define a deflator for wages and aggregate employment is the sum of employment across industries (i.e., equation (3.5.4)). The real components of the aggregates, other than payments to labour, appearing in equations (3.6.9) — (3.6.11) are represented as follows:

$$K_t^{(R)} = \text{Divisia}\left(\boldsymbol{X}_t^{(K)}, \boldsymbol{S}_t^{(K)}, \text{Þ}_t \right); \qquad t = 1, ..., T \qquad (3.6.33)$$

$$N_t^{(R)} = \text{Divisia}\left(\boldsymbol{X}_t^{(N)}, \boldsymbol{S}_t^{(N)}, \text{Þ}_t \right); \qquad t = 1, ..., T \qquad (3.6.34)$$

$$O_t^{(R)} = \text{Divisia}\left(\boldsymbol{X}_t^{(O)}, \boldsymbol{S}_t^{(O)}, \text{Þ}_t \right); \text{ and} \qquad t = 1, ..., T \qquad (3.6.35)$$

$$V_t^{(R)} = \text{Divisia}\left(\boldsymbol{V}_t^{(R)}, \boldsymbol{S}_t^{(V)}, \text{Þ}_t \right). \qquad t = 1, ..., T \qquad (3.6.36)$$

The notation used in equations (3.6.33) — (3.6.36) is similar to that used in equations (3.6.23) - (3.6.32): the $\boldsymbol{X}$s are vectors of quantities; the $\boldsymbol{S}$s are vectors of shares; and **Þ** indicates path dependence. For example:

$$\boldsymbol{X}_t^{(O)} = \{X_{j,t}^{(O)} \mid j=1,2, ...,13\}; \text{ and}$$

$$\boldsymbol{S}_t^{(K)} = \{(P_{j,t}^{(K)} X_{j,t}^{(K)})/K_t \mid j=1,2,...,13\}.$$

Real net indirect tax payments are defined in equation (3.6.36). The vectors $\boldsymbol{V}$ and $\boldsymbol{S}$ each contain six elements. Each element in $\boldsymbol{V}$ represents real net indirect tax payments by: producers; capital creators; households; exporters; government; and importers. The elements in $\boldsymbol{S}$ represent the corresponding shares of these six groups of agents in total net indirect tax revenues. That is:

$$\boldsymbol{V}_t^{(R)} = \{V_t^{(R,1)}, V_t^{(R,2)}, V_t^{(R,3)}, V_t^{(R,4)}, V_t^{(R,5)}, V_t^{(R,6)}\}; \text{ and}$$

$$\boldsymbol{S}_t^{(V)} = \{S_t^{(V,1)}, S_t^{(V,2)}, S_t^{(V,3)}, S_t^{(V,4)}, S_t^{(V,5)}, S_t^{(V,6)}\}.$$

The elements in $\boldsymbol{S}$ can be deduced from equations (3.6.16)—(3.6.22). For example,

$$S^{(V,2)} = V_t^{(2)}/V_t \,.$$

The elements of $\boldsymbol{V}$ are themselves Divisia indexes that can be represented as follows:

$$V_t^{(R,1)} = \text{Divisia}\left(\boldsymbol{X}_t^{(1)}, \boldsymbol{S}_t^{(T1)}, \text{Þ}_t \right); \qquad t = 1, \ldots, T \qquad (3.6.37)$$

$$V_t^{(R,2)} = \text{Divisia}\left(\boldsymbol{X}_t^{(2)}, \boldsymbol{S}_t^{(T2)}, \text{Þ}_t \right); \qquad t = 1, \ldots, T \qquad (3.6.38)$$

$$V_t^{(R,3)} = \text{Divisia}\left(\boldsymbol{X}_t^{(3)}, \boldsymbol{S}_t^{(T3)}, \text{Þ}_t \right); \qquad t = 1, \ldots, T \qquad (3.6.39)$$

$$V_t^{(R,4)} = \text{Divisia}\left(\boldsymbol{X}_t^{(4)}, \boldsymbol{S}_t^{(T4)}, \text{Þ}_t \right); \qquad t = 1, \ldots, T \qquad (3.6.40)$$

$$V_t^{(R,5)} = \text{Divisia}\left(\boldsymbol{X}_t^{(5)}, \boldsymbol{S}_t^{(T5)}, \text{Þ}_t \right); \text{ and} \qquad t = 1, \ldots, T \qquad (3.6.41)$$

$$V_t^{(R,6)} = \text{Divisia}\left(\boldsymbol{X}_t^{(M)}, \boldsymbol{S}_t^{(T6)}, \text{Þ}_t \right). \qquad t = 1, \ldots, T \qquad (3.6.42)$$

The $\boldsymbol{S}$s in equations (3.6.37) - (3.6.42) are shares. For example,

$$\boldsymbol{S}_t^{(T1)} = \{P_{i,s,t}^{(Z)} X_{i,s,j,t}^{(1)} [T_{i,s,j,t}^{(1)} - 1]/V_t^{(1)} \mid i=1,2,\ldots,13;\ s=d,f;\ j=1,2,\ldots,13\}; \text{ and}$$

$$\boldsymbol{S}_t^{(T3)} = \{P_{i,s,t}^{(Z)} X_{i,s,t}^{(3)} [T_{i,s,t}^{(3)} - 1]/V_t^{(3)} \mid i=1,2,\ldots,13;\ s=d,f\} \,.$$

The price deflators corresponding to the quantity indexes defined by equations (3.6.33) - (3.6.42) are as follows:

$$K_t^{(\Pi)} = \text{Divisia}\left(\boldsymbol{P}_t^{(K)}, \boldsymbol{S}_t^{(K)}, \text{Þ}_t \right); \qquad t = 1, \ldots, T \qquad (3.6.43)$$

$$N_t^{(\Pi)} = \text{Divisia}\left(\boldsymbol{P}_t^{(N)}, \boldsymbol{S}_t^{(N)}, \text{Þ}_t \right); \qquad t = 1, \ldots, T \qquad (3.6.44)$$

$$O_t^{(\Pi)} = \text{Divisia}\left(\boldsymbol{P}_t^{(O)}, \boldsymbol{S}_t^{(O)}, \text{Þ}_t \right); \text{ and} \qquad t = 1, \ldots, T \qquad (3.6.45)$$

$$V_t^{(\Pi)} = \text{Divisia}\left(\boldsymbol{V}_t^{(\Pi)}, \boldsymbol{S}_t^{(V)}, \text{Þ}_t \right). \qquad t = 1, \ldots, T \qquad (3.6.46)$$

In equations (3.6.43) — (3.6.45) the $\boldsymbol{P}$s are the price vectors that correspond to the $\boldsymbol{X}$s in equations (3.6.33) — (3.6.35). Similarly, $\boldsymbol{V}^{(\Pi)}$ in equation (3.6.46) is a vector of price deflators corresponding to $\boldsymbol{V}^{(R)}$, the vector of quantity indexes in equation (3.6.36). Each element in $\boldsymbol{V}^{(\Pi)}$ is a Divisia index of the nominal components of net indirect tax payments by: producers; capital creators; households; exporters; government; and importers. The nominal component of net indirect taxes paid by each group of agents includes both prices and tax rates. That is, the nominal component of the indirect taxes collected from each type of expenditure includes all variables that can affect the tax base associated with that expenditure other than quantities. We represent these indexes as follows:

$$V_t^{(\Pi,1)} = \text{Divisia}\left(\boldsymbol{P}_t^{(1)}, \boldsymbol{T}_t^{(1)}, \boldsymbol{S}_t^{(T1)}, Þ_t \right); \qquad t = 1, ..., T \qquad (3.6.47)$$

$$V_t^{(\Pi,2)} = \text{Divisia}\left(\boldsymbol{P}_t^{(2)}, \boldsymbol{T}_t^{(2)}, \boldsymbol{S}_t^{(T2)}, Þ_t \right); \qquad t = 1, ..., T \qquad (3.6.48)$$

$$V_t^{(\Pi,3)} = \text{Divisia}\left(\boldsymbol{P}_t^{(3)}, \boldsymbol{T}_t^{(3)}, \boldsymbol{S}_t^{(T3)}, Þ_t \right); \qquad t = 1, ..., T \qquad (3.6.49)$$

$$V_t^{(\Pi,4)} = \text{Divisia}\left(\boldsymbol{P}_t^{(4)}, \boldsymbol{T}_t^{(4)}, \boldsymbol{S}_t^{(T4)}, Þ_t \right); \qquad t = 1, ..., T \qquad (3.6.50)$$

$$V_t^{(\Pi,5)} = \text{Divisia}\left(\boldsymbol{P}_t^{(5)}, \boldsymbol{T}_t^{(5)}, \boldsymbol{S}_t^{(T5)}, Þ_t \right); \text{ and} \qquad t = 1, ..., T \qquad (3.6.51)$$

$$V_t^{(\Pi,6)} = \text{Divisia}\left(\boldsymbol{P}_t^{(M)}, \boldsymbol{T}_t^{(6)}, \boldsymbol{S}_t^{(T6)}, Þ_t \right). \qquad t = 1, ..., T \qquad (3.6.52)$$

The ***T***s in equations (3.6.47)—(3.6.52) are vectors of tax rates. For example,

$\boldsymbol{T}_t^{(3)} = \{[T_{i,s,t}^{(3)} - 1] \mid i=1,2,...,13;\ s=d,f\}$; and

$\boldsymbol{T}_t^{(6)} = \{[T_{i,t}^{(6)} - 1] \mid i=1,2,...,13\}$.

Nominal GDP from the expenditure side of the national accounts is decomposed into real GDP and a deflator for GDP as follows:

$$GDPE_t^{(R)} = \text{Divisia}\left(\boldsymbol{GDPE}_t^{(R)}, \boldsymbol{S}_t^{(GDPE)}, Þ_t \right); \text{ and} \qquad t = 1, ..., T \qquad (3.6.53)$$

$$GDPE_t^{(\Pi)} = \text{Divisia}\left(\boldsymbol{GDPE}_t^{(\Pi)}, \boldsymbol{S}_t^{(GDPE)}, Þ_t \right). \qquad t = 1, ..., T \qquad (3.6.54)$$

The vector $\boldsymbol{GDPE}^{(R)}$ contains the real expenditure aggregates $C_t^{(R)}$, $I_t^{(R)}$, $G_t^{(R)}$, $E_t^{(R)}$ and $M_t^{(R)}$. The corresponding price deflators $C_t^{(\Pi)}$, $I_t^{(\Pi)}$, $G_t^{(\Pi)}$, $E_t^{(\Pi)}$ and $M_t^{(\Pi)}$ are contained in $\boldsymbol{GDPE}^{(\Pi)}$. The vector ***S*** contains the shares of the expenditure aggregates in GDP. That is,

$\boldsymbol{S}^{(GDPE)} = \{C/GDPE, I/GDPE, G/GDPE, E/GDPE, M/GDPE\}$.

From equations (3.6.53) and (3.6.54) we derive the following definitions of real GNE and the GNE deflator:

$$GNE_t^{(R)} = \text{Divisia}\left(\boldsymbol{GNE}_t^{(R)}, \boldsymbol{S}_t^{(GNE)}, Þ_t \right); \text{ and} \qquad t = 1, ..., T \qquad (3.6.55)$$

$$GNE_t^{(\Pi)} = \text{Divisia}\left(\boldsymbol{GNE}_t^{(\Pi)}, \boldsymbol{S}_t^{(GNE)}, Þ_t \right). \qquad t = 1, ..., T \qquad (3.6.56)$$

The vector $\boldsymbol{GNE}^{(R)}$ contains the real expenditure aggregates $C_t^{(R)}$, $I_t^{(R)}$, and $G_t^{(R)}$. The corresponding price deflators $C_t^{(\Pi)}$, $I_t^{(\Pi)}$, and $G_t^{(\Pi)}$ are contained in $\boldsymbol{GNE}^{(\Pi)}$. The vector ***S*** contains the shares of the expenditure aggregates in GNE. That is,

$\boldsymbol{S}^{(GNE)} = \{C/GNE, I/GNE, G/GNE\}$.

We also decompose nominal GDP from the income side of the national accounts. We derive the following income-side definitions of real GDP and the GDP deflator:

$$\mathrm{GDPI}_t^{(R)} = \mathrm{Divisia}\left(\boldsymbol{GDPI}_t^{(R)}, \boldsymbol{S}_t^{(GDPI)}, Þ_t\right); \text{ and} \qquad t = 1, ..., T \qquad (3.6.57)$$

$$\mathrm{GDPI}_t^{(\Pi)} = \mathrm{Divisia}\left(\boldsymbol{GDPI}_t^{(\Pi)}, \boldsymbol{S}_t^{(GDPI)}, Þ_t\right). \qquad t = 1, ..., T \qquad (3.6.58)$$

The vector $\boldsymbol{GDPI}^{(R)}$ contains $\mathrm{GDPFC}_t^{(R)}$, real GDP at factor cost, and $\mathrm{NIT}_t^{(R)}$, real net indirect taxes. The corresponding deflators, $\mathrm{GDPFC}_t^{(\Pi)}$ and $\mathrm{NIT}_t^{(\Pi)}$, are contained in $\boldsymbol{GDPI}^{(\Pi)}$. The vector $\boldsymbol{S}$ contains the shares of GDPFC_t and NIT_t in GDP.

Real GDP at factor cost (value added) and the factor-cost deflator are defined as follows:

$$\mathrm{GDPFC}_t^{(R)} = \mathrm{Divisia}\left(\mathrm{K}_t^{(R)}, \mathrm{N}_t^{(R)}, \mathrm{L}_t, \boldsymbol{S}_t^{(VA)}, Þ_t\right); \text{ and} \qquad t = 1, ..., T \qquad (3.6.59)$$

$$\mathrm{GDPFC}_t^{(\Pi)} = \mathrm{Divisia}\left(\mathrm{K}_t^{(\Pi)}, \mathrm{N}_t^{(\Pi)}, \mathrm{P}_t^{(L)}, \boldsymbol{S}_t^{(VA)}, Þ_t\right). \qquad t = 1, ..., T \qquad (3.6.60)$$

The vector $\boldsymbol{S}$ in equations (3.6.59) and (3.6.60) contains the shares of labour, capital and agricultural land in value added. Note that because the price of labour is the same across industries we have dropped the industry index from the price of labour in equation (3.6.60). Finally, we define real net indirect taxes and the deflator for net indirect taxes as follows:

$$\mathrm{NIT}_t^{(R)} = \mathrm{Divisia}\left(\mathrm{O}_t^{(R)}, \mathrm{V}_t^{(R)}, \boldsymbol{S}_t^{(NIT)}, Þ_t\right); \text{ and} \qquad t = 1, ..., T \qquad (3.6.61)$$

$$\mathrm{NIT}_t^{(\Pi)} = \mathrm{Divisia}\left(\mathrm{O}_t^{(\Pi)}, \mathrm{V}_t^{(\Pi)}, \boldsymbol{S}_t^{(NIT)}, Þ_t\right). \qquad t = 1, ..., T \qquad (3.6.62)$$

The vector $\boldsymbol{S}$ in equations (3.6.61) and (3.6.62) contains the shares in net indirect taxes of 'other cost' tickets and sales taxes.

Indexing the Price of 'Other Cost' Tickets

The supply of 'other cost' tickets is not formally modelled in ORANI-INT. As explained previously 'other cost' tickets enter the production function in fixed proportions with other inputs (i.e., primary factor composites and commodity composites). Therefore, the option of assuming that the supply of 'other cost' tickets is exogenous is rather limiting. Instead we assume that, $\mathrm{F}_{j,t}^{(O)}$, the real price of 'other cost' tickets is exogenous. With this assumption the usage of 'other cost' tickets is demand determined. The default specification of the real price of 'other cost' tickets is as follows:

$$\frac{\mathrm{P}_{j,t}^{(O)}}{\mathrm{C}_t^{(\Pi)}} = \mathrm{F}_{j,t}^{(O)}. \qquad i = 1, ..., 13;\ s = d,f;\ t = 1, ..., T \qquad (3.6.63)$$

3.7 Chapter Summary

In this chapter we derived all the equations that make up ORANI-INT. Most of the equations are atemporal – they relate variables in the same period. Most of the atemporal equations are borrowed from ORANI, a static CGE model of the Australian economy. Two types of intertemporal equations are used in ORANI-INT. Accounting relationships are used to accumulate capital stocks and net foreign assets over time. The other intertemporal equations model the behaviour of intertemporally optimising consumers and investors.

Five appendices accompany this chapter. Appendix A3.1 contains a consolidated list of the variables and equations that make up ORANI-INT. The next three appendices deal with topics that are central to the theoretical specification of ORANI-INT. Appendix A3.2 deals with the specification of the household budget constraint. In appendix A3.3 we discuss alternative investment specifications. The implications of imposing explicit nonnegativity constraints on investment are dealt with in appendix A3.4. Finally, in appendix A3.5 we briefly discuss the use of Divisia indexes in ORANI-INT.

Appendix A3.1 The Log-linear Form of the ORANI-INT Equation System

A3.1.1 Introduction

This appendix is organised around 3 tables. The main purpose of table A3.1.1 is to present a consolidated list of the equations that make up ORANI-INT. Tables A3.1.2 and A3.1.3 list the variables and parameters in ORANI-INT.

The log-linear forms of the ORANI-INT equations are listed in column 2 of table A3.1.1. In column 1 of table A3.1.1 we map the linearised equations to their non-linear counterparts derived in chapter 3. The numbers that appear in column 1 correspond with the numbers used in chapter 3 to identify the non-linear equations. We have appended the prefix 'A' to all the equation identifiers in column 1 so that we are can refer to the linearised equations in the remainder of the book. In columns 3 and 4 of table A3.1.1 we identify the dimensions of each vector of equations. Column 3 shows the range of the indexes used in each vector of equations and column 4 shows the size of the vector equation. The last column in table A3.1.1 provides a brief description of each vector equation.

In the linearised ORANI-INT equations variables are expressed as levels, percentage changes or ordinary changes. Upper-case letters are used to identify levels variables. Variables expressed as percentage changes are denoted by lower-case italicised letters. For example, $X^{(K)}_{j,t}$ is a levels variable denoting the demand for capital by sector j in year t. The percentage change form of this variable is denoted as $x^{(K)}_{j,t}$.[1] In linearising the ORANI-INT equations we use ordinary changes, rather than percentage changes, for variables whose levels can pass through zero. Variables expressed as ordinary changes are denoted by upper-case letters with a 'd' prefix. For example, the ordinary change form of D_t, the level of net foreign liabilities in year t, is dD_t.

1 Note that $x^{(K)}_{j,t} = 100 \times d\ln X^{(K)}_{j,t}$.

Table A3.1.1: A Log-linear Representation of the ORANI-INT Equation System

Identifier	Equation	Range	No.	Description
1 Final Demands				
1.1 Households				
A3.3.3	$x^{(3)}_{i,s,t} = x^{(3)}_{i,\bullet,t} - \frac{1}{1+\varepsilon}\left\{ p^{(3)}_{i,s,t} - \frac{\sum_k \xi^{1/(1+\varepsilon)}_{i,k,t} P^{(3)\varepsilon/(1+\varepsilon)}_{i,k,t}}{\sum_r \xi^{1/(1+\varepsilon)}_{i,r,t} P^{(3)\varepsilon/(1+\varepsilon)}_{i,r,t}} p^{(3)}_{i,k,t} \right\}$	t=1,...,T i=1,...,I s=1,2	SIT	Household demand for commodities classified by source
A3.3.10	$x^{(3)}_{i,\bullet,t} = \frac{\beta_i C^{(a)}_t}{P^{(3)}_{i,\bullet,t} X^{(3)}_{i,\bullet,t}} \left[c^{(a)}_t - p^{(3)}_{i,\bullet,t} \right] + \frac{P^{(3)}_{i,\bullet,t} Q_t \tilde{\gamma}^{(3)}_{i,\bullet}}{P^{(3)}_{i,\bullet,t} X^{(3)}_{i,\bullet,t}} q_t$	t=1,...,T i=1,...I	IT	Household demand for commodities, undifferentiated by source
A3.3.17a	$c^{(a)}_t - c^{(a)}_{t+1} = q_t - q_{t+1} - \frac{100}{[1 + B_{d,t}]} dB_{d,t} + f^{(3)}_t$	t=1,...T-1	T-1	Distribution of discretionary expenditure through time
1.2 Capital Creators				
A3.3.22	$z^{(K)}_{j,t+1} = \frac{Y_{j,t}}{Z^{(K)}_{j,t+1}} \left\{ y_{j,t} - z^{(K)}_{j,t} \right\} + z^{(K)}_{j,t}$	t=1,...,T j=1,...,J	JT	Accumulation of sectoral capital stocks
A3.3.20	$d\Psi_{j,t} = dB_{d,t} + dH_{j,t} - dF^{(2)}_{j,t}$	t=1,...,T j=1,...,J	JT	Arbitrage condition

....continued

Table A3.1.1 (continued): A Log-linear Representation of the ORANI-INT Equation System

Identifier	Equation	Range	No.	Description
A3.3.33a	$100d\Psi_{j,t} = \frac{P^{(K)}_{j,t+1}}{P^{(A)}_{j,t}}\left\{ p^{(K)}_{j,t+1} - p^{(A)}_{j,t} \right\} + [\,1 - \delta_j\,]\ \frac{P^{(A)}_{j,t+1}}{P^{(A)}_{j,t}}\ \kappa^{(A)}_{j,t+1}$	t=1,...,T-1 j=1,...,J	J(T-1)	Rates of Return on Sectoral Capital
A3.3.33b	$\kappa^{(A)}_{j,t} = \left\{ p^{(A)}_{j,t} - p^{(A)}_{j,t-1} \right\} + f^{(A)}_{j,t}$	t=2,...,T j=1,...,J	J(T-1)	Sectoral capital gains
A3.3.33	$p^{(A)}_{j,t} = \left\{ \frac{P^{(Y)}_{j,t}}{P^{(A)}_{j,t}} p^{(Y)}_{j,t} - \frac{100dF^{(Y)}_{j,t}}{P^{(A)}_{j,t}} \right\}$	t=1,...,T j=1,...,J	JT	Market valuation of sectoral capital
A3.3.38	$z^{(K)}_{j,t+1} - z^{(K)}_{j,t} = f^{(K)}_{j,t}$	t=T j=1,..,J	J	Terminal conditions on sectoral capital
	1.3 Government Demands			
A3.3.43	$x^{(5)}_{i,s,t} - c^{(R)}_{t} = f^{(5)}_{i,s,t} + f^{(5)}_{t}$	t=1,...,T i=1,...,I s=1,2	SIT	Government demands for commodities classified by source
	1.4 Exports			
A3.3.44	$x^{(4)}_{i,t} = \eta_i \left\{ p^{(e)}_{i,t} - f^{(4p)}_{i,t} \right\} + f^{(4q)}_{i,t}$	t=1,...,T i=1,...,I	IT	Export demand functions

....continued

Table A3.1.1 (continued): A Log-linear Representation of the ORANI-INT Equation System

Identifier	Equation	Range	No.	Description
	2 Industry Demands			
	2.1 Primary Factors			
A3.2.9	$x^{(K)}_{j,t} = x^{(F)}_{j,t} - \frac{1}{1+\mu}\left\{\left(p^{(K)}_{j,t} + a^{(K)}_{j,t}\right) - \left(p^{(F)}_{j,t} + a^{(F)}_{j,t}\right)\right\} + \left\{a^{(K)}_{j,t} - a^{(F)}_{j,t}\right\}$	t=1,...,T j=1,...,J	JT	Demand for capital
A3.2.3	$x^{(L)}_{j,t} = x^{(F)}_{j,t} - \frac{1}{1+\mu}\left\{\left(p^{(L)}_{j,t} + a^{(L)}_{j,t}\right) - \left(p^{(F)}_{j,t} + a^{(F)}_{j,t}\right)\right\} + \left\{a^{(L)}_{j,t} - a^{(F)}_{j,t}\right\}$	t=1,...,T j=1,...,J	JT	Demand for labour
A3.2.4	$x^{(N)}_{j,t} = x^{(F)}_{j,t} - \frac{1}{1+\mu}\left\{\left(p^{(N)}_{j,t} + a^{(L)}_{j,t}\right) - \left(p^{(F)}_{j,t} + a^{(F)}_{j,t}\right)\right\} + \left\{a^{(N)}_{j,t} - a^{(F)}_{j,t}\right\}$	t=1,...,T j=1,...,J	JT	Demand for agricultural land
A3.4.2	$x^{(F)}_{j,t} = z^{(1)}_{j,t} + a^{(F)}_{j,t}$	t=1,...,T j=1,...J	JT	Demands for factor composites
	2.2 "Other cost" Tickets			
A3.2.13	$x^{(O)}_{j,t} = z^{(1)}_{j,t} + a^{(O)}_{j,t}$	t=1,...,T j=1,...,J	JT	Demands for "other cost" tickets

....continued

Table A3.1.1 (continued): A Log-linear Representation of the ORANI-INT Equation System

Identifier	Equation	Range	No.	Description
	2.3 Intermediate Inputs			
A3.2.16	$x^{(1)}_{i,s,j,t} = x^{(1)}_{i,\bullet,j,t} - \frac{1}{1+v}\left\{ p^{(1)}_{i,s,j,t} - \frac{\sum_k \varsigma^{1/(1+v)}_{i,k,j,t} P^{(1)v/(1+v)}_{i,k,j,t}}{\sum_r \varsigma^{1/(1+v)}_{i,r,j,t} P^{(1)v/(1+v)}_{i,r,j,t}} p^{(1)}_{i,k,j,t} \right\}$	t=1,...,T i=1,...,I j=1,...J s=1,2	SIJT	Demands for intermediate inputs by source
A3.2.12	$x^{(1)}_{i,\bullet,j,t} = z^{(1)}_{j,t} + a^{(1)}_{i,\bullet,j,t}$	t=1,...,T i=1,...,I j=1,...J	IJT	Demands for intermediate inputs undifferentiated by source
	2.4 Inputs to Capital Creation			
A3.3.42	$x^{(2)}_{i,s,j,t} = y_{j,t} + a^{(2)}_{i,\bullet,j,t} - \frac{1}{1+\upsilon}\left\{ p^{(2)}_{i,s,j,t} - \frac{\sum_k \vartheta^{1/(1+\upsilon)}_{i,k,j,t} P^{(2)\,\upsilon/(1+\upsilon)}_{i,k,j,t}}{\sum_r \vartheta^{1/(1+\upsilon)}_{i,r,j,t} P^{(2)\upsilon/(1+\upsilon)}_{i,r,j,t}} p^{(2)}_{i,k,j,t} \right\}$	t=1,...,T i=1,...,I j=1,...J s=1,2	SIJT	Demands for inputs to capital creation by source

....continued

Table A3.1.1 (continued): A Log-linear Representation of the ORANI-INT Equation System

Identifier	Equation	Range	No.	Description
	3 Pricing Equations			
A3.3.4	$p^{(3)}_{i,\bullet,t} = \left\{ \frac{\sum_{s} \xi^{1/(1+\varepsilon)}_{i,s,t} P^{(3)\varepsilon/(1+\varepsilon)}_{i,s,t}}{\sum_{r} \xi^{1/(1+\varepsilon)}_{i,r,t} P^{(3)\varepsilon/(1+\varepsilon)}_{i,r,t}} p^{(3)}_{i,s,t} \right\}$	t=1,...,T i=1,...I	IT	Price of commodities, undifferentiated by source, to households
A3.2.14	$p^{(1)}_{i,\bullet,j,t} = \left\{ \frac{\sum_{s} \zeta^{1/(1+\nu)}_{i,s,j,t} P^{(1)\nu/(1+\nu)}_{i,s,j,t}}{\sum_{r} \zeta^{1/(1+\nu)}_{i,r,j,t} P^{(1)\nu/(1+\nu)}_{i,r,j,t}} p^{(1)}_{i,s,j,t} \right\}$	t=1,...,T i=1,...,I j=1,...,J	IJT	Price of commodities, undifferentiated by source, to producers
A3.2.7	$p^{(F)}_{j,t} = \zeta^{(L)1/(1+\mu)}_{j,t} \left\{ \frac{P^{(L)}_{j,t} A^{(L)}_{j,t}}{P^{(F)}_{j,t} A^{(F)}_{j,t}} \right\}^{\mu/(1+\mu)} \left(p^{(L)}_{j,t} + a^{(L)}_{j,t} \right)$ $+ \zeta^{(K)1/(1+\mu)}_{j,t} \left\{ \frac{P^{(K)}_{j,t} A^{(K)}_{j,t}}{P^{(F)}_{j,t} A^{(F)}_{j,t}} \right\}^{\mu/(1+\mu)} \left(p^{(K)}_{j,t} + a^{(K)}_{j,t} \right)$ $+ \zeta^{(N)1/(1+\mu)}_{j,t} \left\{ \frac{P^{(N)}_{j,t} A^{(N)}_{j,t}}{P^{(F)}_{j,t} A^{(F)}_{j,t}} \right\}^{\mu/(1+\mu)} \left(p^{(N)}_{j,t} + a^{(N)}_{j,t} \right) - a^{(F)}_{j,t}$	T=1,..., T j=1,...,J	JT	Factor price index

....continued

Table A3.1.1 (continued): A Log-linear Representation of the ORANI-INT Equation System

Identifier	Equation	Range	No.	Description
A3.4.8	$p^{(1)}_{i,s,j,t} = p^{(Z)}_{i,s,t} + t^{(1)}_{i,s,j,t}$	t=1,...,T i=1,...,I j=1,...J s=1,2	SIJT	Purchasers' prices for intermediate inputs
A3.4.9	$p^{(2)}_{i,s,j,t} = p^{(Z)}_{i,s,t} + t^{(2)}_{i,s,j,t}$	t=1,...,T i=1,...,I j=1,...J s=1,2	SIJT	Purchasers' prices for inputs to capital creation
A3.4.10	$p^{(3)}_{i,s,t} = p^{(Z)}_{i,s,t} + t^{(3)}_{i,s,t}$	t=1,...,T i=1,...,I s=1,2	SIT	Zero pure profits in the distribution of goods to households
A3.4.6	$p^{(E)}_{i,t} + \phi_t = p^{(Z)}_{i,d,t} + t^{(4)}_{i,t}$	t=1,...,T i=1,...,I	IT	Zero pure profits in the distribution of goods to foreigners
A3.4.11	$p^{(5)}_{i,s,t} = p^{(Z)}_{i,s,t} + t^{(5)}_{i,s,t}$	t=1,...,T i=1,...,I s=1,2	SIT	Zero pure profits in the distribution of goods to the government
A3.4.7	$p^{(Z)}_{i,f,t} = p^{(M)}_{i,t} + \varphi_t + t^{(6)}_{i,t}$	t=1,...,T i=1,...,I	IT	Zero pure profits in importing

....continued

Table A3.1.1 (continued): A Log-linear Representation of the ORANI-INT Equation System

Identifier	Equation	Range	No.	Description
A3.4.5	$p^{(Y)}_{j,t} = \sum_{i=1}^{13} A^{(2)}_{i,\bullet,j,t}\, a^{(2)}_{i,\bullet,j,t} + \frac{\sum_s \vartheta^{1/(1+\upsilon)}_{i,s,j,t} P^{(2)\upsilon/(1+\upsilon)}_{i,s,j,t}}{\sum_r \vartheta^{1/(1+\upsilon)}_{i,r,j,t} P^{(2)\upsilon/(1+\upsilon)}_{i,r,j,t}} p^{(2)}_{i,s,j,t}$	t=1,...,T j=1,...,J	JT	Zero pure profits in capital creation
A3.4.3	$p^{(Z)}_{j,t} = \frac{P^{(F)}_{j,t} A^{(F)}_{j,t}}{P^{(Z)}_{j,t}} \left\{ p^{(F)}_{j,t} + a^{(F)}_{j,t} \right\} + \frac{P^{(O)}_{j,t} A^{(O)}_{j,t}}{P^{(Z)}_{j,t}} \left\{ p^{(O)}_{j,t} + a^{(O)}_{j,t} \right\} + \sum_{i=1}^{13} \frac{P^{(1)}_{i,\bullet,j,t} A^{(1)}_{i,\bullet,j,t}}{P^{(Z)}_{j,t}} \left\{ p^{(1)}_{i,\bullet,j,t} + a^{(1)}_{i,\bullet,j,t} \right\}$	t=1,...,T j=1,...,J	JT	Zero pure profits in current production
A3.4.4	$p^{(Z)}_{j,t} = p^{(Z)}_{i,d,t}$	t=1,...,T j=1,...,J i=j	JT	Basic price of domestically produced commodity i is equal to unit price of sector j, the sole producer of commodity i
A3.4.12	$100dB_{d,t} = \frac{\Phi_{t+1}}{\Phi_t}[1 + B_{f,t}] \left\{ \varphi_{t+1} - \varphi_t + \frac{100dB_{f,t}}{[1 + B_{f,t}]} \right\}$	t=1,...,T	T	Interest parity condition

....continued

Table A3.1.1 (continued): A Log-linear Representation of the ORANI-INT Equation System

Identifier	Equation	Range	No.	Description
	4 Market Clearing Equations			
	4.1 Primary Factors			
A3.5.2	$z^{(K)}_{j,t} = x^{(K)}_{j,t}$	t=1,...,T j=1,...,J	JT	Supply of sector-specific capital is equal to demand
A3.5.5	$z^{(N)}_{j,t} = x^{(N)}_{j,t}$	t=1,...,T j=1,...,J	JT	Supply of agricultural land is equal to demand
A3.5.3	$l_t = w^{(R)}_t$	t=1,...,T	T	Aggregate supply of labour is equal to aggregate demand for labour
	4.2 Commodities			
A3.5.1	$z^{(1)}_{i,t} = \sum_{j=1}^{13} \frac{X^{(1)}_{i,d,j,t}}{Z^{(1)}_{i,t}} x^{(1)}_{i,d,j,t} + \sum_{j=1}^{13} \frac{X^{(2)}_{i,d,j,t}}{Z^{(1)}_{i,t}} x^{(2)}_{i,d,j,t} + \frac{X^{(3)}_{i,d,t}}{Z^{(1)}_{i,t}} x^{(3)}_{i,d,t} + \frac{X^{(4)}_{i,t}}{Z^{(1)}_{i,t}} x^{(4)}_{i,t} + \frac{X^{(5)}_{i,d,t}}{Z^{(1)}_{i,t}} x^{(5)}_{i,d,t}$	t=1,...,T i=1,...,I	IT	Supply of domestically produced commodities is equal to demand
	5 Indirect Tax Revenue Equations			
A3.6.17	$v^{(1)}_t = \sum_{i=1}^{13} \sum_{s \in d,f} \sum_{j=1}^{13} \frac{P^{(Z)}_{i,s,t} X^{(1)}_{i,s,j,t} [T^{(1)}_{i,s,j,t} - 1]}{V^{(1)}_t} \left\{ p^{(Z)}_{i,s,t} + x^{(1)}_{i,s,j,t} + \frac{T^{(1)}_{i,s,j,t}}{[T^{(1)}_{i,s,j,t} - 1]} t^{(1)}_{i,s,j,t} \right\}$	t=1,...,T	T	Aggregate revenue from taxes on flows of commodities to intermediate users

....continued

Table A3.1.1 (continued): A Log-linear Representation of the ORANI-INT Equation System

Identifier	Equation	Range	No.	Description
A3.6.18	$v_t^{(2)} = \sum_{i=1}^{13} \sum_{s \in d,f} \sum_{j=1}^{13} \frac{P_{i,s,t}^{(Z)} X_{i,s,j,t}^{(2)} [T_{i,s,j,t}^{(2)} - 1]}{V_t^{(2)}} \left\{ p_{i,s,t}^{(Z)} + x_{i,s,j,t}^{(2)} + \frac{T_{i,s,j,t}^{(2)}}{[T_{i,s,j,t}^{(2)} - 1]} t_{i,s,j,t}^{(2)} \right\}$	t=1,...,T	T	Aggregate revenue from taxes on flows of commodities to capital creation
A3.6.19	$v_t^{(3)} = \sum_{i=1}^{13} \sum_{s \in d,f} \frac{P_{i,s,t}^{(Z)} X_{i,s,t}^{(3)} [T_{i,s,t}^{(3)} - 1]}{V_t^{(3)}} \left\{ p_{i,s,t}^{(Z)} + x_{i,s,t}^{(3)} + \frac{T_{i,s,t}^{(3)}}{[T_{i,s,t}^{(3)} - 1]} t_{i,s,t}^{(3)} \right\}$	t=1,...,T	T	Aggregate revenue from taxes on flows of commodities to households
A3.6.20	$v_t^{(4)} = \sum_{i=1}^{13} \frac{P_{i,d,t}^{(Z)} X_{i,t}^{(4)} [T_{i,t}^{(4)} - 1]}{V_t^{(4)}} \left\{ p_{i,d,t}^{(Z)} + x_{i,t}^{(4)} + \frac{T_{i,t}^{(4)}}{[T_{i,t}^{(4)} - 1]} t_{i,t}^{(4)} \right\}$	t=1,...,T	T	Aggregate revenue from taxes on flows of commodities to exports
A3.6.21	$v_t^{(5)} = \sum_{i=1}^{13} \sum_{s \in d,f} \frac{P_{i,s,t}^{(Z)} X_{i,s,t}^{(5)} [T_{i,s,t}^{(5)} - 1]}{V_t^{(5)}} \left\{ p_{i,s,t}^{(Z)} + x_{i,s,t}^{(5)} + \frac{T_{i,s,t}^{(5)}}{[T_{i,s,t}^{(5)} - 1]} t_{i,s,t}^{(5)} \right\}$	t=1,...,T	T	Aggregate revenue from taxes on flows of commodities to "other"
A3.6.22	$v_t^{(6)} = \sum_{i=1}^{13} \frac{P_{i,t}^{(M)} X_{i,t}^{(M)} \Phi_t [T_{i,t}^{(6)} - 1]}{V_t^{(6)}} \left\{ p_{i,t}^{(M)} + x_{i,t}^{(M)} + \phi_t + \frac{T_{i,t}^{(6)}}{[T_{i,t}^{(6)} - 1]} t_{i,t}^{(6)} \right\}$	t=1,...,T	T	Aggregate tariff revenue

....continued

Table A3.1.1 (continued): A Log-linear Representation of the ORANI-INT Equation System

Identifier	Equation	Range	No.	Description
	6 Macroeconomic Aggregates			
A3.6.1	$gdpe_t = \frac{C_t}{GDPE_t} c_t + \frac{I_t}{GDPE_t} i_t + \frac{G_t}{GDPE_t} g_t + \frac{1}{GDPE_t} 100dBoT_t$	t=1,...,T	T	Nominal GDP: expenditure side
A3.6.2	$c_t = \frac{1}{C_t} \sum_{i=1}^{13} P_{i,\bullet,t}^{(3)} X_{i,\bullet,t}^{(3)} \left\{ p_{i,\bullet,t}^{(3)} + x_{i,\bullet,t}^{(3)} \right\}$	t=1,...,T	T	Aggregate nominal consumption
A3.6.3	$i_t = \frac{1}{I_t} \sum_{j=1}^{13} P_{j,t}^{(Y)} Y_{j,t} \left\{ p_{j,t}^{(Y)} + y_{j,t} \right\}$	t=1,...,T	T	Aggregate nominal investment
A3.6.4	$g_t = \frac{1}{G_t} \sum_{i=1}^{13} \sum_{s \in d,f} P_{i,s,t}^{(5)} X_{i,s,t}^{(5)} \left\{ p_{i,s,t}^{(5)} + x_{i,s,t}^{(5)} \right\}$	t=1,...,T	T	Aggregate nominal government consumption
A3.6.5	$100dBoT_t = E_t e_t - M_t m_t$	t=1,...,T	T	Balance of trade
A3.6.6	$e_t = \frac{1}{\Phi_t E_t} \sum_{i=1}^{13} P_{i,t}^{(E)} X_{i,t}^{(4)} \left\{ p_{i,t}^{(E)} + x_{i,t}^{(4)} - \phi_t \right\}$	t=1,...,T	T	Aggregate exports

....continued

Table A3.1.1 (continued): A Log-linear Representation of the ORANI-INT Equation System

Identifier	Equation	Range	No.	Description
A3.6.7	$m_t = \frac{1}{\Phi_t M_t}\sum_{i=1}^{13} P_{i,t}^{(M)} X_{i,t}^{(M)} \left\{ p_{i,t}^{(M)} + x_{i,t}^{(M)} - \phi_t \right\}$	t=1,...,T	T	Aggregate imports
A3.6.8	$x_{i,t}^{(M)} = \frac{1}{X_{i,t}^{(M)}} \left\{ \sum_{j=1}^{13} X_{i,f,j,t}^{(1)} x_{i,f,j,t}^{(1)} + \sum_{j=1}^{13} X_{i,f,j,t}^{(2)} x_{i,f,j,t}^{(2)} + X_{i,f,t}^{(3)} x_{i,f,t}^{(3)} + X_{i,f,t}^{(5)} x_{i,f,t}^{(5)} \right\}$	t=1,...,T i=1,...,I	IT	Aggregate demand for imported good i
A3.6.9	$gdpi_t = \frac{GDPFC_t}{GDPI_t} gdpfc_t + \frac{NIT_t}{GDPI_t} nit_t$	t=1,...,T	T	Nominal GDP: income side
A3.6.10	$gdpfc_t = \frac{W_t}{GDPFC_t} w_t + \frac{K_t}{GDPFC_t} k_t + \frac{N_t}{GDPFC_t} n_t$	t=1,...,T	T	Nominal GDP at factor cost
A3.6.11	$nit_t = \frac{O_t}{NIT_t} o_t + \frac{V_t}{NIT_t} v_t$	t=1,...,T	T	Net indirect tax revenues
A3.6.12	$w_t = \frac{1}{W_t}\sum_{j=1}^{13} P_{j,t}^{(L)} X_{j,t}^{(L)} \left\{ p_{j,t}^{(L)} + x_{j,t}^{(L)} \right\}$	t=1,...,T	T	Aggregate payments to labour

....continued

Table A3.1.1 (continued): A Log-linear Representation of the ORANI-INT Equation System

Identifier	Equation	Range	No.	Description
A3.6.13	$k_t = \frac{1}{K_t}\sum_{j=1}^{13} P_{j,t}^{(K)} X_{j,t}^{(K)} \left\{ p_{j,t}^{(K)} + x_{j,t}^{(K)} \right\}$	t=1,...,T	T	Aggregate payments to capital
A3.6.14	$n_t = \frac{1}{N_t}\sum_{j=1}^{13} P_{j,t}^{(N)} X_{j,t}^{(N)} \left\{ p_{j,t}^{(N)} + x_{j,t}^{(N)} \right\}$	t=1,...,T	T	Aggregate payments to aggricultural land
A3.6.15	$o_t = \frac{1}{O_t}\sum_{j=1}^{13} P_{j,t}^{(O)} X_{j,t}^{(O)} \left\{ p_{j,t}^{(O)} + x_{j,t}^{(O)} \right\}$	t=1,...,T	T	Aggregate "other cost" tickets
A3.6.16	$v_t = \frac{1}{V_t}\left\{ V_t^{(1)} v_t^{(1)} + V_t^{(2)} v_t^{(2)} + V_t^{(3)} v_t^{(3)} + V_t^{(4)} v_t^{(4)} + V_t^{(5)} v_t^{(5)} + V_t^{(6)} v_t^{(6)} \right\}$	t=1,...,T	T	Aggregate commodity taxes
A3.6.23	$c_t^{(R)} = \frac{1}{C_t}\sum_{i=1}^{13} P_{i,\bullet,t}^{(3)} X_{i,\bullet,t}^{(3)} x_{i,\bullet,t}^{(3)}$	t=1,...,T	T	Aggregate real consumption
A3.6.24	$i_t^{(R)} = \frac{1}{I_t}\sum_{j=1}^{13} P_{j,t}^{(Y)} Y_{j,t} y_{j,t}$	t=1,...,T	T	Aggregate real investment

....continued

Table A3.1.1 (continued): A Log-linear Representation of the ORANI-INT Equation System

Identifier	Equation	Range	No.	Description
A3.6.25	$g_t^{(R)} = \frac{1}{G_t}\sum_{i=1}^{13}\sum_{s\in d,f} P_{i,s,t}^{(5)} X_{i,s,t}^{(5)} x_{i,s,t}^{(5)}$	t=1,...,T	T	Aggregate real government spending
A3.6.26	$e_t^{(R)} = \frac{1}{\Phi_t E_t}\sum_{i=1}^{13} P_{i,t}^{(E)} X_{i,t}^{(4)} x_{i,t}^{(4)}$	t=1,...,T	T	Aggregate export volumes
A3.6.27	$m_t^{(R)} = \frac{1}{\Phi_t M_t}\sum_{i=1}^{13} P_{i,t}^{(M)} X_{i,t}^{(M)} x_{i,t}^{(M)}$	t=1,...,T	T	Aggregate import volumes
A3.6.28	$c_t^{(\Pi)} = \frac{1}{C_t}\sum_{i=1}^{13} P_{i,\bullet,t}^{(3)} X_{i,\bullet,t}^{(3)} p_{i,\bullet,t}^{(3)}$	t=1,...,T	T	Consumption deflator
A3.6.29	$i_t^{(\Pi)} = \frac{1}{I_t}\sum_{j=1}^{13} P_{j,t}^{(Y)} Y_{j,t} p_{j,t}^{(Y)}$	t=1,...,T	T	Investment deflator
A3.6.30	$g_t^{(\Pi)} = \frac{1}{G_t}\sum_{i=1}^{13}\sum_{s\in d,f} P_{i,s,t}^{(5)} X_{i,s,t}^{(5)} p_{i,s,t}^{(5)}$	t=1,...,T	T	Government spending deflator

....continued

Table A3.1.1 (continued): A Log-linear Representation of the ORANI-INT Equation System

Identifier	Equation	Range	No.	Description
A3.6.31	$e_t^{(\Pi)} = \frac{1}{\Phi_t E_t} \sum_{i=1}^{13} P_{i,t}^{(E)} X_{i,t}^{(4)} \left\{ p_{i,t}^{(E)} - \phi_t \right\}$	t=1,...,T	T	Export price deflator
A3.6.32	$m_t^{(\Pi)} = \frac{1}{\Phi_t M_t} \sum_{i=1}^{13} P_{i,t}^{(M)} X_{i,t}^{(M)} \left\{ p_{i,t}^{(M)} - \phi_t \right\}$	t=1,...,T	T	Import price deflator
A3.6.33	$k_t^{(R)} = \frac{1}{K_t} \sum_{j=1}^{13} P_{j,t}^{(K)} X_{j,t}^{(K)} x_{j,t}^{(K)}$	t=1,...,T	T	Aggregate real capital stock
A3.5.4	$w_t^{(R)} = \sum_{j=1}^{13} \frac{X_{j,t}^{(L)}}{L_t} x_{j,t}^{(L)}$	t=1,...,T	T	Aggregate demand for labour
A3.6.34	$n_t^{(R)} = \frac{1}{N_t} \sum_{j=1}^{13} P_{j,t}^{(N)} X_{j,t}^{(N)} x_{j,t}^{(N)}$	t=1,...,T	T	Aggregate real agricultural land
A3.6.35	$o_t^{(R)} = \frac{1}{O_t} \sum_{j=1}^{13} P_{j,t}^{(O)} X_{j,t}^{(O)} x_{j,t}^{(O)}$	t=1,...,T	T	Aggregate real "other cost" tickets

....continued

Table A3.1.1 (continued): A Log-linear Representation of the ORANI-INT Equation System

Identifier	Equation	Range	No.	Description
A3.6.36	$v_t^{(R)} = \frac{1}{V_t}\left\{ V_t^{(1)} v_t^{(R,1)} + V_t^{(2)} v_t^{(R,2)} + V_t^{(3)} v_t^{(R,3)} + V_t^{(4)} v_t^{(R,4)} + V_t^{(5)} v_t^{(R,5)} + V_t^{(6)} v_t^{(R,6)} \right\}$	t=1,...,T	T	Aggregate real commodity taxes
A3.6.37	$v_t^{(R,1)} = \frac{1}{V_t^{(1)}} \sum_{i=1}^{13} \sum_{s \in d,f} \sum_{j=1}^{13} P_{i,s,t}^{(Z)} X_{i,s,j,t}^{(1)} [T_{i,s,j,t}^{(1)} - 1]\, x_{i,s,j,t}^{(1)}$	t=1,...,T	T	Aggregate real revenue from taxes on flows of commodities to intermediate users
A3.6.38	$v_t^{(R,2)} = \frac{1}{V_t^{(2)}} \sum_{i=1}^{13} \sum_{s \in d,f} \sum_{j=1}^{13} P_{i,s,t}^{(Z)} X_{i,s,j,t}^{(2)} [T_{i,s,j,t}^{(2)} - 1]\, x_{i,s,j,t}^{(2)}$	t=1,...,T	T	Aggregate real revenue from taxes on flows of commodities to capital creation
A3.6.39	$v_t^{(R,3)} = \frac{1}{V_t^{(3)}} \sum_{i=1}^{13} \sum_{s \in d,f} P_{i,s,t}^{(Z)} X_{i,s,t}^{(3)} [T_{i,s,t}^{(3)} - 1]\, x_{i,s,t}^{(3)}$	t=1,...,T	T	Aggregate real revenue from taxes on flows of commodities to households
A3.6.40	$v_t^{(R,4)} = \frac{1}{V_t^{(4)}} \sum_{i=1}^{13} P_{i,d,t}^{(Z)} X_{i,t}^{(4)} [T_{i,t}^{(4)} - 1]\, x_{i,t}^{(4)}$	t=1,...,T	T	Aggregate real revenue from taxes on flows of commodities to exports
A3.6.41	$v_t^{(R,5)} = \frac{1}{V_t^{(5)}} \sum_{i=1}^{13} \sum_{s \in d,f} P_{i,s,t}^{(Z)} X_{i,s,t}^{(5)} [T_{i,s,t}^{(5)} - 1]\, x_{i,s,t}^{(5)}$	t=1,...,T	T	Aggregate real revenue from taxes on flows of commodities to the government

....continued

Table A3.1.1 (continued): A Log-linear Representation of the ORANI-INT Equation System

Identifier	Equation	Range	No.	Description
A3.6.42	$v_t^{(R,6)} = \frac{1}{V_t^{(6)}} \sum_{i=1}^{13} P_{i,t}^{(M)} X_{i,t}^{(M)} \Phi_t [T_{i,t}^{(6)} - 1]\, x_{i,t}^{(M)}$	t=1,...,T	T	Aggregate real tariff revenue
A3.6.61	$nit_t^{(R)} = \frac{O_t}{NIT_t} o_t^{(R)} + \frac{V_t}{NIT_t} v_t^{(R)}$	t=1,...,T	T	Aggregate real net indirect tax revenues
A3.6.43	$k_t^{(\Pi)} = \frac{1}{K_t} \sum_{j=1}^{13} P_{j,t}^{(K)} X_{j,t}^{(K)} p_{j,t}^{(K)}$	t=1,...,T	T	Deflator for capital rentals
A3.6.44	$n_t^{(\Pi)} = \frac{1}{N_t} \sum_{j=1}^{13} P_{j,t}^{(N)} X_{j,t}^{(N)} p_{j,t}^{(N)}$	t=1,...,T	T	Deflator for returns to agricultural land
A3.6.45	$o_t^{(\Pi)} = \frac{1}{O_t} \sum_{j=1}^{13} P_{j,t}^{(O)} X_{j,t}^{(O)} p_{j,t}^{(O)}$	t=1,...,T	T	Deflator for "other cost" tickets
A3.6.46	$v_t^{(\Pi)} = \frac{1}{V_t} \Big\{ V_t^{(1)} v_t^{(\Pi,1)} + V_t^{(2)} v_t^{(\Pi,2)} + V_t^{(3)} v_t^{(\Pi,3)}$ $+ V_t^{(4)} v_t^{(\Pi,4)} + V_t^{(5)} v_t^{(\Pi,5)} + V_t^{(6)} v_t^{(\Pi,6)} \Big\}$	t=1,...,T	T	Deflator for aggregate commodity taxes

....continued

Table A3.1.1 (continued): A Log-linear Representation of the ORANI-INT Equation System

Identifier	Equation	Range	No.	Description
A3.6.47	$v_t^{(\Pi,1)} = \sum_{i=1}^{13} \sum_{s \in d,f} \sum_{j=1}^{13} \frac{P_{i,s,t}^{(Z)} X_{i,s,j,t}^{(1)} [T_{i,s,j,t}^{(1)} - 1]}{V_t^{(1)}} \left\{ p_{i,s,t}^{(Z)} + \frac{T_{i,s,j,t}^{(1)}}{[T_{i,s,j,t}^{(1)} - 1]} t_{i,s,j,t}^{(1)} \right\}$	t=1,...,T	T	Deflator for taxes on flows of commodities to intermediate users
A3.6.48	$v_t^{(\Pi,2)} = \sum_{i=1}^{13} \sum_{s \in d,f} \sum_{j=1}^{13} \frac{P_{i,s,t}^{(Z)} X_{i,s,j,t}^{(2)} [T_{i,s,j,t}^{(2)} - 1]}{V_t^{(2)}} \left\{ p_{i,s,t}^{(Z)} + \frac{T_{i,s,j,t}^{(2)}}{[T_{i,s,j,t}^{(2)} - 1]} t_{i,s,j,t}^{(2)} \right\}$	t=1,...,T	T	Deflator for taxes on flows of commodities to capital creation
A3.6.49	$v_t^{(\Pi,3)} = \sum_{i=1}^{13} \sum_{s \in d,f} \frac{P_{i,s,t}^{(Z)} X_{i,s,t}^{(3)} [T_{i,s,t}^{(3)} - 1]}{V_t^{(3)}} \left\{ p_{i,s,t}^{(Z)} + \frac{T_{i,s,t}^{(3)}}{[T_{i,s,t}^{(3)} - 1]} t_{i,s,t}^{(3)} \right\}$	t=1,...,T	T	Deflator for taxes on flows of commodities to households
A3.6.50	$v_t^{(\Pi,4)} = \frac{1}{V_t^{(4)}} \sum_{i=1}^{13} \frac{P_{i,d,t}^{(Z)} X_{i,t}^{(4)} [T_{i,t}^{(4)} - 1]}{V_t^{(4)}} \left\{ p_{i,d,t}^{(Z)} + \frac{T_{i,t}^{(4)}}{[T_{i,t}^{(4)} - 1]} t_{i,t}^{(4)} \right\}$	t=1,...,T	T	Deflator for taxes on flows of commodities to foreigners
A3.6.51	$v_t^{(\Pi,5)} = \sum_{i=1}^{13} \sum_{s \in d,f} \frac{P_{i,s,t}^{(Z)} X_{i,s,t}^{(5)} [T_{i,s,t}^{(5)} - 1]}{V_t^{(5)}} \left\{ p_{i,s,t}^{(Z)} + \frac{T_{i,s,t}^{(5)}}{[T_{i,s,t}^{(5)} - 1]} t_{i,s,t}^{(5)} \right\}$	t=1,...,T	T	Deflator for taxes on flows of commodities to the government

....continued

Table A3.1.1 (continued): A Log-linear Representation of the ORANI-INT Equation System

Identifier	Equation	Range	No.	Description
A3.6.52	$v_t^{(\Pi,6)} = \sum_{i=1}^{13} \frac{P_{i,t}^{(M)} X_{i,t}^{(M)} \Phi_t [T_{i,t}^{(6)} - 1]}{V_t^{(6)}} \left\{ p_{i,t}^{(M)} + \phi_t + \frac{T_{i,t}^{(6)}}{[T_{i,t}^{(6)} - 1]} t_{i,t}^{(6)} \right\}$	t=1,...,T	T	Deflator for tariff revenue
A3.6.62	$nit_t^{(\Pi)} = \frac{O_t}{NIT_t} o_t^{(\Pi)} + \frac{V_t}{NIT_t} v_t^{(\Pi)}$	t=1,...,T	T	Deflator for indirect taxes
A3.6.53	$gdpe_t^{(R)} = \frac{C_t}{GDPE_t} c_t^{(R)} + \frac{I_t}{GDPE_t} i_t^{(R)} + \frac{G_t}{GDPE_t} g_t^{(R)} + \frac{E_t}{GDPE_t} e_t^{(R)} - \frac{M_t}{GDPE_t} m_t^{(R)}$	t=1,...,T	T	Real GDP: expenditure side
A3.6.54	$gdpe_t^{(\Pi)} = \frac{C_t}{GDPE_t} c_t^{(\Pi)} + \frac{I_t}{GDPE_t} i_t^{(\Pi)} + \frac{G_t}{GDPE_t} g_t^{(\Pi)} + \frac{E_t}{GDPE_t} e_t^{(\Pi)} - \frac{M_t}{GDPE_t} m_t^{(\Pi)}$	t=1,...,T	T	GDP deflator: expenditure side
A3.6.57	$gdpi_t^{(R)} = \frac{GDPFC_t}{GDPI_t} gdpfc_t^{(R)} + \frac{NIT_t}{GDPI_t} nit_t^{(R)}$	t=1,...,T	T	Real GDP: income side

....continued

Table A3.1.1 (continued): A Log-linear Representation of the ORANI-INT Equation System

Identifier	Equation	Range	No.	Description
A3.6.58	$gdpi_t^{(\Pi)} = \frac{GDPFC_t}{GDPI_t} gdpfc_t^{(\Pi)} + \frac{NIT_t}{GDPI_t} nit_t^{(\Pi)}$	t=1,...,T	T	GDP deflator: income side
A3.6.55	$gne_t^{(R)} = \frac{C_t}{GNE_t} c_t^{(R)} + \frac{I_t}{GNE_t} i_t^{(R)} + \frac{G_t}{GNE_t} g_t^{(R)}$	t=1,...,T	T	Real GNE
A3.6.56	$gne_t^{(\Pi)} = \frac{C_t}{GNE_t} c_t^{(\Pi)} + \frac{I_t}{GNE_t} i_t^{(\Pi)} + \frac{G_t}{GNE_t} g_t^{(\Pi)}$	t=1,...,T	T	GNE deflator
A3.6.59	$gdpfc_t^{(R)} = \frac{W_t}{GDPFC_t} w_t^{(R)} + \frac{K_t}{GDPFC_t} k_t^{(R)} + \frac{N_t}{GDPFC_t} n_t^{(R)}$	t=1,...,T	T	Real GDP at factor cost
A3.6.60	$gdpfc_t^{(\Pi)} = \frac{W_t}{GDPFC_t} w_t^{(\Pi)} + \frac{K_t}{GDPFC_t} k_t^{(\Pi)} + \frac{N_t}{GDPFC_t} n_t^{(\Pi)}$	t=1,...,T	T	Deflator for GDP at factor cost
A3.3.19	$100dD_t = \frac{\Phi_t}{\Phi_{t-1}} \left\{ [1 + B_{f,t-1}]100dD_{t-1} + D_{t-1}100dB_{f,t-1} - E_t e_t + M_t m_t + S_t s_t \right\} - D_t \left\{ \varphi_{t-1} - \varphi_t \right\}$	t=1,...,T	T	Accumulation of net foreign liabilities

....continued

Table A3.1.1 (continued): A Log-linear Representation of the ORANI-INT Equation System

Identifier	Equation	Range	No.	Description
A3.3.18a	$\frac{100dD_t}{D_t} + gdpe_t = \frac{100dD_{t+1}}{D_{t+1}} + gdpe_{t+1} + f^{(3)}_{t+1}$	t=T-1	1	Terminal condition on net foreign liabilities
	6.2 Miscellaneous Equations			
A3.3.11	$c^{(\Pi,a)}_t = \sum_{i=1}^{13} \beta_i \, p^{(3)}_{i,\bullet,t}$	t=1,...,T	T	Deflator for above-subsistence consumption
A3.3.5	$\tilde{u}_t = \sum_{i=1}^{13} \beta_i [\tilde{X}^{(3)}_{i,\bullet,t} - \tilde{\gamma}_{i,\bullet}]^{-1} \tilde{x}^{(3)}_{i,\bullet,t}$	t=1,...,T	T	Aggregate utility in each period (equivalent to aggregate real above-subsistence consumption)
A3.3.12	$u = \sum_{t=1}^{T} \frac{U_t u_t}{U[1+\rho]^t}$		1	Aggregate intertemporal utility
A3.6.63	$p^{(O)}_{j,t} = c^{(\Pi)}_t + f^{(O)}_{j,t}$	t=1,...,T j=1,...,J	JT	Indexing of the prices of "other cost" tickets
A3.4.13	$p^{(L)}_{j,t} = w^{(\Pi)}_t$	t=1,...,T j=1,...,J	JT	Uniformity of the price of labour across sectors
	Total Number of Equations	4SIJT + 4SIT + 2IJT + 7IT +18JT + 68T – J + 1		

Table A3.1.2: The Variables in ORANI-INT

Level	Change form	Range	No.	Description
$X^{(3)}_{i,s,t}$	$x^{(3)}_{i,s,t}$	t=1,...,T i=1,...,I s=1,2	SIT	Demand by households for good i from source s in year t
$X^{(3)}_{i,\bullet,t}$	$x^{(3)}_{i,\bullet,t}$	t=1,...,T i=1,...,I	IT	Demand by households for good i undifferentiated by source in year t
$P^{(3)}_{i,s,t}$	$p^{(3)}_{i,s,t}$	t=1,...,T i=1,...,I s=1,2	SIT	Price paid by households for good i from source s in year t
$P^{(3)}_{i,\bullet,t}$	$p^{(3)}_{i,\bullet,t}$	t=1,...,T i=1,...,I	IT	Price paid by households for good i undifferentiated by source in year t
$C^{(a)}_{t}$	$c^{(a)}_{t}$	t=1,...,T	T	Aggregate above-subsistence consumption in year t
Q_t	q_t	t=1,...,T	T	Number of households in year t
$F^{(3)}_{t}$	$f^{(3)}_{t}$	t=1,...,T	T	Shifter on the equilibrium condition for above-subsistence consumption in year t
$B_{d,t}$	$dB_{d,t}$	t=1,...,T	T	Domestic bond rate in year t
$Z^{(K)}_{j,t}$	$z^{(K)}_{j,t}$	t=1,...,T+1 j=1,...,J	J(T+1)	Supply of capital to sector j in year t
$Y_{j,t}$	$y_{j,t}$	t=1,...,T j=1,...,J	JT	Investment in sector j in year t
$F^{(Y)}_{j,t}$	$dF^{(Y)}_{j,t}$	t=1,...,T j=1,...,J	JT	Wedge between the cost of constructing a unit of sector-specific capital and its market value in year t
$H_{j,t}$	$dH_{j,t}$	t=1,...,T j=1,...,J	JT	Risk premium on capital in sector j in year t
$\Psi_{j,t}$	$d\Psi_{j,t}$	t=1,...,T j=1,...,J	JT	Rate of return on capital in sector j in year t
$P^{(K)}_{j,t}$	$p^{(K)}_{j,t}$	t=1,...,T j=1,...,J	JT	Rental price of a unit of capital in sector j in year t
$P^{(A)}_{j,t}$	$p^{(A)}_{j,t}$	t=1,...,T j=1,...,J	JT	Market value of a unit of capital in sector j in year t

continued...

Table A3.1.2 (continued): The Variables in ORANI-INT

Level	Change form	Range	No.	Description
$P^{(Y)}_{j,t}$	$p^{(Y)}_{j,t}$	t=1,...,T j=1,...,J	JT	Cost of constructing a unit of capital in sector j in year t
$K^{(A)}_{j,t}$	$\kappa^{(A)}_{j,t}$	t=2,...,T j=1,...,J	J(T-1)	Capital gains in sector j in year t
$F^{(2)}_{j,t}$	$dF^{(2)}_{j,t}$	t=1,...,T j=1,...,J	JT	Shifter in the arbitrage condition for sectoral capital
$F^{(A)}_{j,t}$	$f^{(A)}_{j,t}$	t=2,...,T j=1,...,J	J(T-1)	Shifter in the equation for sectoral capital gains
$F^{(K)}_{j,t}$	$f^{(K)}_{j,t}$	t=T j=1,...,J	J	Ratio of sector j's capital stock in year T+1 to its capital stock in year T
$X^{(5)}_{i,s,t}$	$x^{(5)}_{i,s,t}$	t=1,...,T i=1,...,I s=1,2	SIT	Demand by the government for good i from source s in year t
$F^{(5)}_{i,s,t}$	$f^{(5)}_{i,s,t}$	t=1,...,T i=1,...,I s=1,2	SIT	Ratio of the government's demand for good i from source s to total government demand
$F^{(5)}_{t}$	$f^{(5)}_{t}$	t=1,...,T	T	Uniform shifter on the government's commodity demands
$X^{(4)}_{i,t}$	$x^{(4)}_{i,t}$	t=1,...,T i=1,...,I	IT	Demand by foreigners for good i in year t
$P^{(E)}_{i,t}$	$p^{(E)}_{i,t}$	t=1,...,T i=1,...,I	IT	Foreign-currency f.o.b price of exported good i in year t
$F^{(4p)}_{i,t}$	$f^{(4p)}_{i,t}$	t=1,...,T i=1,...,I	IT	Price shifter in export demand function
$F^{(4q)}_{i,t}$	$f^{(4q)}_{i,t}$	t=1,...,T i=1,...,I	IT	Quantity shifter in export demand function
$X^{(K)}_{j,t}$	$x^{(K)}_{j,t}$	t=1,...,T j=1,...,J	JT	Demand for capital by sector j in year t
$X^{(L)}_{j,t}$	$x^{(L)}_{j,t}$	t=1,...,T j=1,...,J	JT	Demand for labour by sector j in year t
$X^{(N)}_{j,t}$	$x^{(N)}_{j,t}$	t=1,...,T j=1,...,J	JT	Demand for agricultural land by sector j in year t

continued...

Table A3.1.2 (continued): The Variables in ORANI-INT

Level	Change form	Range	No.	Description
$A^{(K)}_{j,t}$	$a^{(K)}_{j,t}$	t=1,...,T j=1,...,J	JT	Technical change specific to capital in sector j in year t
$A^{(L)}_{j,t}$	$a^{(L)}_{j,t}$	t=1,...,T j=1,...,J	JT	Technical change specific to labour in sector j in year t
$A^{(N)}_{j,t}$	$a^{(N)}_{j,t}$	t=1,...,T j=1,...,J	JT	Technical change specific to agricultural land in sector j in year t
$X^{(F)}_{j,t}$	$x^{(F)}_{j,t}$	t=1,...,T j=1,...,J	JT	Demand for primary factor composite by sector j in year t
$P^{(L)}_{j,t}$	$p^{(L)}_{j,t}$	t=1,...,T j=1,...,J	JT	Price of labour to sector j in year t
$P^{(N)}_{j,t}$	$p^{(N)}_{j,t}$	t=1,...,T j=1,...,J	JT	Price of agricultural land to sector j in year t
$P^{(F)}_{j,t}$	$p^{(F)}_{j,t}$	t=1,...,T j=1,...,J	JT	Price of the primary factor composite to sector j in year t
$Z^{(1)}_{j,t}$	$z^{(1)}_{j,t}$	t=1,...,T j=1,...,J	JT	Output by sector j in year t
$A^{(F)}_{j,t}$	$a^{(F)}_{j,t}$	t=1,...,T j=1,...,J	JT	Primary factor technical change in sector j in year t
$X^{(O)}_{j,t}$	$x^{(O)}_{j,t}$	t=1,...,T j=1,...,J	JT	Demand for "other cost" tickets by sector j in year t
$P^{(O)}_{j,t}$	$p^{(O)}_{j,t}$	t=1,...,T j=1,...,J	JT	Price of "other cost" tickets to sector j in year t
$A^{(O)}_{j,t}$	$a^{(O)}_{j,t}$	t=1,...,T j=1,...,J	JT	Technical change specific to "other cost" tickets in sector j in year t
$X^{(1)}_{i,s,j,t}$	$x^{(1)}_{i,s,j,t}$	t=1,...,T i=1,...,I j=1,...,J s=1,2	SIJT	Demand by sector j for good i from source s in year t for use in current production
$X^{(1)}_{i,\bullet,j,t}$	$x^{(1)}_{i,\bullet,j,t}$	t=1,...,T i=1,...,I j=1,...,J	IJT	Demand by sector j for good i undifferentiated by source in year t for use in current production
$P^{(1)}_{i,\bullet,j,t}$	$p^{(1)}_{i,\bullet,j,t}$	t=1,...,T i=1,...,I j=1,...,J	IJT	Price paid by sector j for good i, undifferentiated by source, for use in current production in year t

continued...

Table A3.1.2 (continued): The Variables in ORANI-INT

Level	Change form	Range	No.	Description
$P^{(1)}_{i,s,j,t}$	$p^{(1)}_{i,s,j,t}$	t=1,...,T i=1,...,I j=1,...,J s=1,2	SIJT	Price paid by sector j for good i from source s in year t used in current production
$A^{(1)}_{i,\bullet,j,t}$	$a^{(1)}_{i,\bullet,j,t}$	t=1,...,T i=1,...,I j=1,...,J	IJT	Technical change specific to good i undifferentiated by source used by sector j in year t for current production
$X^{(2)}_{i,s,j,t}$	$x^{(2)}_{i,s,j,t}$	t=1,...,T i=1,...,I j=1,...,J s=1,2	SIJT	Demand by sector j for good i from source s in year t for use in capital creation
$A^{(2)}_{i,\bullet,j,t}$	$a^{(2)}_{i,\bullet,j,t}$	t=1,...,T i=1,...,I j=1,...,J	IJT	Technical change specific to good i undifferentiated by source used by sector j in year t for capital creation
$P^{(2)}_{i,s,j,t}$	$p^{(2)}_{i,s,j,t}$	t=1,...,T i=1,...,I j=1,...,J s=1,2	SIJT	Price paid by sector j for good i from source s in year t used in capital creation
Φ_t	ϕ_t	t=0,...,T+1	T+2	Nominal exchange rate in year t
$B_{f,t}$	$dB_{f,t}$	t=0,...,T	T+1	Foreign bond rate in year t
$P^{(Z)}_{i,s,t}$	$p^{(Z)}_{i,s,t}$	t=1,...,T i=1,...,I s=1,2	SIT	Basic price of good i from source s in year t
$P^{(Z)}_{j,t}$	$p^{(Z)}_{j,t}$	t=1,...,T j=1,...,J	JT	Unit cost in sector j in year t
$T^{(1)}_{i,s,j,t}$	$t^{(1)}_{i,s,j,t}$	t=1,...,T i=1,...,I j=1,...,J s=1,2	SIJT	Power of the tax on good i from source s used by sector j for current production in year t
$T^{(2)}_{i,s,j,t}$	$t^{(2)}_{i,s,j,t}$	t=1,...,T i=1,...,I j=1,...,J s=1,2	SIJT	Power of the tax on good i from source s used by sector j for capital creation in year t

continued...

Table A3.1.2 (continued): The Variables in ORANI-INT

Level	Change form	Range	No.	Description
$T^{(3)}_{i,s,t}$	$t^{(3)}_{i,s,t}$	t=1,...,T i=1,...,I s=1,2	SIT	Power of the tax on good i from source s purchased by households in year t
$T^{(4)}_{i,t}$	$t^{(4)}_{i,t}$	t=1,...,T i=1,...,I	IT	Power of the tax on exported good i in year t
$P^{(5)}_{i,s,t}$	$p^{(5)}_{i,s,t}$	t=1,...,T i=1,...,I s=1,2	SIT	Price paid by the government for good i from source s in year t
$T^{(5)}_{i,s,t}$	$t^{(5)}_{i,s,t}$	t=1,...,T i=1,...,I s=1,2	SIT	Power of the tax on good i from source s purchased by the government in year t
$P^{(M)}_{i,t}$	$p^{(M)}_{i,t}$	t=1,...,T i=1,...,I	IT	Foreign (C.I.F) currency price of imported good i in year t
$T^{(6)}_{i,t}$	$t^{(6)}_{i,t}$	t=1,...,T i=1,...,I	IT	Power of the tariff on imported good i in year t
$Z^{(N)}_{j,t}$	$z^{(N)}_{j,t}$	t=1,...,T j=1,...,J	JT	Supply of agricultural land to sector j in year t
L_t	l_t	t=1,...,T	T	Aggregate supply of labour in year t
$V^{(1)}_t$	$v^{(1)}_t$	t=1,...,T	T	Indirect taxes collected from purchases of intermediate inputs in year t
$V^{(2)}_t$	$v^{(2)}_t$	t=1,...,T	T	Indirect taxes collected from purchases of inputs for capital creation in year t
$V^{(3)}_t$	$v^{(3)}_t$	t=1,...,T	T	Indirect taxes collected from sales to households in year t
$V^{(4)}_t$	$v^{(4)}_t$	t=1,...,T	T	Indirect taxes collected from sales to foreigners in year t
$V^{(5)}_t$	$v^{(5)}_t$	t=1,...,T	T	Indirect taxes collected from sales to the government in year t
$V^{(6)}_t$	$v^{(6)}_t$	t=1,...,T	T	Tariff revenue in year t
$GDPE_t$	$gdpe_t$	t=1,...,T	T	Nominal GDP in year t measured on the expenditure side of the National Accounts
C_t	c_t	t=1,...,T	T	Aggregate consumption in year t
I_t	i_t	t=1,...,T	T	Aggregate investment in year t

continued...

Table A3.1.2 (continued): The Variables in ORANI-INT

Level	Change form	Range	No.	Description
G_t	g_t	t=1,...,T	T	Aggregate government spending in year t
BoT_t	$dBoT_t$	t=1,...,T	T	Balance of trade in year t
M_t	m_t	t=1,...,T	T	Aggregate imports in year t
E_t	e_t	t=1,...,T	T	Aggregate exports in year t
$X^{(M)}_{i,t}$	$x^{(M)}_{i,t}$	t=1,...,T i=1,...,I	IT	Demand for imported good i in year t
$GDPI_t$	$gdpi_t$	t=1,...,T	T	Nominal GDP in year t measured on the income side of the National Accounts
$GDPFC_t$	$gdpfc_t$	t=1,...,T	T	Nominal GDP in year t measured at factor cost
NIT_t	nit_t	t=1,...,T	T	Net indirect tax revenues in year t
W_t	w_t	t=1,...,T	T	Payments to labour in year t
K_t	k_t	t=1,...,T	T	Payments to capital in year t
N_t	n_t	t=1,...,T	T	Payments to agricultural land in year t
O_t	o_t	t=1,...,T	T	Payments for other cost tickets in year t
V_t	v_t	t=1,...,T	T	Nominal sales taxes collected in year t
$C^{(R)}_t$	$c^{(R)}_t$	t=1,...,T	T	Real aggregate consumption in year t
$I^{(R)}_t$	$i^{(R)}_t$	t=1,...,T	T	Real aggregate investment in year t
$G^{(R)}_t$	$g^{(R)}_t$	t=1,...,T	T	Real aggregate government spending in year t
$E^{(R)}_t$	$e^{(R)}_t$	t=1,...,T	T	Real aggregate exports in year t
$M^{(R)}_t$	$m^{(R)}_t$	t=1,...,T	T	Real aggregate imports in year t
$C^{(\Pi)}_t$	$c^{(\Pi)}_t$	t=1,...,T	T	Aggregate consumption deflator in year t
$I^{(\Pi)}_t$	$i^{(\Pi)}_t$	t=1,...,T	T	Aggregate investment deflator in year t
$G^{(\Pi)}_t$	$g^{(\Pi)}_t$	t=1,...,T	T	Aggregate government spending deflator in year t

continued...

Table A3.1.2 (continued): The Variables in ORANI-INT

Level	Change form	Range	No.	Description
$E_t^{(\Pi)}$	$e_t^{(\Pi)}$	t=1,...,T	T	Aggregate exports deflator in year t
$M_t^{(\Pi)}$	$m_t^{(\Pi)}$	t=1,...,T	T	Aggregate imports deflator in year t
$K_t^{(R)}$	$k_t^{(R)}$	t=1,...,T	T	Aggregate stock of capital in year t
$N_t^{(R)}$	$n_t^{(R)}$	t=1,...,T	T	Aggregate stock of agricultural land in year t
$O_t^{(R)}$	$o_t^{(R)}$	t=1,...,T	T	Real aggregate other cost tickets in year t
$V_t^{(R)}$	$v_t^{(R)}$	t=1,...,T	T	Real aggregate sales tax revenue collected in year t
$V_t^{(R,1)}$	$v_t^{(R,1)}$	t=1,...,T	T	Real tax revenue collected from purchases of intermediate inputs in year t
$V_t^{(R,2)}$	$v_t^{(R,2)}$	t=1,...,T	T	Real tax revenue collected from sales of inputs to capital creation in year t
$V_t^{(R,3)}$	$v_t^{(R,3)}$	t=1,...,T	T	Real tax revenue collected from sales to households in year t
$V_t^{(R,4)}$	$v_t^{(R,4)}$	t=1,...,T	T	Real tax revenue collected from sales to foreigners in year t
$V_t^{(R,5)}$	$v_t^{(R,5)}$	t=1,...,T	T	Real tax revenue collected from sales to the government in year t
$V_t^{(R,6)}$	$v_t^{(R,6)}$	t=1,...,T	T	Real tariff revenue collected in year t
$NIT_t^{(R)}$	$nit_t^{(R)}$	t=1,...,T	T	Real net indirect tax revenues collected in year t
$K_t^{(\Pi)}$	$k_t^{(\Pi)}$	t=1,...,T	T	Deflator for payments to capital in year t
$N_t^{(\Pi)}$	$n_t^{(\Pi)}$	t=1,...,T	T	Deflator for payments to agricultural land in year t
$O_t^{(\Pi)}$	$o_t^{(\Pi)}$	t=1,...,T	T	Deflator for other cost tickets in year t
$V_t^{(\Pi)}$	$v_t^{(\Pi)}$	t=1,...,T	T	Deflator for aggregate sales taxes in year t
$V_t^{(\Pi,1)}$	$v_t^{(\Pi,1)}$	t=1,...,T	T	Deflator for taxes levied on sales of intermediate inputs in year t
$V_t^{(\Pi,2)}$	$v_t^{(\Pi,2)}$	t=1,...,T	T	Deflator for taxes levied on sales of inputs to capital creation in year t

continued...

Table A3.1.2 (continued): The Variables in ORANI-INT

Level	Change form	Range	No.	Description
$V_t^{(\Pi,3)}$	$v_t^{(\Pi,3)}$	t=1,...,T	T	Deflator for taxes levied on sales to households
$V_t^{(\Pi,4)}$	$v_t^{(\Pi,4)}$	t=1,...,T	T	Deflator for taxes levied on sales to foreigners
$V_t^{(\Pi,5)}$	$v_t^{(\Pi,5)}$	t=1,...,T	T	Deflator for taxes levied on sales to the government in year t
$V_t^{(\Pi,6)}$	$v_t^{(\Pi,6)}$	t=1,...,T	T	Deflator for tariffs in year t
$NIT_t^{(\Pi)}$	$nit_t^{(\Pi)}$	t=1,...,T	T	Deflator for net indirect taxes in year t
$GDP_t^{(R)}$	$gdp_t^{(R)}$	t=1,...,T	T	Real GDP: expenditure side
$GDP_t^{(\Pi)}$	$gdp_t^{(\Pi)}$	t=1,...,T	T	GDP deflator: expenditure side
$GDPI_t^{(R)}$	$gdpi_t^{(R)}$	t=1,...,T	T	Real GDP: income side
$GDPI_t^{(\Pi)}$	$gdpi_t^{(\Pi)}$	t=1,...,T	T	GDP deflator: income side
$GNE_t^{(R)}$	$gne_t^{(R)}$	t=1,...,T	T	Real GNE
$GNE_t^{(\Pi)}$	$gne_t^{(\Pi)}$	t=1,...,T	T	GNE deflator
$GDPFC_t^{(R)}$	$gdpfc_t^{(R)}$	t=1,...,T	T	Real GDP at factor cost in year t
$GDPFC_t^{(\Pi)}$	$gdpfc_t^{(\Pi)}$	t=1,...,T	T	GDP at factor cost deflator in year t
D_t	dD_t	t=0,...,T	T+1	Net foreign liabilities in year t
S_t	s_t	t=1,...,T	T	Net unrequited transfers to foreigners in year t
$C_t^{(\Pi,a)}$	$c_t^{(\Pi,a)}$	t=1,...,T	T	Deflator for above-subsistence consumption in year t
U_t	u_t	t=1,...,T	T	Utility in year t
U	u		1	Intertemporal utility
$F_{j,t}^{(O)}$	$f_{j,t}^{(O)}$	t=1,...,T j=1,...,J	JT	Ratio of the price of "other cost" tickets in sector j to the consumption deflator
$W_t^{(R)}$	$w_t^{(R)}$	t=1,...,T	T	Aggregate employment in year t
$W_t^{(\Pi)}$	$w_t^{(\Pi)}$	t=1,...,T	T	Price of labour in year t
Total Number of Variables			6SITJ + 8SIT + 4IJT + 10IT + 29JT + 75T + 5	

Table A3.1.3: The Parameters in ORANI-INT

Parameter	Range	Description
ε		Substitution parameter in the CES aggregation of household demands for domestic and foreign commodities
$\xi_{i,s,t}$	t=1,...,T i=1,...,I s=1,2	Distribution parameter in the CES aggregation of household demands for domestic and foreign commodities
β_i	i=1,...,I	Households' marginal budget share of good i
$\tilde{\gamma}^{(3)}_{i,\bullet}$	i=1,...,I	Subsistence quantity of good i, undifferentiated by source, consumed by each household
δ_j	j=1,...,J	Rate of depreciation of sector-specific capital
η_i	i=1,...,I	Foreign demand elasticity
μ		Substitution parameter in the CES production function
ν		Substitution parameter in the CES aggregation of producers' demands for domestic and foreign commodities
$\varsigma_{i,s,j,t}$	t=1,...,T j=1,...,J i=1,...,I s=1,2	Distribution parameter in the CES aggregation of producers' demands for domestic and foreign commodities
υ		Substitution parameter in the CES aggregation of capital creators' demands for domestic and foreign commodities
$\vartheta_{i,s,j,t}$	t=1,...,T j=1,...,J i=1,...,I s=1,2	Distribution parameter in the CES aggregation of capital creators' demands for domestic and foreign commodities
$\zeta^{(K)}_{j,t}$	t=1,...,T j=1,...,J	Distribution parameter for capital in the CES production function
$\zeta^{(L)}_{j,t}$	t=1,...,T j=1,...,J	Distribution parameter for labour in the CES production function
$\zeta^{(N)}_{j,t}$	t=1,...,T j=1,...,J	Distribution parameter for agricultural land in the CES production function
ρ		Pure time preference rate

Appendix A3.2 The Intertemporal Budget Constraint

A3.2.1 Introduction

In this appendix we explain how Ω, the present value of the household sector's consumption stream, is determined in ORANI-INT. In the representative household's intertemporal optimisation problem, specified in section 3.3.1, we used Ω as the budget constraint. The value of Ω was assumed to be exogenous to the representative household but endogenous to the economy as a whole. We claimed that a terminal condition on the rate of growth of net foreign liabilities constrained the value of Ω.

A more usual approach to specifying the representative household's intertemporal budget constraint is to equate the present value of consumption to the sum of the household's human and non-human wealth. Human wealth is defined as the present value of the future stream of after-tax labour income plus net transfers from the government. Non-human wealth (or financial wealth) is the value of the household's net holdings of domestic and foreign assets. If private and public savings are assumed to be perfect substitutes it is possible to enforce the household budget constraint in one of two ways: first, by directly constraining the growth of net foreign liabilities; or, second, by imposing a constraint on the accumulation of public debt. Either one of these constraints will imply the other.

In ORANI-INT we assume that all financial assets are perfect substitutes. Since we do not differentiate between private and public debt we can constrain the value of Ω implicitly by imposing an economy-wide budget constraint (i.e., a constraint on total domestic savings). Our economy-wide budget constraint requires that the net-foreign-liabilities-to-GDP ratio stabilises by the terminal year. The advantage of this approach is that there is no need to fully articulate the government sector's financial accounts. For example, there is no need to explicitly model income taxes or government transfers. The public sector's savings are implicit.

In the remainder of this appendix we use a stylised model to show how a constraint on net foreign liabilities impacts on household consumption in ORANI-INT.

A3.2.2 The Effects of Constraining the Growth of Net Foreign Liabilities

To demonstrate how the value of Ω is constrained in ORANI-INT we use a stylised model. The stylised model is designed to capture the key elements in ORANI-INT that are relevant to the economy-wide budget constraint. The equations, parameters and variables of the stylised model are listed in tables A3.2.1 — A3.2.3. The stylised model's exogenous variables are listed in table A3.2.4. The notation used in this appendix should be treated a distinct from that in the body of chapter 3. However, we have tried to reduce the burden on the reader by using notation that is, as much as possible, consistent with that in the body of chapter 3.

The stylised model differs from ORANI-INT in three key respects.

1. The domestic economy is represented by two single-commodity sectors. The export sector sells exclusively to foreigners. The import-competing sector sells to capital creators in the two domestic sectors, to households, and to the government.
2. Output is assumed to be a Cobb-Douglas function of capital and labour only. Like ORANI-INT capital is assumed to be sector specific but labour is not.
3. Imports enter the economy as inputs to capital creation only.
4. Sectoral capital does not depreciate.

The theoretical structure of the stylised model is set out in the equations listed in table A3.2.1. In equation (A3.2.1) we have specified production in each sector as a Cobb-Douglas function of labour and capital. Sectoral demands for labour are specified by equation (A3.2.2). Equation (A3.2.3) reflects the assumption that producers earn zero pure profits. The sector-specific technologies for creating capital are given by equation (A3.2.4). We have assumed that capital is a Cobb-Douglas aggregate of the import-competing commodity and the imported commodity. The demand by capital creators for the import-competing commodity is given by equation (A3.2.5). In equation (A3.2.6) we have assumed that capital creators earn zero pure profits. The demand for exports is given by equation (A3.2.7). Analogous to the treatment in ORANI-INT we have assumed that the demand for exports is an inverse function of the foreign currency price. Equations (A3.2.8) – (A3.2.11) are the market clearing conditions for the export commodity, the import-competing commodity, labour and sectoral capital stocks. The equilibrium condition for sectoral capital stocks is given by equation (A3.2.12).[1] Sectoral capital stocks accumulate according to equation (A3.2.13). A terminal condition, given by equation (A3.2.14) determines sectoral capital stocks

[1] The analogue of equation (A3.2.12) in chapter 3 is equation (3.3.33). Note that we have not incorporated a non-negativity constraint on investment in the stylised model.

Table A3.2.1: The Stylised Model's Equations

Identifier	Equation	Number
(A3.2.1)	$Z_{j,t} = X_{j,t}^{(L)\alpha_j} X_{j,t}^{(K)(1-\alpha_j)}$	t = 1, ..., T j = ic,e
(A3.2.2)	$X_{j,t}^{(L)} = \left\{\frac{P_{j,t}}{P_t^{(L)}}\right\}^{\frac{1}{\alpha_j}} [1-\alpha_j]^{\frac{1}{\alpha_j}} X_{j,t}^{(K)}$	t = 1, ..., T j = ic,e
(A3.2.3)	$P_{j,t}Z_{j,t} = P_t^{(L)}X_{j,t}^{(L)} + P_{j,t}^{(K)}X_{j,t}^{(K)}$	t = 1, ..., T j = ic,e
(A3.2.4)	$Y_{j,t} = X_{ic,j,t}^{(2)\beta_j} X_{m,j,t}^{(2)(1-\beta_j)}$	t = 1, ..., T j = ic,e
(A3.2.5)	$X_{ic,j,t}^{(2)} = \left\{\frac{P_{j,t}^{(Y)}}{P_{ic,t}}\right\}^{\frac{1}{\beta_j}} [1-\beta_j]^{\frac{1}{\beta_j}} X_{m,j,t}^{(2)}$	t = 1, ..., T j = ic,e
(A3.2.6)	$P_{j,t}^{(Y)}Y_{j,t} = P_{ic,t}X_{ic,j,t}^{(2)} + P_{m,t}X_{m,j,t}^{(2)}$	t = 1, ..., T j = ic,e
(A3.2.7)	$X_t^{(4)} = [P_t^{(E)}]^{-\eta}$	t = 1, ..., T
(A3.2.8)	$Z_{e,t} = X_t^{(4)}$	t = 1, ..., T
(A3.2.9)	$Z_{ic,t} = Y_{e,t} + Y_{ic,t} + C_t^{(R)} + G_t^{(R)}$	t = 1, ..., T
(A3.2.10)	$L_t = X_{e,t}^{(L)} + X_{ic,t}^{(L)}$	t = 1, ..., T
(A3.2.11)	$Z_{j,t}^{(K)} = X_{j,t}^{(K)}$	t = 1, ..., T j = ic,e
(A3.2.12)	$P_{j,t+1}^{(K)} = P_{j,t}^{(Y)}\left[1 + B_{d,t}\right] - P_{j,t+1}^{(Y)}$	t = 1, ..., T-1 j = ic,e
(A3.2.13)	$Z_{j,t+1}^{(K)} = Z_{j,t}^{(K)} + Y_{j,t}$	t = 1, ..., T j = ic,e
(A3.2.14)	$Z_{j,t+1}^{(K)} = Z_{j,t}^{(K)}\left[1 + q\right]$	T j = ic,e
(A3.2.15)	$P_{ic,t}C_t^{(R)} = P_{ic,t+1}C_{t+1}^{(R)}\left[\frac{1+\rho}{1+B_{d,t}}\right]\frac{Q_t}{Q_{t+1}}$	t = 1, ..., T-1
(A3.2.16)	$D_t = \frac{\Phi_t}{\Phi_{t-1}}\left\{D_{t-1}\left[1 + B_{f,t-1}\right] - P_{e,t}Z_{e,t} + P_{m,t}M_t^{(R)}\right\}$	t = 1, ..., T
(A3.2.17)	$\frac{D_t}{D_{t-1}} = 1 + q$	T

Continued...

Table A3.2.1(continued): The Stylised Model's Equations

Identifier	Equation	Number
(A3.2.18)	$M_t^{(R)} = X_{m,e,t}^{(2)} + X_{m,ic,t}^{(2)}$	t = 1, ..., T
(A3.2.19)	$\left[1 + B_{f,t}\right]\Phi_t = \left[1 + B_{d,t}\right]\Phi_{t+1}$	t = 1, ..., T
(A3.2.20)	$\frac{Q_{t+1}}{Q_t} = 1 + q$	t = 1, ..., T
(A3.2.21)	$P_{e,t} = P_t^{(E)}\,\Phi_t$	t = 1, ..., T
(A3.2.22)	$P_{m,t} = P_t^{(M)}\,\Phi_t$	t = 1, ..., T
(A3.2.23)	$\Phi_t = 1$	t = 1, ..., T+1
	Total number of equations	9JT+12T+1

Table A3.2.2: The Stylised Model's Parameters

Parameter	Description
α_j	Share in sector j's total costs of payments to labour
β_j	Share in sector j's investment costs of the import-competing commodity
ρ	Pure time preference rate
η	Foreign elasticity of demand
q	Population growth

Table A3.2.3: The Stylised Model's Variables

Variable	Number	Description
$Z_{j,t}$	t = 1, ..., T j = ic,e	Supplies of domestic goods
$X^{(L)}_{j,t}$	t = 1, ..., T j = ic,e	Sectoral demands for labour
$X^{(K)}_{j,t}$	t = 1, ..., T j = ic,e	Sectoral demands for capital
$P_{j,t}$	t = 1, ..., T j = ic,e	Prices of domestic goods
$P^{(L)}_{t}$	t = 1, ..., T	Price of labour inputs
$P^{(K)}_{j,t}$	t = 1, ..., T j = ic,e	Price of capital inputs
$Y_{j,t}$	t = 1, ..., T j = ic,et	Sectoral investment
$X^{(2)}_{ic,j,t}$	t = 1, ..., T j = ic,e	Demand by capital creators for inputs of the import-competing commodity
$X^{(2)}_{m,j,t}$	t = 1, ..., T j = ic,e	Demand by capital creators for inputs of the imported commodity
$P^{(Y)}_{j,t}$	t = 1, ..., T j = ic,e	Cost of constructing a unit of capital
$P_{m,t}$	t = 1, ..., T	Domestic-currency price of imports
$X^{(4)}_{t}$	t = 1, ..., T	Demand for exports
$P^{(E)}_{t}$	t = 1, ..., T	Foreign-currency price of exports
$G^{(R)}_{t}$	t = 1, ..., T	Real government expenditure
$C^{(R)}_{t}$	t = 1, ..., T	Real per-household consumption
$M^{(R)}_{t}$	t = 1, ..., T	Import volume
L_t	t = 1, ..., T	Aggregate supply of labour
$Z^{(K)}_{j,t}$	t = 1, ..., T+1 j = ic,e	Supply of sector-specific capital
Q_t	t = 1, ..., T	Number of households
$B_{f,t}$	t = 0, ..., T	Foreign bond rate
$B_{d,t}$	t = 1, ..., T	Domestic bond rate
D_t	t = 0, ..., T	Net foreign liabilities
$P^{(M)}_{t}$	t = 1, ..., T	Foreign currency price of imports
Φ_t	t = 1, ..., T+1	Nominal exchange rate
10JT+14T+J+3		Total number of variables

Table A3.2.4: The Stylised Model's Exogenous Variables

Variable	Number	Description
$Z_t^{(K)}$	t = 1 j = ic,e	Initial stocks of capital
$G_t^{(R)}$	t = 1, ..., T	Real government spending
D_t	t = 0	Initial stock of net foreign liabilities
L_t	t = 1, ..., T	Aggregate supply of labour
$B_{f,t}$	t = 0, ..., T	Foreign bond rate
$P_t^{(M)}$	t = 1, ..., T	Foreign-currency price of imports
	4T+J+2	Total number of exogenous variables

in period T+1. The equilibrium condition for consumption is given by equation (A3.2.15). This condition differs slightly from the specification in ORANI-INT (i.e., equation (3.3.17) in chapter 3) because it applies to total consumption rather than to above-subsistence consumption. The accumulation of net foreign liabilities is given by equation (A3.2.16). Terminal condition (A3.2.17) determines the growth of net foreign liabilities in the terminal period. Aggregate demand for the imported commodity is defined by equation (A3.2.18). In equation (A3.2.19) we have assumed uncovered interest parity. The growth in the number of households is assumed to be constant over time in equation (A3.2.20). The relationship between the foreign and domestic currency prices of exports and imports are given by equations (A3.2.21) and (A3.2.22). Finally, equation (A3.2.23) specifies the nominal exchange rate as the numeraire.

The stylised model consists of 10JT + 14T + J + 3 variables in 9JT + 12T + 1 equations. Thus, JT + 2T + J +2 variables must be specified exogenously.[2] The exogenous variables, which are listed in table A3.2.4, are chosen to mimic as closely as possible the standard closure of ORANI-INT. Whilst the stylised model can be easily solved numerically, it is not possible to obtain a closed-loop analytic solution. Fortunately it is not necessary to derive such a solution to show that the value of Ω is tied down. To show that the value of Ω is tied down it is sufficient to show that the value of nominal consumption is tied down in the steady state. This can be seen by re-writing the intertemporal consumption function as follows:

$$C_t = C_T \left[\frac{1+\rho}{1+q}\right]^{t-T} \prod_{u=t}^{T-1} [1 + B_{f,u}]^{-1}. \qquad t = 1, ..., T-1 \quad \text{(A3.2.24)}$$

where, $C_t = P_{ic,t} C_t^{(R)}$. Note that in deriving (A3.2.24) we used equations (A3.2.20), (A3.2.19) and (A3.2.23) to substitute Q_t and $B_{d,t}$ out of equation (A3.2.15). Given

2 In table A3.2.4 we have listed 4T + J +2 exogenous variables. Given that J = 2, 4T + J +2 = JT + 2T + J + 2.

that the path of $B_{f,t}$ is exogenous, all that is required to determine the entire path of consumption is the value of C_t at any point in time. We assume that C_T is equal to the steady-state value of consumption. This assumption allows us to show that Ω is tied down if the steady state value of consumption is tied down.

Using equation (A3.2.24) we can re-write the household budget constraint (i.e., equation (3.3.13) in chapter 3) as follows:

$$\Omega = C_T\left[\frac{1+\rho}{1+q}\right]^T \prod_{u=1}^{T-1}[1+B_{f,u}]^{-1}\sum_{t=1}^{T}\left\{\left[\frac{1+q}{1+\rho}\right]^t \frac{1}{[1+B_{f,t}]}\right\} . \qquad \text{(A3.2.25)}$$

Apart from C_T the variables on the RHS of equation (A3.2.25) are exogenous. Our task in the remainder of this appendix is to show that C_T, and therefore Ω, is tied down.

In the stylised model's steady state all real variables should grow at the rate q and all price variables should be stationary. The growth of price variables in the steady state is governed by the growth in the numeriare. In this case the exchange rate is the numeraire and, as indicated by equation (A3.2.23), it is assumed to be constant. Whether the stylised model possesses a steady state depends on the numerical values assigned to the parameters and to the exogenous variables. It is beyond the scope of this appendix to show the conditions under which the stylised model will possess a steady state. However, we assume, but do not prove, that the stylised model will have a steady state if the values assigned to the parameters and exogenous variables are similar to those used in ORANI-INT.[3] We also assume that T is a period long enough for the model to converge to its steady state (if such a state exists).

Conditional on the above assumptions, we can derive a steady-state form of the stylised model by replacing all lead and lag variables with their steady state counterparts. In the case of real variables that lead or lag we use the assumption that real variables grow at the rate q in the steady state. Similarly, in the case of price variables that lead or lag we use the assumption that price variables are stationary in the steady state. In deriving the steady state form of the stylised model we must also assume that ρ, the pure time preference rate, is equal to $B_{d,T}$, the domestic bond rate in the steady state. The necessity of this assumption can be deduced from equation (A3.2.15). This equation can hold in a steady state characterised by stationary prices and real variables growing at the rate q only if $B_{d,T} = \rho$. As is the case in ORANI-INT we have also assumed that q is equal to $B_{f,T}$. An implication of this assumption is that the level of debt that the economy enters the steady state with is irrelevant.[4]

---

[3] In chapters 5 – 7 we provide numerical evidence that ORANI-INT possesses a steady state with the values we assigned to its parameters and exogenous variables.

[4] Note that it is inadmissible to assume that $B_f < q$ in the steady state because foreign debt will be unbounded. However, the steady-state level of foreign debt is bounded if $B_f > q$. This latter assumption is less stringent than the assumption that we have adopted. See Blanchard and Fischer (1989, chapter 2) for further discussion on this topic.

The steady state form of the stylised model is presented in table A3.2.5. The steady state model consists of 9J + 8 variables in 8J + 6 equations. In specifying the steady-state form of the stylised model we have eliminated $Z_{j,T}^{(K)}$, Q_T, Φ_T, $B_{d,T}$, $P_T^{(E)}$ and $P_{m,T}$ from the system using equations (A3.2.11) and (A3.2.19) – (A3.2.23). We have also used the assumption that $B_{d,T} = q$ to derive equation (A3.2.16s). As mentioned above, this latter assumption also allows us to eliminate D_T from the steady-state model. To solve the steady state model we must specify four (J + 2) variables exogenously. The exogenous variables are the same as those listed in table A3.2.4 except for $Z_{j,1}^{(K)}$ and D_0, which do not appear in the steady-state model. Whilst the steady-state model can be solved to obtain an expression that relates nominal consumption in the steady state to the exogenous variables and to the parameters we find it convenient to solve the log-linear form of the steady-state model. The log-linear form of the steady-state model is presented in table A3.2.6.

We define c_T, the percentage change in nominal consumption in period T, as follows:

$$c_T = c_T^{(R)} + p_{ic,T}. \tag{A3.2.26}$$

In equation (A3.2.26) $c_T^{(R)}$ is the percentage change in real consumption and $p_{ic,T}$ is the percentage change in the price of the import-competing commodity. From the solution of the log-linear form of the steady-state model presented in table A3.2.6 we derive the elasticities of $c_T^{(R)}$ and $p_{ic,T}$ with respect to the model's exogenous variables and parameters. We can express these elasticities as follows:[5]

$$\begin{aligned} c_T^{(R)} = {} & \left\{\frac{C_T^{(R)} + G_T^{(R)}}{C_T^{(R)}}\right\}\left[\frac{\text{COEF2}}{\text{COEF1}}\right] l_T - \left\{\frac{G_T^{(R)}}{C_T^{(R)}}\right\} g_T^{(R)} \\ & - \left\{\frac{C_T^{(R)} + G_T^{(R)}}{C_T^{(R)}}\right\}\left[\frac{\text{COEF3}}{\text{COEF1}}\right] p_T^{(M)} + \left[\frac{\text{COEF4}}{\text{COEF1}}\right]\frac{100dB_{f,T}}{[1+B_{f,T}]}. \end{aligned} \tag{A3.2.27}$$

and

$$p_{ic,T} = \left[\frac{\text{COEF6}}{\text{COEF5}}\right]\frac{100dB_{f,T}}{[1+B_{f,T}]} - \left[\frac{\alpha_{ic}}{\text{COEF5}}\right] l_T + \left[\frac{\text{COEF7}}{\text{COEF5}}\right] p_T^{(M)}. \tag{A3.2.28}$$

The coefficients in equations (A3.2.27) and (A3.2.28) are as follows:

$$\begin{aligned} \text{COEF1} = {} & [1 - \beta_{ic}(1-\alpha_{ic})]\,[\eta + (1-\eta)(1-\alpha_e)(1-\beta_e)] \\ & + (1-\eta)\beta_e(1-\alpha_e)(1-\alpha_{ic})(1-\beta_{ic}). \end{aligned} \tag{A3.2.29}$$

---

5 These elasticities are derived using a simple but tedious algorithm of successively eliminating variables and equations through substitution. To economise on space we have not provided detailed derivations. We have checked our algebra by solving the stylised model numerically.

Table A3.2.5: The Steady-state Form of the Stylised Model

Identifier	Equation	Number
(A3.2.1s)	$Z_{j,T} = X_{j,T}^{(L)\alpha_j} X_{j,T}^{(K)(1-\alpha_j)}$	j = ic,e
(A3.2.2s)	$X_{j,T}^{(L)} = \left\{\frac{P_{j,T}}{P_T^{(L)}}\right\}^{\frac{1}{\alpha_j}} [1-\alpha_j]^{\frac{1}{\alpha_j}} X_{j,T}^{(K)}$	j = ic,e
(A3.2.3s)	$P_{j,T}Z_{j,T} = P_T^{(L)}X_{j,T}^{(L)} + P_{j,T}^{(K)}X_{j,T}^{(K)}$	j = ic,e
(A3.2.4s)	$Y_{j,T} = X_{ic,j,T}^{(2)\beta_j} X_{m,j,T}^{(2)(1-\beta_j)}$	j = ic,e
(A3.2.5s)	$X_{ic,j,T}^{(2)} = \left\{\frac{P_{j,T}^{(Y)}}{P_{ic,T}}\right\}^{\frac{1}{\beta_j}} [1-\beta_j]^{\frac{1}{\beta_j}} X_{m,j,T}^{(2)}$	j = ic,e
(A3.2.6s)	$P_{j,T}^{(Y)}Y_{j,T} = P_{ic,T}X_{ic,j,T}^{(2)} + P_T^{(M)}X_{m,j,T}^{(2)}$	j = ic,e
(A3.2.7s)	$X_T^{(4)} = [P_{e,T}]^{-\eta}$	1
(A3.2.8s)	$Z_{e,T} = X_T^{(4)}$	1
(A3.2.9s)	$Z_{ic,T} = Y_{e,T} + Y_{ic,T} + C_T^{(R)} + G_T^{(R)}$	1
(A3.2.10s)	$L_T = X_{e,T}^{(L)} + X_{ic,T}^{(L)}$	1
(A3.2.12s)	$P_{j,T}^{(K)} = P_{j,T}^{(Y)} B_{f,T}$	j = ic,e
(A3.2.13s)	$Y_{j,T} = q\, X_{j,T}^{(K)}$	j = ic,e
(A3.2.16s)	$P_{e,T}Z_{e,T} = P_T^{(M)}M_T^{(R)}$	1
(A3.2.18s)	$M_T^{(R)} = X_{m,e,T}^{(2)} + X_{m,ic,T}^{(2)}$	1
	Total number of equations	8J + 6

Table A3.2.6: The Log-linear Form of the Stylised Model's Steady State

Identifier	Equation	Number
(A3.2.1p)	$z_{j,T} = \alpha_j\, x^{(L)}_{j,T} + (1 - \alpha_j)\, x^{(K)}_{j,T}$	j = ic,e
(A3.2.2p)	$x^{(L)}_{j,T} = z_{j,T} + p_{j,T} - p^{(L)}_{jT}$	j = ic,e
(A3.2.3p)	$p_{j,T} + z_{j,T} = \alpha_j \left[x^{(L)}_{j,T} + p^{(L)}_{T} \right] + (1 - \alpha_j) \left[x^{(K)}_{j,T} + p^{(K)}_{j,T} \right]$	j = ic,e
(A3.2.4p)	$y_{j,T} = \beta_j\, x^{(2)}_{ic,j,T} + (1 - \beta_j)\, x^{(2)}_{m,j,T}$	j = ic,e
(A3.2.5p)	$x^{(2)}_{ic,j,T} = y_{j,T} + p^{(Y)}_{j,T} - p_{ic,T}$	j = ic,e
(A3.2.6p)	$p^{(Y)}_{j,T} + y_{j,T} = \beta_j \left[x^{(2)}_{ic,j,T} + p_{ic,T} \right] + (1 - \beta_j) \left[x^{(2)}_{m,j,T} + p^{(M)}_{T} \right]$	j = ic,e
(A3.2.7p)	$x^{(4)}_{T} = -\eta\, p_{e,T}$	1
(A3.2.8p)	$z_{e,T} = x^{(4)}_{T}$	1
(A3.2.9p)	$z_{ic,T} = \frac{Y_{e,T}}{Z_{ic,T}} y_{e,T} + \frac{Y_{ic,T}}{Z_{ic,T}} y_{ic,T} + \frac{C^{(R)}_{T}}{Z_{ic,T}} c^{(R)}_{T} + \frac{G^{(R)}_{T}}{Z_{ic,T}} g^{(R)}_{T}$	1
(A3.2.10p)	$l_T = \frac{X^{(L)}_{e,T}}{L_T} x^{(L)}_{e,T} + \frac{X^{(L)}_{ic,T}}{L_T} x^{(L)}_{ic,T}$	1
(A3.2.12p)	$p^{(K)}_{j,T} = p^{(Y)}_{j,T} + \frac{dB_{f,T}}{B_{f,T}}$	j = ic,e
(A3.2.13p)	$x^{(K)}_{j,T} = y_{j,T}$	j = ic,e
(A3.2.16p)	$p_{e,T} + z_{e,T} = p^{(M)}_{T} + m^{(R)}_{T}$	1
(A3.2.18p)	$m^{(R)}_{T} = \frac{X^{(2)}_{m,e,T}}{M^{(R)}_{T}} x^{(2)}_{m,e,T} + \frac{X^{(2)}_{m,ic,T}}{M^{(R)}_{T}} x^{(2)}_{m,ic,T}$	1
	Total number of equations	13T

$$COEF2 = \alpha_{ic}[\eta + (1-\eta)(1-\alpha_e)(1-\beta_e)] - \alpha_e(1-\eta)(1-\alpha_{ic})(1-\beta_{ic}) \qquad (A3.2.30)$$

$$COEF3 = \eta(1-\alpha_{ic})(1-\beta_{ic}). \qquad (A3.2.31)$$

$$COEF4 = \left\{\frac{C_T^{(R)} + G_T^{(R)}}{C_T^{(R)}}\right\}\left[(1-\alpha_e) + \alpha_e \frac{M_T^{(R)}}{X_{m,ic,T}^{(2)}}\frac{X_{ic,T}^{(L)}}{L_T}\right](1-\eta)(1-\alpha_{ic})(1-\beta_{ic})]$$

$$-\left\{\frac{C_T^{(R)} + G_T^{(R)}}{C_T^{(R)}}\right\}\left[(1-\alpha_{ic}) + \alpha_{ic} \frac{M_T^{(R)}}{X_{m,ic,T}^{(2)}}\frac{X_{ic,T}^{(L)}}{L_T}\right][\eta + (1-\eta)(1-\alpha_e)(1-\beta_e)]$$

$$+\left[\left(\frac{Y_{e,T} + Y_{ic,T}}{C_T^{(R)}}\right) + \frac{M_T^{(R)}}{X_{m,ic,T}^{(2)}}\left(\frac{Z_{ic,T} - Y_{ic,T}}{C_T^{(R)}}\right)\right]COEF1 \qquad (A3.2.32)$$

$$COEF5 = COEF1 \qquad (A3.2.33)$$

$$COEF6 = \left[(1-\alpha_{ic}) + \alpha_{ic} \frac{M_T^{(R)}}{X_{m,ic,T}^{(2)}}\frac{X_{ic,T}^{(L)}}{L_T}\right][1 - \alpha_e(1-\eta)]$$

$$+\left[(1-\alpha_e) + \alpha_e \frac{M_T^{(R)}}{X_{m,ic,T}^{(2)}}\frac{X_{ic,T}^{(L)}}{L_T}\right]\alpha_{ic}(1-\eta)\,. \qquad (A3.2.34)$$

$$COEF7 = COEF5 - \alpha_{ic}\,\eta. \qquad (A3.2.35)$$

In combination equations (A3.2.27) and (A3.2.28) imply that Ω, the household budget constraint, can be expressed as a function of the steady state values of: employment; real government expenditure; the foreign currency price of imports; the foreign bond rate; and the parameters listed in table A3.2.2. Coefficients COEF1, COEF5 and COEF3 are unambiguously positive. The signs on the remaining coefficients are ambiguous. Thus, the only unambiguous results that we can deduce from equations (A3.2.25) — (A3.2.28) without assigning values to the parameters in these equations are: (a) real consumption and, therefore, nominal consumption and the household budget constraint are inversely related to real government expenditure; (b) real consumption is inversely related to the foreign currency price of imports; and (c) the price of the import-competing commodity is inversely related to employment.

One of the key determinants of the signs on the coefficients COEF2, COEF4, COEF6 and COEF7 is η, the elasticity of foreign demand. The value of η is constrained to be greater than zero. The bigger is η the less market power exporters are assumed to have on world markets. The mechanism through which η impacts on the household budget constraint is the terms of trade. As in ORANI-INT, labour is assumed to be the immobile factor in the stylised model. An improvement in the terms of trade is accommodated by an increase in the payments to labour and vice versa. For example, other things constant, a given increase in the foreign currency price of imports will have a bigger negative impact on real consumption (and therefore nominal consumption and the budget constraint) the larger is the value of η. Conversely, other things constant, a given increase in employment will have a larger positive impact on real consumption the larger is the value of η.

To exploit the stylised model beyond the few qualitative results discussed above we must assign values to the parameters in equations (A3.2.27) — (A3.2.35). In table A3.2.7 we report values for these parameters that are chosen to mimic as closely as possible the analogous parameters in ORANI-INT. The key features of ORANI-INT's representation of the Australian economy reflected in the parameter values reported in table A3.2.7 are: (a) the relatively small size of the export sector; (b) the relatively high, but less than infinite, foreign demand elasticity; and (c) the relatively large share in final demand of private consumption.

Using the parameter values reported in table A3.2.7 we can calibrate equations (A3.2.27) and (A3.2.28) to derive the elasticities of the endogenous variables $C_T^{(R)}$, $P_{ic,T}$ and C_T with respect to the exogenous variables L_T, $P_T^{(M)}$, $G_T^{(R)}$ and $B_{f,T}$. These elasticities are reported in table A3.2.8. Note that the elasticities of Ω with respect to L_T, $P_T^{(M)}$ and $G_T^{(R)}$ are identical to those reported for C_T. The elasticity of Ω with respect to $B_{f,T}$ cannot be easily deduced because Ω is a function of the whole path of $B_{f,t}$.[6]

We can make three observations about the results in table A3.2.28. First, they are qualitatively and quantitatively similar to the elasticities generated by ORANI-INT. Second, the results are qualitatively and quantitatively robust to plausible alternative parameter values. That is, parameter values that are not obviously inconsistent with Australian data. Third, the results accord with our priors. For example: (i) an increase in employment boosts the household's budget and, therefore, consumption; (ii) increases in public consumption crowd out private consumption; (iii) the terms of trade deterioration resulting from an increase in the foreign price of imports reduces the household's budget and, therefore, consumption; and (iv) by increasing domestic costs (specifically the cost of capital) an increase in the foreign bond rate reduces the economy's competitiveness. This loss in competitiveness induces a contraction in both domestic sectors as export sales are lost and imports gain a larger share of the domestic market. With aggregate employment held constant the contraction in domestic production is accommodated by a decrease in the economy's capital-labour ratio. This reduces the marginal product of labour and, consequently, consumption.

---

6 To arrive at a new steady state in which the value of $B_{f,T}$ is higher (relative to the control scenario) implies that the values of $B_{f,t}$ must also be higher for at least some periods prior to T.

Table A3.2.7: Plausible Values for the Stylised Model's Parameters

Parameter	Value	Description
α_e	0.58	Share of labour costs in the export sector's total costs
α_{ic}	0.65	Share of labour costs in the import-competing sector's total costs
β_e	0.72	Share in the export sector's investment costs of the import-competing commodity
β_{ic}	0.78	Share in the import-competing sector's investment costs of the import-competing commodity
$C_T^{(R)}/Z_{ic,T}$	0.60	Share of private consumption in total sales by the import-competing sector
$G_T^{(R)}/Z_{ic,T}$	0.20	Share of public consumption in total sales by the import-competing sector
$Y_{e,T}/Z_{ic,T}$	0.05	Share of investment by the export sector in total sales by the import-competing sector
$Y_{ic,T}/Z_{ic,T}$	0.15	Share of investment by the import-competing sector in total sales by the import-competing sector
$X_{m,ic,T}^{(2)}/M_T^{(R)}$	0.94	Share in total imports of imports purchased by the import-competing sector's for the purpose of creating capital
$X_{ic,T}^{(L)}/L_T$	0.95	The import-competing sector's share of total employment
$B_{f,T}$	0.03	Foreign bond rate
ρ	0.03	Pure time preference rate
η	11	Foreign elasticity of demand
q	0.03	Population growth

Table A3 2.8: Elasticities of Selected Variables with Respect to the Exogenous Variables

Endogenous Variables	Exogenous Variables			
	L_T	$P_T^{(M)}$	$G_T^{(R)}$	$B_{f,T}$ (a)
$C_T^{(R)}$	1.32	-0.16	-0.33	-0.22
$P_{ic,T}$	-0.09	-0.04	0.00	0.05
C_T	1.22	-0.20	-0.33	-0.17

(a) The shock to $B_{f,T}$ is 1 percent (i.e., $dB_{f,T} = 0.0103$).

Appendix A3.3 Alternative Investment Specifications

A3.3.1 Introduction

In this appendix we compare the investment specification implemented in ORANI-INT with the 'cost of adjustment' approach that is adopted in most intertemporal CGE models. Investment is an inherently intertemporal process as it involves trading off current consumption possibilities for future consumption possibilities. The survey of investment models by Chirinko (1993) identifies a range of conceptual and empirical issues that must be confronted by economists modelling investment behaviour. A comparison of Chirinko's survey with Jorgenson's (1971) survey reveals that there have been some key changes in the modelling of investment behaviour over the two decades separating the studies. In particular, there appears to be growing consensus in the literature that investment should be modelled as an intertemporal optimisation problem in which expectations are treated explicitly. However, there is less consensus about the form of the optimisation problem and about the way in which investors form expectations. Researchers have struggled to specify an optimisation problem that yields an investment specification with reasonable empirical properties. A key empirical regularity that has proved difficult to model on microeconomic principles is inertia in investment. Adjustment costs and/or time-to-build characteristics are just two of the approaches that introduce inertia into investment decisions that have been explored in the literature. A survey of these and other approaches is provided in Chirinko (1993).

In the remainder of this appendix we describe a standard cost of adjustment investment model. A number of difficulties with using such a specification in a multisectoral model are identified. We then explain the reasons for adopting a time-to-build model of investment in ORANI-INT. Finally, we offer some general comments about the treatment of investment in applied models.

A3.3.2 Cost of Adjustment Models of Investment

Whilst there is a wide variety of adjustment cost models of investment, they all postulate that firms adjust their capital stocks gradually rather than abruptly because the marginal cost of investment is an increasing function of investment.[1] The key differences relate to whether the adjustment costs are internal or external to the firm [see Mussa (1977)]. In most CGE models adjustment costs are assumed to be internal to the firm. A popular version of the adjustment cost model postulates that it is costly for firms to install (or uninstall) capital. Thus, to augment its capital stock, a firm must use resources (existing factors or goods and services) to install new capital. The quantity of resources needed for installation is assumed to be an increasing and convex function of investment. For example, McKibbin and Wilcoxen (1995) use an adjustment cost model that puts a wedge between the quantity of investment undertaken and the increment to capital stocks.[2] Using the notation developed in chapter 3, the representative firm in sector j purchases $Y_{j,t}$ units of investment goods but $N_{j,t}$, the increment to its capital stock, is less. In this case the technological relationship between investment and the increment to capital stock is represented by the following function:

$$Y_{j,t} = N_{j,t}\left\{1 + \frac{\omega}{2}\frac{N_{j,t}}{K_{j,t}}\right\}; \qquad j = 1, ..., 13, t = 1, ..., T \qquad \text{(A3.3.1)}$$

The second term on the RHS of (A3.3.1) represents the costs of adjustment. The parameter ω indicates the significance of these costs. The larger value of ω the greater the penalty for fast adjustment. Note that when ω is zero equation (A3.3.1) reduces to equation (3.3.23) [see section 3.3.2 in chapter 3].

An investment demand function for the representative producer in the jth sector can be obtained from the solution to a maximisation similar to that presented in chapter 3, section 3.3.2. As before the representative producer takes the time paths of all prices as given. The choice variables in the producer's intertemporal optimisation problem are $Z^{(K)}_{j,t}$, the supply of sector-specific capital in year t, for t=1, ...,T-1 and $Y_{j,t}$, gross investment in year t, for t=1, ...,T-1. Note that in contrast to the problem specified in chapter 3, the capital stock in the first period of the planning horizon is a choice variable in this case. This reflects the absence of a gestation or installation lag. The producer's maximand, which is the same as that represented by equation (3.3.21) in chapter 3, is the present value of the expected future stream of profits accruing from the ownership of capital. That is:

$$\chi_j = \sum_{t=1}^{T}\left\{\frac{P^{(K)}_{j,t}Z^{(K)}_{j,t} - P^{(Y)}_{j,t}Y_{j,t}}{\prod_{u=0}^{t-1}[1 + \Psi_{j,u}]}\right\} \qquad j = 1, ..., 13 \qquad \text{(A3.3.2)}$$

---

1 The adjustment cost model of investment was introduced by Eisner and Strotz (1963). Key contributions to the development of adjustment cost models were made by Lucas (1967), Treadway (1969), Gould (1968), Uzawa (1969) and Mussa (1977 & 1978). Brechling (1975) explores the implications of alternative adjustment cost specifications and the issues that arise in estimation of such models. Nickell (1978) discusses the implications of adjustment cost models under different assumptions about product and factor market structures and under different assumptions about the way expectations are formed.

2 This approach to modelling adjustment costs is due to Uzawa (1969).

where the notation is as described in chapter 3. The constraints faced by the producer are:

$$Z^{(K)}_{j,t} = Z^{(K)}_{j,t-1}[1 - \delta_j] + N_{j,t}\,; \qquad j = 1, \ldots, 13, t = 1, \ldots, T \qquad \text{(A3.3.3)}$$

$$Z^{(K)}_{j,0} = \hat{Z}^{(K)}_{j,0}\,; \qquad j = 1, \ldots, 13 \qquad \text{(A3.3.4)}$$

$$Z^{(K)}_{j,T} = \hat{Z}^{(K)}_{j,T}\,; \qquad j = 1, \ldots, 13 \qquad \text{(A3.3.5)}$$

and the investment technology represented by equation (A3.3.1). Note that the accumulation relationship reflects the absence of gestation lags. Investment undertaken in period t comes on stream in the same period. We have also not included a nonnegativity constraint for investment. Nonnegativity constraints are typically not made explicit in adjustment cost models of investment. The terminal condition represented by equation (A3.3.5) is typically specified as a transversality condition that ensures the value of the firm and the value of the capital stock are bounded as T tends to infinity.

The first order conditions from the above maximisation problem are:

$$\frac{N_{j,t+1}}{Z^{(K)}_{j,t+1}} + \frac{P^{(Y)}_{j,t}}{P^{(Y)}_{j,t+1}} \frac{[1 + \Psi_{j,t}]}{[1 - \delta_j]} \frac{N_{j,t}}{Z^{(K)}_{j,t}} \left\{ \frac{1}{2} \frac{N_{j,t}}{Z^{(K)}_{j,t}} + 1 \right\} = \frac{1}{\omega} \frac{[1 + \Psi_{j,t}]}{[1 - \delta_j]} \left\{ \frac{P^{(Y)}_{j,t}}{P^{(Y)}_{j,t+1}} - \frac{P^{(K)}_{j,t}}{P^{(Y)}_{j,t+1}} - \frac{[1 + \Psi_{j,t}]}{[1 - \delta_j]} \right\}$$

$$j = 1, \ldots, 13, t = 1, \ldots, T\text{-}1 \qquad \text{(A3.3.6)}$$

and the constraints (A3.3.3) – (A3.3.5). Because of the nonlinear form of difference equation (A3.3.6) an explicit form of the investment demand function cannot be derived from these first order conditions if expectations are assumed to be rational. However, a numerical solution for these first order conditions is easily obtained under rational expectations.

The key feature of the adjustment cost model is that it introduces inertia into the investment process. A firm that receives a new piece of information in period t (e.g., an unexpected increase in demand) will not adjusts its capital stock completely in that period even though it is technically possible to do so. The faster the firm tries to adjust its capital stock to the new equilibrium value the more costly such an adjustment will be. These costs of rapid adjustment must be traded-off against the benefits of having the capital stock at its equilibrium level. For example, in the case of an unexpected increase in demand, the slower the firm is in adjusting its capital stock the greater will be the foregone profit opportunities.

There are many variations of the internal cost of adjustment investment model. The price used to value the adjustment costs differs in the various models to reflect the perceived source of these costs. For example, Bovenberg and Goulder (1991) use the price of the firm's output to value adjustment costs because they assume that the firm absorbs some of its output (which is a function of capital, labour and intermediate goods) when it expands its capital stock. Other studies use the price of labour to value adjustment costs to reflect the idea that additional labour is used to install new capital [e.g., Dixon, Parmenter, Powell and Wilcoxen (1992)]. Similarly, depending on ones view about the nature of the adjustment costs the investment technology may be specified in terms of net investment rather than gross investment as in equation (A3.3.1) above. Such an approach is justified on the grounds adjustment costs arise mainly because of disruption to the production process (i.e., workers need to be trained and teething problems with new capital must be overcome) rather than because of installation costs. Some adjustment cost models assume that there are diminishing returns to investment (i.e., the adjustment cost function is not homogeneous of degree one in real variables (usually investment and capital). This approach implies that high levels of investment rather than rapid growth in investment give rise to adjustment costs. In most cases adjustment cost models of this kind are adopted for their analytical tractability (i.e., closed form decision rules for investment) rather than for their empirical properties [see for example Dixon, Parmenter, Powell and Wilcoxen (1992)]. We also note that many implementations of the adjustment cost model of investment include a one period gestation lag. This is often implicit and follows from the conversion of differential equations (i.e., the first-order conditions derived from the solution of a continuous-time optimisation problem) into difference equations.

Whilst the adjustment cost specification has been adopted in most intertemporal CGE models[3] we felt it would be useful to explore an alternative investment specification for several reasons. First, the specific nature of adjustment costs is typically not made clear. In the context of a macroeconomic model or a single-equation model the exact nature of the adjustment costs is probably of secondary importance. In such a model one can appeal to factors exogenous to model to justify the existence of adjustment costs. However, in the context of a multisectoral model the adjustment cost specification is less compelling if the nature of these costs is not made explicit. The key point is that the more disaggregated the representation of the supply side of the economy the less reason there should be to leave the nature of the adjustment costs unspecified. If adjustment costs are assumed to be related to installation costs then it may be appropriate to specify which sector supplies the installation services and what makes the costs of these services a convex function of investment (e.g., a supply constraint). For example, in the ORANI-INT database we find that the *Construction* sector supplies most of the economy's requirements for inputs to capital creation. Some of these inputs may represent installation services. If the *Construction* sector's production technology exhibits decreasing returns, then the price of the *Construction* sector's output will be an increasing function of the demand for this output. Under such conditions the capital creators that use inputs of the *Construction* commodity will face convex (external) costs of adjustment.[4]

---

3 Exceptions to this are Jorgenson and Wilcoxen (1993), whose investment specification does not have convex adjustment costs, and Mercenier and Sampiao de Souza (1993), whose investment specification allows for adjustment costs and gestation lags.

4 In the time-to-build approach that we use in ORANI-INT the *Construction* sector is unable to adjust its capital stock in the first year of the planning horizon. Thus, in the first

A second reason for looking beyond the adjustment cost model of investment is that the empirical support for the model is not strong [see Chirinko (1993)]. This lack of empirical support may reflect data difficulties and estimation problems (e.g., the treatment of expectations). However, the poor empirical performance of adjustment cost models may also reflect conceptual difficulties. For example, it is conceivable that in some cases internal costs of adjustment may be concave rather than convex.[5] It is conceivable that rapid adjustment of some types of capital is less costly than gradual adjustment.

A3.3.3 Time-to-build Models of Investment

The time-to-build investment models postulate that there is a lag between the time a firm decides to invest and the time at which the investment becomes productive capital. For convenience we will refer to this lag as a gestation lag. A variety of sources for this gestation lag are identified, including the time that elapses between the placement of an order for capital goods, their delivery and subsequent installation.

In ORANI-INT the representative firm in industry j creates capital by combining inputs of goods and services using a sector-specific technology. We assume that it takes the firm a year on average to construct and install a new unit of capital. Thus, to put in place a productive unit of capital in year t+1 the firm must purchase the inputs to its capital creation process in year t. A more general time-to-build specification would allow for gestation lags of variable length. A more general time-to-build investment technology may be specified as follows:

$$Y_{j,t} = \sum_{g=1}^{G} \pi_g N_{j,t+g}; \qquad j = 1, ..., 13, t = 1, ..., T \qquad \text{(A3.3.7)}$$

where G is the length of the gestation period and π_g is the proportion of investment in period t that is devoted to increments to capital stock that are g periods from completion.

Our choice of a one-year gestation lag for all sectors is arbitrary. Without any empirical evidence for guidance we conjectured that at the level of disaggregation adopted in ORANI-INT (i.e., 13 sectors) the plausibility of lengthier gestation lags is questionable.[6] In fact it is highly likely that for some sectors the gestation lag

---

year there are diminishing returns to the *Construction* sector's capital stock. The higher the level of investment activity in the economy the higher will be the demand for the *Construction* sector's output and the higher will be the price of this output. As is explained in chapters 6 and 7 the forward-looking producers anticipate that full adjustment of the capital stock in year 2 is more costly than is gradual adjustment over a number of years.

5 See Brechling (1975) for a discussion about of alternative adjustment cost specifications.

6 A possible exception to this claim is the *Utilities* sector. Capital in this sector is often lumpy and lengthy construction periods are plausible (e.g., power stations and water dams).

will be less than one year. For such sectors the disaggregation of time in ORANI-INT is too coarse to capture the implications of the time-to-build technology. The time-to-build approach is probably easier to apply in models with a finer degree of sectoral disaggregation than ORANI-INT. This is because it is easier to identify the specific capital items used by each sector. For example, it is probably easier to identify the capital items used by typical firms in the *Motor Vehicle* sector than for the *Manufacturing* sector. The ability to match specific capital items to sectors may be useful for determining the appropriate length of the gestation period in each sector on *a priori* grounds. For example, if the main capital item used by the *Finance* sector is computers it is plausible that the appropriate gestation lag for that sector is quite short. In contrast, if the capital used by the *Oil Extraction* sector consists mainly of oil rigs a more lengthy gestation lag may be appropriate.

Another key reason for adopting a one-year gestation lag is to keep the model tractable. Whilst the implementation of gestation lags of greater than one year in some sectors does not pose any technical difficulties, the complexity of the model's projections increases. In the context of the sectoral investment responses, this complexity is exacerbated by the implementation of nonnegativity constraints on investment. Without any strong empirical justification for gestation lags greater than one year we opted for the simplest possible form of the time-to-build model. As the results in chapters 6 and 7 demonstrate the investment specification in ORANI-INT, although simple, generates interesting and complicated dynamics.

A3.3.4 Concluding Remarks

Whilst we have opted to use the time-to-build approach rather than the adjustment cost approach in ORANI-INT, this choice is not based on any strong conviction about their relative merits. Both approaches fail to account for a key feature of investment behaviour — uncertainty. In ORANI-INT, and in most other intertemporal CGE models, investors are assumed to have perfect foresight. This assumption is adopted for computational convenience rather than for empirical reasons. It is possible that an adequate treatment of uncertainty in the modelling of investment will go a long way towards accounting for the inertia observed in investment responses. Investors may not react immediately and fully to new information if they are uncertain about the implications of that information.

The roles of uncertainty and irreversibility in investment decisions are gaining prominence in the literature [see Pindyck (1991) and Dixit (1992) for a summary]. A key point to emerge from this literature is that uncertainty and irreversibility introduce inertia into investment decisions. This inertia arises because there is an incentive for investors to delay their decisions to learn more about the expected returns.[7] In ORANI-INT we have adopted the irreversibility aspect of investment

7 In the literature this type of investment behaviour is likened to the purchase of a financial call option.

decisions emphasised by the recent literature but not uncertainty.[8] The dynamics introduced by irreversibility constraints are discussed in appendix A3.4.

Two other aspects of investment behaviour that deserve more attention than they receive in ORANI-INT are the supply of funds and lumpiness of capital goods. In common with most applied models we have assumed that there is an infinitely elastic supply of funds[9] and that capital stocks can be adjusted incrementally.

Firms can finance investment by using retained earnings, by issuing debt, or by issuing equity. In ORANI-INT we have implicitly assumed that capital market are perfectly competitive and that there are no tax biases. Under these conditions firms will, after adjusting for risk, be indifferent between the alternative financing arrangements. This assumption warrants further investigation. Although the empirical evidence is not conclusive (see Chirinko, 1993), it does suggest that capital market imperfections may have significant implications for the way investment is financed. In the context of intertemporal CGE models, McKibbin and Sachs (1991) and McKibbin and Wilcoxen (1995) have explicitly allowed for liquidity-constrained investment behaviour.[10] Dixon and Malakellis (1996) examine sectoral investment responses when the supply of funds is less than infinitely elastic.[11]

---

8 Whilst irreversibility of investment decisions is emphasised in the recent literature, the concept has received attention in earlier literature. For example, Arrow (1968) provides a formal treatment of irreversibility. The innovation in the recent literature has been to examine irreversibility in the context of uncertainty.

9 Investors can borrow as much as they like at the domestic bond rate adjusted for an exogenous sector-specific risk premium. Under the standard closure of the model the domestic bond rate is equal to the foreign bond rate (see chapter 5).

10 In both studies the modelling of liquidity constrained behaviour is ad hoc in that it does not follow explicitly from the firms optimisation problem. The inclusion of liquidity constrained behaviour is justified on the basis that it improves the empirical properties of the investment function.

11 The specification used by Dixon and Malakellis (1996) is ad hoc. They assume that the sector-specific risk premium required by suppliers of funds is an increasing function of the rate of growth of a particular sector relative to some benchmark (e.g., trend growth in that sector).

Appendix A3.4 The Implications of the Irreversibility Constraint on Investment

A3.4.1 Introduction

In this appendix we examine the behavioural implications of the nonnegativity constraints on sectoral investment.[1] We do this in two parts: first, we examine the theoretical implications of the constraints using a hypothetical example. In the second part we reconcile the theoretical implications of the nonnegativity constraints with the results obtained from an experiment, reported in chapter 7.

A3.4.2 Theoretical Implications

To examine the theoretical implications of the nonnegativity constraints we start with equation (3.3.33), the equilibrium condition for sectoral capital demands, which was derived in section 3.3.2 of chapter 3. For convenience we repeat this equation below:

$$P^{(K)}_{j,t} = \left[1 + \Psi_{j,t-1}\right]\left(P^{(Y)}_{j,t-1} + \Gamma^{*}_{j,t-1}\right) - \left[1 - \delta_j\right]\left(P^{(Y)}_{j,t} + \Gamma^{*}_{j,t}\right),$$

$$j = 1, \ldots, 13, \; t = 2, \ldots, T \qquad \text{(A3.4.1)}$$

For simplicity we assume that $\Psi_{j,t}$, the risk-adjusted return to capital, is constant over time. Under these conditions we can re-write equation (A3.4.1) as:

$$\left(P^{(Y)}_{j,1} + \Gamma^{*}_{j,1}\right) = \left(P^{(Y)}_{j,T+1} + \Gamma^{*}_{j,T+1}\right)\left[\frac{1-\delta_j}{1+\Psi_j}\right]^{T} + \left[\frac{1}{1-\delta_j}\right]\sum_{u=1}^{T} P^{(K)}_{j,u+1}\left[\frac{1-\delta_j}{1+\Psi_j}\right]^{u} \qquad \text{(A3.4.2)}$$

The term on the LHS of equation (A3.4.2) is the value in year 1 of purchasing an asset that yields a stream of sector-specific capital services. Because we have assumed that there is a gestation lag of one year in the investment process, an asset

[1] For a more general discussion of irreversible investment decisions in the context of certainty see Arrow (1968).

that is purchased in year 1 will not come on stream until year 2. In its first year of productive use the asset will yield a unit of sector-specific capital services. In subsequent years, the asset will yield a diminishing stream of services due to depreciation. Hereafter, we shall refer to such an asset as a *machine*. In equation (A3.4.2) the value in year 1 of a machine is equal to the appropriately discounted and depreciated stream of imputed rental income accruing to the producer from using the machine for T periods [second term on RHS of (A3.4.2)], plus the residual value of the machine after T periods of use [first term on RHS of (A3.4.2)].

The complementary slackness condition, given by condition (3.3.28) in section 3.3.2 of chapter 3, implies that $\Gamma^*_{j,t} \geq 0, \forall_{j,t}$. It follows, therefore, that the value of a machine can never exceed $P^{(Y)}_{j,t}$, the cost of constructing it. If the value of a machine is greater than the cost of constructing it, the firm would not be optimising since it could improve its position by investing more.

We assume that a *serious slump* is characterised by an exogenous shock, in a specific period, that induces the rate of decline in the *desired* level of capital stock to be greater than the rate of depreciation in that period. If investment decisions are reversible, a firm that anticipates a serious slump in some period can, without loss, divest itself of excess capital stock.

Imposing nonnegativity constraints on investment means that the firm is unable to sell its capital stock. Thus, the firm must consider the profitability of a machine for its entire life and must act upon information about impending serious slumps earlier than would be the case if investment was unconstrained. For example, a serious slump in period k implies that the nonnegativity constraint on investment in period k-1 will be binding (i.e., $\Gamma^*_{j,k-1} > 0$) and the firm must adjust its investment plans not only in period k-1 but also in period k-2 and possibly, depending on the severity of the serious slump, in previous periods.

Figure A3.4.1 depicts a hypothetical investment plan that will be used to highlight the key implications of nonnegativity constraints on investment. We have scaled the price variables depicted in the figure A3.1.4 (i.e., $P^{(Y)}_{j,t}$, $P^{(K)}_{j,t}$ and $\Gamma^*_{j,t}$) so that the quantity variables (i.e., investment and capital) can be depicted on the same chart.

For ease of exposition, an interval of time in which the first and last periods are characterised by non-binding nonnegativity constraints is labelled an *off-off* interval. An *on-off* interval refers to the situation where the nonnegativity constraints on investment are binding in the first period of the interval but not the last (and *vice versa* for an *off-on* interval).

In the hypothetical investment plan depicted in figure A3.4.1, one example of an off-off interval is that starting in period s and ending in period s+4 (i.e., $\Gamma^*_{j,s} = \Gamma^*_{j,s+4} = 0$). The path of the capital stock over this interval must satisfy the following equilibrium condition:

$$P^{(Y)}_{j,s} = P^{(Y)}_{j,s+4}\left[\frac{1-\delta_j}{1+\Psi_j}\right]^4 + \left[\frac{1}{1-\delta_j}\right]\sum_{u=1}^{4} P^{(K)}_{j,s+u}\left[\frac{1-\delta_j}{1+\Psi_j}\right]^u \qquad \text{(A3.4.3)}$$

In equation (A3.4.3) $P^{(Y)}_{j,s}$, the cost of obtaining an additional machine in period s, is equal to the benefits derived from having that machine for 4 periods. Over the interval (s, s+4), therefore, there is no gain to the firm for doing any more, or less, investment in period s. The net gain to the firm of having an additional machine over any off-off interval must be zero. If this is not the case, the firm could improve its position by increasing or decreasing its investment in, at least, the first period of the interval. In the hypothetical investment plan the nonnegativity constraints are binding in the periods between (but not including) s and s+4. However, the implications of equation (A3.4.3) are independent of the status of the nonnegativity constraints in all but the first and last periods of the interval.

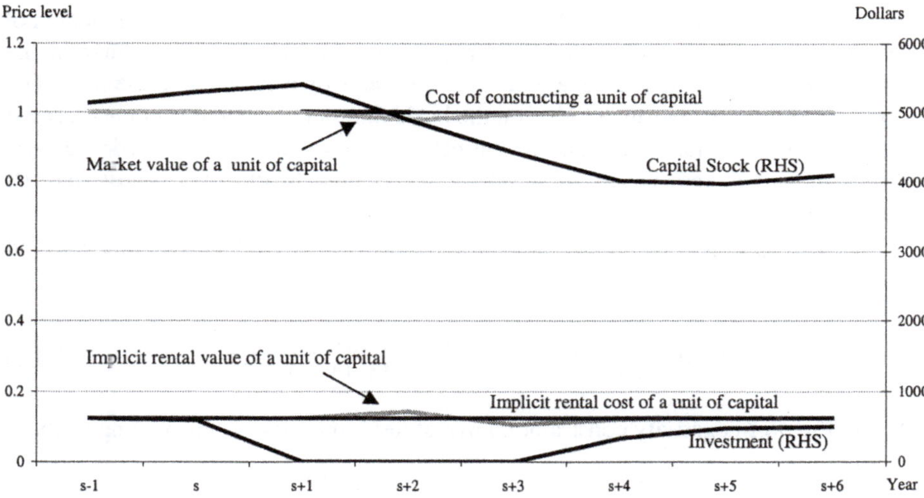

Figure A3.4.1: A Hypothetical Investment Plan

Because the nonnegativity constraints are binding in some periods within the off-off interval (s, s+4), the hypothetical investment plan must contain at least one period in which a serious slump is expected to occur. The nonnegativity constraint on investment is binding in period s+3 but not in s+4, (i.e., $\Gamma^{*}_{j,s+3} > 0$ and $\Gamma^{*}_{j,s+4} = 0$); therefore, a serious slump must be expected in, at least, period s+4. The serious slump expected in period s+4 may be severe enough to induce the firm to cease investing several periods prior. It is possible, however, that more than one serious slump is expected. Since the nonnegativity constraint on investment is not binding in the first period of an off-off interval, a serious slump cannot be expected in the second period of such an interval. An off-off interval may contain serious slumps in some, or all other, periods in the interval except the second.

Equation (A3.4.3) shows that the imputed stream of rental income derived from having an additional machine over the off-off interval must equal the cost of obtaining the machine less its replacement cost at the end of the interval. This result does not hold for on-off or off-on intervals, however. For example, the equilibrium condition for capital stock over an off-on interval beginning in period s and ending in period s+γ, γ < 4, is:

$$P^{(Y)}_{j,s} = \left(P^{(Y)}_{j,s+\gamma} + \Gamma^{*}_{j,s+\gamma}\right)\left[\frac{1-\delta_j}{1+\Psi_j}\right]^{\gamma} + \left[\frac{1}{1-\delta_j}\right]\sum_{u=1}^{\gamma} P^{(K)}_{j,u+1}\left[\frac{1-\delta_j}{1+\Psi_j}\right]^{u} \qquad \text{(A3.4.4)}$$

and since the non-negativity constraint on investment in period s+γ is binding, (i.e., $\Gamma^{*}_{j,s+\gamma} > 0$) then:

$$P^{(Y)}_{j,s} < P^{(Y)}_{j,s+\gamma}\left[\frac{1-\delta_j}{1+\Psi_j}\right]^{\gamma} + \left[\frac{1}{1-\delta_j}\right]\sum_{u=1}^{\gamma} P^{(K)}_{j,u+1}\left[\frac{1-\delta_j}{1+\Psi_j}\right]^{u} \qquad \text{(A3.4.5)}$$

Thus, over any off-on interval the stream of imputed rentals derived from having an additional machine over this interval will exceed the cost of the machine less its replacement cost at the end of the interval. This situation does not encourage the firm to invest more because at the end of the off-on interval the replacement cost of an additional machine is greater than its value to the firm. The firm formulates its investment plan on the basis that once a machine is purchased it can never be re-sold. At the end of the off-on interval the firm is burdened with excess machines and, hence, the value of a machine to the firm is less than its replacement.

Alternatively, for an on-off interval beginning in period s+γ, 1 ≤ γ < 4, and ending in period s+4:

$$\left(P^{(Y)}_{j,s+\gamma} + \Gamma^{*}_{j,s+\gamma}\right) = P^{(Y)}_{j,s+4}\left[\frac{1-\delta_j}{1+\Psi_j}\right]^{4-\gamma} + \left[\frac{1}{1-\delta_j}\right]\sum_{u=1}^{4-\gamma} P^{(K)}_{j,u+1}\left[\frac{1-\delta_j}{1+\Psi_j}\right]^{u} \qquad \text{(A3.4.6)}$$

Again, the non-negativity constraint on investment in period s+γ is binding so that:

$$P^{(Y)}_{j,s+\gamma} > P^{(Y)}_{j,s+4}\left[\frac{1-\delta_j}{1+\Psi_j}\right]^{4-\gamma} + \left[\frac{1}{1-\delta_j}\right]\sum_{u=1}^{4-\gamma} P^{(K)}_{j,u+1}\left[\frac{1-\delta_j}{1+\Psi_j}\right]^{u} \qquad \text{(A3.4.7)}$$

Over an on-off interval the stream of rentals derived from having an additional machine will be less than the cost of owning it (i.e., the cost of the machine less its replacement cost at the end of the interval). In the last period of the interval the value to the firm of a machine is equal to its replacement cost. In the first period, and possibly all other periods except the last, of the on-off interval, however, the replacement cost of a machine exceeds its value to the firm.

Equations (A3.4.4)—(A3.4.7) imply that the implicit rental *value* of capital (i.e., the amount that the firm would, if it was allowed, pay to rent a machine for one period) will rise above the implicit rental *cost* of capital (i.e., the implicit cost to the firm of using a machine that it owns for one period) for some portion of the hypothetical investment plan beginning in period s and will fall below the implicit rental cost of capital for some other portion of the plan ending in period s+4. Although difficult to detect in figure A3.4.1, the rental value of capital rises above the rental cost of capital in periods s+1 and s+2 and below it in periods s+3 and s+4. Since equation (A3.4.3) must hold over any off-off interval, the gains implied when the rental value of capital rises above its rental cost must be exactly offset by the losses implied when the rental value of capital falls below the rental cost.

Because investment decisions are irreversible, the firm is unable to take advantage of the gains implied by an off-on interval nor is it able to avoid the losses implied by an on-off interval. In the first and last periods of the off-off interval the capital stock held by the firm is equal to its desired level. This will not be true for the other periods in the plan, however. Since the optimal policy for the firm is to cease investing prior to the occurrence of a serious slump, the actual capital stock held in at least some periods prior to the occurrence of the serious slump will be less than the "desired" capital stock (i.e., the amount of capital that would be held if investment decisions were reversible). In those periods the implicit rental value of capital rises above the rental cost. In at least the period immediately prior to the occurrence of a serious slump the firm will be holding more capital stock than "desired" even if it has reduced its capital stock by ceasing to invest in prior periods. This is because capital gains/losses make it cheaper for the firm to adjust its capital stock gradually rather than abruptly. In the periods that the actual stock of capital is above the desired level the rental value of capital will be less than the rental cost. This occurs in periods t+3 and t+4 in the hypothetical plan.

A3.4.3 Results from ORANI-INT

In the anticipated tariff-cut experiment, reported in section 7.3 of chapter 7, the nonnegativity constraint on the *Construction* sector's investment (i.e., sector 5) is binding in years 10 and 11, the two years prior to the implementation of the announced tariff cut. In all other years, the *Construction* sector's investment is positive and the nonnegativity constraints are not binding. This configuration of the nonnegativity constraints corresponds to the *off-off* interval discussed in the previous section.

In figures A3.4.2 – A3.4.4 we depict a selection of results for the *Construction* sector that are taken from the anticipated tariff-cut experiment. Note that the paths depicted in these charts represent the levels values of the variables.

The deviations from the control scenario of the *Construction* sector's output are shown in chart S5 in chapter 7, section 7.3. From this chart we can deduce that in year 12, the year that the anticipated tariff cut is implemented, the *Construction* sector's output falls about 10 per cent below control. This result is reflected in figure A3.4.2 by the fall in the *Construction* sector's capital stock between years 10 and 12. The fact that the nonnegativity constraint is binding in years 10 and 11 indicates that the fall in the *Construction* sector's activity level in year 12 is sufficiently strong that it constitutes a *serious slump*. That is, if investment in the *Construction* sector was not constrained, the rate of decline in this sector's capital stock would be greater than the depreciation rate and investment would be

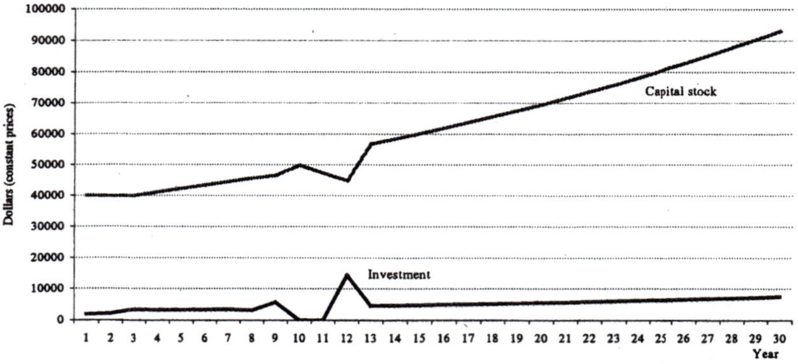

Figure A3.4.2: The *Construction* Sector's Capital and Investment Paths

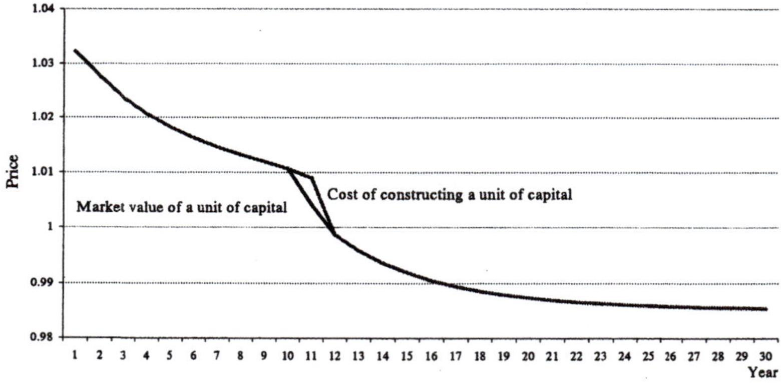

Figure A3.4.3: The Asset Value and Cost of the *Construction* Sector's Capital

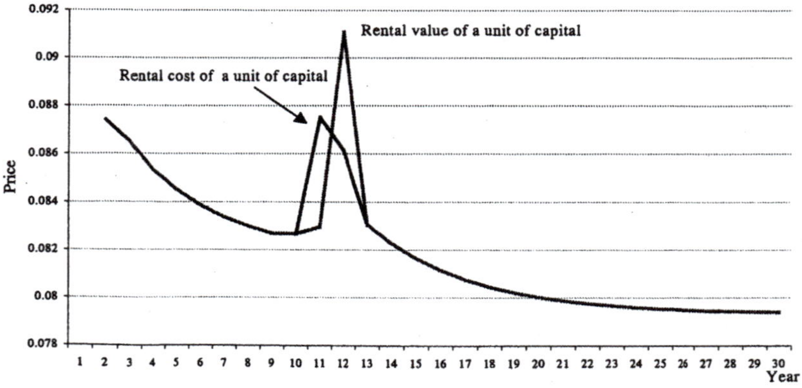

Figure A3.4.4: The Rental Value and Cost of the *Construction* Sector's Capital

negative. However, as figure A3.4.2 shows, the binding nonnegativity constraint in years 10 and 11 ensures that the *Construction* sector's investment does not fall below zero. In the previous section we explained that when the nonnegativity constraint is binding the asset value of capital stock is less than its construction cost. Figure A3.4.3 shows that this is the case for the *Construction* sector in years 10 and 11.[2]

Figure A3.4.4 shows that in year 12, the year in which the serious slump occurs, the returns to the *Construction* sector from its capital stock (i.e., the implicit rental value) are less than the implicit rental costs of this capital.[3]

---

2 In year 10 the asset of value of the *Construction* sector's capital is only marginally less than the construction cost.

3 The reason that the paths of the rentals are depicted as starting in year 2 rather than in year 1 is that capital stocks in year 1 are exogenous and the equilibrium condition for capital stocks does not hold.

Appendix A3.5 A Note on Divisia Indexes

A3.5.1 Introduction

In this appendix we explain how Divisia indexes are used to decompose value indexes into price and quantity components. In aggregating prices or quantities between α_0, an initial point, and α_1, a final point, the weights adopted in typically used indexes are fixed.[1] For example, initial-point weights are used in Laspeyres' indexes and final-point weights are used in Paasche indexes. In contrast, the weights used in Divisia indexes are continually revised to account for price and quantity changes along the path connecting α_0 to α_1. Given such a weighting scheme, a Divisia index of the quantities X_i, $i=1, ..., N$, can be loosely interpreted as some average of a Laspeyres index and a Paasche index of those quantities. A Divisia index can also be interpreted as a chained Laspeyres index.

In the next section we use the definition of nominal consumption as an example to show how the differential forms of Divisia price and quantity indexes can be easily derived. We then derive the levels form of these indexes. Finally, we explain why Divisia indexes are preferred to Laspeyres and Paasche indexes in ORANI-INT.

A3.5.2 The Differential Form of Divisia Indexes

The levels form of a Divisia index is a complicated path-dependent line integral. However, Divisia indexes have very simple differential forms. This is a convenient feature given that we use GEMPACK, a general purpose software package for solving systems of non-linear equations [see Pearson (1991)], to solve ORANI-INT.[2] As will be explained in more detail in chapter 4, the algorithm used in GEMPACK to solve systems of non-linear equations is based on Euler's method.

---

1 In this context the terms 'initial point' and 'final point' may refer to points in time or to points on the paths of exogenous variables at a particular point in time. For example, the 'initial point' may refer to a situation in 1996 in which the foreign bond rate (an exogenous variable) is 6 per cent while the 'final point' may refer to a situation at the same point in time (i.e., 1996) but in which the foreign bond rate is 5 percent.

2 A more detailed discussion about Divisia price and quantity indexes in the context of a CGE model implemented in GEMPACK can be found in Dixon and Rimmer (1998b).

Euler's method is a derivative approach to solving non-linear equations. Computations involve moving from a known solution of the non-linear equation system to a sought-after solution (i.e., one in which the exogenous variables are assigned their forecast or desired values) in a series of small steps. The rules for moving from one solution to another are provided by the differential form of the non-linear equation system. GEMPACK users have the option of implementing each of their model's equations its non-linear or differential form. Before performing any computations the software symbolically differentiates any equation implemented in non-linear form to derive its corresponding analytical derivative formula.

The levels form of a Divisia index is too complicated for GEMPACK's symbolic differentiation routines. However, the differential form of a Divisia index is easily derived by hand. More importantly, the differential forms of Divisia indexes used in ORANI-INT can be derived trivially from value indexes already specified in the model. That is, the price and quantity indexes in ORANI-INT are derived by a trivial decomposition of nominal macroeconomic variables already specified. To demonstrate this we use the definition of aggregate nominal consumption, presented in chapter 3 as equation (3.6.2), to derive the differential forms of Divisia indexes of consumer prices and real consumption. For convenience we repeat the definition of nominal consumption below:

$$C_t = \sum_{i=1}^{13} P^{(3)}_{i,\bullet,t} X^{(3)}_{i,\bullet,t} \qquad t = 1, \ldots, T \qquad \text{(A3.5.1)}$$

The differential form of equation (A3.5.1) is:

$$c_t = \sum_{i=1}^{13} \frac{P^{(3)}_{i,\bullet,t} X^{(3)}_{i,\bullet,t}}{C_t} \left\{ p^{(3)}_{i,\bullet,t} + x^{(3)}_{i,\bullet,t} \right\} \qquad t = 1, \ldots, T \qquad \text{(A3.5.2)}$$

In equation (A3.5.2) the variables expressed in lower-case Italics denote percentage changes in the corresponding levels variables. The differential forms of the Divisia indexes of consumer prices and real consumption can be derived by additively decomposing equation (A3.5.2) as follows:

$$c^{(\Pi)}_t = \sum_{i=1}^{13} \frac{P^{(3)}_{i,\bullet,t} X^{(3)}_{i,\bullet,t}}{C_t} p^{(3)}_{i,\bullet,t} \text{ ; and} \qquad t = 1, \ldots, T \qquad \text{(A3.5.3)}$$

$$c^{(R)}_t = \sum_{i=1}^{13} \frac{P^{(3)}_{i,\bullet,t} X^{(3)}_{i,\bullet,t}}{C_t} x^{(3)}_{i,\bullet,t}. \qquad t = 1, \ldots, T \qquad \text{(A3.5.4)}$$

Note that the coefficients in equations (A3.5.2) — (A3.5.4) are identical. These coefficients can be interpreted as the shares in total nominal consumption of expenditure on good i. At the nth step of an N-step Euler computation the values of these coefficients is revised to reflect changes in the exogenous and endogenous variables between steps n-1 and n.

A3.5.3 The Levels Form of Divisia Indexes

To derive explicit levels forms of equations (A3.5.3) and (A3.5.4) we need to introduce some new notation. Implicit in the ORANI-INT solution algorithm is a vector equation of the following form:

$$\mathbf{Z} = \mathbf{Z}_I + \gamma[\mathbf{Z}_F - \mathbf{Z}_I] \tag{A3.5.5}$$

where: $\mathbf{Z}$ is a vector of the model's exogenous variables; $\mathbf{Z}_I$ is a vector containing the values of the exogenous variables in the initial solution[3]; $\mathbf{Z}_F$ is a vector containing the preferred values of the exogenous variables; and γ is a scalar. Differences in the values of $\mathbf{Z}_I$ and $\mathbf{Z}_F$ reflect perturbations to the economic environment imposed by the modeller. For example, if the modeller is interested in examining the effects of increasing government expenditure (an exogenous variable in ORANI-INT) by 5 percent then the value of this variable in $\mathbf{Z}_F$ will be 10 percent bigger than in $\mathbf{Z}_I$. In computations of ORANI-INT $\mathbf{Z}_I$ and $\mathbf{Z}_F$ are treated as parameters.

We can deduce from ORANI-INT implicit functions for $P^{(3)}_{i,\bullet,t}$ and $X^{(3)}_{i,\bullet,t}$. We assume that these can be expressed explicitly as follows:

$$\mathbf{P} = \mathbf{P}(\gamma) \tag{A3.5.6}$$

$$\mathbf{X} = \mathbf{X}(\gamma) \tag{A3.5.7}$$

where $\mathbf{X}$ is the vector $\{X^{(3)}_{1,\bullet,t}, X^{(3)}_{2,\bullet,t}, \ldots, X^{(3)}_{13,\bullet,t}\}$ and $\mathbf{P}$ is the vector $\{P^{(3)}_{1,\bullet,t}, P^{(3)}_{2,\bullet,t}, \ldots, P^{(3)}_{13,\bullet,t}\}$ so that if $\mathbf{Z} = \mathbf{Z}_I$ then $d\mathbf{X} = d\mathbf{P} = dC_t = 0$.

An initial solution for ORANI-INT will contain values for C_t, $\mathbf{P}$, $\mathbf{X}$, $\mathbf{Z}$, $\mathbf{Z}_I$, $\mathbf{Z}_F$ and γ, say $\mathbf{S}_0 = \{C_{t,0}, \mathbf{P}_0, \mathbf{X}_0, \gamma_0, \mathbf{Z}_0, \mathbf{Z}_I, \mathbf{Z}_F\}$, that jointly satisfy equations (A3.5.1) and (A3.5.5) — (A3.5.7). Note that the subscript 0 does not refer to time. Rather it refers to the initial solution of the equation system. We have not put 0 subscripts on $\mathbf{Z}_I$ and $\mathbf{Z}_F$ because they do not vary between solutions. In the initial solution γ is set to zero (i.e.,$\gamma_0 = 0$) and $\mathbf{Z}_0 = \mathbf{Z}_I$. The vector $\mathbf{Z}_F$ contains revised values of the model's exogenous variables. As will be explained in chapter 4 the ORANI-INT solution method involves moving from the initial solution, $\mathbf{S}_0$, to the final solution $\mathbf{S}_F$ (i.e., the solution in which the exogenous variables are set to the desired values) in a series of N steps. Under this system a computation involves perturbing the scalar γ from γ_{n-1} to γ_n (i.e., $\gamma_n = \gamma_{n-1} + d\gamma$) and finding a new solution to equations (A3.5.1) and (A3.5.5) — (A3.5.7), say $\mathbf{S}_n = \{C_{t,n}, \mathbf{P}_n, \mathbf{X}_n, \gamma_n, \mathbf{Z}_n, \mathbf{Z}_I, \mathbf{Z}_F\}$. In the final solution, $\mathbf{S}_N = \{C_{t,N}, \mathbf{P}_N, \mathbf{X}_N, \gamma_N, \mathbf{Z}_N, \mathbf{Z}_I, \mathbf{Z}_F\}$, γ equals one (i.e., $\gamma_N = 1$) and $\mathbf{Z}_N = \mathbf{Z}_F$.

The two points $\mathbf{S}_{n-1}$ and $\mathbf{S}_n$ are connected by *P*, a path which is characterised by $\{C_t(\gamma), \mathbf{P}(\gamma), \mathbf{X}(\gamma)\}$, $\gamma \in [\gamma_{n-1}, \gamma_n]$. At any point on the path *P*,

$$C_t(\gamma) = \sum_{i=1}^{13} P^{(3)}_{i,\bullet,t}(\gamma) X^{(3)}_{i,\bullet,t}(\gamma) \qquad t = 1, \ldots, T \tag{A3.5.8}$$

3 See chapter 5 for a discussion about an initial solution of ORANI-INT.

and the rules for moving along this path can be derived by differentiating the logarithmic form of equation (A3.5.8) with respect to γ as follows:

$$\frac{d\ln C_t(\gamma)}{d\gamma} = \frac{\dot{C}_t(\gamma)}{C_t(\gamma)} = \sum_{i=1}^{13} \frac{\dot{P}^{(3)}_{i,\bullet,t}(\gamma) X^{(3)}_{i,\bullet,t}(\gamma)}{C_t(\gamma)} + \sum_{i=1}^{13} \frac{P^{(3)}_{i,\bullet,t}(\gamma) \dot{X}^{(3)}_{i,\bullet,t}(\gamma)}{C_t(\gamma)}; \qquad t = 1, \ldots, T \qquad \text{(A3.5.9)}$$

where,

$$\dot{P}^{(3)}_{i,\bullet,t}(\gamma) = \frac{\partial P^{(3)}_{i,\bullet,t}(\gamma)}{\partial \gamma} \text{ and } \dot{X}^{(3)}_{i,\bullet,t}(\gamma) = \frac{\partial X^{(3)}_{i,\bullet,t}(\gamma)}{\partial \gamma}.$$

We additively decompose movements along *P* into those emanating from changes in quantities only and those emanating from changes in prices only. That is:

$$\frac{\dot{C}_t(\gamma)}{C_t(\gamma)} = \frac{\dot{C}_t^{(R)}(\gamma)}{C_t^{(R)}(\gamma)} + \frac{\dot{C}_t^{(\Pi)}(\gamma)}{C_t^{(\Pi)}(\gamma)}; \qquad t = 1, \ldots, T \qquad \text{(A3.5.10)}$$

where,

$$\frac{\dot{C}_t^{(\Pi)}(\gamma)}{C_t^{(\Pi)}(\gamma)} = \sum_{i=1}^{13} \frac{\dot{P}^{(3)}_{i,\bullet,t}(\gamma) X^{(3)}_{i,\bullet,t}(\gamma)}{C_t(\gamma)}; \text{ and} \qquad t = 1, \ldots, T \qquad \text{(A3.5.11)}$$

$$\frac{\dot{C}_t^{(R)}(\gamma)}{C_t^{(R)}(\gamma)} = \sum_{i=1}^{13} \frac{P^{(3)}_{i,\bullet,t}(\gamma) \dot{X}^{(3)}_{i,\bullet,t}(\gamma)}{C_t(\gamma)}. \qquad t = 1, \ldots, T \qquad \text{(A3.5.12)}$$

Note that equations (A3.5.11) and (A3.5.12) are analogous to equations (A3.5.3) and (A3.5.4). The levels forms of the price and quantity index used in ORANI-INT can be derived by integrating equations (A3.5.11) and (A3.5.12) as follows:

$$\frac{C_t^{(\Pi)}(\gamma)}{C_t^{(\Pi)}(\gamma_0)} = \exp \int_{\gamma_0}^{\gamma} \sum_{i=1}^{13} \frac{\dot{P}^{(3)}_{i,\bullet,t}(g) X^{(3)}_{i,\bullet,t}(g)}{C_t(g)} dg \text{ ;and} \qquad t = 1, \ldots, T \qquad \text{(A3.5.13)}$$

$$\frac{C_t^{(R)}(\gamma)}{C_t^{(R)}(\gamma_0)} = \exp \int_{\gamma_0}^{\gamma} \sum_{i=1}^{13} \frac{P^{(3)}_{i,\bullet}(g) \dot{X}^{(3)}_{i,\bullet}(g)}{C_t(g)} dg \qquad t = 1, \ldots, T \qquad \text{(A3.5.14)}$$

Note that at all points γ along the path from γ_0 to γ_N,

$$C_t^{(\Pi)}(\gamma) \times C_t^{(R)}(\gamma) = \frac{C_t(\gamma)}{C_t(\gamma_0)}. \qquad t = 1, \ldots, T \qquad \text{(A3.5.15)}$$

A3.5.4 Why Use Divisia Indexes?

Whether the path dependence property of Divisia indexes poses serious practical problems for ORANI-INT remains an open question. In our experience the consequences of path dependent price and quantity indexes have not been perceptible in ORANI-INT solutions. This is not surprising since our use of Divisia indexes is confined, with one exception[4], to the construction of useful reporting variables. These variables are useful for understanding and communicating the model's results but do not impact upon the rest of the model.

Whilst the path dependence property of Divisia indexes may not pose serious practical problems for ORANI-INT, our use of such indexes, rather than Laspeyres or Paasche indexes, warrants further explanation. As indicated above, our justification for using Divisia indexes in ORANI-INT is computational convenience. The ease with which Divisia indexes can be implemented in GEMPACK has already been explained. Laspeyres indexes are a little more tedious to implement in GEMPACK than are Divisia indexes. The Laspeyres indexes corresponding to equations (A3.5.3) and (A3.5.4) can be written as follows:

$$c_t^{(\Pi,\mathrm{Las})} = \sum_{i=1}^{13} \bar{S}_{i,\bullet,t}^{(3)}\, p_{i,\bullet,t}^{(3)} \text{ ; and} \qquad t = 1, \ldots, T \quad \text{(A3.5.16)}$$

$$c_t^{(\mathrm{R},\mathrm{Las})} = \sum_{i=1}^{13} \bar{S}_{i,\bullet,t}^{(3)}\, x_{i,\bullet,t}^{(3)}. \qquad t = 1, \ldots, T \quad \text{(A3.5.17)}$$

In equations (A3.5.16) and (A3.5.17),

$$\bar{S}_{i,\bullet,t}^{(3)} = \frac{P_{i,\bullet,t}^{(3)}(\gamma_0)X_{i,\bullet,t}^{(3)}(\gamma_0)}{C_t(\gamma_0)}. \qquad t = 1, \ldots, T \quad \text{(A3.5.18)}$$

The key difference between the Divisia indexes, equations (A3.5.3) and (A3.5.4), and their Laspeyres counterparts, equations (A3.5.16) and (A3.5.17), is that the coefficients in the latter are constant. In the context of GEMPACK the coefficients (or weights) in the Laspeyres indexes, given by equation (A3.5.18), are evaluated in the initial step (i.e., γ_0) of an N-step Euler computation only. The values of these coefficients remain unchanged throughout an N-step computation. Thus, relative to Divisia indexes, Laspeyres indexes such as (A3.5.16) and (A3.5.17) introduce a small additional computational burden — the initial solution values of the coefficients (weights) that appear in Laspeyres indexes must be retained throughout an N-step Euler computation.[5]

---

4 The exception is the Divisia index that defines real government spending. This variable is exogenous and may, if shocked, impact on other variables in the model.

5 The procedure for retaining the initial-solution values of coefficients has become routine in recent versions of GEMPACK.

Paasche indexes are harder to implement in GEMPACK than both Divisia and Laspeyres indexes. Paasche indexes have the same form as Laspeyres indexes such as (A3.5.16) and (A3.5.17). The key difference between Laspeyres and Paasche indexes is that the former use initial-solution weights (i.e., the coefficients are evaluated at γ_0) whilst the latter use final-solution weights (i.e., the coefficients are evaluated at γ_N). Since the values of the coefficients in Paasche indexes are unknown until the N-step Euler computation has been completed, a preliminary guess of the values of the coefficients must be provided and an iterative scheme for revising this guess must be implemented.

Chapter 4 Solution Method

4.1 Introduction

As explained in chapter 1 intertemporal CGE models such as ORANI-INT have the potential to be powerful tools for economic analysis. However, because of their size and complexity detailed intertemporal CGE models will be of practical use to policy-makers only if accurate solutions can be obtained at reasonable cost. In a survey of CGE modelling, Manne (1985) observed that for the purposes of computational tractability, the dimensions of intertemporal CGE models are typically reduced by adopting two assumptions; first, that "capital stocks are homogeneous (not specific to sectors or to regions), and that there are only a few types of capital stock variables" and second, that there are always interior solutions. The purpose of this chapter is to describe how a hybrid of the Euler and Newton-Raphson methods can be used to solve ORANI-INT without resorting to such dimensionality reduction schemes.

4.1.1 A Note on the Semantics Used in this Chapter

Euler's method is used to integrate an equation system from one solution to another. For this reason, the method can be used to solve *initial value* problems only. An initial value problem is characterised by at least one known solution of the equation system. However, the integration of an equation system via Euler's method may, or may not, be through time. For example, in solving ORANI, a single period model, Dixon *et al* (1982) use Euler's method to integrate their equation system over different values of exogenous variables but at a single point in time. Their computations start from a solution that represents the economy in equilibrium in a particular period. Euler's method is used to find a different equilibrium state of the economy for the same period but in which the values of the exogenous variables are different.

Euler's method can also be used to integrate an equation system through time. For example, if we had a model in which time appeared as an explicit variable and for which solution values of all variables in some period, say $t = 0$, are known, then Euler's method could be used to obtain solutions for other periods by integrating the model through time.

To solve ORANI-INT we use Euler's method in the same way that it is used in Dixon *et al* (1982). That is, time is not an explicit variable. Instead, the variables of the model are given time subscripts and Euler's method is used to integrate our equation system over different values of the exogenous variables.

Often the solution from which the Euler integration process begins is referred to as the *initial* solution. Since the integration of the equation system need not be through time, the adjective *initial* does not have any temporal connotations. To avoid confusion we avoid using the term initial solution. Instead, we refer to the solution from which the integration process begins as the *base* solution. For an intertemporal model such as ORANI-INT, the base solution consists of time-paths for all variables that satisfy all the static and intertemporal equations of the model. Where necessary we distinguish a base solution for a single period model from that of a multi period model by adding the qualifier *intertemporal* when we refer to the base solution of the latter.

In this, and subsequent, chapters we also refer to a *control* path solution. A control path solution (or control path for short) is a special type of intertemporal base solution. An intertemporal base solution qualifies as a control path solution if the paths of the exogenous variables are set to their expected or preferred trajectories.[1]

4.2 Alternative Solution Methods

A multi-period CGE model such as ORANI-INT may be represented as follows:

$$
\begin{array}{ll}
F_{1,t}(V_t) = 0 & \\
\vdots & \\
F_{h,t}(V_t) = 0 & \\
\hline
 & t = 1, \ldots, T \qquad (4.2.1) \\
F_{h+1}(V_0, V_1 \ldots, V_{T+1}) = 0 & \\
\vdots & \\
F_{h+m}(V_0, V_1 \ldots, V_{T+1}) = 0 &
\end{array}
$$

In system (4.2.1) the $F_{i,t}$, i=1,...,h, and F_{h+j}, j=1,...,m, are h+m differentiable functions (some or all of which may be non-linear). The first h of these functions represent the atemporal equations which inter-relate V, the variables, at the same point in time (i.e., they represent the single-period CGE submodels). The remaining m functions represent the dynamic equations which relate variables at

1 See chapter 5 for further discussion on the nature of a control path solution.

different, often adjacent, points in time (i.e., they link the single-period CGE sub-models through time). There are two main strategies for solving such multi-period models:

(a) solve for each period in turn; and,

(b) solve all periods simultaneously.

If agents in the model represented by system (4.2.1) had static (or backward-looking) expectations, method (a) would be ideal. A model without forward-looking expectations can be treated as an initial value problem. If current decisions are not affected by future variables, the values of all variables in the first period can be inferred from historical data. Thus, the endogenous variables in any future period may be obtained by solving the model recursively through time (i.e., period by period).

Forward-looking behaviour complicates solution of a system such as (4.2.1) because the values of some variables in period t depend on the values of variables in future periods. In order to solve such a problem uniquely, terminal period values (i.e., terminal conditions) must be specified for those variables for which initial period values are not available (i.e., initial conditions). An equation system with these types of boundary conditions, (i.e., some that hold in the initial period and some that hold in the terminal period) is typically treated as a two-point boundary value problem.

Two-point boundary value problems are much harder to solve than initial value problems [see Press, *et al.* (1986)]. The numerical methods used for solving such problems fall into two main categories, namely; *shooting* and *relaxation.* The relative merits of these methods[2] for solving intertemporal CGE models are discussed in Dixon, *et al.* (1992). Although most economic models with rational expectations are solved using shooting type techniques some modellers, including Bovenberg (1985), Hall (1985) and Wilcoxen (1985), have experimented with relaxation methods.

4.2.1 Shooting Methods

Shooting algorithms use initial value methods to integrate the equation system from the initial to the terminal period. The values of some of the time dependent variables are known in the initial period (i.e., they can be inferred from observed data) while the remainder are known in the terminal period (i.e., they are exogenously specified or implied by economic theory). In order to use initial value methods to integrate the equation system forward through time, a trial solution consisting of the values of all time dependent variables must be specified in the first period. The values of variables for which initial conditions are unavailable must be guessed. Starting from the trial solution the equation system is integrated forward one period at a time. Since the terminal values of some variables are known prior to the integration procedure, a solution will obtain when there are no

---

2 Dixon *et al* (1992) refer to the relaxation method as the finite difference method.

significant discrepancies between the previously known and the computed terminal values of these variables. If there are intolerable discrepancies, the guesses made about the values of variables whose initial conditions are unknown must be revised and the procedure repeated.

The 'pure' shooting method, described above, is prone to numerical instability. A small error in the trial values assigned to the unknown initial conditions can result in very large and uncontrollable errors after integration over a small number of periods. To overcome the problem of numerical instability, the 'multiple' shooting method divides the period over which the model is to be integrated into a number of smaller sub-periods (see Lipton *et al*, 1982). The 'pure' shooting method is then used over these smaller sub-periods.

The gain in numerical stability achieved via the 'multiple' shooting method comes at considerable cost in terms of computing effort. For example, if the model is to be integrated over 20 periods the atemporal equations of the model must be solved at least that many times. In practice, the atemporal core of the model will have to be solved many more times since there will be as many sets of trial values of the unknown initial conditions as there are sub-periods. Revision of any one of these trial solutions will require the model to be integrated again over the 20 periods hence requiring the atemporal core of the model to be solved another 20 times. In the example given, if the 20 period time horizon was divided into 5 even sub-periods then a single revision of each of the five sets of trial values of the unknown initial conditions would require the atemporal core of the model to be solved 100 times.

The most commonly used algorithms for solving economic models with model-consistent expectations are based on the extended path method developed by Fair and Taylor (1983). The Fair-Taylor technique is a special case of multiple shooting. However, it is far more efficient than standard multiple shooting techniques because the algorithm exploits the structure of the model. In variants of the Fair-Taylor technique different approaches to exploiting the structure of the equation system are used to speed up computations (see, for example, Powell and Murphy, 1997).

For a model of the size and structure of ORANI-INT shooting methods may be overly restrictive. The temptation with such methods is to minimise the number of unknown initial conditions by reducing the number of intertemporal linkages modelled. This is often achieved, for example, by modelling a single type of capital only. Alternatively, the efficiency of a shooting algorithm can be improved by clever exploitation of a model's structure. The disadvantage of this latter approach is that the improvement in efficiency gained be exploiting the structure of a model comes at the cost of reducing the flexibility of the algorithm. For example, it may not be possible to change the model's theoretical structure and database or to change the partitioning of variables between the endogenous and exogenous categories without re-crafting the solution algorithm.

4.2.2 Relaxation Methods

Relaxation methods differ from the shooting algorithms in that endogenous variables at all periods are solved simultaneously. This method requires that there be as many independent equations in the model as there are endogenous variables. Typically, a trial solution consisting of the values of all variables at each point in time is iteratively revised ('relaxed') until all the equations of the model (including all difference equations and boundary conditions) are satisfied.

For models specified in continuous time, the solution process is preceded by the replacement of differential equations with finite difference equations. A mesh or grid is then defined, dividing the time horizon of interest into intervals of time over which the finite difference equations are assumed to approximate the original differential equations. In this case, the trial solution consists of the values of all variables at each grid point. This technique is used, for example, by Wilcoxen (1985) to solve an illustrative investment model and by Dixon *et al* (1992) to solve a small intertemporal CGE model.

Because the endogenous variables at all periods are solved simultaneously, relaxation methods allow complete freedom in the structure of intertemporal links; the end-point conditions appear explicitly as part of the equation system. However, as argued by Press *et al.* (1986), solving systems of nonlinear simultaneous equations via relaxation methods may be very inefficient. They suggest that the Newton-Raphson method might be efficient in finding a solution to such a problem if provided with a trial solution that is in the neighbourhood of the true solution. For large models however, it is very difficult to provide a trial solution (i.e., guesses of the time paths of all endogenous variables) that is close to the true solution and then to revise it iteratively. Again, the temptation is to keep the size of the model small, particularly by minimising the number of intertemporal linkages. Wilcoxen (1985) for example, concludes that "it may be impossible to model each sector's investment independently in a highly disaggregated model".

4.3 The ORANI-INT Solution Algorithm

The method used to solve ORANI-INT falls into the relaxation class of solution methods in that the values of all endogenous variables are determined in a single computational process. The model is initially formulated in discrete time so that the finite differencing process is not required. The inefficiency problems associated with relaxation methods are avoided by ensuring that computations always start from an intertemporal base solution.

The algorithm exploits the ability of the GEMPACK software (see Pearson (1988)) to solve large systems of simultaneous non-linear equations using Euler's method. Since the solution of a rational expectations model involves solving a two-point boundary value problem the choice of Euler's method, which can be used to solve initial value problems only, is not natural. For a special class of rational expectations models however, initial value methods, such as Euler's, may be used.

This class of models includes those for which an intertemporal base solution is already known. The problem then becomes one of moving from the known solution to the sought-after solution. Since this process characterises exactly an initial value problem, Euler's method can be used solve it.

The use of Euler's method to solve intertemporal economic models is discussed in Codsi, Pearson and Wilcoxen (1991). It is used successfully by Dixon *et al* (1992) to solve their small intertemporal CGE model. They use a steady state intertemporal base solution (i.e., the values of the variables are the same in each period), constructed from hypothetical data, as the starting point for Euler calculations. This solution is obtained via a side calculation in which all time differences in the model are exogenous. The model is then used to examine the effects of perturbations about the steady state solution. Thus, in Dixon *et al* the steady state solution serves as the intertemporal base solution as well as the control path solution.

Dixon *et al* argue that a steady state solution constitutes a perfectly acceptable control path for many policy experiments and that any limitations are offset by the ease with which it can be constructed. To assess this argument it is helpful to keep the computational and economic issues separate.

From the computational perspective the steady state solution provides an intertemporal base solution that allows Euler's method to be used to find other solutions. Euler's method cannot, however, be used to compute the steady state solution. It is not obvious that a steady state solution will be easy to obtain for all intertemporal CGE models. The side calculation required to obtain the steady state solution involves solving a system of simultaneous nonlinear equations (i.e., the static version of the model). For large models this may not be a trivial task.

The use of the steady state solution as a control path for comparative dynamic simulations may be quite limiting. There are good economic reasons why computational expediency should, as far as possible, not constrain the choice of control path used. If the model were to be used for forecasting, for example, it would be appropriate to use a control path in which the values of variables in the first year reflect the most recently available data about the state of the economy. Similarly, in many comparative dynamic experiments interest lies in what effects a change in policy (or circumstance) will have on the current, not hypothetical steady state, growth path of the economy.[3] In principle, if a steady state solution is available it can be treated as an intertemporal base solution and Euler's method may be used to generate alternative control path scenarios. Non-steady state control paths have not been widely exploited despite their potential advantages.

The ORANI-INT solution algorithm is a hybrid of the Euler and Newton-Raphson methods. In the following sub-sections we review the Euler method and outline a scheme by which it can be modified to avoid the problems associated with obtaining an intertemporal base solution. The modifications to Euler's method

---

[3] The current growth path of the economy is not known with any certainty and must itself be forecast. Comparative dynamic experiments of this type constitute sensitivity analysis on the forecast growth path of the economy.

result in an algorithm, which is very similar to the Newton-Raphson method. As will be explained, these similarities are exploited to obtain a hybrid of the two methods which allows inequality constraints to be handled efficiently and makes the process of generating alternative control path scenarios very easy.

4.3.1 The Euler Method

The intertemporal CGE model represented by system (4.2.1) may be further summarised as:

$$F(Y, X) = 0. \tag{4.3.1}$$

The notation used here is different from that used in (4.2.1); specifically, F is a matrix of differentiable functions, Y is a vector of endogenous variables and X is a vector of exogenous variables. In system (4.3.1) no distinction is made between difference (in time) equations and other equations in the model. Similarly, no distinction is made between time dependent variables and other variables.

Suppose particular values {X, Y} satisfy (4.3.1). Since F is differentiable, it may be locally represented by a system of first-order differential equations:

$$F'_Y(Y, X)dY + F'_X(Y, X)dX = 0 \tag{4.3.2}$$

where $F'_Y(Y, X)$ is the derivative matrix corresponding to the endogenous variables and $F'_X(Y, X)$ is the derivative matrix corresponding to the exogenous variables. The differential equations (4.3.2) provide the rules for moving from (Y_0, X_0), an intertemporal base solution, to (Y_n, X_n), some other intertemporal solution.

Having specified an intertemporal base solution [i.e., the vector (Y_0, X_0)], a solution for the changes in the values of the endogenous variables brought about by changes in the values of the exogenous variables may be obtained via:

$$dY = -F'_Y(Y_0, X_0)^{-1} F'_X(Y_0, X_0)\, dX \tag{4.3.3}$$

where,

$$dX = X_F - X_0 \tag{4.3.4}$$

and the subscript F denotes the forecast or final value of the exogenous variables. Note that the subscripts in (4.3.3) and (4.3.4) do not have any temporal connotations. This convention will be maintained for the remainder of the chapter.

The solution method implied by (4.3.3) corresponds closely to the Johansen method used to solve ORANI. The difference is that ORANI uses percentage changes rather than ordinary changes. A base solution or equilibrium is typically provided by input-output data (supplemented by external parameter estimates) and results are interpreted as percentage deviations from the initial equilibrium.

There are three key reasons why, even for very large models, the Johansen method is computationally tractable. First, the levels equations of the model [i.e., system (4.3.1)] need not be evaluated since a base solution satisfying these equations is assumed. Second, approximating the model by a system of simultaneous linear equations [i.e., (4.3.2)] means that the model may be easily condensed via substitution – this process is not always straightforward with the original non-linear equation system. Third, the homogeneity properties of economic models (i.e., units of measurement are irrelevant) are exploited so that the formulae for percentage change derivative matrices tend to be very simple. All coefficients are either dimensionless parameters or ratios of flows (i.e., price × quantity).

The simplicity of the derivative formulae can be demonstrated by comparing a non-linear CES factor demand function to its linearised counterpart. The non-linear form of the CES factor demand equation can be expressed as follows:

$$Y_{i,j} = Q_j \delta_{i,j}^{[1/(1+\rho)]} P_{i,j}^{-[1/(1+\rho)]} \left\{ \sum_k \delta_{k,j}^{[1/(1+\rho)]} P_{k,j}^{-[\rho/(1+\rho)]} \right\}^{\frac{1}{\rho}},$$

while its linearised counterpart is:

$$y_{i,j} = q_j - \sigma_j \left(p_{i,j} - \sum_k S_{k,j} p_{k,j} \right).$$

In these equations the subscripts i and j denote factors and industries. In the non-linear equation δ and ρ are parameters (with $-1 < \rho \neq 0$ and $\Sigma_i \delta_i = 0$) and Y, Q, and P denote factor demands, the activity level and factor prices respectively. In the linearised equation σ is the elasticity of substitution between factors, S is the share of factor i in industry j's factor costs and y, q and p denote the percentage changes in the variables Y, Q and P. Calibration of the non-linear factor demand equation is tedious whereas for the linear equation we simply require estimates of the dimensionless parameters σ_i as well as values for the coefficients $S_{k,j}$. The parameters σ_i are typically obtained from econometric studies while the coefficients $S_{k,j}$ are ratios of flows that can be read directly from input-output data.

Since system (4.3.3) is only a local representation of the levels equations (4.3.1) suggested by economic theory, the results obtained via (4.3.3) are valid for 'small' changes in the exogenous variables only. Figure 4.1 illustrates this for a simple model with only two scalar variables.[4] Given an intertemporal base solution at H, the function F(Y, X) is approximated in the neighbourhood of H by its slope at that point. An exogenous shock to variable X, which moves it from X_0 to X_F, results in Y moving from Y_0 to Y_1. Clearly, the solution obtained via (4.3.3) introduces an approximation error (in this case equivalent to $Y_{TRUE} - Y_1$) which can be ignored only for small changes in the exogenous variables.

There is no formal guidance as to what constitutes a 'small' change in an exogenous variable. The 'small' change concept is relative to both the particular model to be solved and to the particular application (i.e., which variables are exogenous and which of these variables are shocked). In general, there is no simple

---

4 All diagrams in this paper employ the vector notation used in the text but for simplicity assume that the variables are scalars.

way of determining *a priori* whether the degree of approximation error introduced by the Johansen solution procedure will be significant.

To control the degree of approximation error the Euler method divides the shocks to the exogenous variables into a sequence of N smaller parts. That is:

$$dX_n = \frac{X_F - X_0}{N}. \tag{4.3.5}$$

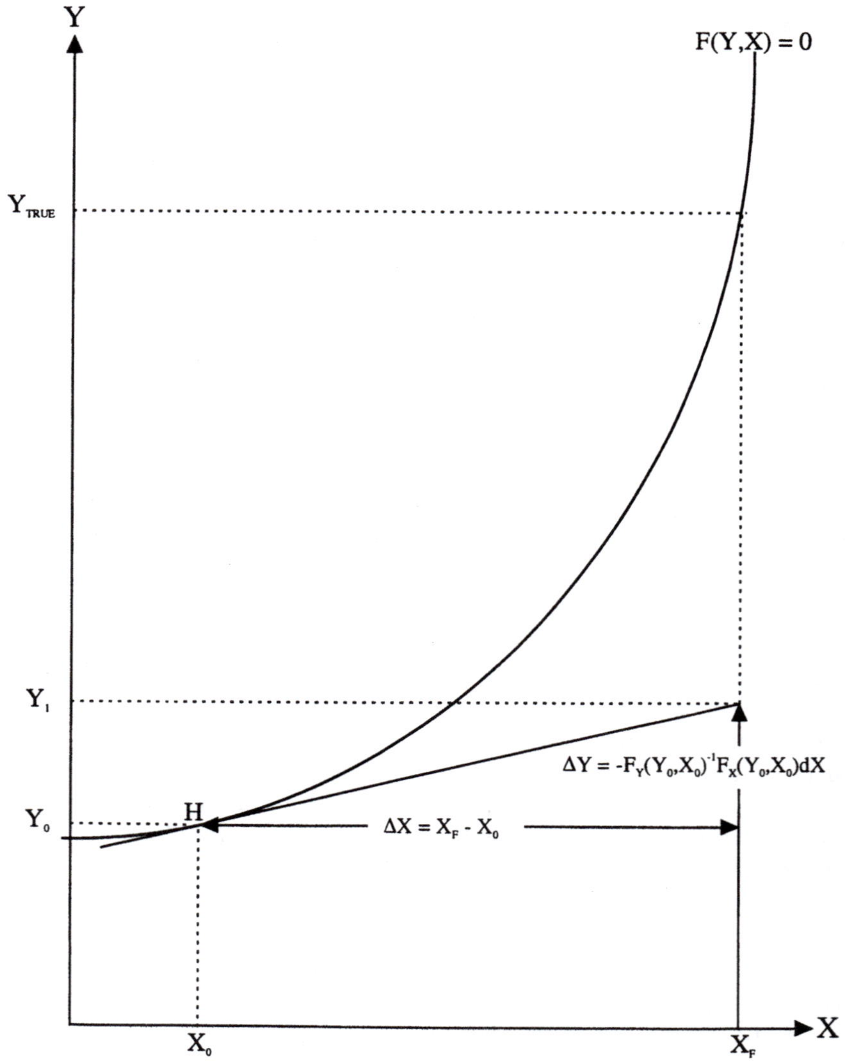

Figure 4.1: The Johansen or 1-Step Euler Method

The first part of the shock is applied and the effects on the endogenous variables are calculated. The database is then revised to account for the exogenous and endogenous consequences of the first part of the shock using the revision rules:

$$X_{n+1} = X_n + \frac{(X_F - X_0)}{N} \qquad n = 0,1, \ldots, N-1 \qquad (4.3.6)$$

and,

$$Y_{n+1} = Y_n - F_Y'(Y_n, X_n)^{-1} F_X'(Y_n, X_n) \frac{(X_F - X_0)}{N}. \qquad n = 0,1, \ldots, N-1 \qquad (4.3.7)$$

At the next step, the derivative matrices in system (4.3.3) are re-evaluated using the revised data (i.e., Y_n, X_n). In the CES example above, this means that the shares $S_{k,j}$ are revised at each step. This procedure is repeated N times and is known as the N-step Euler method. Note that when N=1 the Euler method corresponds to Johansen's method.

If F is continuous and differentiable over the relevant ranges of X and Y, and if derivatives are bounded in these ranges, results which are as close to the exact solution as machine accuracy allows may be obtained by choosing N large enough (see Dixon, Parmenter, Sutton and Vincent (1982) and Pearson (1991)). Figure 4.2 illustrates how taking more Euler steps may reduce the linearisation error. The larger is N, the closer are the approximate solutions generated at each step to the genuine root vectors along the curve F(Y, X) = 0, and the more accurately do the derivatives at each step approximate the slope of that curve.[5]

From a computational point of view, Euler's method may be rather inefficient. Convergence to a result that is free of significant linearisation errors may require a large number of steps. Indeed, the number of steps may be required to increase by a factor of ten for each additional significant figure of accuracy in the endogenous variables. One way of minimising this convergence problem is to supplement Euler's method with an extrapolation technique such as Richardson's (see Dixon *et al*, 1982 and Pearson, 1991), so that results which are free of significant linearisation errors may be obtained with a smaller number of calculations. A pathological case in which the Euler method will fail is illustrated in figure 4.3; for the intertemporal base solution, $\{Y_0, X_0\}$, the derivative matrix $F_Y'(Y_0, X_0)$ is singular.

A problem of more practical significance with Euler's method is that an intertemporal base solution to the model is required. In the above discussion we assumed that an intertemporal base solution (Y_0, X_0) that satisfied (4.3.1) exactly was available. For atemporal models this is normally provided by an observed or historical set of data; for intertemporal models, however, a solution consists of time-series data that are consistent with the equations of the model. Unfortunately, such data are rarely available.

---

5 Comparison of results for different values of N also allows us to place bounds on the error associated with a particular finite value of N.

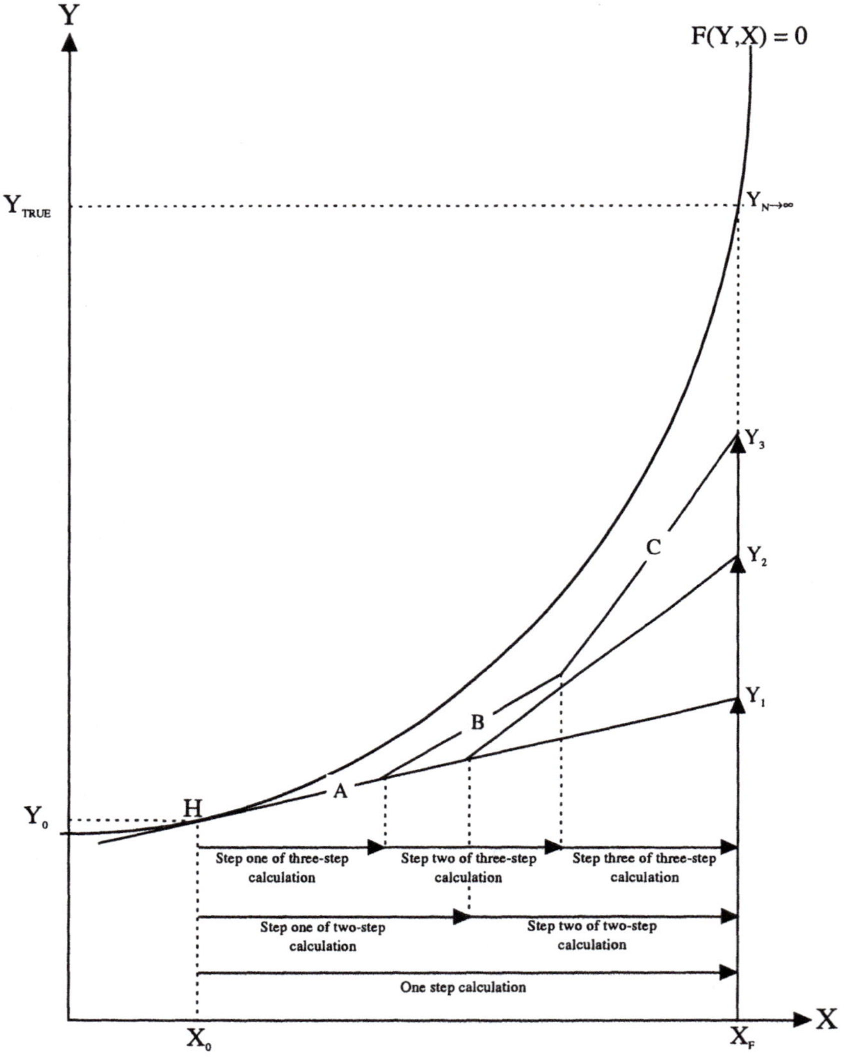

Figure 4.2: Euler Multi-step Method

The homotopy principle (see Zangwill and Garcia, 1981) can be conveniently employed to modify system (4.3.1) so that an intertemporal base solution will always be available. Rather than starting by attempting to find a database which satisfies the given non-linear equations of the intertemporal model the strategy is to temporarily modify the equation system to satisfy a database which is easily constructed. Having obtained a solution for the modified equation system it is then possible to find other solutions (including a solution of the original equation system) using Euler's method. We do this by modifying system (4.3.1) as follows:

$$G(Y, X, S,) = F(Y, X) - S = 0. \tag{4.3.8}$$

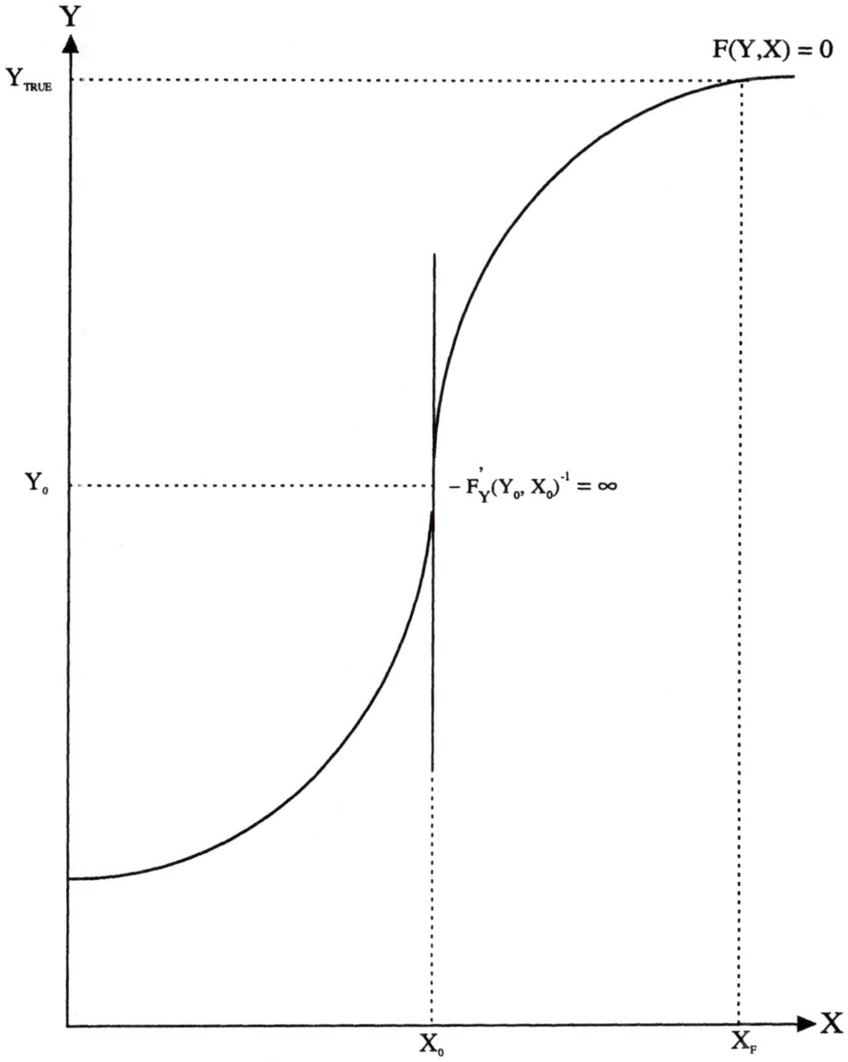

Figure 4.3: Euler Method: A Pathological Case

In contrast to (4.3.1), system (4.3.8) includes S, an additive slack vector variable (formally, a vector of homotopy parameters). Note that when S = 0 systems (4.3.1) and (4.3.8) are equivalent.

If an intertemporal base solution for (4.3.1) is not available $\tilde{Y}_0$, a guess of the timepaths of all endogenous variables must be made. Given this guess, the slack vector will adopt a value that satisfies (4.3.8). That is:

$$S_0 = F(\tilde{Y}_0, X_0) . \qquad (4.3.9)$$

The vector variable S will only adopt a zero value if the initial solution vector exactly satisfies (4.3.1). Having obtained (by construction) an initial solution for the augmented equation system (4.3.8), it is then possible to find other solutions using Euler's method.

Since the objective is to obtain an intertemporal base solution for the original equation system (4.3.1), the slack variables in (4.3.8) must always be shocked back to zero as follows:

$$dS_n = -\frac{S_0}{N} = -\frac{F(\tilde{Y}_0, X_0)}{N}. \qquad n = 0, 1, ..., N \qquad (4.3.10)$$

Assuming that X, the exogenous variables from the original equation system, are held constant, shocking the slack variables to zero will yield an intertemporal base solution that satisfies system (4.3.1). In this scheme, the rule for revising the values of the slack variables after each step of the solution process is:

$$S_{n+1} = S_n + \frac{(S_F - S_0)}{N}. \qquad n = 0,1,2, ..., N-1 \qquad (4.3.11)$$

By construction S_F, the final value of the slack variables, is zero. The revision rule for the endogenous variables can be written as:

$$Y_{n+1} = Y_n - F_Y'(Y_n, X_n)^{-1}\frac{F(\tilde{Y}_0, X_0)}{N}. \qquad n = 0,1,2, ..., N-1 \qquad (4.3.12)$$

Figure 4.4 shows the effects of administering the shock to the slack variables in three steps. Again, more steps would lead to a more accurate solution. Note that the horizontal axis in this figure refers to S, not X.

As long as the slack variables are exogenously set to zero, any closure of the model (and any shocks to the other exogenous variables) could be used to construct an arbitrary intertemporal base solution to the original equation system. When both types of exogenous variables (i.e., S and X) in equation (4.3.8) are shocked simultaneously, the rules for revising the database will be:

$$X_{n+1} = X_n + \frac{(X_F - X_0)}{N} \qquad n = 0, 1, 2, ..., N-1 \qquad (4.3.13)$$

and

$$Y_{n+1} = Y_n - F_Y'(Y_n, X_n)^{-1}\left[F_X'(Y_n, X_n)\frac{(X_F - X_0)}{N} - \frac{F(\tilde{Y}_0, X_0)}{N}\right].$$

$$n = 0, 1, 2, ..., N-1 \qquad (4.3.14)$$

Since this process is difficult to represent diagrammatically because of its three dimensional nature, figure 4.5 is a projection of the implicit 3-dimensional {S, X, Y} figure onto the Y – X plane. The vectors A, B and C represent the changes in Y, the endogenous variables, with respect to changes in X, the exogenous variables. These vectors are similar to the A, B and C vectors in Figure 4.2 except that they are evaluated at different values of the endogenous variables. The new vectors a, b and c represent the changes in the endogenous variables with respect to changes in the slack variables; that is, the term:

$$F_Y'(Y_n, X_n)^{-1}\frac{F(\tilde{Y}_0, X_0)}{N}$$

in equation (4.3.14). They may also be seen in figure 4.4. Note that the derivative matrix corresponding to the endogenous variables in this expression is re-evaluated after each step of the solution procedure while the other term, the shock to the slack variables, is always evaluated at the values provided by the original guess (i.e., Y_n).

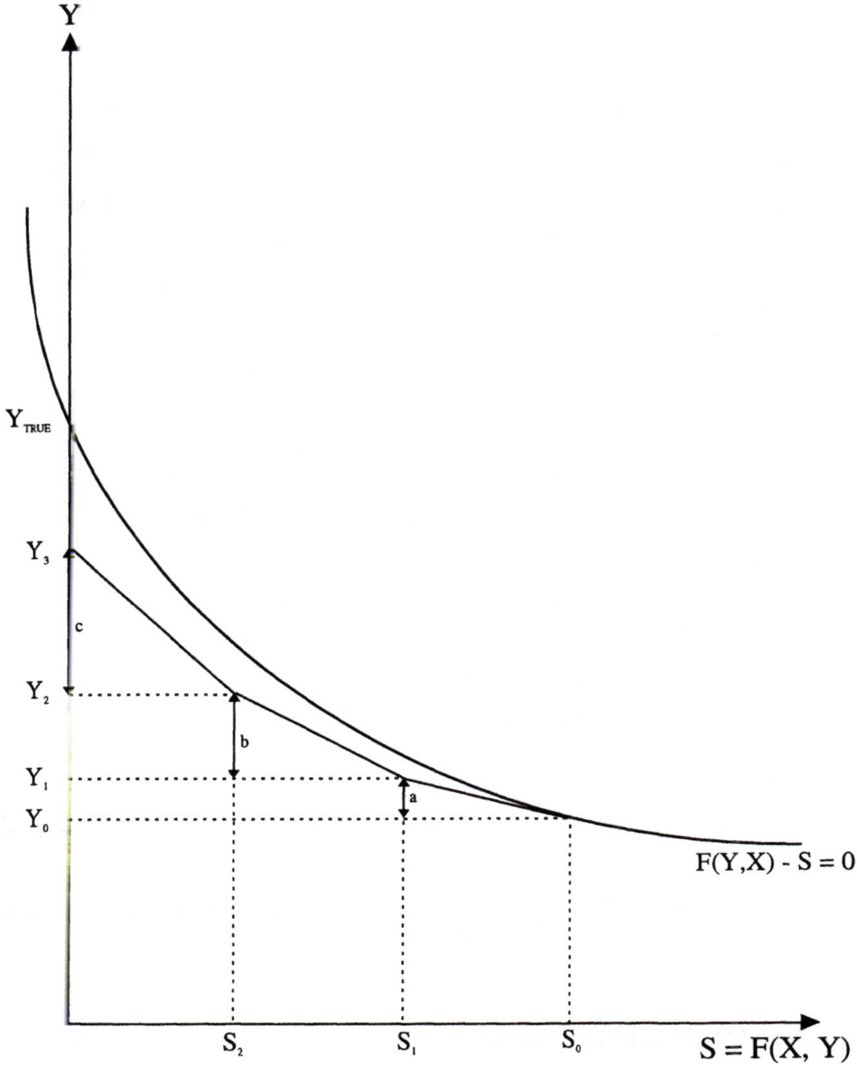

Figure 4.4: Three Step Euler Method Where the Initial Solution is Unknown and Exogenous Variable X is Held Constant

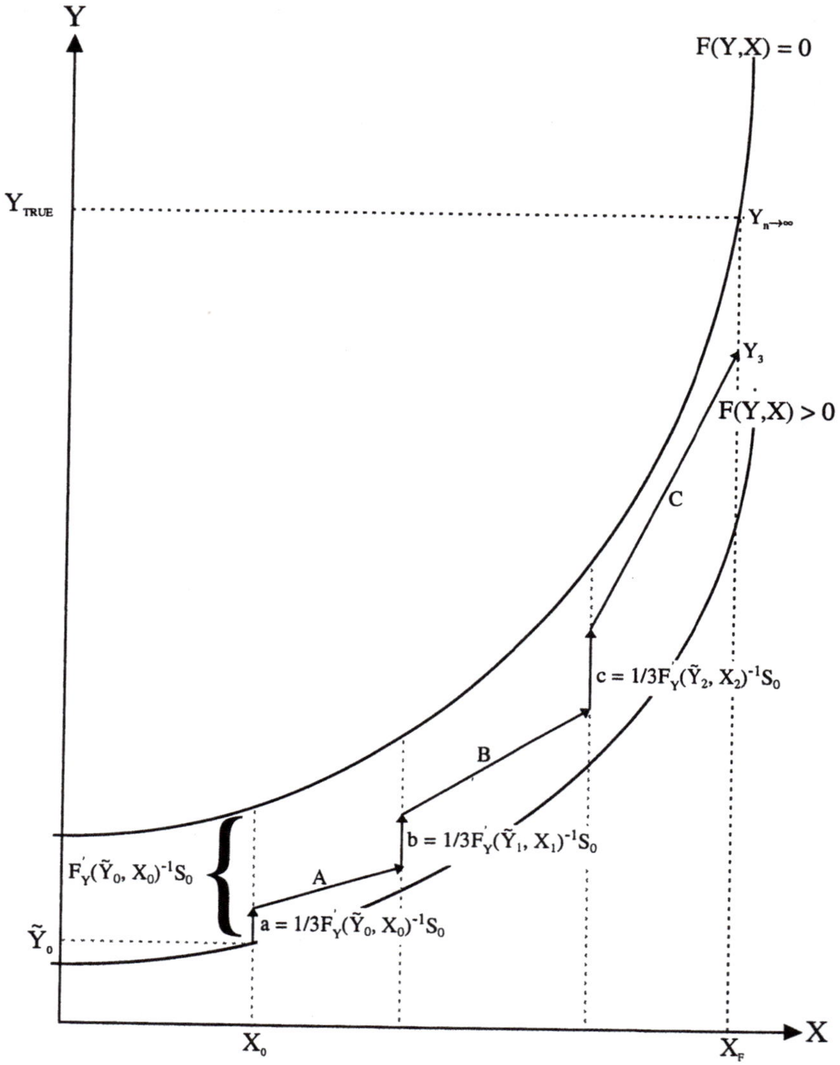

Figure 4.5: Three Step Euler Method: Initial Solution Unknown and Exogenous Variables X set to Forecast Values

4.3.2 Newton-Raphson Method

An alternative method for solving a system of simultaneous non-linear equations like (4.3.1) is the Newton-Raphson method. As normally used the Newton-Raphson method is similar to the method described above for obtaining an intertemporal base solution using Euler's method. To use the Newton-Raphson method system (4.3.1) is expressed as:

$$F(Y, X_F) = E. \tag{4.3.15}$$

A 'guess' or trial solution to system (4.3.1) must be specified. In the 'guess' or trial solution the exogenous variables are assigned their final or forecast values, X_F, and the values of the endogenous variables, Y, are 'guessed'. Using this trial solution the value of E is calculated. The solution to (4.3.15) sought is that where E = 0. The rules for moving from the trial solution to the desired solution are provided by the following system of first-order differential equations:

$$F'_Y(Y, X_F)\, dY + F'_X(Y, X_F)dX = dE\,. \tag{4.3.16}$$

Since the exogenous variables have been assigned their forecast values, they do not change (i.e., dX = 0). The change in the value of the error vector, dE, is set to –E and a revised solution of the endogenous variables is obtained via:

$$dY = -\,F'_Y(Y, X_F)^{-1}F(Y, X_F)\,. \tag{4.3.17}$$

Iterative revision of Y via (4.3.17) can reduce E to arbitrarily small values. The rule for revising the solution is as follows:

$$Y^{i+1} = Y^i - F'_Y(Y^i, X_F)^{-1}F(Y^i, X_F) \qquad i = 0,1,2, \ldots, I-1 \tag{4.3.18}$$

where the superscript i refers to the iteration number. The larger is I, the number of iterations, the more nearly Y^i approximates the true solution. Figure 4.6 shows how the Newton-Raphson method converges to the root vector from the original trial solution. While figure 4.6 shows the effects of 3 iterations only, in this example, the more iterations allowed, the greater the accuracy of the solution.

4.3.3 The Hybrid Method

The Newton-Raphson method is very efficient when the original 'guess' is in the neighbourhood of the root vector sought. Each additional iteration may halve any error in the endogenous variables. However, if the original 'guess' is far from the root vector sought, there is no guarantee of convergence. In contrast, Euler's method has slower convergence properties but, since calculations start from a known solution, it is possible to stay close to a root vector by choosing N, the number of steps, large enough.

The respective strengths of the two solution methods appear to be complementary so that a hybrid of the two is appealing. One strategy which has proved useful for dealing with highly non-linear equations (e.g., corner constraints) involves using a multi-step Euler calculation in which the approximation error accumulated in the previous step (n–1) is reduced via a single Newton-Raphson type calculation in the current step (n). The desirable stability properties of the Euler method are preserved by starting from an existing solution and by applying exogenous shocks in small steps. At small additional cost, a single Newton-Raphson error correction greatly reduces the approximation errors accumulated at each step of the Euler procedure.

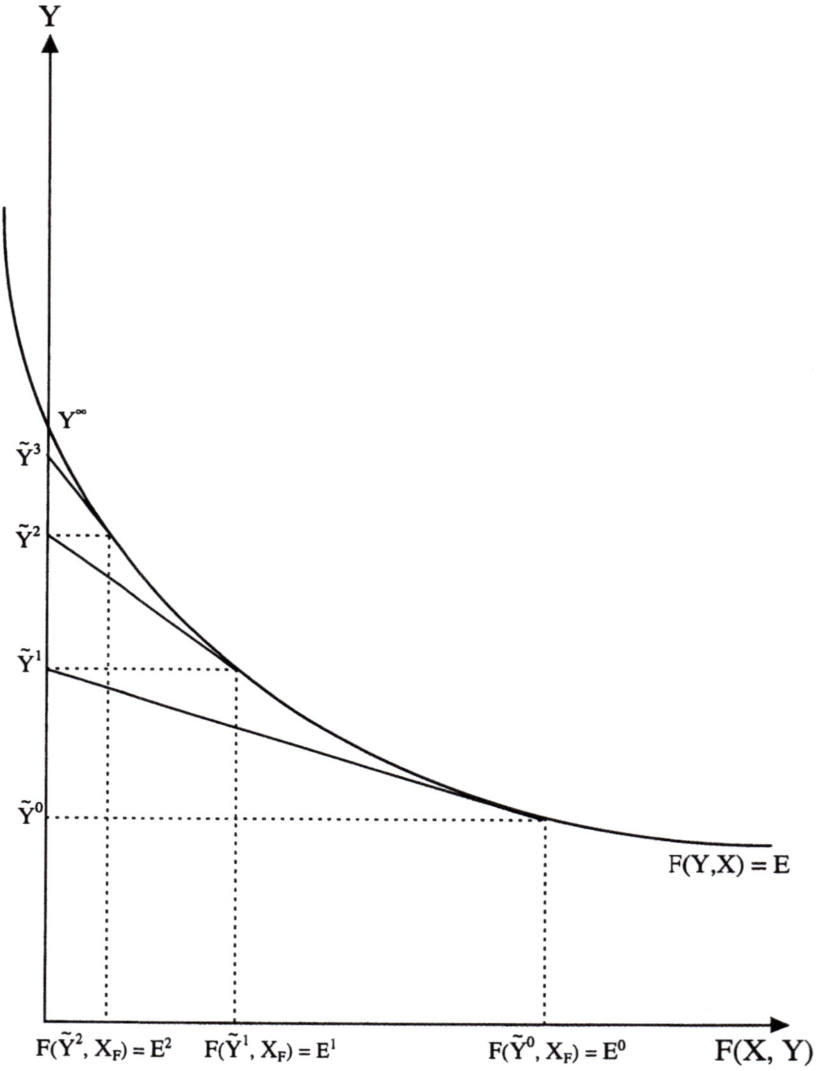

Figure 4.6: Three Iteration Standard Newton-Raphson Method

To describe the hybrid solution method, we assume for simplicity that $\{X_0, Y_0\}$, an intertemporal base solution that satisfies (4.3.1), is available. Equation (4.3.1) may be expressed as:

$$F(Y, X) = E . \qquad (4.3.19)$$

The error vector in (4.3.19) is equal to zero in the intertemporal base solution (i.e., n = 0). After the nth Euler step its value is:

$$E_n = F(Y_n, X_n) . \qquad n = 1, ..., N \qquad (4.3.20)$$

The rules for moving from the intertemporal base solution to the desired solution are provided by the following system of first-order differential equations:

$$F'_Y(Y_n, X_n)dY + F'_X(Y_n, X_n)dX = dE \,. \qquad n = 0, 1, ..., N-1 \qquad (4.3.21)$$

The change in the error vector in (4.3.21) is always exogenously set to $-E_n$. The shocks to X, the exogenous variables, are administered as per equation (4.3.4). A revised solution of the endogenous variables at each of the N steps is therefore obtained as follows:

$$Y_{n+1} = Y_n - F'_Y(Y_n, X_n)^{-1}\left[F'_Y(Y_n, X_n)\frac{(X_F - X_0)}{N} - F(Y_n, X_n)\right] .$$

$$n = 0, 1, ... N-1 \qquad (4.3.22)$$

Note that the only difference between (4.3.22) and (4.3.7) is $F(Y_n, X_n)$, the last term on the RHS of (4.3.22). The effect of this term on Y_{n+1} is to reduce the approximation errors accumulated at the previous step in a manner analogous to a single Newton-Raphson iteration. This can be seen by comparing figure 4.7 with figure 4.2. In both diagrams the vectors A, B and C show the effect on Y of changes in X. The vector β shows the effect of the Newton-Raphson correction implemented at the second step, which aims to remove any errors accumulated at the first step. Similarly, γ attempts to account for errors accumulated in the first and second steps.

Since the equation system is already written in differential form, the matrix inversion process is by far the most costly part of either the Euler or Newton-Raphson solution procedures. As can be seen from (4.3.22), a single Newton-Raphson error correction performed at each step of the solution procedure does not require any additional matrix inversions. Compared to the Euler method, the hybrid method imposes a small additional cost: the evaluation of the non-linear equations of the model at each of the N steps.

If necessary the Newton-Raphson method can be used to further 'polish' the approximation Y_N^0. That is, after the Nth step of the solution process the endogenous variables may be further revised as follows:

$$Y_N^{i+1} = Y_N^i - F'_Y(Y_N^i, X_N)^{-1}F(Y_N^i, X_N) \,. \qquad i = 0,1,2, ...,I\text{-}1 \qquad (4.3.23)$$

In figure 4.7 the effects of two such iterations are shown by the adjustments δ_1 and δ_2.

As before, the unavailability of an intertemporal base solution may be overcome by augmenting the system with a slack vector S. Analogous to (4.3.8) and (4.3.9) the augmented system is expressed as follows:

$$G(Y, X, S,) = F(Y, X) - S = E \qquad (4.2.24)$$

where

$$S_0 = F(\tilde{Y}_0, X_0) \text{ and } E_0 = 0 \,. \qquad (4.2.25)$$

Having obtained an intertemporal base solution for the augmented system other solutions may then be obtained via:

$$dY = -F'_Y(Y_n, X_n)^{-1}[F'_Y(Y_n, X_n)dX - dS - dE_n] . \qquad n = 0,1,2, ..., N \qquad (4.2.26)$$

The slack variables are shocked to zero as per equation (4.3.10) and the other exogenous variables are shocked to their forecast values as per equation (4.3.4). The error vector E in (4.2.24) is equal to zero when evaluated at the intertemporal base solution (n = 0). In subsequent steps its value is given by:

$$E_n = G(Y_n, X_n, S_n) = F(Y_n, X_n) - \frac{n}{N} S_0 . \qquad n = 1,2, ...,N \qquad (4.2.27)$$

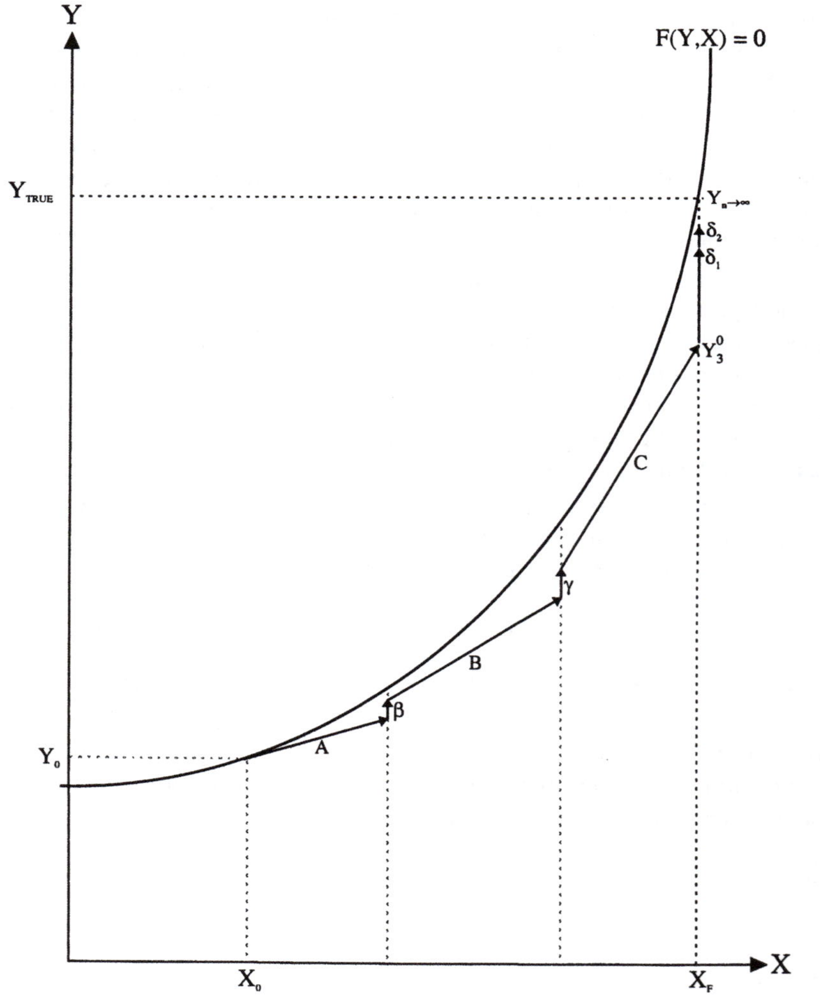

Figure 4.7: Hybrid Method

The change in the value of the error vector in (4.2.26) is always set to $-E_n$. A revised solution of the endogenous variables at each of the N steps is therefore obtained as follows:

$$Y_{n+1} = Y_n - F_Y'(Y_n,X_n)^{-1}[F_X'(Y_n,X_n)\frac{(X_F - X_0)}{N} + \frac{F(\tilde{Y}_0,X_0)}{N} + F(Y_n,X_n) - \frac{n}{N}S_0].$$

$$n = 0,1,2, \ldots,N-1 \qquad (4.2.28)$$

The hybrid solution method requires that the theoretical structure of the model can be expressed as a system of equations. Incorporating sign constraints appears to be problematic. However, the approach adopted by Horridge (1992) for solving the non-linear water-pricing model described in Dixon and Baker (1992) is readily extended to allow sign constraints to be accommodated by the hybrid solution method.

4.4 Modelling Sign Constraints

An optimisation problem involving sign constraints may be specified as follows:[6]

Choose: V_k $\qquad k = 1,2, ..,K \qquad (4.4.1)$

To Maximise: $f(V_k)$ $\qquad k = 1,2, ..,K \qquad (4.4.2)$

Subject to the constraints:

$$g^m(V_k) = 0\,; \qquad k = 1,2, ..,K,\ m = 1,2, ..,M \qquad (4.4.3)$$

and $\quad V_k \geq 0\,. \qquad k = 1,2, ..,K \qquad (4.4.4)$

Using vector notation the Lagrangian function, L, for this problem is:

$$L = f(V) + \Lambda g(V) \qquad (4.4.5)$$

where Λ is a vector of Lagrange Multipliers, length M. The first-order conditions are the constraints (4.4.3) and:

$$\frac{\partial L}{\partial V} = \frac{\partial f(V)}{\partial V} + \Lambda\frac{\partial g(V)}{\partial V} \leq 0; \qquad V \geq 0; \quad \text{and} \quad V\frac{\partial L}{\partial V} = 0\,. \qquad (4.4.6)$$

Condition (4.4.6) implies that either (i) the marginal condition holds as an equality and V, the choice variable, adopts a nonnegative value, or (ii) the marginal condition holds as an inequality and V adopts a value of zero.

---

6 Note that for simplicity it is assumed that g^m, the constraint functions, hold as equalities. Nonnegative slack variables of the form $d_m = g^m(V_k)$ could be introduced to handle inequality constraints.

The marginal conditions (4.4.6) may be transformed into an equality via the inclusion of a vector of slack variables, length K, as follows:

$$-H = \frac{\partial L}{\partial V}. \qquad H \geq 0 \tag{4.4.7}$$

This approach overcomes the problems posed by inequalities but makes choosing the appropriate closure very difficult. Since it is not possible to deduce, *ex ante*, whether a particular shock (or set of shocks) will violate a nonnegativity constraint, the partitioning of variables between the exogenous and endogenous categories will be an iterative process requiring manual intervention.

To highlight this problem consider using Johansen's method to solve the system of simultaneous equations implied by (4.4.6). Assume that in this equation system the marginal conditions are transformed into equalities as per (4.4.7). The inclusion of the K slack variables means that there will be K more variables than there are equations. Either V, the choice variable, or H, the corresponding slack variable, must be exogenously set to zero. Initially the slack variables are held exogenous at zero. The results obtained from the Johansen calculation are then inspected and if any of the V are negative, the solution procedure must be repeated using a different closure (i.e., setting the offending V to zero and allowing the corresponding marginal condition to be slack by endogenising the appropriate H). If several V are found to be negative, the process of adjusting the closure becomes an intricate combinatorial problem (because of simultaneity), possibly requiring many revisions of the closure until all sign constraints are satisfied.

This process is far more tedious if the Euler method is used since shocks to exogenous variables are applied in N steps rather than one. Thus, the procedure described above must be repeated N times. Fortunately, GEMPACK is sufficiently flexible to allow the above procedure to be automated. Prior to running a multi-step (Euler) simulation in GEMPACK the user must specify the closure, the shocks to be administered, the number of steps over which the shocks are to be applied and how the database is to be revised after each step. To avoid resorting to manual intervention, the incorporation of sign constraints requires the inclusion of a mechanism that triggers a switch in closure when such constraints start to bind.

Condition (4.4.6) can be used to illustrate how sign constraints may be implemented in GEMPACK. First, the complementary slackness conditions (4.4.6) are expressed as:

$$\text{Min}\{H, V\} = 0, \tag{4.4.8}$$

where in general, $\text{Min}\{a, b\} \equiv a$ if $a < b$, otherwise $\equiv b$. Totally differentiating (4.4.8) gives:

$$dH = 0 \qquad \text{for } H < V \tag{4.4.9}$$

and,

$$dV = 0. \qquad \text{for } H \geq V \tag{4.4.10}$$

A set of K binary coefficients are then defined as follows:

$$D = 0 \qquad \text{for } H \geq V \tag{4.4.11}$$

and,

$$D = 1 . \qquad \text{for } H < V \tag{4.4.12}$$

The binary coefficients are then used to combine conditions (4.4.9) and (4.4.10) giving:

$$D\, dH + (1-D)\, dV = 0 . \tag{4.4.13}$$

Equation (4.4.13) may be considered as two separate equations; one that holds some of the time and another that holds at other times.

The scheme for handling sign constraints in GEMPACK exploits the fact that an intertemporal base solution (albeit sometimes to an augmented equation system) is known and, hence, the marginal conditions that are initially active (i.e., those in which the slack variable is zero) are also known. The basic idea is to move from the known intertemporal base solution to some other solution in a sequence of small steps; at each step, the closure is automatically changed as required.

The mechanism that effectively switches the closure is the value of the binary coefficients. The values of these coefficients are determined by the levels values of the marginal conditions and the appropriate choice variables. In GEMPACK the database is automatically revised after the application of each of the N parts of the shock. For example, the variable V is typically updated according to the formula:

$$V_{n+1} = V_n + dV. \qquad n = 0, 1, 2, \ldots, N-1 \tag{4.4.14}$$

Note that the new value of V affects the value of D via (4.4.11) and (4.4.12).

A shortcoming of the above method for incorporating sign constraints is that the nth part of the shock may cause V_n to become negative. For example, if after the nth step of the Euler solution V_n is negative, then in the next step (n+1) of the solution procedure, D_{n+1} will adopt a value of zero and hence equation (4.4.10) will hold. With equation (4.4.10) holding, the choice variable is effectively exogenous and its value remains the same as it was in the previous step of the solution procedure (i.e., $V_n = V_{n+1}$). Thus, after the final step of the Euler solution it is possible that the value of the choice variable, which should be zero, is in fact (perhaps slightly) negative. It is possible, although very costly in terms of computing resources, to obtain a more accurate value for the choice variable by choosing N large enough. Note however, that errors are not *necessarily* reduced for small increases in N – they may in fact increase.

A more efficient way of obtaining the 'correct' value of the choice variable is to include in equation (4.4.13) an error correction mechanism that ensures that the complementary slackness conditions, (4.4.8), are arbitrarily close to being satisfied. We use the Newton error correction mechanism described by equation (4.2.28). Equation (4.4.8) is modified as follows:

$$\text{Min}\{H, V\} = e. \tag{4.4.15}$$

The binary coefficients are defined as before while e, the error term, is given by e = H for D = 1 (i.e., H < V) and e = V for D = 0 (i.e., H ≥ V). Equation (4.4.9) is modified accordingly, that is:

$$D[dH + H] + (1 - D)\,[dV + V] = 0\,. \tag{4.4.16}$$

The new equation not only switches closure as appropriate but also moves the newly exogenous variables to zero. For example, when D is equal to zero (i.e., the nonnegativity constraint on the choice variable is binding) equation (4.4.16) reduces to:

$$dV = -V\,. \tag{4.4.17}$$

Figure 4.8 illustrates the operation of sign constraints in the hybrid method. The choice variable is depicted on the horizontal axis; assume that it denotes irreversible (i.e., nonnegative) sector-specific investment expenditure. On the vertical axis the marginal condition is depicted; assume that it takes the form:

$$H = T - RR \tag{4.4.18}$$

where RR is the sectoral rate of return, T is the target rate of return and H is a slack variable similar to that in (4.4.7).

Analogous to (4.4.16) the change form of the complementary slackness condition for this example may be expressed as follows:

$$D[dH - H] + (1 - D)\,[dI + I] = 0\,. \tag{4.4.19}$$

The line QQ′ passing through the origin divides the H – I plane and determines the value of D; to the left of QQ′, H > I and D = 0, while, on, and to the right of QQ′, H ≤ I and D = 1.

In figure 4.8 the lines labelled p_n, n = 0, 1, ,...,N, describe the relationship between H and I for a given value of T, the target rate of return.[7] The slope of the curves p_n implies that RR, the rate of return, is negatively related to I, the rate of investment. More precisely:

$$RR = U(I, \Omega)$$

where Ω denotes a vector of other exogenous variables in the model and

$$\frac{\partial U}{\partial I} < 0.$$

The function U derives from the rest of the model (i.e., it is a function of the cost of capital creation and the rental price of capital). The target rate of return is exogenous to the model (perhaps set to the safe bond rate).

---

7 In figure 4.8 the linear relationship between H and I is assumed for convenience only.

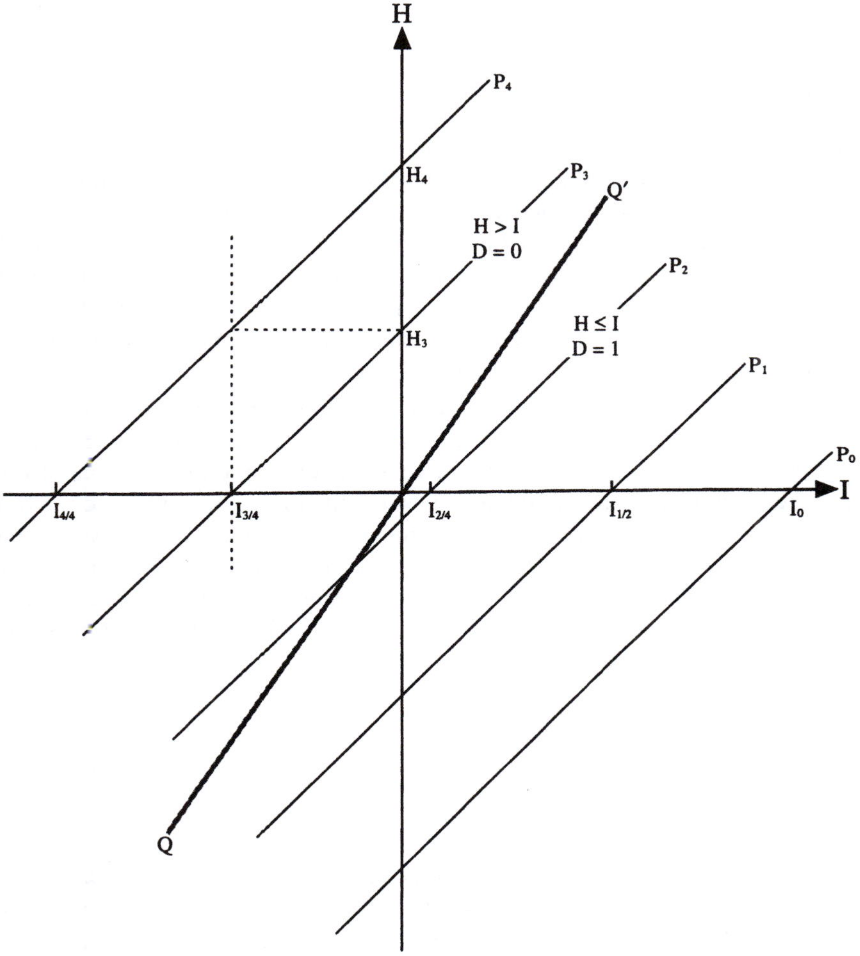

Figure 4.8: Sign Constraints

The point I_0 indicates the intertemporal base solution — at this point I is positive and H is equal to zero (i.e., the sectoral rate of return is equal to its target). Since I > H, D = 1 and (4.4.19) reduces to:

$$dH = -H = 0. \tag{4.4.20}$$

Consider now an Euler type calculation in which a set of shocks is administered to the model in four steps. Assume that these shocks have the effect of moving the p_n schedules to the left. With equation (4.4.20) active, the first part of the shock results in a move to $I_{\frac{1}{4}}$. The database is revised and again, D = 1 so the second part of the shock results in a movement to $I_{\frac{2}{4}}$; still D = 1 so that the third part of the shock moves investment to $I_{\frac{3}{4}}$ — a negative value. At this point, revision of the database reveals that I < H and hence D = 0. A closure switch occurs — equation (4.4.20) is replaced by:

$$dI = -I_{\frac{3}{4}}$$

Thus, the application of the last part of the shock moves investment back towards zero rather than $I_{\frac{4}{4}}$ (which would be the solution if I was not constrained to be nonnegative). The slack variable H, which is now endogenous, absorbs the impact both of the final set of shocks and of this error correction and moves towards H_4. Note that without the error correction mechanism in place, the application of the final instalment of shocks in the above example results in investment being held fixed at $I_{\frac{3}{4}}$ and H moving to H_3. The error correction mechanism moves both I and H closer to their true solutions (i.e., 0 and H_4 respectively).

The final solution may not be exactly at H_4 because of approximation errors. If the correction to investment in the final step is large then these approximation errors may be significant. To obtain a more accurate solution the number of Euler steps taken could be increased so that the switch in closure occurs very close to I = 0 and the correction required to investment in the next step is very small. Alternatively, after the final (in this case fourth) instalment of shocks to the exogenous variables, additional 'polishing' Newton-Raphson [see equation (4.4.23)] corrections designed to reduce the error in I to some arbitrarily small number may be performed.

4.5 Chapter Summary

In the following three chapters we report computations performed using the solution algorithm outlined in this chapter. The algorithm allowed us to solve ORANI-INT quickly and accurately under a variety of different theoretical assumptions. Two features of the algorithm should appeal to economic modellers. First, the algorithm is generic. This means that it can be applied to a wide range of models, including macro-dynamic models and intertemporal CGE models. Moreover, because the algorithm is independent of the model's structure the modeller is provided with maximum scope for model modifications (e.g., altering or adding equations, changing the data, and the partitioning of variables between the endogenous and exogenous categories). This flexibility is a desirable feature for applied economic analysis as the specification of a model is constrained by economic theory or data rather than by computational considerations. For example, there is no special need to constrain the number of forward-looking variables nor is there is any special need to assume interior solutions. Corner constraints suggested by economic theory (e.g., quotas, inventories, and some investments) can be incorporated explicitly. The second appealing feature of the algorithm is that it is readily accessible to other modellers. The algorithm can be easily implemented in GEMPACK, a commercially available software package, by modellers with no source-code programming skills.

Chapter 5 Generating the Control Path Solution

5.1 Introduction

In this chapter we describe how a control path solution (or control scenario) is generated for ORANI-INT. The control scenario is an intertemporal base solution in which: (a) all the nonlinear equations in ORANI-INT are satisfied, and (b) the time paths of the exogenous variables are set to their expected or preferred trajectories. The control path solution should be a suitable reference scenario for performing comparative-dynamic simulations or a good starting point for performing forecasting simulations.[1] We produce two control scenarios. The first is a balanced growth (BG) scenario in which all real variables grow by 3 per cent per annum and in which there is no growth in prices. In the second scenario (labelled CBG) the economy *converges* to a balanced growth path, but does not start on one.

As explained in the previous chapter, the ORANI-INT solution method is an initial value method; it starts from a known intertemporal base solution and then, following a perturbation to one or more exogenous variables, finds a new solution.[2] Thus, before we can generate a control scenario we must have available an intertemporal base solution of the model. For convenience, we use different intertemporal base solutions to generate our two control scenarios.

For atemporal models, such as ORANI, a base solution is normally provided by an observed or historical set of data—usually the latest available input-output data.[3] For intertemporal models like ORANI-INT, however, a solution consists of time-series data that are less readily available. In chapter 4 we outlined a strategy for obtaining an intertemporal base solution. Below we explain how this strategy is used to construct such solutions for ORANI-INT. We then explain how the BG and CBG control scenarios, which are used in the experiments discussed in chapters 6 and 7, are generated.

---

1 See Dixon, Parmenter and Horridge (1986) for a discussion on the importance of the control scenario and on the problems of constructing it.

2 A solution of ORANI-INT consists of time paths for all variables that satisfy all the nonlinear equations of the model.

3 See Dixon *et al* (1982) for a discussion about the conditions necessary for input-output data to constitute a base solution to models such as ORANI.

In practice, the processes of obtaining an intertemporal base solution and a control scenario are combined into a single operation. However, the two processes are conceptually distinct; the intertemporal base solution need not have any sensible economic interpretation whereas the control path solution must. For these reasons we discuss the intertemporal base solution and control scenario separately.

5.2 Constructing an Intertemporal Base Solution

Our method for obtaining an intertemporal base solution is indirect. Rather than starting by attempting to find time-series data that satisfy the non-linear equations of ORANI-INT, we start by modifying the equation system (temporarily) so that it satisfies time-series data that are easily constructed. We call this set of time-series data a *quasi-solution.*

As explained in chapter 2 the bulk of ORANI-INT's equations are contained in the sequence of T identical ORANI-13 sub-models. A base solution of ORANI-13, which is a static model, is readily available from input-output data. We use two modified versions of the ORANI-13 database to generate the two quasi-solutions required. The ORANI-13A database is produced by modifying the ORANI-13 database to reflect the structure of the economy in a typical year on a balanced growth path with 3 percent per annum growth in all real variables and no growth in prices. To generate the ORANI-13B database we reduce, but do not eliminate, the disequilibrium (relative to a balanced-growth steady state) reflected in the ORANI-13 database. The original ORANI-13 database and the two modified versions referred to above are described in appendix A5.1.

Since ORANI-INT contains dynamic equations a quasi-solution of the model will include values for all variables in periods 1 to T and for some variables in periods 0 (i.e., anterior endpoint conditions) and T+1 (i.e., posterior endpoint conditions). We can easily replicate the ORANI-13A and ORANI-13B databases T+2 times to obtain the two required quasi-solutions (say QSA and QSB). By construction, both QSA and QSB will satisfy all the atemporal equations in ORANI-INT. However, since neither the ORANI-13A or ORANI-13B databases reflect the economy in a no-growth steady state, QSA and QSB will not satisfy the dynamic equations in ORANI-INT.

The dynamic equations in ORANI-INT were derived in chapter 3. Our strategy for obtaining an intertemporal base solution is to modify these equations by adding to each a unique slack variable (formally a homotopy parameter but hereafter referred to as a *calibration variable*). These calibration variables adopt values that ensure that the modified equations are satisfied, in the levels, by our quasi-solutions.

Having obtained, by construction, an intertemporal base solution for the augmented equation system it is then possible to find other solutions using the ORANI-INT solution method. If the calibration variables, which are exogenous, are assigned appropriate values (zero if the calibration variable enters the equation additively and one if it is multiplicative), the augmented equation system can be made equivalent to the original equation system. That is, with appropriate shocks administered to the calibration variables, an intertemporal base solution of the augmented equation system will also be an intertemporal base solution of ORANI-INT.

To illustrate this approach we can refer to the capital accumulation relations described in chapter 3. These are:

$$Z^{(K)}_{j,t+1} = Z^{(K)}_{j,t}(1 - \delta_j) + N_{j,t} . \qquad j = 1, ..., 13, t = 1, ..., T \qquad (5.2.1)$$

This equation will not be consistent with our quasi-solution unless the input-output data represents the economy in a steady state. That is, a state in which the rates of growth in sectoral capital stocks are equal to sectoral depreciation rates. We augment each accumulation equation with a multiplicative calibration variable, $F^{(CV,K)}_{j,t}$, as follows:

$$Z^{(K)}_{j,t+1} = [Z^{(K)}_{j,t}(1 - \delta_j) + N_{j,t}]F^{(CV,K)}_{j,t} . \qquad j = 1, ..., 13, t = 1, ..., T \qquad (5.2.2)$$

The next step is to calculate the levels value of $F^{(CV,K)}_{j,t}$ in the quasi-solution. Since each calibration variable is unique and appears in one equation only, it is easy to derive the values of these variables in the quasi-solution. Having obtained a solution to the augmented equations, the calibration variables are shocked to unity so that a solution to the original accumulation equations (5.2.1) is obtained. For example, in the case of the quasi-solution generated by replicating the ORANI-13A database, the value of $F^{(CV,K)}_{j,t}$, for all j and for all t, is 0.9708738.[4] A solution to the original unaugmented accumulation equations (5.2.1) is obtained by shocking the $F^{(CV,K)}_{j,t}$ by 3 percent.

5.3 The Control Scenarios

Once an intertemporal base solution of ORANI-INT is available we are able to use the model to generate any control scenario desired. As mentioned above we construct two control scenarios. The BG scenario is a hypothetical characterisation of the economy in which all real variables grow by 3 per cent per annum and in which there is no growth in prices. The CBG scenario is also hypothetical but its characterisation of the economy in the first year is based more closely on a historically observed state of the economy[5] than is the case in the BG scenario.

---

4 In ORANI-13A the net investment-capital ratio is 3 percent. Under these conditions accumulation equation (5.2.2) can be expressed as follows:

$$Z^{(K)}_{j,t+1} = [Z^{(K)}_{j,t}(1.03)]F^{(CV,K)}_{j,t} .$$

Since in the quasi-solution we assume that $Z^{(K)}_{j,t+1} = Z^{(K)}_{j,t}$, the value of $F^{(CV,K)}_{j,t}$ in the quasi-solution is 0.9708738 (i.e., 1/1.03).

5 As will be explained in sub-section 5.3.3 the historically observed state of the economy that we use to characterise the first year of the CBG scenario is a modified version of the

Beyond the first year, the economy tends towards a balanced growth path in which all real variables grow by 3 percent per annum and in which there is no growth in prices. In the CBG scenario convergence to balanced growth is achieved, asymptotically, in the last years of the chosen time horizon.

ORANI-INT has many more variables than it has equations and, therefore, some variables must be specified exogenously. This issue was not addressed explicitly in our discussion about obtaining an intertemporal base solution. Because the intertemporal base solution need not have any sensible economic interpretation, the closure of the model for that purpose can be treated rather mechanically; the key requirement is that the calibration variables are exogenous. The choice of closure is far more important in the construction of a control scenario. In practice, because the processes of obtaining an intertemporal base solution and generating a control scenario are combined into a single operation, we need a single closure only—we call this the *standard* closure. Before explaining how the two control scenarios are computed we describe briefly the key features of the standard closure.

5.3.1 The Standard Closure

The standard closure is one of many closures of ORANI-INT that are legitimate on economic grounds. In this section we explain the implications that our choice of exogenous variables has on the behaviour of agents in the model. The complete listing of the exogenous variables in the standard closure is provided in table 5.3.1. In appendix A3.1 we listed the equations and variables in ORANI-INT. In total 4SIJT + 4SIT + 2IJT + 7IT +18JT + 68T – J + 1 equations and 6SITJ + 8SIT + 4IJT + 10IT + 29JT + 75T + 5 variables are listed in tables A3.1.1 and A3.1.2.[6] This implies that 2SITJ + 4SIT + 2IJT + 3IT + 11JT + 7T + J + 4 variables must be exogenous. In table 5.3.1 we have listed 2SITJ + 3SIT + 2IJT + 5IT + 10JT + 6T + J + 4 exogenous variables. Noting that 2IT = SIT we appear to be JT exogenous variables short. The reason for this is that the equations that implement the nonnegativity constraints on sectoral investment were not included in table A3.1.1.[7] This vector equation, which is analogous to equation (4.4.19) in chapter 4, has dimensions JT. Note that the calibration variables discussed in section 5.2 have not been included in table 5.3.[8] The

ORANI-13 database. The reasons for these modifications will also be explained in sub-section 5.3.3.

6 With J=13, I=13, S=2 and T=30 we have 65,598 equations and 104,795 variables.

7 The main reason for not including this equation in table A3.1.1 in appendix A3.1 is that we consider it to be a device for implementing behavioural assumptions contained in other equations.

8 These calibration variables were also not included in table A3.1.2 in appendix A3.1. There are 2JT + T + 1 calibration variables corresponding to: (i) the JT sectoral capital accumulation equations; (ii) the JT equilibrium conditions for sectoral investment; (iii) the T foreign liabilities accumulation equations; and (iv) the intertemporal consumption function.

calibration variables, which are always exogenous, are included in ORANI-INT for computational convenience only.

The past behaviour of agents is taken as given in ORANI-INT. This implies that any variable defined for year 0 is exogenous. Because we have specified a 1-year gestation lag in the capital creation process the amount of capital that sectors have at their disposal in year 1 is determined by decisions taken in the past. Therefore, year 1 is characterised by a short-run equilibrium in which the supply of sectoral capital stocks (i.e., $Z^{(K)}_{j,1}$) cannot be altered and sectoral rates of return are allowed to vary. Beyond year one, however, the supply of sectoral capital stocks is allowed to vary whilst sectoral rates of return are required to equalise. Arbitrage conditions that relate risk-adjusted sectoral rates of return to the interest rate are enforced by exogenising the shifter $F^{(2)}_{j,t}$.

Investment behaviour in ORANI-INT is distinguished on the basis of the degree of government involvement. The activities of two sectors in ORANI-INT (i.e., *Public Administration* and *Community Services*) are dominated by the government. Capital stocks in these sectors are exogenous in all periods because the investment theory outlined in chapter 3 is considered inappropriate. The *Non-competing Imports* sector is a dummy sector for dealing with non-competing imports. This sector is endowed with a negligible capital stock that we assume is exogenous in all periods. Sectoral capital stocks in year T+1 and, hence, sectoral investments in year T are determined by a terminal condition. These terminal conditions, which are discussed in chapter 3, are imposed by exogenising the $F^{(K)}_{j,T}$.

For many variables ORANI-INT has no formal theory and, typically, the values of these variables are specified exogenously. This group of variables includes: technical change and consumer tastes (i.e., the As in table 5.3.1); indirect tax rates (the Ts); risk factors ($H_{j,t}$); foreign demand conditions (summarised by $F^{(4p)}_{i,t}$ and $F^{(4q)}_{i,t}$); foreign prices ($P^{(M)}_{i,t}$); foreign interest rates ($B_{f,t}$); transfers overseas (S_t); population (Q_t); aggregate real government expenditure ($G^{(R)}_t$); and the composition of government demands ($F^{(5)}_{i,s,t}$). The price of 'other cost tickets' is indexed to the consumption deflator by making $F^{(O)}_{j,t}$ exogenous.

ORANI-INT does not model the supply of labour or of agricultural land. We assume that the aggregate supply of labour (L_t) is exogenous in all periods with the real wage adjusting to clear the labour market. A similar assumption is made for sectoral supplies of agricultural land ($Z^{(N)}_{j,t}$).

The treatment of exports in ORANI-INT distinguishes between those commodities that Australia is assumed to be a price-taker (non-traditional exports) and those whose world price is influenced by Australian sales (traditional exports). Three commodities, *Rural*, *Mining*, and *Manufacturing* are treated as traditional exports with their foreign currency prices and sales overseas endogenously determined. The commodities associated with the remaining ten sectors (the subset **N** in table 5.3.1) are treated as non-traditional exports. Sales of these commodities overseas (i.e., $X^{(4)}_{i,t}$, $i \in \mathbf{N}$) are exogenous. An endogenous export subsidy ensures that the exogenously specified sales of non-traditional exports are achieved. This subsidy, which is represented as $T^{(4)}_{i,t}$ in table 5.3.1, is exogenous for all

Table 5.3.1: The Standard Closure of ORANI-INT

Level	Change form	Range	No.	Description
$Z_{j,t}^{(K)}$	$z_{j,t}^{(K)}$	t=1 j=1,...,J	J	Supply of capital to sector j in year 1
$Z_{j,t}^{(K)}$	$z_{j,t}^{(K)}$	t=1,...,T $j \in \mathbf{G}^{(a)}$	G^*T	Supply of capital to sector j in year t
$F_{j,t}^{(2)}$	$dF_{j,t}^{(2)}$	t=1,...,T $j \in \mathbf{K}^{(b)}$	K^*T	Shifter in the arbitrage condition for sectoral capital stocks
$F_{j,t}^{(K)}$	$f_{j,t}^{(K)}$	t=T j=1,...,J	J	Ratio of sector j's capital stock in year T+1 to its capital stock in year T
$H_{j,t}$	$dH_{j,t}$	t=1,...,T j=1,...,J	JT	Risk premium on capital in sector j in year t
$F_t^{(3)}$	$f_t^{(3)}$	t=1,...,T	T	Shifter in the consumption function
$F_{j,t}^{(A)}$	$f_{j,t}^{(A)}$	t=2,...,T j=1,...,J	J(T-1)	Shifter in the equation for sectoral capital gains
$F_{i,s,t}^{(5)}$	$f_{i,s,t}^{(5)}$	t=1,...,T i=1,...,I s=1,2	SIT	Ratio of the government's demand for good i from source s to total government demand
S_t	s_t	t=1,...,T	T	Net unrequited transfers to foreigners in year t
Q_t	q_t	t=1,...,T	T	Number of households in year t
$X_{i,t}^{(4)}$	$x_{i,t}^{(4)}$	t=1,...,T $i \in \mathbf{N}^{(c)}$	N^*T	Demand by foreigners for good i in year t
$F_{i,t}^{(4p)}$	$f_{i,t}^{(4p)}$	t=1,...,T i=1,...,I	IT	Price shifter in export demand function
$F_{i,t}^{(4q)}$	$f_{i,t}^{(4q)}$	t=1,...,T i=1,...,I	IT	Quantity shifter in export demand function
Φ_t	ϕ_t	t=0,...,T+1	T+2	Nominal exchange rate in year t
D_t	dD_t	t=0	1	Net foreign liabilities in year 0
$B_{f,t}$	$dB_{f,t}$	t=0,...,T	T+1	Foreign bond rate in year t
$A_{j,t}^{(K)}$	$a_{j,t}^{(K)}$	t=1,...,T j=1,...,J	JT	Technical change specific to capital in sector j in year t
$A_{j,t}^{(L)}$	$a_{j,t}^{(L)}$	t=1,...,T j=1,...,J	JT	Technical change specific to labour in sector j in year t
$A_{j,t}^{(N)}$	$a_{j,t}^{(N)}$	t=1,...,T j=1,...,J	JT	Technical change specific to agricultural land in sector j in year t
$A_{j,t}^{(F)}$	$a_{j,t}^{(F)}$	t=1,...,T j=1,...,J	JT	Primary factor technical change in sector j in t
$A_{j,t}^{(O)}$	$a_{j,t}^{(O)}$	t=1,...,T j=1,...,J	JT	Technical change specific to "other cost" tickets in sector j in year t

...continued

Table 5.3.1(continued): The Standard Closure of ORANI-INT

Level	Change form	Range	No.	Description
$A^{(1)}_{i,\bullet,j,t}$	$a^{(1)}_{i,\bullet,j,t}$	t=1,...,T i=1,...,I j=1,...,J	IJT	Technical change specific to good i undifferentiated by source used by sector j in year t for current production
$A^{(2)}_{i,\bullet,j,t}$	$a^{(2)}_{i,\bullet,j,t}$	t=1,...,T i=1,...,I j=1,...,J	IJT	Technical change specific to good i undifferentiated by source used by sector j in year t for capital creation
$T^{(1)}_{i,s,j,t}$	$t^{(1)}_{i,s,j,t}$	t=1,...,T i=1,...,I j=1,...,J s=1,2	SIJT	Power of the tax on good i from source s used by sector j for current production in year t
$T^{(2)}_{i,s,j,t}$	$t^{(2)}_{i,s,j,t}$	t=1,...,T i=1,...,I j=1,...,J s=1,2	SIJT	Power of the tax on good i from source s used by sector j for capital creation in year t
$T^{(3)}_{i,s,t}$	$t^{(3)}_{i,s,t}$	t=1,...,T i=1,...,I s=1,2	SIT	Power of the tax on good i from source s purchased by households in year t
$T^{(4)}_{i,t}$	$t^{(4)}_{i,t}$	t=1,...,T $i \in \mathbf{D}^{(d)}$	$D^{*}T$	Power of the tax on exported good i in year t
$T^{(5)}_{i,s,t}$	$t^{(5)}_{i,s,t}$	t=1,...,T i=1,...,I s=1,2	SIT	Power of the tax on good i from source s purchased by the government in year t
$P^{(M)}_{i,t}$	$p^{(M)}_{i,t}$	t=1,...,T i=1,...,I	IT	Foreign (C.I.F) currency price of imported good i in year t
$T^{(6)}_{i,t}$	$t^{(6)}_{i,t}$	t=1,...,T i=1,...,I	IT	Power of the tariff on imported good i in year t
$Z^{(N)}_{j,t}$	$z^{(N)}_{j,t}$	t=1,...,T j=1,...,J	JT	Supply of agricultural land to sector j in year t
L_t	l_t	t=1,...,T	T	Aggregate supply of labour in year t
$G^{(R)}_t$	$g^{(R)}_t$	t=1,...,T	T	Real aggregate government spending in year t
$F^{(O)}_{j,t}$	$f^{(O)}_{j,t}$	t=1,...,T j=1,...,J	JT	Ratio of the price of "other cost" tickets in sector j to the consumption deflator
Total Number of Exogenous Variables			2SITJ + 3SIT + 2IJT + 5IT + 10JT + 6T + J + 4	

(a) **G** is a subset containing 3 sectors. These are: *Public Administration*, *Community Services* and *Non-competing Imports*. G* is the number of elements in the set **G**.

(b) **K** is a subset containing the sectors not in **G**. K* is the number of elements in **K**.

(c) **N** is a subset containing the N*=10 commodities treated as non-traditional exports.

(d) **D** is a subset containing the D*=3 commodities treated as traditional exports. These are: *Rural*, *Mining* and *Manufacturing*.

commodities not in the set **N**. The foreign elasticities of demand for non-traditional export commodities are relatively high (see table 5.1.4) hence the foreign currency prices of non-traditional exports are not sensitive to domestic cost conditions.

The variables $F_t^{(3)}$ and $F_{j,t}^{(A)}$ are shifters that are exogenous in the standard closure. When these shifters are exogenous and not shocked they have no impact on the model. However, as explained in chapter 6, we use these shifters to explore alternative assumptions about investment and consumption behaviour. For example, we make consumption exogenous by endogenising $F_t^{(3)}$.

All real endogenous variables in ORANI-INT are homogeneous of degree zero with respect to nominal variables.[9] Therefore, to tie down the absolute price level in ORANI-INT we must specify a numeraire sequence. This is achieved by exogenously specifying the time path of the nominal exchange rate (Φ_t). The homogeneity properties of ORANI-INT imply that a 1 per cent increase in the nominal exchange rate in each period will increase all prices by 1 per cent in every period and leave real variables unchanged (in all periods). A 1 per cent increase in the nominal exchange rate in period t will increase all prices in period t by 1 per cent and leave all other variables, including prices in other periods, unchanged. Such an increase in the nominal exchange rate will be offset by movements in the nominal interest rate so that inflation cannot have real effects in ORANI-INT.[10]

5.3.2 The BG Control Scenario

To produce the BG scenario we perform a simulation with ORANI-INT. Using the intertemporal base solution of ORANI-INT derived from QSA as the starting point, we compute the desired control scenario in which all real variables are growing at 3 per cent per annum and all price variables are stationary. We choose a time horizon of 30 years (i.e., T=30) and use the standard closure described in the previous section. We obtained an accurate control path solution by using Richardson's procedure to extrapolate the results produced by 4-, 8- and 16-step Euler computations (see section 4.3.1 in chapter 4 for details).

In this simulation the values of the exogenous variables conform to a predictable pattern. Shocks are applied to all exogenous real variables from years 1 to T. These shocks are commensurate with growth of 3 per cent compounded annually. Since no other shocks are administered in this simulation, the percentage changes in all other exogenous variables in all periods are zero. This includes all variables in year 0, all calibration variables and all exogenous nominal variables.

---

9 These homogeneity properties of ORANI-INT stem from the assumption of constant returns to scale in all production activities and from the assumption that per-capita consumption is constant. Since the number of households is allowed to vary, the non-homotheticity of the utility function specified in ORANI-INT does not affect the model's homogeneity properties.

10 Tests to see if these formal homogeneity requirements were satisfied exactly were among the procedures used to check our implementation of ORANI-INT for errors.

ORANI-INT is homogeneous of degree 1 in real variables. Thus, if the annual growth rate of all exogenous real variables, including the number of households, is 3 percent, then the annual growth rate of all the endogenous real variables will also be 3 percent (and all prices will remain stationary). Because the results of this simulation simply confirm the homogeneity properties of ORANI-INT, we do not present them here.

5.3.3 The CBG Control Scenario

Intertemporal CGE models are typically used for comparative-dynamic analysis (rather than for forecasting). For such analyses, a balanced growth scenario like that described above is typically used. In chapter 4 we argued that there are good economic reasons why computational expediency should not constrain the choice of control path used. Here we demonstrate that with the ORANI-INT solution method the computational burden of generating any arbitrary control scenario is no different to that required to generate a balanced growth control scenario. In addition, we highlight the economic issues that must be tackled to generate realistic control scenarios (i.e., control scenarios that reflect our best guess of how the economy will evolve over time).

The CBG scenario simulation and results

The CBG scenario is generated in a similar manner to the BG scenario. The BG and CBG simulations share the same closure of the model, the same shocks to the exogenous variables and the same time horizon. The difference between the two simulations is that computations start from different intertemporal base solutions. To generate the CBG scenario we use the intertemporal base solution derived from QSB. As in the BG simulation we obtained an accurate control path solution by using Richardson's procedure to extrapolate the results produced by 4-, 8- and 16-step Euler computations.

A selection of results from this simulation is presented in figures 5.1 - 5.3. The results in these figures show the annual percentage growth rates of selected variables. As expected real variables converge towards steady growth of 3 percent per annum and prices converge to zero growth. In the early periods a degree of structural change is occurring in the economy (see figure 5.3). The structural changes observed in the early periods of the control scenario reflect, mainly, the adjustments that sectors must make in order to re-configure their investment-to-capital ratios in a way that is consistent with the equilibrium conditions for investment (i.e., equation (3.3.33) in chapter 3) and with the growth of the rest of the economy.

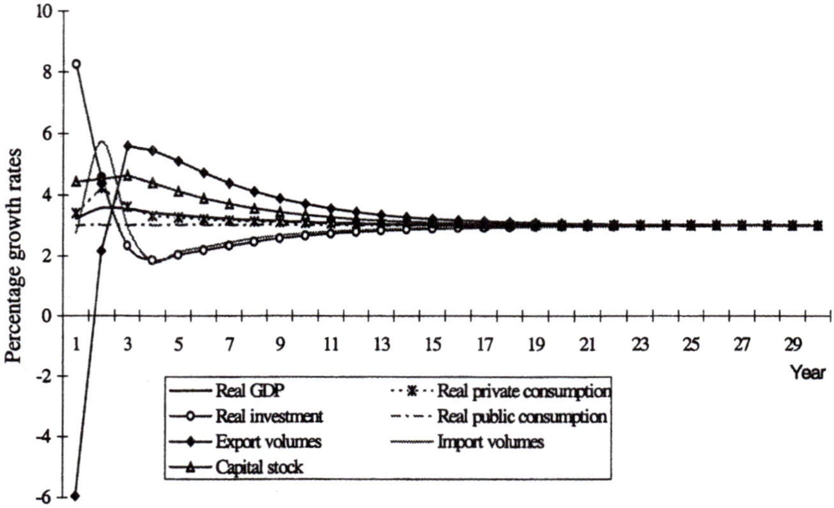

Figure 5.1: CBG Scenario Projections for Selected Real Macro Variables

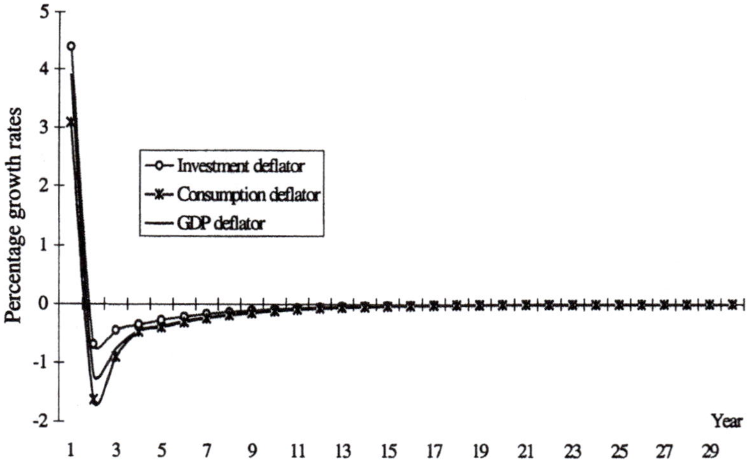

Figure 5.2: CBG Scenario Projections for Selected Deflators

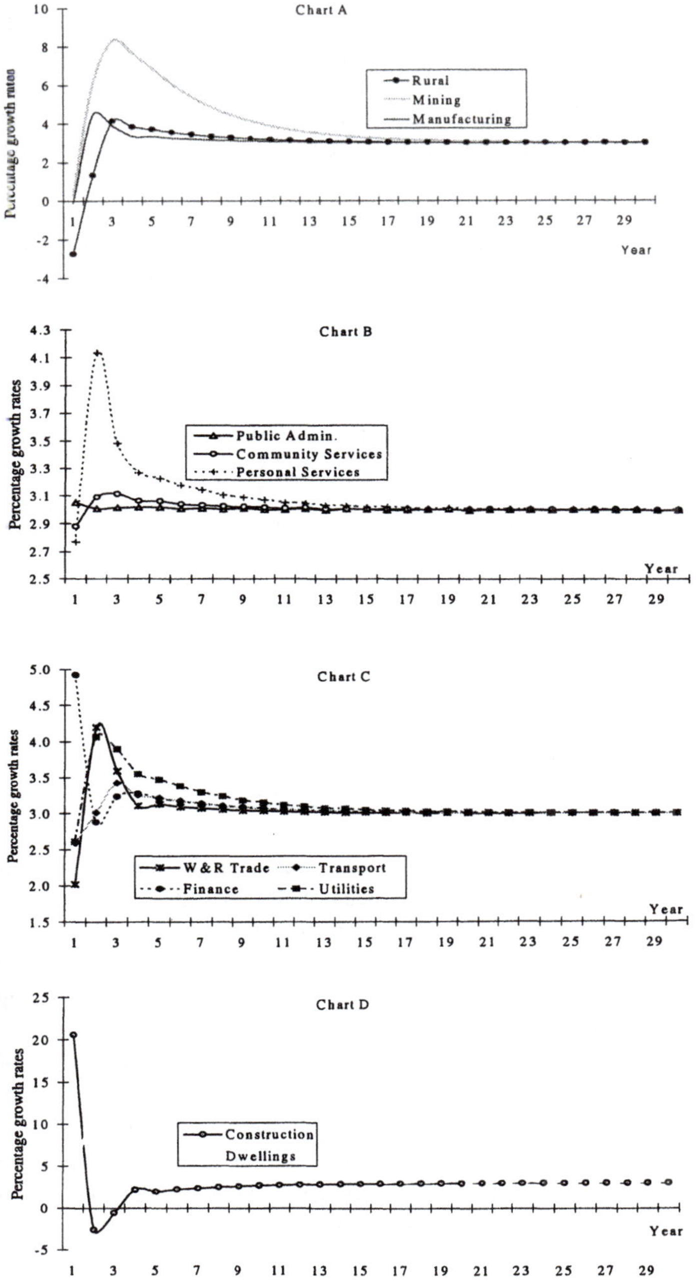

Figure 5.3: CBG Scenario Projections for Sectoral Activity Levels

Since the amount of capital that sectors have at their disposal in year 1 is determined by investment decisions taken in the past, the growth of sectoral capital stocks in year 1 reflects the net investment-to-capital ratios in year 0. The single-period database (ORANI-13B) used to construct the quasi-solution (QSB) remains unchanged in year 0. Hence, the percentage growth rates of sectoral capital stocks in year 1 coincide with the net investment-to-capital ratios in ORANI-13B. These are listed in column 2 of table 5.3.2.

Table 5.3.2: Sectoral Investment-capital Ratios and Rates of Return

Sector	Net Investment-to-capital ratio (per cent)	Risk Adjusted Rate of Return (per cent)
Rural	1.2	3.2
Mining	9.6	5.2
Manufacturing	3.6	4.1
Utilities	3.1	3.1
Construction	4.1	2.3
W&R Trade	5.9	3.7
Transport	3.4	2.6
Finance	8.0	5.1
Housing	3.9	5.2
Public administration	-1.3	-5.1
Community services	1.9	-5.5
Personal services	3.3	5.0
Non-competing imports	-7.2	0.0

Ignoring sector 13, which is endowed with a negligible stock of capital, the initial rates of growth in the capital stocks of three of the remaining sectors listed in table 5.3.2 (i.e., *Rural*, *Public Administration*, and *Community Services*) are less than the long-run equilibrium growth rate of 3 per cent per annum to which the economy is tending. These sectors tend to re-adjust their investment-capital ratios upward. Capital stocks in the other sectors are initially growing faster than 3 per cent per annum and the tendency for these sectors is to decrease their investment-capital ratios.

The structural changes induced by the re-configuration of the sectoral investment-capital ratios are compounded by the imposition in year 2 of the sectoral equilibrium conditions for investment. These condition require the risk adjusted sectoral rates of return to equal 3 per cent, the exogenously specified world interest rate. Column 2 in table 5.3.2 shows the degree of disequilibrium in sectoral rates of return in year 1. Five sectors, *Construction*, *Transport*, *Public administration*, *Community services* and *Non-competing imports* have rates of return below the equilibrium rate. Since investment in the latter three sectors is assumed to be exogenous, the degree of disequilibrium in their rates of return is unimportant. The *Rural* and *Utilities* sectors have rates of return close to the equilibrium rate. In the remaining sectors rates of return are greater than 3 per cent. Sectors with rates of return higher than the equilibrium rate tend to increase their capital stock by doing more investment and *vice versa* for sectors with rates of return below the equilibrium rate.

In year 1 the average rate of return in the economy is higher than 3 per cent. To satisfy the equilibrium condition that sectoral rates of return are equal to 3 per cent in year 2 and beyond, the economy's capital stock must grow faster in year 2 than in year 1 (see figure 5.1). This generates strong investment growth in year 1. Of particular importance is investment by the *Housing* sector, which accounts for about 27 per cent of the economy's capital stock and about 20 per cent of aggregate investment. The gap between this sector's rate of return and the equilibrium rate of 3 per cent is 2.2 percentage points. This gap is the biggest recorded by any sector (it is equalled by the *Mining* sector). In the ORANI-13B database the *Housing* sector's net investment-capital ratio is 3.9 per cent. Capital is the only primary factor used by the *Housing* sector hence its growth in the first year of the CBG scenario is also 3.9 per cent (see chart D in figure 5.3). To reduce its rate of return in year 2 to 3 per cent the *Housing* sector needs to grow its capital stock by close to 10 per cent in year 2. This induces an increase in investment by the *Housing* sector in year 1 that contributes about 16 percentage points to the growth in aggregate investment in year 1. Partially offsetting this contribution to aggregate investment growth is the reduction in investment in year 1 by the *Construction* and *Transport* sectors which need to reduce their capital stocks to meet the rate of return target in year 2.

The strong growth in investment in the first year stimulates growth in the *Construction* sector (see chart D in figure 5.3) which supplies about 60 per cent of the economy's input requirements for capital creation. The fall in the growth of aggregate investment after year 1 is reflected in the *Construction* sector's output growth path. The negative growth of the *Housing* sector in years 2 and 3 is related to the decrease in investment in the sector that is necessary to increase the rate of return to the target rate.

The capital creation process is relatively import intensive. This is reflected by the similarity of the growth paths for aggregate investment and import volumes after year 1 (figure 5.1). Import growth in year 1 is lower than in year 2 partly because consumption growth in year 1 is low relative to year 2 and partly because the growth in the *Manufacturing* sector in year 1 is low relative to year 2. In year 1 growth in the economy's productive capacity is constrained. Employment grows by 3 per cent and the growth in the capital stock is determined by past investment decision. The strong growth in investment causes domestic prices to rise. In year 2 and beyond aggregate employment continues to grow at 3 per cent but the economy's capacity is less constrained than in year 1 because capital stocks can expand. This is reflected by the fall in the growth of domestic prices after year 1. The forward-looking consumers anticipate this pattern in the path of domestic prices. They react by skewing consumption in favour of the first few years where the growth in prices is negative.

The *Manufacturing* sector's poor growth performance in year 1 is related to the fall in its exports and to the increase in imports of the *Manufacturing* commodity. Chart A in figure 5.3 shows that the other export oriented sectors, *Rural* and *Mining*, are also adversely affected by the sharp fall in the growth of exports in year 1. With the growth in the economy's capacity constrained in year 1, the strong growth in investment crowds out exports. The growth of domestic prices in year 1 reduces the competitiveness of domestic commodities on world markets. This causes export growth to fall and encourages import growth. This tendency towards trade deficit must be reversed in later years to accommodate the constraint on net foreign liabilities. With the foreign rate of interest set at 3 per cent, net foreign liabilities will converge to 3 per cent growth only if the trade surplus is equal to net unrequited transfers.[11] In the ORANI-13B database the trade deficit and unrequited transfers represent 1.3 per cent of GDP. Unrequited transfers are exogenous and grow by 3 per cent per annum. Thus, the trade deficit widens in the first few years but, as shown in figure 5.1, this pattern is reversed in year 3 and beyond with exports growing more strongly than imports.

Generating Realistic Control Scenarios

The CBG scenario may be considered more realistic than the BG scenario because it does not exhibit balanced growth in all years. However, the realism of the CBG scenario should not be overstated for two reasons. First, the database representing the structure of the economy in year 0 (i.e., the ORANI-13B database) is not a historically observed state of the economy. As explained in appendix A5.1, the ORANI-13B database is a modified version of the ORANI-13 database, which is the Australian Bureau of Statistic's representation of the structure of the Australian economy in 1980-81. The second limitation of the CBG scenario is that the exogenous variables have not been assigned plausible values. Year 1 in the CBG scenario should represent 1981-82 and year 30 should represent 2010-11. The paths of most of the exogenous variables are observable for about half of this time horizon (i.e., at least for 1981-82 to 1997-98). We have simply assumed that all real exogenous variables grow by 3 per cent per annum and that prices, tax rates

---

[11] To show this we repeat the accumulation condition for net foreign liabilities given by equation (3.3.19) in chapter 3. That is,

$$\frac{D_t}{\Phi_t} = \frac{1}{\Phi_{t-1}}\left\{ D_{t-1}[1 + B_{f,t-1}] - (E_t - M_t) + S_t \right\}, \qquad t = 1, \ldots, T \qquad (3.3.19)$$

where: D is the nominal Australian dollar ($A) value of net foreign liabilities; Φ is the nominal exchange rate ($A/$F); $B_{f,t}$ is the foreign interest rate; E and M are the $A values of exports and imports; and S is net unrequited transfers. In the CBG scenario Φ has the same value in all years and $B_{f,t}$ is set to 0.03 in all years. Under these conditions D will grow at 3 per cent only if the trade surplus (E - M) is equal to S. In the steady state D will accumulate passively at the rate of 3 per cent (i.e., through interest charges on existing liabilities) hence the active accumulation of D (i.e., through trade deficits or unrequited transfers) must be zero.

and unobservable variables, such as technical changes and taste changes and risk premia, remain constant over the 30 year time horizon.

In common with most intertemporal CGE modellers we have avoided tackling the difficult problems that must be resolved if a realistic control scenario is to be generated. In our initial attempts to produce a realistic control scenario we used unmodified historical data (i.e., the ORANI-13 database) to represent the structure of the economy in year 0 and, where available, we used historically observed growth rates for the exogenous variables. The main difficulty that we encountered with this approach was controlling the sectoral investment responses. The sectoral investment responses that we obtained bore little resemblance to the historical data. For some sectors investment jumped to the corner constraint in year 1 and remained there for the entire time horizon. For other sectors, investment growth in the first few years was very high. There are several possible explanations for the implausible investment responses that we encountered.

i. The theoretical structure of ORANI-INT may be inadequate. In particular, the specification of investment behaviour in the model may be deficient. Three aspects of our investment theory are likely to cause abrupt investment responses. First, the assumption that sectoral rates of return are unconstrained in year 1[12] but must be equal to the domestic interest rate in year 2 and beyond. In year 1 the sectoral rates of return were very disparate. Some sectors recorded negative rates of return while other sectors recorded rates of return that were significantly higher than the domestic interest rate. To accommodate the rate of return target in year 2, most sectors required a dramatic turnaround in their fortunes from year 1 to 2. The second critical assumption in our investment specification is that expectations are model-consistent. Even if the information set that investors base their expectations on is the same as that modelled, it is probable that expectations are not held with certainty as is assumed in the model. Thus, the investment responses in ORANI-INT will be more volatile than those observed because investors are assumed to react less cautiously to new information in ORANI-INT than they do in reality. Thirdly, our investment specification does not allow for the differential treatment of taxes/subsidies on capital income in the 13 sectors (e.g., capital gains and imputed rentals on owner-occupied dwellings are not taxed).

ii. The sectors whose investment responses were least plausible have one of the following sets of characteristics in the ORANI-13 database: the rental value of their capital stock is very low/high relative to the replacement value of the capital stock (e.g., on the low side are *Construction* and *Transport* and on the high side are *Mining* and *Finance*); or their rate of depreciation is high relative to the ratio of the rental-to-replacement values of their capital stock (e.g., *Rural*). The rental and replacement values of sectoral capital stocks and

---

[12] Recall that year 1 is supposed to represent a short run equilibrium in which sectoral capital stocks are assumed to be held constant with sectoral rates of return adjusting to clear capital markets.

the corresponding depreciation rates are probably the least reliable pieces of data contained on the ORANI-13 database. The measurement problems peculiar to these variables are described in Australian Bureau of Statistics (1990). Sectoral rates of return are sensitive to small measurement errors in these variables, particularly the rental value of sectoral capital stocks and the depreciation rates. Given our assumption that sectoral rates of return are equal to the domestic rate of interest in year 2 and beyond, errors in the measurement of capital stocks and depreciation rates in year 1 may accentuate the investment responses in that year.

iii. We have assumed that investors and consumers form model-consistent expectations. If the paths of all the exogenous variables are not consistent with the information set actually used by agents, then the investment and consumption responses produced by ORANI-INT may be inconsistent with observed responses (where observations are available) or may be implausible relative to historical responses. For example, the abrupt investment responses obtained for year 1 may indicate that the information set upon which investment decisions are based changed from year 0 to year 1. This may reflect changes in economic policies or circumstances that were unanticipated year 0 or it may reflect differences in the information set assumed in ORANI-INT and the actual information set used by investors. In setting the paths of the exogenous variables we opted for the convenient, but questionable, approach of assuming that the information set used by the forward-looking agents did not change over time. That is, we assumed that expectations formed in year 0 of the paths of the exogenous variables are realised. In a more appropriate treatment of the information set, expectations of exogenous variables will not always be realised. However, we avoided the challenging task of modelling an information set that changes over time for practical reasons. To do this task the modeller must first speculate about what information was available to agents in each year of the control scenario horizon. For example, did agents anticipate in 1981-82, the first year of the control scenario, the budget cuts that took place in 1996-97. The model must then be solved to reflect any changes in the information set over time. This involves solving the model conditional on the information set available in year 1 then, taking the results for year 1 as given, re-solving the model conditional on the information set available in year 2 and so on.[13]

[13] The computational burden of generating such a control scenario is greater than that required to generate a balanced growth scenario. To produce a balanced growth scenario ORANI-INT must be solved once only. In the case of a scenario in which the information set is changing over time the model must be solved as many times as the (annual) information set changes. However, given the efficiency of the ORANI-INT solution algorithm modellers are likely to be constrained by data limitations (e.g., what was contained in the information set in year t) long before the computational burden becomes prohibitive.

iv. Finally, the difficulties that we encountered with sectoral investment responses may stem from a combination of some or all of the above three explanations.

Two options that allowed us to represent the structure of the economy in year 0 with unmodified historical data (i.e., the ORANI-13 database) and at the same time to control the sectoral investment responses were explored. The first option involved the implementation of a variety of adjustment cost models in the spirit of Lucas (1967) and Treadway (1969). The second option involved the specification of an ad hoc partial adjustment mechanism to eliminate the disequilibrium in sectoral rates of return observed in the first year of the control scenario gradually rather than in one year as is assumed in the default specification of investment in ORANI-INT. In both cases judicious calibration of the parameters[14] was required to control the investment responses.

Despite the apparent success of the above two options for controlling investment responses we have chosen not to use them. The main reason for this is that neither approach deals with the problems canvassed above, particularly those relating to the veracity of key data items and to the availability and use of information by forward-looking agents. The arbitrary nature of the calibration procedure used in both approaches may in fact mask potential deficiencies in the model's theoretical specification and database. A related issue that must be considered is the appropriateness of the values assigned to the adjustment parameters in different modelling exercises. ORANI-INT can be used for forecasting or for comparative-dynamic analysis. The control scenario is a forecast that will serve as a reference solution in comparative dynamic simulations. Our aim in calibrating the adjustment parameters was to subdue the investment responses in the control scenario. It is not clear that the parameter values obtained in this manner will be appropriate when the model is used for comparative dynamic analysis.[15]

In constructing the CBG scenario our approach was to avoid changing the theoretical structure of the model and to control the investment responses by modifying the data representing the structure of the economy in year 0 (i.e., the ORANI-13 database). These modifications are detailed in appendix A5.1. The modifications were designed to eliminate from the ORANI-13 database as much of the disequilibrium (relative to an intertemporal equilibrium in which all real variables are growing by three percent per annum and prices are stationary) as was necessary to control the investment responses.[16] While this approach does not

---

14 In the case of the adjustment cost specification these were the sectoral adjustment cost parameters and in the case of the ad hoc partial adjustment mechanism these were the sectoral parameters governing the speed with which disequilibrium in sectoral rates of return is eliminated.

15 Ideally, these adjustment parameters should be estimated econometrically. Such an exercise is beyond the scope of this monograph. We were unable to find estimates of these parameters at the required level of disaggregation in the literature.

16 Other modellers, including McKibbin and Sachs (1991), choose to account for intertemporal disequilibrium in the base year as risk premia. The dilemma then is how to

solve any of the conceptual and data problems associated with producing a realistic control scenario, it does have the advantage of being transparent.

5.4 Chapter Summary

In this chapter we explained how a control scenario for ORANI-INT can be generated from an input-output database. We produced two such control scenarios. The BG scenario is characterised by balanced growth in all periods. The CBG scenario converges to balanced growth asymptotically. In generating the control scenarios we identified several difficulties that must be confronted before models like ORANI-INT can be used to produce realistic control scenarios (forecasts). In particular, we found that it is difficult to control the sectoral investment responses without resorting to *ad hoc* theoretical specifications and/or data manipulation. We also highlighted the difficulties faced by the modeller in assigning values to the paths of the exogenous variables. Judgements must be made about what is contained in the agents' information set at all points in time.

Apart from generating control scenarios that will be used in the next two chapters, the computations reported in this chapter also demonstrate the ability of ORANI-INT to converge to a balanced steady-growth path. This serves two purposes: first, it provides the reader with a useful reference point by identifying ORANI-INT within the class of neo-classical growth models; second, it allows an infinite period solution to be approximated by computing only the solution to the first T periods—in this case 30 years. The exogenous variables are on steady growth paths by design while the paths of the endogenous variables show strong evidence of convergence to steady growth by year 20. It is plausible to assume that the paths of the endogenous variables at time points t > T, would, if actually computed, conform to the steady growth path. Moreover, the paths of the endogenous variables over the interval [0, 30] should not be significantly affected by the choice of a new T (T*, say) arbitrarily larger than the originally chosen T.

---

model the evolution of these risk premia. The approach taken by McKibbin and Sachs is to hold the risk premia constant over time.

Appendix A5.1 The ORANI-13 Database

A5.1 Introduction

In this appendix we present the ORANI-13, ORANI-13A, and ORANI-13B databases. The latter two are the single-period databases that we use to construct the quasi-solutions QSA and QSB. The ORANI-13 database is based on the 13-sector aggregation of the 1980-81 ORANI database (see Parmenter, Meagher and Higgs (1994) for a description of this database). Hereafter, we refer to the aggregated ORANI database as the PMH database. The ORANI-13A, and ORANI-13B databases are modified version of the ORANI-13 database.

The remainder of this appendix is organised as follows. The PMH database is presented schematically in section A5.2. The relationship between the PMH and ORANI-13 databases is established. The complete ORANI-13 database is presented in section A5.3. Sections A5.4 and A5.5 document the ORANI-13A and ORANI-13B databases. This documentation includes only those parts of the databases that differ from the ORANI-13 database.

A5.2 The PMH Database

Figure A5.1.1 is a schematic representation of the PMH database. The columns identify 5 groups of agents: producers; capital-creators; households; foreigners; and governments. The cells in figure A5.1.1 contain data for 1980-81 showing the flows of commodities, indirect taxes and primary factors to the 5 groups of agents. Table A5.1.1 contains a description of the typical element of each matrix identified in figure A5.1.1 as well as a mapping of these elements to the notation used in chapter 3. Note that the direct flows identified in figure A5.1.1 are valued at basic prices (i.e., producer prices). The basic values of imports are calculated using f.o.b. prices. The data outlined in figure A5.1.1 is derived from the input-output accounts published by the Australian Bureau of Statistics. In addition to this data, the PMH database contains data on: import duties; the asset value of sectoral capital stocks; rates of depreciation on sectoral capital stocks; elasticities of substitution between primary factors; elasticities of substitution between domestic and foreign commodities; foreign elasticites of demand; and marginal budget shares.

		ABSORPTION MATRIX				
		1	2	3	4	5
		Producers	Investors	Household	Export	Govt.
	Size	← j →	← j →	← 1 →	← 1 →	← 1 →
Direct Flows	↑ i×s ↓	BAS1	BAS2	BAS3	BAS4	BAS5
Margins	↑ i×s×r ↓	MAR1	MAR2	MAR3	MAR4	MAR5
Taxes	↑ i×s ↓	TAX1	TAX2	TAX3	TAX4	TAX5
Labour	↑ o ↓	LAB				
Capital	↑ 1 ↓	CAPR				
Land	↑ 1 ↓	LAND				
Other Costs	↑ 1 ↓	OCT				

i = 13 = Number of Commodities

j = 13 = Number of Sectors

r = 4 = Number of Commodities used as Margins

s = 2 = Source (domestic, foreign)

o = 8 = Number of occupations

Figure A5.1.1: A Schematic Representation of the PMH Database

Table A5.1.1: A Description of the Flows in Figure A5.1.1

Matrix	Typical element in matrix	Ch 3 Notation
BAS1	flow of commodity i from source s to sector j	$P^{(Z)}_{i,s}X^{(1)}_{i,s,j}$
BAS2	flow of commodity i from source s to capital-creators in sector j	$P^{(Z)}_{i,s}X^{(2)}_{i,s,j}$
BAS3	flow of commodity i from source s to households	$P^{(Z)}_{i,s}X^{(3)}_{i,s}$
BAS4	flow of domestic commodity i to foreigners[(a)]	$P^{(Z)}_{i,d}X^{(4)}_{i,d}$
BAS5	flow of commodity i from source s to government	$P^{(Z)}_{i,s}X^{(5)}_{i,s}$
MAR1	flow of domestic commodity r used as a margin to facilitate the flow of commodity i from source s to sector j	na
MAR2	flow of domestic commodity r used as a margin to facilitate the flow of domestic commodity i from source s to capital-creators in sector j	na
MAR3	flow of domestic commodity r used as a margin to facilitate the flow of domestic commodity i from source s to households	na
MAR4	flow of domestic commodity r used as a margin to facilitate the flow of domestic commodity i foreigners	na
MAR5	flow of domestic commodity r used as a margin to facilitate the flow of domestic commodity i from source s to governments	na
TAX1	flow of taxes(subsidies) associated with the delivery of commodity i from source s to sector j	$P^{(Z)}_{i,s}X^{(1)}_{i,s,j}\tau^{(1)}_{i,s,j}$
TAX2	flow of taxes(subsidies) associated with the delivery of commodity i from source s to capital-creators in sector j	$P^{(Z)}_{i,s}X^{(2)}_{i,s,j}\tau^{(2)}_{i,s,j}$
TAX3	flow of taxes(subsidies) associated with the delivery of commodity i from source s to households	$P^{(Z)}_{i,s}X^{(3)}_{i,s}\tau^{(3)}_{i,s}$
TAX4	flow of taxes(subsidies) associated with the delivery of domestic commodity i to foreigners	$P^{(Z)}_{i,d}X^{(4)}_{i,d}\tau^{(4)}_{i}$
TAX5	flow of taxes(subsidies) associated with the delivery of commodity i from source s to government	$P^{(Z)}_{i,s}X^{(5)}_{i,s}\tau^{(5)}_{i,s}$
LAB	flow of labour of occupation type o to sector j	na
CAPR	flow of capital (rental value) to sector j	$P^{(K)}_{i,s,j}X^{(K)}_{i,s,j}$
LAND	flow of land (rental value) to sector j	$P^{(N)}_{i,s,j}X^{(N)}_{i,s,j}$
OCT	flow of "other cost tickets" to sector j	$P^{(O)}_{i,s,j}X^{(O)}_{i,s,j}$

(a) While the matrix BAS4 in figure A5.1.1 has dimensions ixs, only domestically produced commodities are exported. Thus the elements in BAS4 for s=2(=imports) are zero.

The PMH database is designed for a model that differs from ORANI in the level of sectoral disaggregation only. As explained in chapter 3, there are several other differences between the dimensions of ORANI and ORANI-13. The former model recognises 8 occupational categories and 4 margin commodities: ORANI-13 has a single occupational category only and treats margin commodities as if they were direct demands. Thus, in forming the ORANI-13 database we aggregate the PMH database to accommodate these differences. The shaded cells in figure A5.1.1 indicate the parts of the PMH data that we modified. To accommodate the assumption of a single occupational category in ORANI-13 the matrix LAB is aggregated by summing over o, the 8 occupational categories. To accommodate the assumption in ORANI-13 that margins are treated as final demands we add the matrices labelled MAR to their BAS counterparts.

The ORANI-13 database contains some additional data items not in the PMH database. For each year, the intertemporal equations in ORANI-INT introduce four scalar variables and one vector variable that do not appear in ORANI-13. These are: the foreign bond rate, the domestic bond rate,. net foreign liabilities, net unrequited transfers overseas, and sector-specific risk premia The intertemporal equations in ORANI-INT also introduce one new parameter, the time preference rate, that is not contained on the PMH database.

A5.3 The ORANI-13 Database

The presentation of the database is organised in tables A5.1.3 — A5.1.14. Table A5.1.2 contains a list of the sectors and commodities distinguished in the database and their identifiers. Apart from the interest rates in table A5.1.3 and the parameter values in table A5.1.4, the values in the remaining tables are expressed in millions of Australian dollars for the financial year 1981-82. To help the reader relate the ORANI-13 database to figure A5.1.1 we indicate in brackets in the table headings (or column headings) the correspondence between the data in each table and the matrices in figure A5.1.1. Note that because margins have been treated as final demands in ORANI-13 (i.e., in the notation of figure A5.1.1, we added the matrices labelled MAR to their BAS counterparts) we use an asterisk to differentiate the basic flows in the ORANI-13 database from those in the PMH database. For example, BAS1* in the ORANI-13 database is equal to the sum (over commodities) of BAS1 and MAR1 in the PMH database. In the tables below we have presented domestic and imported flows separately. This is indicated by the suffixes D and M. For example, BAS3D* is the flow of domestic commodities to households and BAS3M* is the flow of imported commodities to households.

Table A5.1.2: Sectors, Commodities and their Identifiers

	Sector/commodity	Identifier: Sector	Identifier: Commodity
1	Rural	I1	C1
2	Mining	I2	C2
3	Manufacturing	I3	C3
4	Utilities	I4	C4
5	Construction	I5	C5
6	W&R Trade	I6	C6
7	Transport	I7	C7
8	Finance	I8	C8
9	Housing	I9	C9
10	Public administration	I10	C10
11	Community services	I11	C11
12	Personal services	I12	C12
13	Non-competing imports	I13	C13

Table A5.1.3: Sundry Data Items (not in the PMH Database)

Foreign interest rate %	Domestic interest rate %	Time preference rate %	Net foreign liabilities	Net transfers overseas
3.0	3.0	3.0	14582	80

Table A5.1.4: Parameter Values

	Depreciation rate	Risk premium	Elas. of factor substitution
I1	0.11	0	1.28
I2	0.09	0	1.28
I3	0.09	0	1.28
I4	0.06	0	1.28
I5	0.05	0	1.28
I6	0.09	0	1.28
I7	0.06	0	1.28
I8	0.07	0	1.28
I9	0.03	0	1.28
I10	0.06	0	1.28
I11	0.08	0	1.28
I12	0.08	0	1.28
I13	0.08	0	1.28

	Armington elasticity	Export demand elas.	Marginal budget share
C1	1.61	-7.21	0.0076
C2	36.53	-13.39	0.0007
C3	1.65	-6.92	0.3562
C4	0.00	-20.00	0.0203
C5	0.00	-20.00	0.0000
C6	0.00	-20.00	0.0355
C7	1.26	-20.00	0.0607
C8	0.00	-20.00	0.0509
C9	0.00	-20.00	0.2714
C10	0.00	-20.00	0.0037
C11	0.00	-20.00	0.1028
C12	0.00	-20.00	0.0813
C13	0.00	-20.00	0.0090

Table A5.1.5: Flows of Domestic Commodities into Current Production (BAS1D*)

	I1	I2	I3	I4	I5	I6	I7	I8	I9	I10	I11	I12	I13
C1	883	23	6334	1	22	2	11	6	0	11	15	30	0
C2	4	1190	3487	599	240	24	52	9	2	15	26	16	0
C3	1488	828	22142	349	8489	2208	2460	992	531	895	1427	685	0
C4	129	230	1214	1405	74	188	155	576	818	199	333	274	0
C5	15	148	90	32	0	68	203	64	671	133	131	17	0
C6	391	290	3418	76	1127	857	1036	372	66	156	600	233	0
C7	233	404	2845	179	856	918	992	889	27	370	555	197	0
C8	323	672	2256	212	1286	3319	1083	3658	1482	808	1635	676	0
C9	0	0	0	0	0	0	0	0	0	0	0	0	0
C10	15	9	209	18	70	72	67	81	4	13	93	18	0
C11	80	54	128	7	46	67	70	178	2	67	191	47	0
C12	16	37	521	8	26	156	65	339	0	54	110	253	0
C13	0	0	0	0	0	0	0	0	0	0	0	0	0

Table A5.1.6: Flows of Imported Commodities into Current Production (BAS1M*)

	I1	I2	I3	I4	I5	I6	I7	I8	I9	I10	I11	I12	I13
C1	12	0	126	0	0	0	0	1	0	0	0	24	0
C2	3	4	2075	0	7	0	0	0	0	0	0	0	0
C3	206	374	6397	142	1282	452	810	281	107	592	517	276	0
C4	0	1	3	4	0	0	0	1	0	1	1	1	0
C5	0	0	0	0	0	0	0	0	0	0	0	0	0
C6	1	1	1	0	0	3	0	1	0	0	1	0	0
C7	6	101	78	4	18	97	324	52	0	39	35	11	0
C8	2	18	30	1	5	48	8	47	5	11	9	7	0
C9	0	0	0	0	0	0	0	0	0	0	0	0	0
C10	0	0	0	0	0	0	0	0	0	0	0	0	0
C11	0	0	0	0	0	0	0	1	0	0	0	0	0
C12	0	1	16	0	1	3	1	7	0	5	24	13	0
C13	1	8	374	4	35	58	11	37	0	303	11	15	0

Table A5.1.7: Flows of Domestic Commodities into Capital Creation (BAS2D*)

	I1	I2	I3	I4	I5	I6	I7	I8	I9	I10	I11	I12	I13
C1	121	0	0	0	0	0	0	0	0	0	0	0	0
C2	0	899	0	0	0	0	0	0	0	0	0	0	0
C3	373	385	1479	532	1042	535	925	250	0	55	171	121	0
C4	0	0	0	0	0	0	0	0	0	0	0	0	0
C5	1044	846	1476	1443	1290	1545	1994	2571	6295	429	1290	771	0
C6	101	104	393	143	279	234	248	73	0	15	48	34	0
C7	22	22	84	31	60	31	53	16	0	3	10	7	0
C8	94	66	133	23	116	139	59	231	392	7	24	69	0
C9	0	0	0	0	0	0	0	0	0	0	0	0	0
C10	0	0	0	0	0	0	0	0	0	0	0	0	0
C11	0	0	0	0	0	0	0	0	0	0	0	0	0
C12	0	0	0	0	0	0	0	0	0	0	0	0	0
C13	0	0	0	0	0	0	0	0	0	0	0	0	0

Table A5.1.8: Flows of Imported Commodities into Capital Creation (BAS2M*)

	I1	I2	I3	I4	I5	I6	I7	I8	I9	I10	I11	I12	I13
C1	0	0	0	0	0	0	0	0	0	0	0	0	0
C2	0	0	0	0	0	0	0	0	0	0	0	0	0
C3	246	254	976	351	688	353	610	165	0	36	113	80	0
C4	0	0	0	0	0	0	0	0	0	0	0	0	0
C5	0	0	0	0	0	0	0	0	0	0	0	0	0
C6	0	0	0	0	0	0	0	0	0	0	0	0	0
C7	0	0	0	0	0	0	0	0	0	0	0	0	0
C8	1	0	1	0	1	1	0	2	3	0	0	0	0
C9	0	0	0	0	0	0	0	0	0	0	0	0	0
C10	0	0	0	0	0	0	0	0	0	0	0	0	0
C11	0	0	0	0	0	0	0	0	0	0	0	0	0
C12	0	0	0	0	0	0	0	0	0	0	0	0	0
C13	0	0	0	0	0	0	0	0	0	0	0	0	0

Table A5.1.9: Taxes on Flows of Domestic Commodities into Current Production (TAX1D)

	I1	I2	I3	I4	I5	I6	I7	I8	I9	I10	I11	I12	I13
C1	-7	0	-95	0	0	0	0	0	0	0	0	0	0
C2	0	3	1865	4	1	1	6	1	0	0	4	1	0
C3	29	21	138	1	32	134	147	46	3	0	49	17	0
C4	-1	1	7	7	0	1	0	-3	-13	0	1	0	0
C5	0	0	0	0	0	0	0	0	0	0	0	0	0
C6	0	0	0	0	0	0	0	0	0	0	0	0	0
C7	0	0	-2	0	0	-2	0	-2	0	0	-1	0	0
C8	3	8	16	3	10	13	11	24	71	0	11	3	0
C9	0	0	0	0	0	0	0	0	0	0	0	0	0
C10	0	0	0	0	0	0	0	0	0	0	0	0	0
C11	0	0	0	0	0	0	0	0	0	0	0	0	0
C12	0	0	13	0	0	2	1	5	0	0	0	0	0
C13	0	0	0	0	0	0	0	0	0	0	0	0	0

Table A5.1.10: Taxes on Flows of Imported Commodities into Current Production (TAX1M)

	I1	I2	I3	I4	I5	I6	I7	I8	I9	I10	I11	I12	I13
C1	0	0	-2	0	0	0	0	0	0	0	0	0	0
C2	0	0	1110	0	0	0	0	0	0	0	0	0	0
C3	4	9	40	0	5	27	49	13	1	0	18	7	0
C4	0	0	0	0	0	0	0	0	0	0	0	0	0
C5	0	0	0	0	0	0	0	0	0	0	0	0	0
C6	0	0	0	0	0	0	0	0	0	0	0	0	0
C7	0	0	0	0	0	0	0	0	0	0	0	0	0
C8	0	0	0	0	0	0	0	0	0	0	0	0	0
C9	0	0	0	0	0	0	0	0	0	0	0	0	0
C10	0	0	0	0	0	0	0	0	0	0	0	0	0
C11	0	0	0	0	0	0	0	0	0	0	0	0	0
C12	0	0	0	0	0	0	0	0	0	0	0	0	0
C13	0	0	0	0	0	0	0	0	0	0	0	0	0

Table A5.1.11: Taxes on Flows of Domestic Commodities into Capital Creation (TAX2D)

	I1	I2	I3	I4	I5	I6	I7	I8	I9	I10	I11	I12	I13
C1	0	0	0	0	0	0	0	0	0	0	0	0	0
C2	0	0	0	0	0	0	0	0	0	0	0	0	0
C3	5	6	21	8	15	8	13	4	0	1	2	2	0
C4	0	0	0	0	0	0	0	0	0	0	0	0	0
C5	0	0	0	0	0	0	-1	-1	-2	0	0	0	0
C6	0	0	0	0	0	0	0	0	0	0	0	0	0
C7	0	0	0	0	0	0	0	0	0	0	0	0	0
C8	0	0	0	0	0	0	0	0	0	0	0	0	0
C9	0	0	0	0	0	0	0	0	0	0	0	0	0
C10	0	0	0	0	0	0	0	0	0	0	0	0	0
C11	0	0	0	0	0	0	0	0	0	0	0	0	0
C12	0	0	0	0	0	0	0	0	0	0	0	0	0
C13	0	0	0	0	0	0	0	0	0	0	0	0	0

Table A5 1.12: Taxes on Flows of Imported Commodities into Capital Creation (TAX2M)

	I1	I2	I3	I4	I5	I6	I7	I8	I9	I10	I11	I12	I13
C1	0	0	0	0	0	0	0	0	0	0	0	0	0
C2	0	0	0	0	0	0	0	0	0	0	0	0	0
C3	4	4	14	5	10	5	9	2	0	1	2	1	0
C4	0	0	0	0	0	0	0	0	0	0	0	0	0
C5	0	0	0	0	0	0	0	0	0	0	0	0	0
C6	0	0	0	0	0	0	0	0	0	0	0	0	0
C7	0	0	0	0	0	0	0	0	0	0	0	0	0
C8	0	0	0	0	0	0	0	0	0	0	0	0	0
C9	0	0	0	0	0	0	0	0	0	0	0	0	0
C10	0	0	0	0	0	0	0	0	0	0	0	0	0
C11	0	0	0	0	0	0	0	0	0	0	0	0	0
C12	0	0	0	0	0	0	0	0	0	0	0	0	0
C13	0	0	0	0	0	0	0	0	0	0	0	0	0

Table A5.1.13: Sundry Commodity Flows and Indirect Taxes

	Household Consumption				Exports		Other Demands				Import duty
	Domestic flows (BAS3D*)	Tax on domestic (TAX3D)	Import (BAS3M*)	Tax on imports (TAX3M)	Basic flow (BAS4*)	Tax (TAX4)	Domestic flows (BAS5D*)	Tax on domestic (TAX5D)	Import (BAS5M*)	Tax on imports (TAX5M)	(DUTY)
C1	1110	-26	71	-2	4007	22	176	0	1	0	6
C2	36	6	0	0	3461	133	28	0	0	0	2
C3	20632	3387	4218	692	9034	-10	43	0	3	0	1506
C4	1643	21	4	0	14	0	101	0	0	0	0
C5	0	0	0	0	0	0	0	0	0	0	0
C6	15825	0	0	0	1338	0	0	0	0	0	0
C7	4849	-407	579	-60	3427	0	329	0	28	0	0
C8	3101	72	17	0	184	3	468	0	2	0	0
C9	13666	-4	0	0	0	0	0	0	0	0	0
C10	226	0	0	0	33	0	8246	0	0	0	0
C11	6394	0	2	0	21	0	12766	0	1	0	0
C12	5751	461	59	6	43	1	529	0	5	0	0
C13	0	0	440	0	0	0	0	0	0	0	0

Table A5.1.14: Flows of Primary Factors, 'Other Costs' and the Asset Value of Capital Stocks

	Primary factors			Other cost tickets	Capital stock
	Wage bill (LAB)	Capital rents (CAPR)	Land rents (LAND)	(OCT)	(KS)
I1	4796	1365	2436	319	17927
I2	2114	2394	0	1146	13657
I3	15854	4224	0	3159	35247
I4	1740	2131	0	426	27984
I5	7553	818	0	563	38407
I6	12855	2430	0	3452	19011
I7	7664	1498	0	686	42642
I8	8251	4333	0	2258	21446
I9	0	9824	0	64	93264
I10	5435	60	0	7	12993
I11	13576	415	0	334	16870
I12	3319	851	0	922	8155
I13	0	0	0	0	0

A5.4 The ORANI-13A Database

We generate the ORANI-13A database by re-configuring the ORANI-13 database so that it is consistent with an intertemporal equilibrium in which all real variables grow by 3 percent and all prices are stationary. To meet these requirements the ORANI-13A database must meet three criteria. First, the net-investment-to-capital ratios must equal 3 percent. Second, the risk-adjusted sectoral rates of return must equal 3 percent. Finally, the trade deficit must equal net transfers overseas. For convenience we set net transfers overseas to zero in the ORANI-13A database. The remaining differences between the ORANI-13 and ORANI-13A databases are recorded in tables A5.1.15 and A5.1.16. Details about how the adjustments were made are provided beneath each table.

The ORANI-13 database is consistent with the usual input-output accounting conventions. In making adjustments to the database we are careful to observe these conventions. For example, we ensure that the ORANI-13A database is balanced. That is, we ensure that the adjustments that we make do not upset the equality between costs and sales in each industry. Similarly, we ensure that the equality between income and expenditure is preserved (e.g., GDP measured from the expenditure and income sides is identical).

A5.5 The ORANI-13B Database

The ORANI-13B database is also a modified version of the ORANI-13 database. The differences between these two databases are recorded in tables A5.1.17 and A5.1.18. Arbitrary alterations were made to the ORANI-13 database to reduce, but not eliminate, the degree of disequilibrium (relative to a long-run balanced 3 per cent growth equilibrium) reflected in it. Table A5.1.19 provides a comparison of the net-investment-to-capital ratios and the risk adjusted rates of return in the ORANI-13 and ORANI-13B databases.

Tables A5.1.17—A5.1.19 show that we have made adjustments to seven of the twelve sectors. Our aim was to make the minimal adjustments to the data necessary to control sectoral investment responses. In so doing the binding criteria was that no sector has zero investment (i.e., the corner constraint is not binding) in the year 1 of the CBG scenario. A more flexible criterion was to confine sectoral investment growth rates in year 1 of the CBG scenario in a band of ±50 per cent. Two notable outliers were the *Transport* and *Housing* sectors. Investment growth in year 1 of the CBG scenario is minus 90 per cent for *Transport* and plus 85 per cent for *Housing*.

Table A5.1.15: Changes to Commodity Flows

	Domestic household consumption (BAS3D*)[a]		Tax on domestic household consumption (TAX3D)[b]		Exports (BAS4*)[c]		Taxes on exports (TAX4)[d]	
	ORANI-13	***ORANI-13A***	ORANI-13	***ORANI-13A***	ORANI-13	***ORANI-13A***	ORANI-13	***ORANI-13A***
C1	1110	***800***	-26	***-28***	4007	***4318***	22	***24***
C2	36	***36***	6	***-5***	3461	***3729***	133	***143***
C3	20632	***19932***	3387	***3388***	9034	***9733***	-10	***-11***
C4	1643	***1642***	21	***21***	14	***15***	0	***-0***
C5	0	***0***	0	***0***	0	***0***	0	***0***
C6	15825	***15722***	0	***0***	1338	***1442***	0	***0***
C7	4849	***4584***	-407	***-407***	3427	***3692***	0	***0***
C8	3101	***3086***	72	***72***	184	***199***	3	***3***
C9	13666	***13666***	-4	***-4***	0	***0***	0	***0***
C10	226	***224***	0	***0***	33	***36***	0	***0***
C11	6394	***6392***	0	***0***	21	***23***	0	***0***
C12	5751	***5748***	461	***461***	43	***46***	1	***1***
C13	0	***0***	0	***0***	0	***0***	0	***0***

Notes:

(a) Adjustments to the domestic household consumption vector are made as follows:

$$\text{BAS3D}_i^A = \text{BAS3D}_i - [\text{BAS4D}_i^A - \text{BAS4D}_i] \qquad i \neq 2$$

$$\text{BAS3D}_i^A = \text{BAS3D}_i \qquad i = 2$$

The variable names used correspond to the column headings in the tables containing the data. We have dropped the * superscript for convenience and have used the A superscript to differentiate the variables in the ORANI-13A database from their counterparts in the ORANI-13 database. These conventions will be maintained below.

(b) To balance the trade account we make the following adjustments to the export vector:

$$\text{BAS4D}_i^A = \text{BAS4D}_i \times \frac{\text{IMPORTS}}{\text{EXPORTS}}$$

where,

$$\text{IMPORTS} = \sum_{i=1}^{13}\sum_{j=1}^{13}[\text{BAS1M}_{i,j} + \text{BAS2M}_{i,j} + \text{BAS3M}_i + \text{BAS5M}_i - \text{DUTY}_i]$$

and

$$\text{EXPORTS} = \sum_{i=1}^{13}[\text{BAS4}_i + \text{TAX4}_i] .$$

(c) In the trade balance exports are valued at f.o.b prices. Thus, we adjust the export tax vector in the same way as the export vector. That is:

$$\text{TAX4D}_i^A = \text{TAX4D}_i \times \frac{\text{IMPORTS}}{\text{EXPORTS}} .$$

(d) The adjustments made to export taxes are offset by the following adjustments to consumption taxes:

$$\text{TAX3D}_i^A = \text{TAX3D}_i - [\text{TAX4D}_i^A - \text{TAX4D}_i] .$$

Table A5.1.16: Changes to Industry Flows

	Primary factors									
	Wage bill (LAB)[e]		Capital rents (CAPR)[f]		Other cost tickets (OCT)[g]		Capital stocks (KS)[h]		Risk premium % (RP)[i]	
	O-13	*O-13A*	O-13	*O-13A*	O-13	*O-13A*	O-13	*O-13A*	O-13	*O-13A*
I1	4796	*4473*	1365	*2011*	319	*-4*	17927	*15471*	0	*0*
I2	2114	*2018*	2394	*2586*	1146	*1319*	13657	*20957*	0	*0*
I3	15854	*15677*	4224	*4578*	3159	*2982*	35247	*37062*	0	*0*
I4	1740	*1537*	2131	*2536*	426	*224*	27984	*28235*	0	*0*
I5	7553	*6212*	818	*3499*	563	*-778*	38407	*43472*	0	*0*
I6	12855	*12645*	2430	*2851*	3452	*3242*	19011	*23519*	0	*0*
I7	7664	*6458*	1498	*3912*	686	*-521*	42642	*44357*	0	*0*
I8	8251	*8761*	4333	*3312*	2258	*2769*	21446	*31855*	0	*0*
I9	0	*0*	9824	*9877*	64	*12*	93264	*106278*	0	*3.0*
I10	5435	*5192*	60	*547*	7	*-237*	12993	*6427*	0	*0*
I11	13576	*12953*	415	*1661*	334	*-289*	16870	*15112*	0	*0*
I12	3319	*3201*	851	*1086*	922	*805*	8155	*10300*	0	*0*
I13	0	*0*	0	*0*	0	*0*	0	*0*	0	*0*

Notes:

(a) Sectoral wage bills were altered to compensate for adjustments in sectoral capital rentals as follows:

$$LAB_j^A = LAB_j - 0.5\times[CAPR_j^A - CAPR_j] \qquad j\neq 9$$

$$LAB_j^A = LAB_j \qquad j=9$$

(b) Sectoral capital rentals were adjusted to be consistent with a risk-adjusted net return of 3 per cent:

$$CAPR_j^A = [0.03 + \delta_j^A + RP_j^A]\times KS_j^A$$

where δ is the depreciation rate, RP is the risk premium and KS is the asset value of the capital stock.

(c) The asset values of sectoral capital are configured so that the net investment-capital ratio is 3 per cent:

$$\sum_{i=1}^{13}[BAS2D_{i,j} + BAS2M_{i,j} + TAX2D_{i,j} + TAX2M_{i,j}] = INVEST_j = KS_j^A\ [0.03 + \delta_j^A]$$

(d) Some of the adjustments to sectoral capital rentals were offset by adjustments to sectoral wage bills (see note (e) above). The remainder is offset by adjustment to other cost tickets as follows:

$$OCT_j^A = OCT_j - 0.5\times[CAPR_j^A - CAPR_j] \qquad j\neq 2,9$$

and $$OCT_j^A = OCT_j - [CAPR_j^A - CAPR_j]\ . \qquad j=9$$

For sector 2, the adjustment to 'other costs' also allows for that part of the adjustment to exports of commodity 2 not offset by the adjustment to consumption (see table A5.1.15, note (a)). That is:

$$OCT_j^A = OCT_j - 0.5\times[CAPR_j^A - CAPR_j] + [BAS4D_i^A - BAS4D_i] \qquad j=2$$

(e) The risk premium for sector 9 is set to 3 per cent. We choose not to make adjustments to sector 9's cost or sales data. The adjustments necessary to equate this sector's risk-adjusted net return to 3 per cent were considered too large because they changed the fundamental nature of the industry.

The adjustments made to the database are arbitrary hence we offer little justification for them. The key to controlling the sectoral investment responses is to adjust the data relating to sectoral capital rentals. Such adjustments then have to be offset by adjustments to sectoral costs (e.g., payments to labour) or sales (e.g., sales to governments) to preserve the balancing properties of the database. To control the investment responses of the *Mining*, *Finance* and *Housing* sectors we have allowed their rates of return to be higher than the market rate of interest by assigning to each a risk premium. Controlling the investment responses of these sectors without resorting to risk premiums required large adjustments to their cost and sales structures. Such large changes were deemed to be undesirable because they altered the fundamental nature of these sectors and their relationships with the rest of the economy.

Table A5.1.17: Changes to Sectoral Variables

	Primary factors									
	Wage bill (LAB)		Capital rents (CAPR)		Land rents (LAND)		Other cost tickets (OCT)		Capital stocks (KS)	
	ORANI-13	***O-13B***	O-13	***O-13B***	O-13	***O-13B***	O-13	***O-13B***	O-13	***O-13B***
I1	4796	***4296***	1365	***2365***	2436	***2186***	319	***69***	17927	17927
I2	2114	2114	2394	2394	0	0	1146	1146	13657	13657
I3	15854	15854	4224	***4724***	0	0	3159	***2659***	35247	35247
I4	1740	1740	2131	***2531***	0	0	426	***26***	27984	27984
I5	7553	***6353***	818	***2818***	0	0	563	***63***	38407	38407
I6	12855	12855	2430	2430	0	0	3452	3452	19011	19011
I7	7664	***6514***	1498	***3598***	0	0	686	***36***	42642	42642
I8	8251	***9251***	4333	***3333***	0	0	2258	2258	21446	21446
I9	0	0	9824	9824	0	0	64	64	93264	93264
I10	5435	5435	60	60	0	0	7	7	12993	12993
I11	13576	13576	415	415	0	0	334	334	16870	16870
I12	3319	3319	851	***1251***	0	0	922	***522***	8155	***10000***
I13	0	0	0	***0***	0	0	0	0	0	0

Table A5.1.18: Sundry Adjustments to Database

	Depreciation rate		Risk premium % (RP)	
	ORANI-13	*ORANI-13B*	ORANI-13	*ORANI-13B*
I1	0.11	***0.10***	0	0
I2	0.09	0.09	0	0
I3	0.09	0.09	0	***3.0***
I4	0.06	0.06	0	0
I5	0.05	0.05	0	0
I6	0.09	0.09	0	0
I7	0.06	0.06	0	0
I8	0.07	0.07	0	***3.0***
I9	0.03	0.03	0	***2.0***
I10	0.06	0.06	0	0
I11	0.08	0.08	0	0
I12	0.08	0.08	0	0
I13	0.08	0.08	0	0

	Other domestic demands (BAS5D*)	
	ORANI-13	*ORANI-13B*
C1	176	176
C2	28	28
C3	43	43
C4	101	101
C5	0	***300***
C6	0	0
C7	329	***629***
C8	468	468
C9	0	0
C10	8246	8246
C11	12766	12766
C12	529	529
C13	0	0

Table A5.1.19: Sectoral Investment-Capital Ratios and Rates of Return

	Net-investment-to-capital ratio (per cent)		Risk adjusted rate of return (per cent)	
Sector	ORANI-13	*ORANI-13B*	ORANI-13	*ORANI-13B*
Rural	-0.2	***1.2***	-3.8	***3.2***
Mining	9.6	9.6	8.2	***5.2***
Manufacturing	3.6	3.6	2.6	***4.1***
Utilities	3.1	3.1	1.6	***3.1***
Construction	4.1	4.1	-2.9	***2.3***
W&R Trade	5.9	5.9	3.7	3.7
Transport	3.4	3.4	-2.3	***2.6***
Finance	8.0	8.0	12.8	***5.1***
Housing	3.9	3.9	7.2	***5.2***
Public administration	-1.3	-1.3	-5.1	-5.1
Community services	1.9	1.9	-5.5	-5.5
Personal services	5.8	***3.3***	2.9	***5.0***
Non-competing imports	-7.5	-7.5	0.0	0.0

Chapter 6 ORANI-INT's Simulation Properties With and Without Forward-looking Behaviour

6.1 Introduction

In this chapter we demonstrate how ORANI-INT can be used to conduct comparative-dynamic simulations. The role of the intertemporal mechanisms in the model are highlighted via a detailed analysis of the results of five illustrative experiments. These experiments have in common a permanent expansion in government expenditure. The effects of such a shock are examined both with and without forward-looking behaviour. Also, the effects of announcing such a policy in advance of its implementation are compared to the case where the shock is implemented without warning.

The purpose of the illustrative experiments is not to shed light on actual policy issues but, rather, to investigate the properties of the model itself. A set of more policy-oriented simulations is presented in the next chapter. By reconciling the results of the five illustrative simulations with ORANI-INT's theoretical structure and database we aim to provide some evidence that the model is free of implementation errors. This process of justifying the simulation results should also provide the reader with a basis for assessing the plausibility of the model's projections by bringing to the fore critical theoretical assumptions and critical elements of the database. The experience gained in interpreting the results of relatively simple experiments will also be of benefit when more realistic, but more complicated, experiments are analysed in the next chapter.

6.2 An Overview of the Illustrative Experiments

The time horizon of the five illustrative experiments is 30 years. We use the BG scenario (described in chapter 5) as the control solution. In each experiment real government expenditure is assumed to be 1 per cent higher than it is in the BG scenario in each of years 10 through 30. The identifying characteristics of the five experiments are listed in table 6.2.1. The experiments are designed to highlight the roles, individually and jointly, of the static and forward-looking mechanisms in ORANI-INT. We disentangle the effects of these mechanisms by first stripping away all forward-looking behaviour and then reinstating the forward-looking mechanisms separately. This decomposition allows us to explain the static and intertemporal mechanisms in ORANI-INT separately.

Table 6.2.1: Key Feature of the Five Illustrative Simulations

Feature *Experiment*	Forward-looking consumption	Forward-looking investment	Number of years of anticipation
1. Benchmark	No	No	10
2. Investment	No	Yes	10
3. Consumption	Yes	No	10
4. Full intertemporal	Yes	Yes	10
5. Surprise	Yes	Yes	0

In the first experiment all forward-looking behaviour in the model is removed. The results obtained from this experiment constitute the benchmark against which results from subsequent experiments will be compared. For this reason, we also refer to experiment 1 as the *benchmark* experiment. Removing the forward-looking behaviour from ORANI-INT reduces the model to a sequence of static ORANI models that are linked through time by stock-flow accounting relations only. The results produced by ORANI-INT in this configuration can be treated as comparative static and explained by the same types of mechanisms used to account for ORANI results.

The mechanisms underlying the results of the *benchmark* experiment are also present in the results of the other four simulations. In all simulations the long-run results generated by ORANI-INT are consistent with a balanced-growth steady state. The long-run results can, therefore, be replicated by a single-period model (ORANI). Thus, like the results of the *benchmark* experiment, the long-run results of the other experiments can be explained without appealing to intertemporal mechanisms. In the experiments with forward-looking behaviour the long-run results also provide insights about the behaviour of agents in the short and medium run by indicating the direction in which the economy is tending. Thus, the static mechanisms in ORANI-INT are crucial not only for explaining the steady-state results but also the transition of the economy to the steady state.

Having established the static results produced by ORANI-INT as the benchmark, we then proceed to reinstate forward-looking behaviour into the model. There are two sources of forward-looking behaviour in ORANI-INT. The first emanates from the modelling of capital gains in the equilibrium conditions for sectoral capital stocks (i.e., equation (3.3.33) in chapter 3). The second emanates from the equilibrium condition for aggregate consumption (i.e., equation (3.3.17) in chapter) which implies that households smooth their consumption over time. Forward-looking investment and consumption behaviour are examined separately in the second and third experiments respectively. For short, we call the former the *investment* experiment and the latter the *consumption* experiment.

In the fourth experiment, which we label the *full intertemporal* experiment, both forward-looking mechanisms are allowed to operate simultaneously. The final experiment, referred to as the *surprise* experiment, is identical to the full intertemporal experiment except that agents do not anticipate the shock to government expenditure.

6.3 Interpretation of Results

Following the imposition of a shock, or set of shocks, ORANI-INT produces projections of the per-cent deviations of each endogenous variable (in each year of the 30-year time horizon) from its corresponding value in the control scenario (in this case the BG scenario).

The results of the five illustrative simulations are presented in a series of charts. These charts depict the time paths of the per-cent deviations of variables from their control-scenario values. When referring to the charts the qualifier that indicates that the results are per-cent deviations from the control scenario will often be suppressed. For example, where the meaning is obvious from the context, we will refer to the path of the per-cent deviations in real GDP as simply the path of real GDP.

To analyse the results of each simulation it is convenient to divide the 30-year time horizon of the experiments into four sub-intervals. These intervals are depicted in figure 6.3.1. Following the shock to government expenditure we expect the model to converge to a new steady state by year 30 – that is, a state in which all real variables are growing at a common rate (in this case 3 per cent) and all price variables are stationary. As mentioned above, this property implies that the long-run results (marked in figure 6.3.1 by the interval **A**) can be treated as if they were produced by a comparative-static model. The comparative static nature of the long-run results makes their interpretation less difficult. For this reason, we discuss the long-run results first. The second sub-interval analysed includes year 10, the year in which the government shock is initially implemented, as well as the years immediately prior and after (i.e., years 9 and 11). This interval is marked **B** in figure 6.3.1. Next, the transition from year 10 to the long run, marked **C** in figure 6.3.1, is discussed. Finally, anticipation effects are examined with reference to the results pertaining to the pre-shock years (i.e., the interval marked **D**).

6.4 The Benchmark Experiment

The only links between the periods that are allowed in this experiment are those provided by the accumulation relations between trade deficits and foreign liabilities, and between sectoral investment and capital. In this configuration ORANI-INT is recursive and the values of variables in period t depend on past decisions but not on any future variables. To suppress all forward-looking behaviour, the closure that we use in this experiment differs in several ways from the standard one described in chapter 6. In each year aggregate real consumption is fixed[1] — that is, it is exogenous and held at its control-scenario values.[2] There is no constraint on foreign liabilities.[3] The absence of a foreign-liabilities constraint means that accumulation equation (3.3.19) plays a passive role in this experiment. The level of foreign liabilities does not have any feedback effects on any other variable. In the final alteration to the standard closure we suppress forward-looking investment behaviour by endowing investors with static expectations.[4]

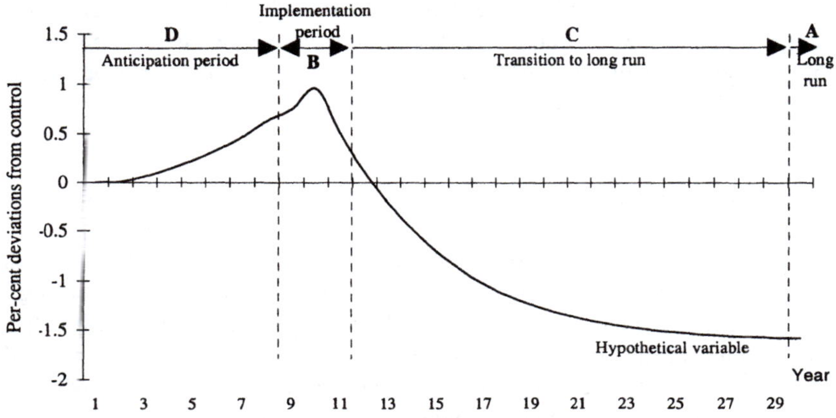

Figure 6.3.1: Division of the 30 Year Horizon into Four Sub-intervals

With static expectations the equilibrium condition for sectoral investment (i.e., equation (3.3.33) in chapter 3) can be expressed as:

$$P^{(K)}_{j,t} = [\Psi_{d,t-1} + \delta_j]P^{(Y)}_{j,t}. \qquad j = 1, ..., 13, t = 2, ..., T \qquad (6.4.1)$$

In this equation $P^{(K)}_{j,t}$ is the rental price of a unit of capital in sector j in year t, $P^{(Y)}_{j,t}$ is the price of a unit of investment in sector j in year t, $\Psi_{d,t}$ is the risk-adjusted rate of

---

1 We do this via a closure swap involving $C^{(R)}_t$, aggregate real consumption, and $F^{(3)}_t$, the shifter on the intertemporal consumption function (see section 3.3.1 in chapter 3). In the standard closure described in section 5.3.1 of chapter 5 $C^{(R)}_t$ is endogenous for all t and $F^{(3)}_t$ is exogenous for all t. In the *Benchmark* and *Investment* experiments we modify the standard closure so that $C^{(R)}_t$ is exogenous for all t and $F^{(3)}_t$ is endogenous for all t.

2 Hereafter a variable that is exogenous and held at its control scenario value will be referred to as being 'fixed'.

3 This follows from the closure swap described in footnote 1 above. Recall that the shifter $F^{(3)}_t$ for t=T relates to the terminal condition on the accumulation of foreign liabilities (see section 3.3.1 in chapter 3).

4 In the standard closure $K^{(A)}_t$, capital gains, is endogenous and $F^{(A)}_t$, the shifter on the equation defining capital gains, is exogenous. In the *Benchmark* and *Consumption* experiments we make $K^{(A)}_t$ exogenous and $F^{(A)}_t$ endogenous.

return in sector j in year t and δ_j is the rate of depreciation of capital in sector j. Note that in equation (6.4.1) we have abstracted from the complications of binding nonnegativity constraints on investment. With $\Psi_{d,t}$ and δ_j held at their control scenario values[5], the key implication of equation (6.4.1) for the *benchmark* experiment is that changes in $P^{(K)}_{j,t}$ and $P^{(Y)}_{j,t}$ will be proportional.

A selection of results from the *benchmark* experiment is presented in figures 6.4.2—6.4.4. There are several notable features in these results. The first is that even though the shock to government expenditure does not commence until year 10, agents react prior to its implementation. A second notable feature is that the economy becomes less capital intensive even though returns to capital remain unchanged. Finally, we observe that the model converges to its new long-run equilibrium growth path in year 10, the same year in which the permanent 1 per cent increase in government expenditure is implemented.

6.4.1 Long-run Results

The increase in government expenditure may be accommodated by crowding-out some other component of aggregate demand and/or by increasing the economy's productive capacity. In ORANI-INT, aggregate output is a function of the endowments of the primary factors: agricultural land; labour; and capital. With aggregate labour and land endowments fixed, aggregate output depends on the capital stock only. The nominal exchange rate, the foreign interest rate and the sector-specific risk premia are all fixed. These conditions, together with our arbitrage assumptions, imply that sectoral rates of return remain at their control scenario values. Because sectoral rates of return remain at their control scenario values we might expect that demands for capital, and hence investment, will also remain at their control scenario levels. If this were the case, any expansion in government expenditure would, given that real consumption expenditure is fixed, be fully absorbed by a deterioration in the balance of trade.

The results in figure 6.4.2 show that the increase in government expenditure, which is equivalent to about 0.16 per cent of GDP in year 30 of the control scenario, is accommodated largely by a deterioration in the balance of trade and partly by an increase in the economy's productive capacity. The crowding-out of the trade balance is achieved by the 0.18 per cent appreciation of the real exchange rate (see figure 6.4.3). ORANI-INT projects that in year 30 export volumes will be 0.85 per cent below control and that import volumes will be 0.34 per cent above control. In the BG control scenario trade is balanced with exports and imports each accounting for about 17 per cent of GDP. Thus, the projected decrease in exports

---

[5] Whilst $\Psi_{d,t}$ is an endogenous variable we can deduce that it remains at its control scenario values from arbitrage condition (3.3.20) in chapter 3. Two of the three variables on the RHS of equation (3.3.20) are exogenous. These are $H_{j,t}$, the sector-specific risk premium, and $F^{(2)}_{j,t}$, the shifter on the arbitrage condition. The other variable, the domestic bond rate is related, via uncovered interest parity, to the foreign bond rate and the exchange rate. The paths of the foreign bond rate and the exchange rate are exogenous and not shocked.

and increase in imports causes the trade balance, in volume terms, to deteriorate by about 0.2 per cent of the BG scenario level of GDP in year 30. Since Australia is assumed to have some market power in its export markets, the decrease in export volumes causes the terms of trade to improve by about 0.017 per cent.[6] Consequently, the deterioration in the nominal trade balance is about 0.18 per cent of the BG scenario level of GDP in year 30.

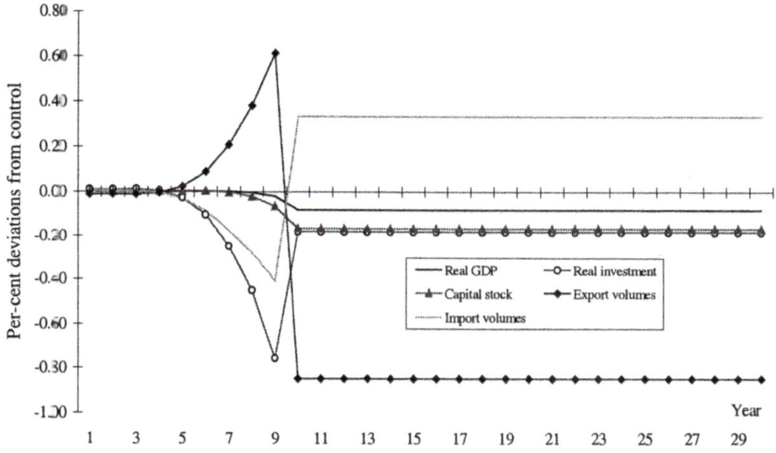

Figure 6.4.2: *Benchmark* Simulation Projections for Selected Real Macro Variables

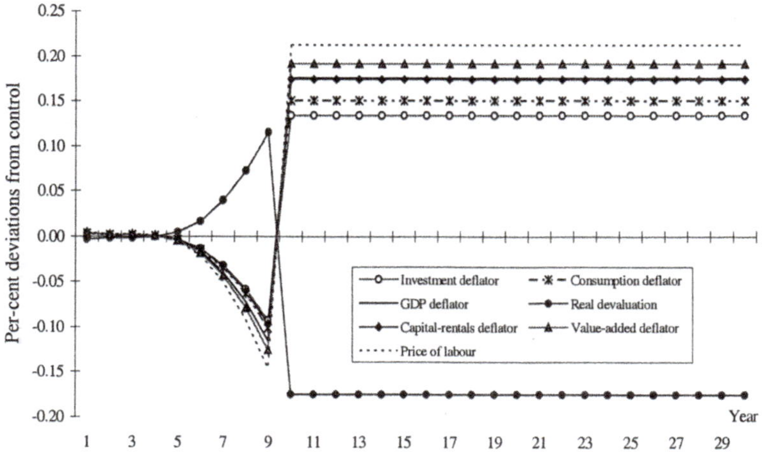

Figure 6.4.3: *Benchmark* Simulation Projections for Selected Deflators

6 Since the paths of the foreign currency prices of imports are exogenous and unshocked, the improvement in the terms of trade emanates from increases in the foreign currency prices of exports.

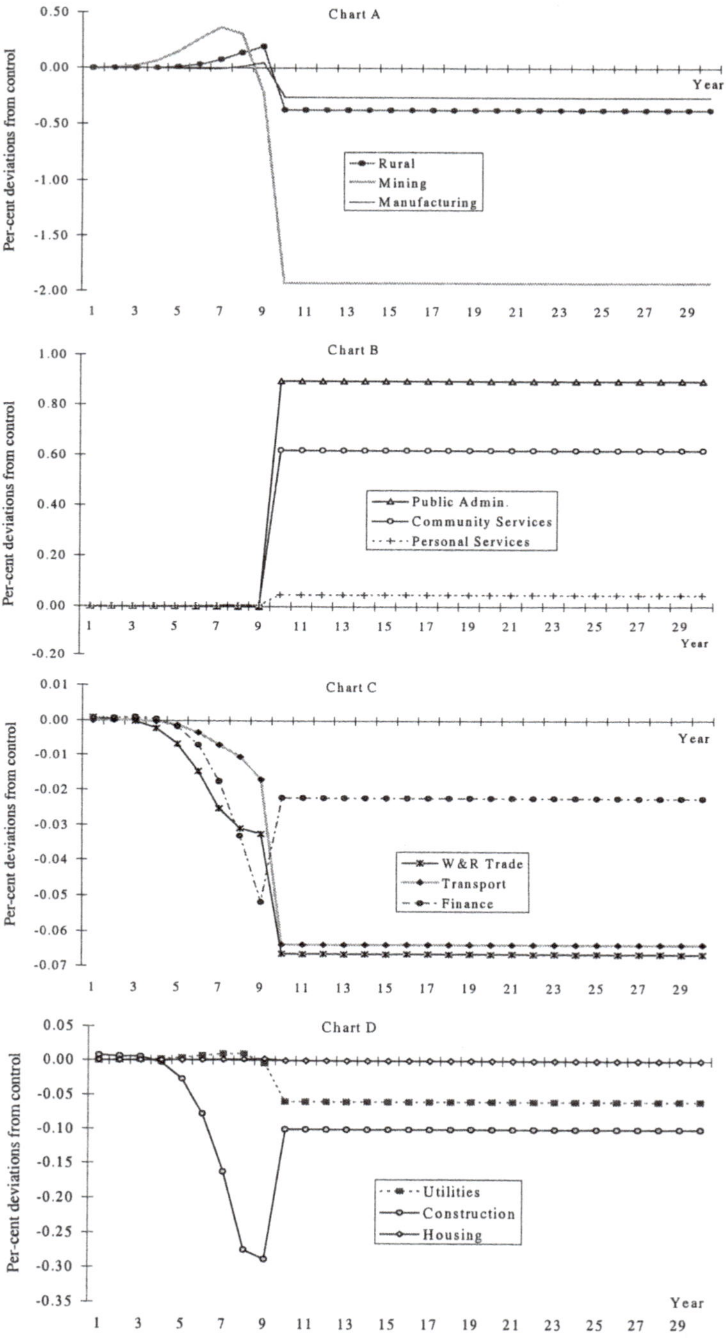

Figure 6.4.4: *Benchmark* Simulation Projections for Sectoral Activity Levels

The deterioration in the trade balance is accompanied by a small contraction in the economy's productive capacity (i.e., in value added). With aggregate employment and agricultural land held fixed, the economy's productive capacity can change via changes in the capital stock only. As figure 6.4.2 shows aggregate capital stocks decrease by about 0.16 per cent. With capital accounting for 32 per cent of value added the increase in capital stocks generates a 0.05 per cent decrease in productive capacity.

In ORANI-INT, GDP is measured in market prices. Indirect taxes put a wedge between the resource cost and market value of a unit of output. Changes in real GDP can be traced to changes in the usage of resources and/or to changes in the efficiency with which resources are used. To explore this idea further we use the differential form of the Divisia index of real GDP measured from the income side. This is listed in table A3.1.1 of appendix A3.1 as equation (A3.6.57) and repeated below for convenience:

$$gdpi_t^{(R)} = \frac{GDPFC_t}{GDPI_t} gdpfc_t^{(R)} + \frac{NIT_t}{GDPI_t} nit_t^{(R)} . \qquad t = 1, ..., T \qquad (6.4.2)$$

In equation (6.4.2) GDPI, GDPFC and NIT are the levels of: GDP measured from the income side; GDP measured at factor cost; and net indirect taxes. The percentage changes in these three variables are expressed in lower-case italics. The superscript (R) indicates a real variable. Figure 6.4.2 shows that in year 30 real GDP falls by about 0.08 per cent. In the BG control scenario the share of GDP at factor cost (i.e., value added) in GDP is 0.86 and the share in GDP of net indirect taxes is 0.14. Using these values as our estimates of the coefficients in (6.4.2)[7] and using the year-30 simulation results for $gdpfc^{(R)}$ and $nit^{(R)}$ we can decompose $gdpi^{(R)}$ as follows:

$$gdpi_{30}^{(R)} = -0.08 \approx 0.86\times(-0.053) + 0.14\times(-0.255) = -0.08 .$$

To two decimal places, our estimate of $gdpi^{(R)}$ concords with the model's projection. This decomposition shows that just over half of the decrease in real GDP emanates from the decrease in real value added with the remainder being accounted for by the decrease in real indirect tax revenues. Since capital is the only variable factor, the entire decrease in real value added in year 30 emanates from the 0.16 per cent decrease in the aggregate capital stock.

Net indirect taxes can change if the tax rates change and/or if the tax bases change. The tax bases can change through price or quantity movements. The model distinguishes production taxes by sector, sales taxes by user (i.e., producers, investors, households, governments, and foreigners) and tariffs. The corresponding bases are the basic values of outputs, the basic values of sales of commodities (domestic and foreign) and the c.i.f. values of imports. In ORANI-INT $nit^{(R)}$ is defined as that part of the percentage change in net indirect taxes that is due to

---

7 While ORANI-INT is solved in its non-linear form, we simplify the reconciliation of the simulation results with the model's theory and data by using first-order approximations. That is, we use the linear percentage change forms of the model's equations and data from the control solution to calibrate these linearised equations.

changes in the tax bases caused by changes in quantities. This definition, which is derived from the equations listed in table A3.1.1 of appendix A3.1[8], can be expressed follows:

$$\begin{aligned} nit_t^{(R)} = \frac{1}{NIT_t}\Bigg[& \sum_{j=1}^{13} P_{j,t}^{(O)} X_{j,t}^{(O)} x_{j,t}^{(O)} \\ & + \sum_{i=1}^{13}\sum_{s=1}^{2}\sum_{j=1}^{13} P_{i,s,t}^{(Z)} X_{i,s,j,t}^{(1)} [T_{i,s,j,t}^{(1)} - 1]\, x_{i,s,j,t}^{(1)} \\ & + \sum_{i=1}^{13}\sum_{s=1}^{2}\sum_{j=1}^{13} P_{i,s,t}^{(Z)} X_{i,s,j,t}^{(2)} [T_{i,s,j,t}^{(2)} - 1]\, x_{i,s,j,t}^{(2)} \\ & + \sum_{i=1}^{13}\sum_{s=1}^{2} P_{i,s,t}^{(Z)} X_{i,s,t}^{(3)} [T_{i,s,t}^{(3)} - 1]\, x_{i,s,t}^{(3)} \\ & + \sum_{i=1}^{13} P_{i,1,t}^{(Z)} X_{i,t}^{(4)} [T_{i,t}^{(4)} - 1]\, x_{i,t}^{(4)} \\ & + \sum_{i=1}^{13}\sum_{s=1}^{2} P_{i,s,t}^{(Z)} X_{i,s,t}^{(5)} [T_{i,s,t}^{(5)} - 1]\, x_{i,s,t}^{(5)} \\ & + \sum_{i=1}^{13} P_{i,t}^{(M)} X_{i,t}^{(M)} \Phi_t [T_{i,t}^{(6)} - 1]\, x_{i,t}^{(M)} \Bigg]. \qquad t = 1, \ldots, T \qquad (6.4.3) \end{aligned}$$

The notation in equation (6.4.3) is set out in chapter 3. The coefficients in equation (6.4.3) are shares in net indirect taxes of 'other cost' tickets (mainly production taxes) and of the various sales taxes. The *x*s are percentages changes in outputs and sales volumes. These are distinguished by the superscripts. The sales are to: (1) intermediate users; (2) capital creators; (3) households; (4) exporters; (5) government; and (M) importers. The superscript (O) denotes 'other cost' tickets.

In the absence of any changes in the composition of sectoral outputs and sales, the *x*s in equation (6.4.3) will move together. Under these conditions $nit^{(R)}$, and therefore $gdpi^{(R)}$ [via equation (6.4.2)], will be equal to $gdpfc^{(R)}$ (which is the weighted sum of sectoral outputs). However, the government expenditure shock induces a change in the economy's production and sales structures in favour of commodities that are relatively lightly taxed. This compositional change causes $nit^{(R)}$ and, therefore, $gdpi^{(R)}$ to fall by more than $gdpfc^{(R)}$. The excess of $gdpfc^{(R)}$ over $gdpi^{(R)}$ represents the allocative efficiency losses from changing the composition of the economy against activities that were already discouraged (relative to optimum) in the BG scenario. In the BG scenario sales tax rates, tariff rates and production tax rates are not uniform across commodities or activities. This causes resources to be allocated sub-optimally. Sales will be skewed in favour of commodities that attract relatively low tax rates. Similarly, production will be skewed against activities that are relatively highly taxed.

In the *benchmark* experiment most of the excess of $gdpfc^{(R)}$ over $gdpi^{(R)}$ can be traced to the change in the structure of output and sales against the domestic

---

[8] Equation (6.4.3) can be derived from equations listed in table A3.1.1 of appendix A3.1 by substituting equations (A3.6.37) – (A3.6.42) into equation (A3.6.36) then substituting the resultant expression, and equation (A3.6.35), into equation (A3.6.61).

Mining commodity. According to the BG scenario the highest production tax (i.e., 'other cost' tickets) rate in the economy is the 13 per cent levied on the *Mining* sector. Figure 6.4.4 shows that the 1.93 per cent fall in the *Mining* sector's output is the largest recorded in this experiment. In combination, the relatively high production tax rate and the relatively large fall in *Mining* output will tend to reduce $nit^{(R)}$ relative to $gdpfc^{(R)}$. Reinforcing this effect will be the expansion in the outputs of the *Public administration* and *Community services* sectors, which receive small production subsidies (2.5 and 1.4 per cent respectively). On the sales side, the domestic *Mining* commodity is also highly taxed. Sales of the *Mining* commodity to the *Manufacturing* sector attract a 53 per cent tax making this the most heavily taxed flow in the BG scenario. The *Mining* sector sells about 35 per cent of its output to the *Manufacturing* sector. The contraction in the *Manufacturing* sector reduces the demand for the *Mining* commodity. This tends to reduce $nit^{(R)}$ relative to $gdpfc^{(R)}$.

The remaining puzzle in the macro results is the contraction in the capital stock. This result is puzzling because sectoral rates of return are held at their control scenario values beyond year 1. There are two competing mechanisms underlying this result. The dominant mechanism relates to the sectoral bias of the government expenditure shock. The mitigating mechanism relates to the distinction in ORANI-INT between the rate of return and the real user-cost of capital. These two mechanisms are detailed below.

In ORANI-INT producers will alter their factor input ratios only if the real cost of employing a particular factor changes. However, the *aggregate* factor input ratios can change, even if *sectoral* factor input ratios remain at their control scenario values. To simplify the exposition, consider an economy consisting of a traded-goods sector and a non-traded-goods sector. Assume that:

- the production technology is characterised by CRS;
- zero pure profits are earned;
- labour and capital are the only inputs to the production process;
- capital is sector specific; and
- labour is mobile across sectors but fixed in aggregate.

Under these conditions holding the real cost of employing capital fixed implies that the marginal product of capital is fixed. In percentage changes, this implies:

$$p_j^{out} = p_j^{cap} . \qquad j \in \{\text{non-trad., trade}\} \qquad (6.4.4)$$

In equation (6.4.4) p^{out} and p^{cap} are the percentage changes in the prices of output and capital. With zero pure profits p^{out} is equal to the share-weighted average of p^{cap} and p^{lab}, the percentage change in the price of labour. That is:

$$p_j^{out} = S_j^{cap,costs} p_j^{cap} + S_j^{lab,costs} p^{lab} ; \qquad j \in \{\text{non-trad., trade}\} \qquad (6.4.5)$$

In each sector $S^{cap,costs}$ and $S^{lab,costs}$ are the shares in total costs of capital and labour. Because labour is mobile its price is the same in both sectors hence the absence of the j subscript. Substituting equation (6.4.4) into equation (6.4.5) and recognising that for each sector $S^{cap,costs} + S^{lab,costs} = 1$ yields:

$$p_j^{out} = p_j^{lab} \, . \qquad j \in \{\text{non-trad., trade}\} \qquad (6.4.6)$$

Thus, holding the real cost of employing capital fixed implies that the real cost of using labour will also be fixed. In this situation producers have no incentive to alter their labour-capital ratios.

Suppose that in the hypothetical economy described above there is an increase in demand that favours a particular sector of the economy, say the non-traded goods sector. In the absence of any relative factor price movements this sector will wish to increase its use of both labour and capital by the same proportion as the increase in demand for its output. Since the aggregate supply of labour is fixed, the demand shock will cause the price of labour to rise. Our assumptions about price relativities imply that the percentage increases in all domestic prices will be the same. The rise in domestic prices results in a contraction in the traded-goods sector as export sales are lost and imports replace domestic outputs. Again, since relative factor prices have not changed, the traded-goods sector will wish to decrease its demand for both labour and capital by the same proportion as the decrease in the demand for its output.

With aggregate labour held fixed, the increased usage of labour by the non-traded-goods sector must be matched by an equal decrease in the usage of labour by the traded-goods sector. Producers in both sectors will want to maintain their labour-capital ratios at their control scenario values. Thus, the non-traded goods sector increases its use of capital and the traded goods sector decreases its use of capital. Whether the aggregate level of capital stock changes, depends on the relative factor intensities of the two sectors. If both sectors have identical labour-capital ratios, an expansion in demand will have no net effect on output – the expansion in the non-traded goods sector will be exactly offset by the contraction in the traded goods sector (i.e., complete crowding-out). If the non-traded goods sector is relatively capital intensive, however, the demand expansion will result in an increase in aggregate capital stocks and, hence, aggregate output. The opposite will be true if the non-traded goods sector is relatively labour intensive.

In ORANI-INT an increase in government expenditure favours the non-traded goods sectors of the economy. These are very labour intensive. A $1 increase in government expenditure requires, directly and indirectly, about 71 cents worth of labour. The government purchases about 28 per cent of its total requirements from the *Public administration* sector and about 43 per cent from the *Community Services* sector. These two sectors, which figure 6.4.4 shows benefit most from the expansion in government expenditure, are the most labour intensive sectors in the economy with labour costs accounting for about 90 per cent of value added in both. The sector that is most adversely affected by the shock is *Mining*, which is the third most capital intensive sector (behind *Housing* and *Transport*). Thus, the sectoral bias of the expansion in government expenditure in favour of the most labour intensive sectors of the economy is consistent with the projected contraction in the aggregate capital stock.

The negative effect that the sectoral bias of the government expenditure shock has on capital stocks is mitigated by a reduction in the real cost of using capital. Despite the fact that sectoral rates of return remain at their control scenario values, the real cost of *using* capital is able to vary. In ORANI-INT the *suppliers* and *users* of capital do not respond to the same real cost of capital.

In ORANI-INT international capital markets are assumed to be competitive. This implies that capital is abundantly available to Australians at the exogenous foreign bond rate. In the illustrative experiments the nominal exchange rate and the foreign bond rate are fixed. This implies that the domestic bond rate will also be fixed. Investors have static expectations, hence, sectoral capital gains do not influence investment decisions. We also observe that the non-negativity constraints on sectoral investment are never binding. Under these conditions changes in the rental price of capital and the asset price of capital will be proportional. That is, the real cost of *supplying* capital is fixed. This can be deduced from the differential form of equation (6.4.1). That is, from:

$$p_{j,t}^{(K)} = p_{j,t}^{(Y)} ; \qquad j = 1, \ldots, 13, t = 2, \ldots, T \qquad (6.4.7)$$

where $p_{j,t}^{(K)}$ is the percentage change in the rental price of capital in sector j and $p_{j,t}^{(Y)}$ is the percentage change in the price of a unit of investment in sector j.

An increase in the demand for capital is possible if the real cost of *using* it falls. Users of capital are concerned with movements in the rental price of capital relative to movements in the price of their output (i.e., the movement in the marginal product of capital). The assumption of zero pure profits in all activities implies that output prices will move with production costs. Similarly, movements in the asset price of capital will reflect movements in the cost of constructing that capital.[9] For a particular sector, therefore, it is likely that movements in the cost of producing a unit of output will differ from movements in the cost of producing a unit of capital.

One key reason for the difference in the cost structures of current and capital outputs is that the latter process is typically more import intensive. In the absence of relative price movements, a $1 increase in final demand requires, directly and indirectly, about 16 cents worth of imports. The direct and indirect import requirements resulting from a $1 increase in investment expenditure however, are about 20 cents. Since import prices are assumed to be independent of domestic conditions, an increase in domestic demand, which increases domestic costs, allows the real cost of using capital to fall. That is, import prices remain unchanged and the relatively high import intensity of the capital creation process allows the rental price of capital to rise less rapidly than domestic costs.

---

9 Inspection of figure 6.4.3 reveals that the percentage increase in the *average* construction cost of capital (i.e., the investment deflator) is less than the percentage increase in the *average* rental price of capital (i.e., the capital-rentals deflator). There are two reasons for this discrepancy. First, the equilibrium condition for investment does not apply to the *Public administration* and *Community services* sectors. Investment in these two sectors is exogenous. This means that the rental price of their capital need not move in line with their investment costs. The second reason for the discrepancy in the investment and capital-rentals deflators is that the weights used to construct these indexes are different.

An additional reason for the divergence in the movements of output prices and capital costs is that the terms of trade improve. Because Australia is assumed to have some market power in its export markets, the increase in domestic costs causes the foreign currency prices of some exports to rise. These price increases will be reflected in some measure of producer prices but not in any measure of investment costs. Expenditure deflators, such as the investment deflator, include import prices but not export prices.

The average price received by producers for their output is measured by the factor cost (or value-added) deflator. Figure 6.4.3 shows that this deflator rises by 0.19 per cent whilst the average rental price of capital, as measured by the rental price of capital deflator, rises by about 0.17 per cent. In aggregate, therefore, the real cost of using capital falls. The typical producer will tend to become more capital intensive. However, as indicated by the results, the stimulus to capital usage generated by the fall in the real cost of using capital is not sufficient to offset the negative effect on capital usage of the sectoral bias of the increase in government spending.

Because of the constraint on aggregate employment, and to a lesser extent the constraint on the supply of agricultural land, the increase in real government expenditure puts upward pressure on domestic prices. The nominal exchange rate is fixed, as are the foreign currency prices of imports, hence the increase in domestic prices causes the real exchange rate to appreciate. This is the mechanism by which resources are re-directed towards the non-traded sectors that satisfy the governments increased demands. The appreciation of the real exchange rate induces a contraction in the traded goods sectors of the economy as export sales are lost and imports replace the relatively more expensive domestic commodities.

Figure 6.4.4 confirms that the three traded-goods sectors (i.e., *Rural*, *Mining* and *Manufacturing*) bear the brunt of real exchange rate appreciation. The main, but not sole, reason for the *Rural* sector's contraction is the loss of export sales. Although not reported, exports of the *Rural* commodity fall by 0.7 per cent. Since this sector sells about 34 per cent of its output to foreigners, about two thirds of the 0.37 per cent fall in its output (see chart A in figure 6.4.4) is accounted for by the 0.7 per cent fall in *Rural* exports (i.e., 0.34(-0.7) = -0.24). The *Rural* sector also contracts because its main domestic customer, the *Manufacturing* sector[10], contracts.

The *Manufacturing* sector sells about 12 per cent of its output to foreigners. Exports of the *Manufacturing* commodity fall by 0.93 per cent. This accounts for just under half of the 0.26 per cent fall in the *Manufacturing* sector's output. The *Manufacturing* sector also loses domestic sales, particularly sales of intermediate inputs. This is because the domestic *Manufacturing* commodity faces strong competition from foreign substitutes.[11] The appreciation of the real exchange rate

10 The *Rural* sector sells about 50 per cent of its output to the *Manufacturing* sector.

11 This can be deduced from two key pieces of data: first, the imported variety accounts for about 20 per cent of total sales of the *Manufacturing* commodity; and, second, the

adversely affects the competitiveness of the domestically produced *Manufacturing* commodity.

In the long run the *Mining* sector records the largest output contraction (i.e., 1.93 per cent). The *Mining* commodity is assumed to be highly tradeable. About 36 per cent of the *Mining* sector's output is sold to foreigners. Moreover, the imported and domestic *Mining* commodities are assumed to be close substitutes (i.e., the elasticity of substitution is 36) with the former accounting for almost 17 per cent of total sales of the *Mining* commodity. The real appreciation causes the *Mining* sector to lose export sales and domestic market share. Exports of the *Mining* commodity fall by about 2 per cent. This contributes about 0.74 percentage points to the fall in the *Mining* sector's output. Most of the remaining output contraction is accounted for by the loss of sales to other domestic sectors, particularly to the *Manufacturing* sector.[12] Note that the loss of domestic sales involves an activity effect and a substitution effect. For example, the fall in the *Manufacturing* sector's activity level causes a fall in demand for inputs of both *Mining* commodities (i.e., domestic and foreign). The fall in the price of the imported *Mining* commodity relative to the domestic variety causes the market share of the domestic variety to shrink.

6.4.2 Results Coinciding With the Implementation of Shock

In this experiment the economy reaches its new long-run equilibrium growth path in the same year (i.e., year 10) that the permanent 1 per cent increase in real government expenditure is initiated. All necessary adjustments in the economy are made in the pre-shock years. It follows that the explanation of the year-30 results in sub-section 6.4.1 also applies to the year-10 results.

The year-10 results are related to the results in adjacent periods by the sectoral capital accumulation relationships. The flat path of capital stocks after year 9 implies that investment and capital will move together in year 10 and beyond. This can be deduced from the percentage change form of the sectoral capital accumulation equations, which are listed in table A3.1.1 in appendix A3.1.1. For convenience these equations are repeated below:

$$z_{j,t+1}^{(K)} = \frac{Y_{j,t}}{Z_{j,t+1}^{(K)}}\left\{y_{j,t} - z_{j,t}^{(K)}\right\} + z_{j,t}^{(K)} \qquad j = 1, \ldots, 13,\ t = 1, \ldots, T \qquad (6.4.8)$$

The zs are percentage changes in $Z_{j,t+1}^{(K)}$, sectoral capital stocks, and the ys are percentage changes in $Y_{j,t}$, sectoral investment. When the percentage deviations in capital in adjacent periods are equal, then it follows that $z_{j,t+1}^{(K)} = z_{j,t}^{(K)} = y_{j,t}$. Figure 6.4.2 shows that this relationship is not preserved precisely at the aggregate level (i.e., aggregate capital stocks in each of years 10 and 11 decrease by 0.16 per cent

---

elasticity of substitution between the domestic and foreign *Manufacturing* commodities (i.e., the Armington elasticity) is 1.65.

12 The *Mining* sector sells about 33 per cent of its output to the *Manufacturing* sector.

but aggregate investment in year 10 decreases by 0.18 per cent). This discrepancy at the aggregate level is accounted for by aggregation effects. The weights used to aggregate sectoral capital and investment are different.

The one-year gestation lag in the capital creation process implies that investment in year 9 must fall to generate the decrease in capital stocks in year 10. We discuss this result further in section 6.4.3.

6.4.3 Results Over the Duration of the Shock

The economy reaches its new long-run equilibrium growth path in year 10. Therefore, the explanation of the long-run results in sub-section 6.4.1 applies to all years beyond year 9. The resources attracted into the government sector in year 10, via appreciation of the real exchange rate, can be maintained there permanently without any further exchange rate adjustments. Appreciation of the real exchange rate in year 10 implies that capital gains will occur in that year. However, investors do not anticipate these gains. In this experiment there is no mechanism in the model that allows the stock of capital and the rate of investment in year 10 to deviate from their long-run values.

6.4.4 Pre-shock (Anticipation) Effects

The pre-shock results obtained in this experiment are attributable solely to the assumption of a one-year gestation lag in the capital creation process. The decrease in the demand for capital in year 10 brought about by the increase in government expenditure means that an appropriate reduction in investment must be made in the previous year (i.e., year 9). The decrease in investment in year 9 also induces a decrease in the demand for capital in year 9. In turn, the decrease in the demand for capital in year 9 induces a decrease in investment in year 8. This backward input-output linkage effect continues (in attenuated form) back to the first year.

Figure 6.4.4 (chart D) shows that the main loser from the decrease in investment in the pre-shock periods is the *Construction* sector, which supplies about 60 per cent of the economy's total requirements of inputs for capital creation. In the years leading up to the implementation of the shock the trade balance moves increasingly towards surplus. Over this period the *Construction* sector contracts in line with the gradual decrease in investment. Because aggregate employment is fixed the labour released by the *Construction* sector, which is relatively labour intensive, must be absorbed by other sectors. The price of labour falls tending to reduce domestic prices. The real exchange rate devalues thereby improving the competitiveness of the traded-goods sectors. As chart A in figure 6.4.4 shows, the traded-goods sectors, *Rural*, *Mining* and *Manufacturing*, expand in the pre-shock years. The fall in imports over this period also reflects the fact that the capital creation process is relatively import intensive.

6.5 The Investment Experiment

This experiment is identical to the *benchmark* experiment in all respects except that investors are forward-looking. As in the *benchmark* experiment, sectoral rates of return remain at their control scenario values after year 1. However, in contrast to the *benchmark* experiment, the forward-looking investors respond to capital gains/losses. Inspection of the results reveals that the non-negativity constraints on sectoral investment are never binding. Therefore, the equilibrium conditions governing sectoral investment in this experiment may be expressed, in their linear forms, as:

$$p^{(K)}_{j,t+1} = p^{(Y)}_{j,t} - \left[1 - \delta_j\right]\frac{P^{(A)}_{j,t+1}}{P^{(K)}_{j,t+1}}\left\{p^{(Y)}_{j,t} - p^{(Y)}_{j,t-1}\right\} \qquad j = 1, \ldots, 13,\ t = 1, \ldots, T\text{-}1 \qquad (6.5.1)$$

Equation (6.5.1) is derived from equations (A3.3.33) and (A3.3.33a), listed in table A3.1.1 of appendix A3.1, under the assumptions that: $p^{(Y)}_{j,t} = p^{(A)}_{j,t}$ (i.e., the non-negativity constraints on sectoral investment are not binding); and $d\Psi_{j,t} = 0$ (i.e., sectoral rates of return remain at their control scenario values).

Equation (6.5.1) implies that in the absence of capital gains/losses (i.e., where $p^{(Y)}_{j,t} = p^{(Y)}_{j,t+1}$) the percentage change in the rental price of a unit of capital in period t+1 will be equal to the percentage change in the cost of constructing that capital (i.e., $p^{(K)}_{j,t+1} = p^{(Y)}_{j,t+1}$). This situation prevails when the economy is at a steady state. When $p^{(Y)}_{j,t} \neq p^{(Y)}_{j,t+1}$ a capital gain or loss accrues to agents investing in period t. Other things constant, capital gains(losses) allow the rental price of capital to fall(rise). This will tend to stimulate(depress) the demand for capital.

A selection of results obtained from this experiment is presented in figures 6.5.1—6.5.3. Notably, the long-run (i.e., year-30) results obtained in the *benchmark* and *investment* experiments are almost identical. However, in the *investment* experiment the economy converges to its new long-run equilibrium less rapidly than in the *benchmark* experiment. Another key difference between the *benchmark* and *investment* experiments is that the projected responses in the pre-shock years are bigger in the latter.

6.5.1 Long-run Results

Differences between the results obtained in the *benchmark* and *investment* experiments can be attributed solely to the effects of capital gains/losses. As the economy converges to its long-run equilibrium growth path capital gains/losses become arbitrarily small. It is not surprising, therefore, that the long-run results of the *benchmark* and *investment* experiments are almost identical and that the mechanisms that generate these results are the same.

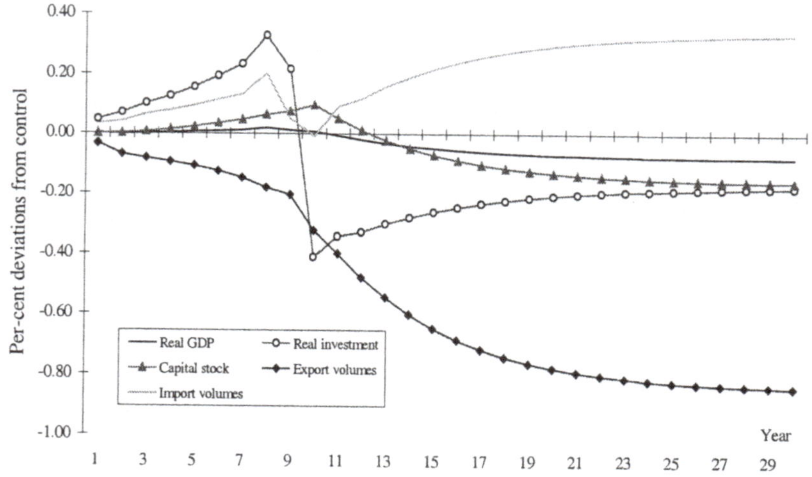

Figure 6.5.1: *Investment* Simulation Projections for Selected Real Macro Variables

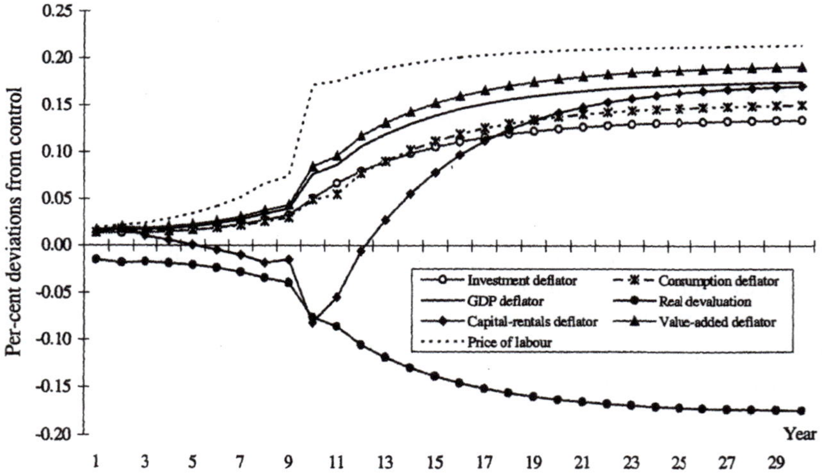

Figure 6.5.2: *Investment* Simulation Projections for Selected Deflators

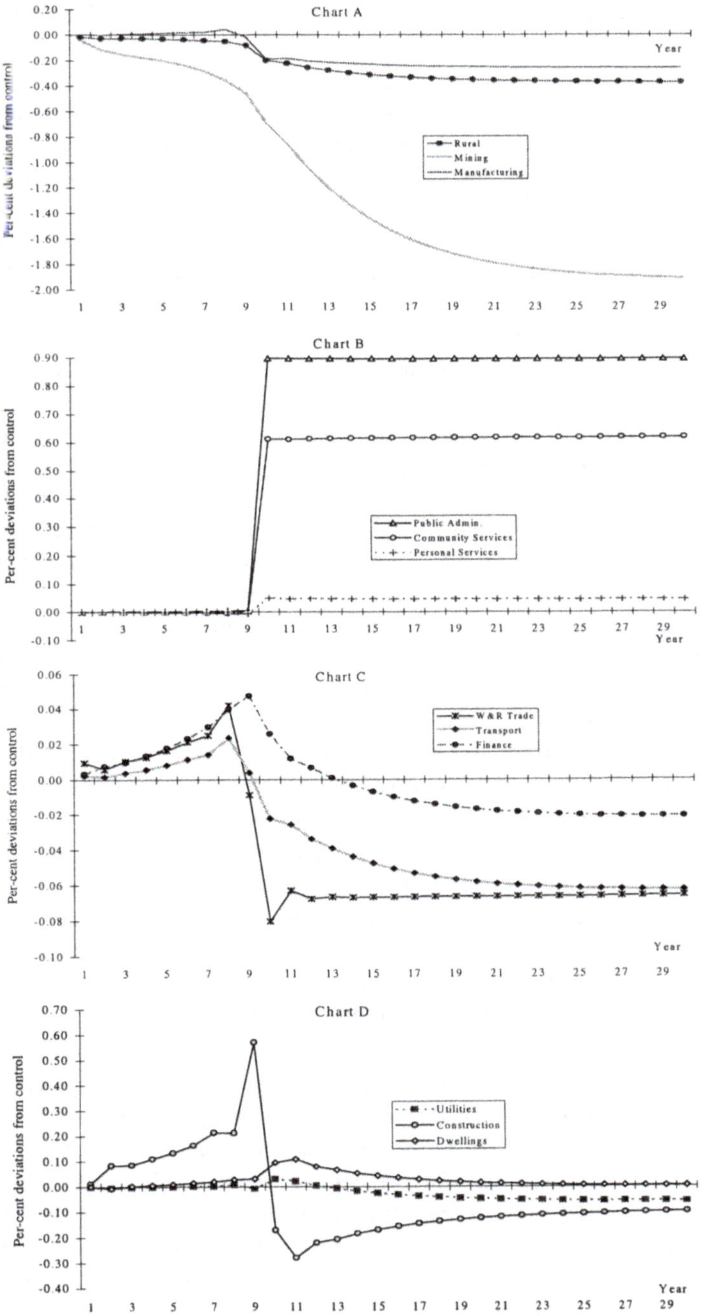

Figure 6.5.3: *Investment* Simulation Projections for Sectoral Activity Levels

6.5.2 Results Coinciding With the Implementation of Shock

In the *benchmark* experiment the economy reaches its new long-run equilibrium in year 10. In contrast, the results of this experiment indicate that many of the variables diverge from their new long-run equilibrium growth path by the greatest margin in year 10. The increase in government expenditure in year 10 is accommodated partially by crowding out investment and the balance of trade and partially by an increase in productive capacity. Figure 6.5.1 shows that aggregate investment falls by 0.41 per cent in year 10. In the same year the 0.32 per cent fall in export volumes and the 0.01 per cent fall in import volumes generate a trade balance deterioration worth about 0.06 per cent of GDP.

The economy becomes more capital intensive in year 10 with aggregate capital stocks expanding by 0.10 per cent. The mechanisms that generate the increase in the capital intensity of the economy are analogous to those used in the explanation of the long-run results of the *benchmark* experiment (see section 6.4.1). In contrast to the long-run results, the stimulatory effect on the demand for capital by the fall in the real user cost of capital outweighs the contractionary effect on the capital stock of the sectoral bias of the increase in government expenditure. Chart B in figure 6.5.3 shows that in year 10, just as in the long run, the increase in government spending favours the most labour-intensive sectors of the economy (i.e., *Public administration* and *Community services*). However, this compositional bias in favour of labour-intensive sectors is weaker in year 10 than in the long run. There are two reasons for this. First, the fall in exports, which are supplied by relatively capital-intensive sectors (e.g., *Mining*), is weaker in year 10 than in the long run. Secondly, the fall in investment activity, which is relatively labour intensive, is stronger in year 10 than in the long run.

The fall in the user cost of capital is stronger in year 10 than in the long run. Figure 6.5.2 shows that in year 10 the average rental price of capital ($K_t^{(\Pi)}$) falls by 0.08 per cent whilst the average price of output received by producers, represented by the value-added deflator ($GDPFC_t^{(\Pi)}$), rises by about 0.08 per cent. Thus, in year 10 the ratio $K_t^{(\Pi)}/GDPFC_t^{(\Pi)}$ falls by about 0.16 percentage points. The same ratio falls by about 0.02 percentage points in the long run.

In the explanation of the long-run results, the fall in the real cost of using capital was attributed to the relatively high import intensity of the capital creation process. The explanation of the fall in the real cost of using capital in year 10 is not as straightforward because of the presence of capital gains. The results in figure 6.5.2 show that $K_t^{(\Pi)}$ decreases by 0.08 per cent in year 10 whilst the average cost of constructing capital (given by the investment price deflator, $I_t^{(\Pi)}$) rises by 0.03 per cent in year 9. From equation (6.5.1) these results imply that investors expect capital gains in year 10. The results in figure 6.5.2 confirm this expectation with the investment price deflator in year 9 rising by less than in year 10 (i.e., 0.03 per cent compared with 0.05 per cent).

In our discussion of the long-run results we explained why the government spending shock causes domestic prices to rise. Given that the shock is introduced in year 10, it is reasonable to expect that, relative to control, the *growth* in domestic prices between years 9 and 10 will be positive. This pattern in domestic prices is consistent with the capital gains observed in the year-10 results. The results in figure 6.5.2 confirm that domestic prices do grow between years 9 and 10. However, the reason for this growth in prices is more complicated than that offered above. It is true that real government expenditure grows between years 9 and 10. However, the growth in real GNE over this period is very small (i.e., real GNE increases by 0.055 per cent in year 9 and 0.059 per cent in year 10). With real consumption held fixed, changes in real GNE can occur only through changes in real investment and real government spending.

The impacts on the economy of an increase in aggregate real investment will be *qualitatively* similar to the impacts of an increase in government expenditure. However, our results suggest that *quantitatively* it matters whether investment spending or government spending drives the increase in real GNE. In year 9 the increase in real GNE emanates exclusively from the increase in investment. In year 10, however, the increase in real GNE generated by the increase in government spending is partially offset by the decrease in investment. The increase in domestic prices required to accommodate the 0.055 per cent increase real GNE in year 9 is smaller than that required to accommodate a similar increase in real GNE in year 10. There are two reasons for this result. The first reason relates to the relative import intensities of investment and government spending. The second reason relates to the relative labour intensities of investment and government spending.

The investment process is more import intensive than is government expenditure. The direct and indirect import requirements resulting from a $1 increase in GNE due to investment is 91 cents. The same increase in GNE via government expenditure requires 40 cents worth of imports only. This means that an increase in investment places less pressure on the demand for domestic resources than does an equivalent (in terms of GNE) increase in government expenditure. Therefore, the required deterioration in the balance of trade can be achieved with less real appreciation in the case of an increase in real GNE brought about by an increase in investment.

Investment activity is less labour intensive than is government spending. Given that aggregate employment is fixed, an increase in government spending will place greater upward pressure on wages than an equivalent increase in investment spending. This is evident in the path of wages, which rises sharply between years 9 and 10 (see figure 6.5.2).

6.5.3 Results Over the Duration of the Shock

In contrast to the *benchmark* experiment, figure 6.5.2 shows that in the *investment* experiment domestic prices continue to rise (albeit at an increasingly slower rate) beyond year 10 in order to maintain the required resources in the government sector. This is reflected by the real exchange rate, which continues to appreciate after year 10. The persistent increase in domestic prices is consistent with the gradual increase in real GNE over the interval between years 10 and 30. Despite the fact that the government expenditure shock is fully implemented in year 10 real

GNE continues to increase after that year because real investment is growing (i.e., relative to control the fall in real investment gets smaller beyond year 10).

The persistent increase in domestic prices generates capital gains over the interval between years 10 and 30. Since investors in this experiment anticipate these capital gains, the stock of capital and rate of investment over this interval will differ from their long-run values. The magnitude of the capital gains decreases gradually from a peak in year 10 to negligible values in year 30. Capital gains of the same order of magnitude as those observed in year 10 cannot persist beyond that year. There are two reasons for this: first, beyond year 10 the growth in real GNE is modest and gets progressively smaller; and, second, there are no large changes in the composition of GNE, such as those observed in year 10, that cause sharp changes in the rate of growth in domestic prices.

With investors trading off capital gains for rentals, the declining value of the capital gains beyond year 10 is reflected in the gradual convergence of the investment price deflator and the capital-rentals deflator. The relationship between capital usage and the real cost of using capital is evident in figures 6.5.1 and 6.5.2. The percentage decrease in the average real cost of using capital is indicated by the (positive) gap between paths of the value-added and capital-rentals deflators (see figure 6.5.2). This gap gets progressively smaller beyond year 10. Commensurately, the demand for capital falls over this period.

Although capital stocks can be adjusted fully to their new long run equilibrium values in year 10 (as was the case in the *investment* experiment), producers choose not to do this. It is cheaper for producers to contract their capital stocks gradually rather than abruptly. Other things constant, rapid contraction of investment in year t generates capital gains in that year (i.e., $p^{(Y)}_{j,t} < p^{(Y)}_{j,t+1}$) which are traded off for lower rentals in year t+1. However, the lower rentals in year t+1 encourage the use of capital by producers in that year tending to mitigate the investment response in year t.

The contraction in capital stocks between years 10 and 11 implies that investment in year 10 is below its long-run equilibrium value. To show this, we can rearrange equation (6.4.8), the linearised capital accumulation relationships, as follows:

$$y_{j,t} - z^{(K)}_{j,t} = \frac{Z^{(K)}_{j,t+1}}{Y_{j,t}} \left\{ z^{(K)}_{j,t+1} - z^{(K)}_{j,t} \right\} \qquad j = 1, ..., 13, t = 1, ..., T \qquad (6.5.2)$$

Since the ratio $Z^{(K)}_{j,t+1}/Y_{j,t}$ is always positive, it follows that if $z^{(K)}_{j,t+1} > z^{(K)}_{j,t}$ then $y_{j,t} > z^{(K)}_{j,t}$ and *vice versa*. In the long run (t=ss), $y_{j,ss} = z^{(K)}_{j,ss}$. Thus, if $y_{j,t} < z^{(K)}_{j,t}$ and $z^{(K)}_{j,t} > z^{(K)}_{j,ss}$, then $y_{j,t} < y_{j,ss}$. This pattern in the paths of investment and aggregate capital is consistent with the results in figure 6.5.1 for the interval between years 10 and 30. Over this interval aggregate capital stocks are falling gradually and aggregate investment is below, but asymptoting towards, its new long-run equilibrium value.

6.5.4 Pre-shock (Anticipation) Effects

In the *benchmark* experiment the pre-shock results are explained by the backward input-output linkage effect introduced by the one-year gestation lag in the investment process. This effect accounts only partly for the pre-shock results in the *investment* experiment. In the *benchmark* experiment the paths of aggregate investment and aggregate capital stocks fell gradually over the pre-shock period, with the paths of both variables below control in year 9. In the *investment* experiment, however, the path of aggregate capital stocks is above control and growing in all pre-shock years. Similarly, the path of investment is above control in all pre-shock years and is growing in all but the last of these years.

For the reasons explained in the section 6.5.2 the aggregate stock of capital is 0.10 per cent above control in year 10. To achieve this expansion in capital stocks net investment in the preceding 9 years must, on average, be above control. Because of capital gains it is less costly to expand capital stocks gradually. Hence, investment grows gradually over the pre-shock period.

The slightly smaller increase in investment in year 9 relative to year 10 appears to be inconsistent with equation (6.5.2) which suggests that the gap between the percentage changes in investment and capital stocks will be bigger the larger is the *growth* in capital stocks relative to control.[13] While equation (6.5.2) holds at the sectoral level, figure 6.5.1 shows that it does not hold at the aggregate level. Relative to control, capital stocks grow faster between years 9 and 10 than they do between years 8 and 9 yet the gap between the capital and investment paths is greater in year 8 than in year 9. A subtle compositional effect underlies this result.

In year 8 the increase in aggregate investment is largely accounted for by the increase in investment by the *Construction* sector. This sector contributes about 0.48 percentage points to the 0.33 per cent increase in aggregate investment in year 8. Most other sectors decrease their investment slightly. In year 9, however, the *Construction* sector decreases its investment (contributing about -0.60 percentage points to the 0.22 per cent increase in aggregate investment) and most other sectors increase their investment. Relative to the economy-wide average, the rate of depreciation of the *Construction* sector's capital stock is low (i.e., 0.05 compared with 0.06).[14] Moreover, the sectors that contribute more to aggregate investment in year 9 than in year 8 have higher depreciation rates than the *Construction* sector. For example, the *Finance* sector, which contributes about 0.02 percentage points to the increase in aggregate investment in year 8 and about 0.17 percentage points in year 9, has a depreciation rate of 0.74. Similarly, the *Wholesale & retail trade* (*WRT*) sector, which contributes about -0.02 percentage points to the increase in

---

13 In the levels this means that the ratio of net investment to capital must be equal to the rate of growth in capital stocks. Put another way, net investment is the first derivative of the capital path.

14 With balanced 3 per cent growth in the BG scenario the coefficient $Z^{(K)}_{j,t+1}/Y_{j,t}$ in equation (6.5.2) will differ across sectors only if the rates of depreciation differ across sectors.

aggregate investment in year 8 and about 0.10 percentage points in year 9, has a depreciation rate of 0.09.

The investment and capital paths in figure 6.5.1 are consistent with the bias in the composition of aggregate investment in favour of sectors with low depreciation rates in year 8 and high depreciation rates in year 9. Because of this compositional bias, the 0.22 per cent increase in aggregate investment in year 9 generates a bigger increase in aggregate capital stock *growth* than does the 0.32 per cent increase in aggregate investment in year 8.

The turn-around in the *Construction* sector's investment behaviour between years 8 and 9 reflects its role as the economy's major supplier of inputs to capital creation (i.e., it supplies about 60 per cent of the economy's requirements for inputs to capital creation). In the pre-shock years the growth in aggregate investment stimulates activity in the *Construction* sector. To accommodate the increase in demand for its output the *Construction* sector expands its capital stock (as well as its employment of labour) in the pre-shock years. However, activity in the *Construction* sector falls in year 10 in line with the sharp fall in aggregate investment. The *Construction* sector's capital stock remains above control in year 10 but is significantly lower than in year 9 (i.e., in year 9 its capital stock is about 0.65 per cent above control compared with 0.13 per cent in year 10). To achieve this reduction in its capital stock the *Construction* sector reduces its investment in year 9.

6.6 The Consumption Experiment

The *consumption* experiment is identical to the *benchmark* experiment in all respects except that aggregate real consumption is endogenous in all periods and growth in terminal-period net foreign liabilities (NFL) is constrained. The NFL-to-GDP ratios in the last two years of the experiment are constrained to be identical. This ensures that the balance of trade surplus in the long run is sufficient to service the interest repayments on accumulated foreign debt.[15]

Projections of the paths of selected macroeconomic variables are presented in figures 6.6.1—6.6.3. In contrast to the *benchmark* experiment the results of the *consumption* experiment show that: the magnitudes of the variables in the pre-shock years are bigger; the economy is less capital intensive in the long-run; and, there is no deterioration in the trade balance in the long-run. In this experiment the increase in government expenditure is accommodated largely by the reduction in aggregate real consumption.

---

[15] In this experiment all exogenous real variables grow by 3 per cent per annum except government spending, which is shocked. Real government spending grows by 3 per cent in all years but 10. With the shock, real government expenditure grows by 4.03 per cent in year 10 (i.e., 3 per cent underlying growth plus 1.03 per cent additional growth imparted by the shock. Under this configuration of the exogenous variables the economy will converge to 3 per cent growth in the long run.

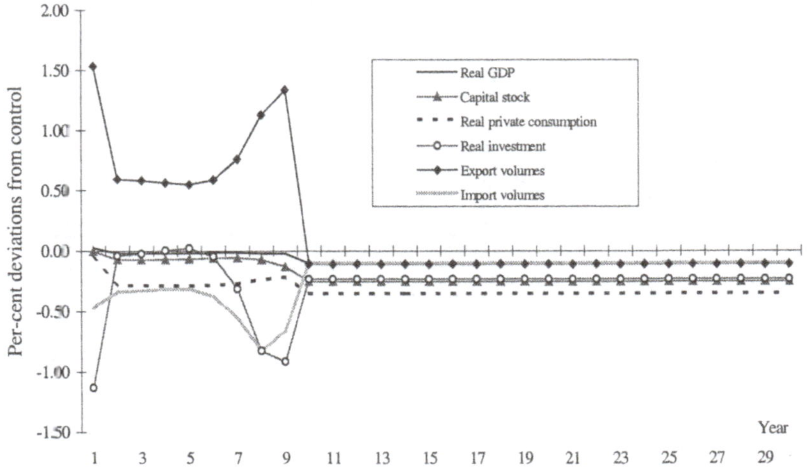

Figure 6.6.1: *Consumption* Simulation Projections for Selected Real Macro Variables

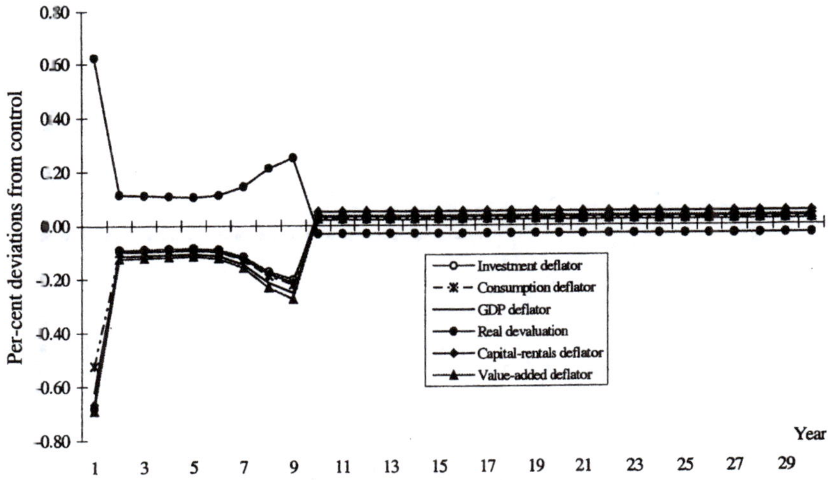

Figure 6.6.2: *Consumption* Simulation Projections for Selected Deflators

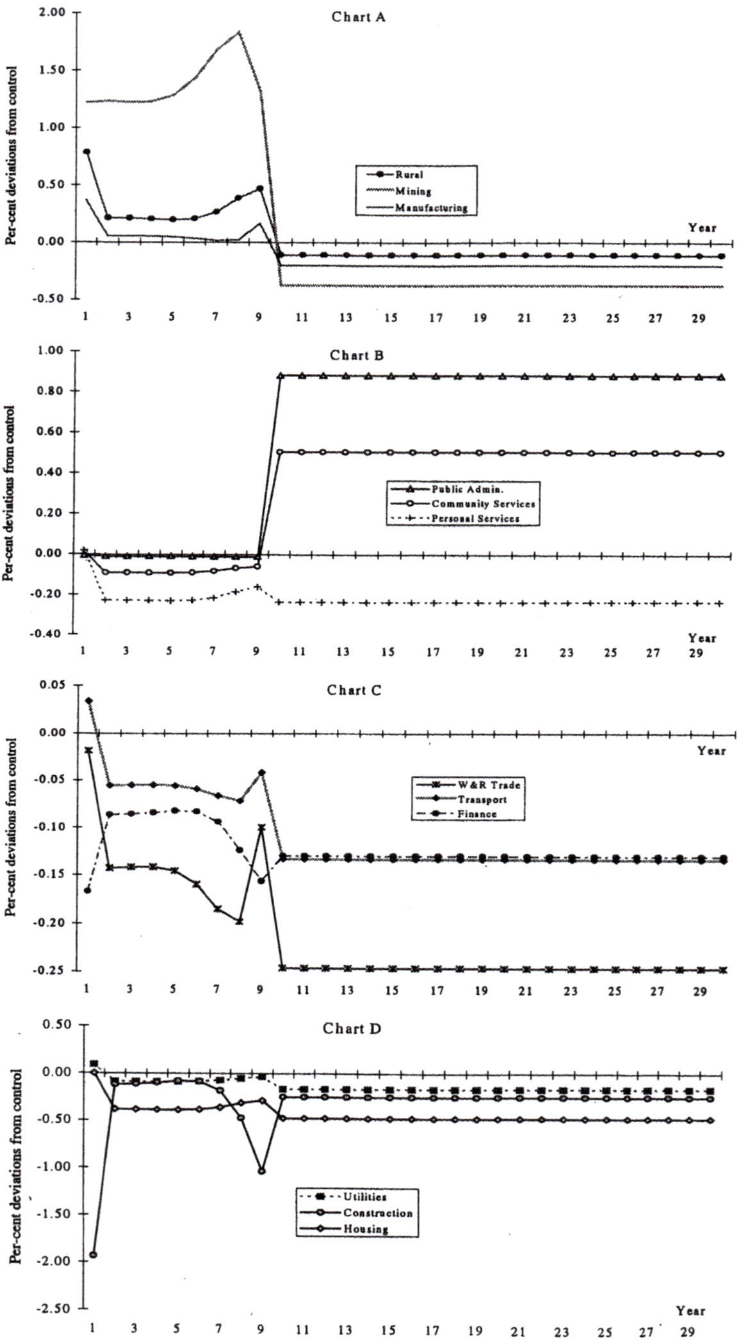

Figure 6.6.3: *Consumption* Simulation Projections for Sectoral Activity Levels

6.6.1 Long-run Results

As in the *benchmark* experiment, the ability of the economy to respond to the demand shock by increasing output is limited. Aggregate labour and agricultural land are fixed and the demands for sectoral capital stocks are constrained because sectoral rates of return remain at their control scenario values. In the *benchmark* experiment the increase in government expenditure is accommodated in the long run largely by a deterioration in the trade balance. In this experiment the constraint on net foreign liabilities means that the trade balance is not allowed to deteriorate in response to the government shock. Instead, the increase in government expenditure is accommodated largely by the 0.35 per cent fall in aggregate real consumption. In addition, the contraction in the economy's productive capacity is greater in the *consumption* experiment than it is in the *benchmark* experiment (i.e., aggregate capital stocks fall by 0.25 per cent in the former and by 0.16 per cent in the latter).

In the *benchmark* experiment, the contractionary effect on the demand for capital, induced by the sectoral bias of the shock, is mitigated by the stimulus to the demand for capital associated with the fall in its user cost. In the *consumption* experiment, the sectoral bias effect is stronger and the fall in the user cost of capital weaker. Therefore, the contraction in capital stocks is stronger in the *consumption* experiment than in the *benchmark* experiment. As explained in section 6.4.1, the real user cost of capital falls when domestic prices rise relative to foreign prices. Since the balance of trade cannot move into deficit in this experiment, the scope for such a price movement is more limited than in the *benchmark* experiment. This shows up in the results as a smaller appreciation of the real exchange rate (i.e., 0.03 per cent compared to 0.18 per cent in the *benchmark* experiment).

Figure 6.6.2 shows that the average rental price of capital, indicated by the capital-rentals deflator, rises by 0.05 per cent whilst the average price of output, indicated by the value-added deflator, rises by 0.04 per cent. Seemingly contrary to the claim made above, this suggest that the *average* real cost of using capital *rises* slightly. However, the real cost of using capital falls for all sectors except *Public administration* and *Community services*. Because investment in these sectors is exogenous, the real cost of capital does not affect their investment decisions. The rental price of capital in these two sectors is not constrained to move in line with investment costs [i.e., equilibrium condition (6.4.1) does not apply]. Under these conditions the rental price of capital will reflect the scarcity of capital rather than the cost of constructing it. The marginal product of capital (i.e., the ratio of the rental price of capital to the price of output) rises in the *Public administration* and *Community services* sectors because their capital stocks are not allowed to respond to the government spending shock. Capital becomes relatively scarce in these sectors, which are strongly favoured by the increase in government spending. Thus, the *Public administration* and *Community services* sectors contribute more to the increase in the capital-rentals deflator than they do to the increase in the value-added deflator. This allows the former deflator to rise relative to the latter.

The sectoral-bias effect is reinforced in this experiment by the fall in aggregate real consumption, which is the most capital-intensive component of GDP. Of particular importance is the 0.47 per cent contraction in the *Housing* sector's activity level. This sector, which sells all of its output to households, is the biggest loser in the *consumption* experiment. The *Housing* sector owns about 26 per cent of the economy's capital stock and does not use any labour directly in its production process. Thus, without any relative price stimulus, the contraction in the *Housing* sector contributes about 0.12 percentage points to the 0.25 per cent decrease in aggregate capital stocks.

The results presented in figure 6.6.3 indicate that the fortunes of the traded-goods sectors (i.e., *Rural*, *Mining* and *Manufacturing*) are less adversely affected in this experiment than in the *benchmark* experiment. This is because the appreciation of the real exchange rate is smaller in this experiment. Whilst the *Manufacturing* sector is better off in the *consumption* experiment, it still records a fall in its activity level because of its exposure to household demands.

6.6.2 Results Coinciding With the Commencement of the Shock

As in the *benchmark* experiment, the economy reaches its new long-run equilibrium growth path in the same year (i.e., year 10) that the permanent 10 per cent increase in real government expenditure is initiated. Since the economy reaches its new long-run equilibrium in year 10, the explanation of the long-run results offered in section 6.6.1 applies.

In the *benchmark* experiment the sectoral capital accumulation relations provided the only links between the periods. In this experiment there are two additional temporal links: a transition equation relating consumption in adjacent years; and, an accumulation relation between foreign liabilities and balance of trade deficits.

In the five illustrative simulations the domestic interest rate is equal to the time preference discount rate.[16] Under these conditions, the transition equation which relates consumption in adjacent years (i.e., equilibrium condition (3.3.17) presented in section 3.3.1 of chapter 3) implies the rate of growth of the representative household's *nominal* discretionary consumption will be zero. The growth in the representative household's *real* discretionary consumption is inversely related to the growth in $C_t^{(\Pi,a)}$, the deflator for discretionary consumption. Although not reported, nominal discretionary consumption falls by 0.62 per cent in all years. Figure 6.6.1 shows that the path of real aggregate consumption (which consists of subsistence and discretionary consumption) is below control in all years

---

[16] Formally, the time preference rate is assumed to be equal to the exogenous long-run value of the foreign bond rate. The domestic bond rate is related to the foreign bond rate via uncovered interest parity. In the illustrative experiments the foreign bond rate is the same in all years and is not shocked. The path of the exchange rate is also exogenous and not shocked. Hence, we can deduce that the domestic bond rate is equal to the time preference rate.

but is flat beyond year 9 only. This is because real subsistence consumption is fixed[17] and because there is no further growth in $C_t^{(\Pi,a)}$. Prior to year 10 the path of real consumption is not flat. For example, in year 9 real aggregate consumption falls by 0.22 per cent compared with the 0.35 per cent fall in each of the subsequent years. The reasons for this result will be explained in section 6.6.4, which deals with the pre-shock results.

Aggregate capital stocks fall by 0.25 per cent in year 10. This fall is slightly more than that recorded in the *benchmark* experiment. The reasons for this difference are the same as those offered for the difference in the long run results. With capital stocks falling further below control between years 9 and 10, aggregate investment falls by 0.91 per cent in year 9.

Although not reported, net foreign liabilities decrease by about 0.34 per cent of year-10 GDP between years 9 and 10. This is consistent with the move towards trade surplus in year 9. In that year export volumes increase by 1.34 per cent and import volumes contract by 0.66 per cent. This generates a trade surplus equivalent to about 0.30 per cent of year-10 GDP. The difference between the decrease in net foreign liabilities between years 9 and 10 and the increase in the trade surplus in year 9 is accounted for by the interest charges saved from the decrease in net foreign liabilities in year 9. The decrease in net foreign liabilities in year 9 is equivalent to 1.43 per cent of year-10 GDP. The foreign interest rate is 3 per cent hence the interest charges saved in year 9 is equivalent to 0.04 per cent of year-10 GDP.

6.6.3 Results Over the Duration of the Shock

The economy converges to its new long run equilibrium in year 10. Thus, the explanation of the long-run results presented in section 6.6.1 applies to year 10 and beyond.

6.6.4 Pre-shock (Anticipation) Effects

In this subsection we focus on two notable pre-shock results. First, we explain why the path of aggregate real consumption is not flat. Second, we explain the sharp decrease in aggregate investment in year 1.

Real aggregate consumption is the sum of subsistence and discretionary consumption. Subsistence consumption is constant over time and is assumed to be unaffected by the government expenditure shock. Households distribute their discretionary consumption over time to maximise utility subject to an intertemporal budget constraint. An implication of the intertemporal consumption specification in ORANI-INT is that the rate of growth of the representative household's *nominal* discretionary expenditure is positively related to the ratio of

---

[17]Recall, that a constant level of subsistence consumption is a key feature of the Stone-Geary utility function used in ORANI-INT.

the interest rate to the time preference rate (i.e., see equilibrium condition (3.3.17) presented in section 3.3.1 of chapter 3). That is, if the interest rate in year t is higher than the time preference rate then the household will tend to save in year t hence skewing its expenditure in favour of future years. As mentioned previously, the rate of interest is equal to the time preference rate in all years. Under these conditions the rate of growth of the representative household's *nominal* discretionary consumption will be zero.

To show the relationship between $C_t^{(R)}$, real aggregate consumption, and $C_t^{(a)}$, nominal discretionary consumption, we use the differential equations listed in table A3.1.1 in appendix A3.1. Substituting equation (A3.3.10) into equation (A3.6.23) and re-arranging gives:

$$c_t^{(R)} = \frac{C_t^{(a)}}{C_t}\left[c_t^{(a)} - \sum_{i=1}^{13} \beta_i \, p_{i,\bullet,t}^{(3)} \right] + \frac{1}{C_t} \sum_{i=1}^{13} P_{i,\bullet,t}^{(3)} Q_t \, \tilde{\gamma}_{i,\bullet}^{(3)} \, q_t \, . \qquad t = 1, \ldots, T \qquad (6.6.1)$$

We note that the second term in square brackets is equal to the percentage change in the deflator for above-subsistence consumption [see equation (A3.3.11) in table A3.1.1, appendix A3.1]. We also note that q_t, the percentage change in the number of households, is equal to zero in the experiments reported in this chapter. Thus, equation (6.6.1) can be re-written as follows:

$$c_t^{(R)} = \frac{C_t^{(a)}}{C_t}\left[c_t^{(a)} - c_t^{(\Pi,a)} \right] \qquad t = 1, \ldots, T \qquad (6.6.2)$$

Equation (6.6.2) implies that movements in aggregate real consumption are proportional to movements in *real* discretionary consumption. In the five illustrative simulations the percentage change in *nominal* discretionary consumption is the same in all years. This can be deduced from the differential form of the household's equilibrium condition [i.e., equation (A3.3.17) in table A3.1.1, appendix A3.1]. Under the assumptions that the domestic bond rate and the number of households is unaffected by the increase in government spending we can re-write this condition as follows:

$$c_t^{(a)} = c_{t+1}^{(a)} \qquad t = 1, \ldots, T\text{-}1 \qquad (6.6.3)$$

Equation (6.6.2) indicates that the path of $c_t^{(a)}$ will vary inversely with the path of $c_t^{(\Pi,a)}$. Figure 6.6.2 shows that domestic prices fall in all pre-shock years but rise in all years after year 9. Since domestic prices rise by the same proportion in all years in which government expenditure rises (i.e. years 10 to 30), the path of real aggregate consumption after year 9 is flat. Between years 2 and 9, domestic prices are fairly stable so, again, the path of aggregate consumption is relatively flat over this period. Because prices fall in the pre-shock years and rise after year 9, the flat portion of the consumption path over years 2 to 9 will be higher than the flat portion of the consumption path over years 10 and 30.

The sharp fall in aggregate investment in year 1 can be traced to the behaviour of the *Housing* sector. Nominal discretionary expenditure falls 0.62 per cent below control in all years. The expenditure elasticity for *Housing* services is high (1.34). Other things constant, the 0.62 per cent fall in $c_t^{(a)}$ reduces demand for *Housing* services by about 0.83 percentage points in each year. A special feature of the

Housing sector is that capital is the only primary factor that it employs. Together with the assumption that primary factors and intermediate inputs are combined in fixed proportions, this means that the *Housing* sector's output and capital stock will change proportionally. In year 1 sectoral capital stocks are assumed to be fixed. In that year, therefore, the supply of *Housing* services cannot change.[18] The decrease in demand for *Housing* services is accommodated in year 1 by a fall in the price of these services relative to other consumption goods and services. This induces households to increase the share of *Housing* services in total consumption. The decrease in the price of *Housing* services in year 1 is absorbed by a fall in the rental price of the *Housing* sector's capital stock.

Beyond year 1 the rental price of capital is constrained to move in line with investment costs [via equilibrium condition (6.4.1)]. Between years 2 and 9 investment costs fall, allowing the rental price of the *Housing* sector's capital stock to fall. Over this period, the fall in demand for *Housing* services is accommodated partially by a contraction of the *Housing* sector's output (see chart D in figure 6.6.3) and partially by the price reductions induced by the fall in the cost of capital. In year 10 and beyond capital costs rise slightly above control. Therefore, relative to the pre-shock period, a bigger reduction in the *Housing* sector's output is required in years 10 and beyond (see chart D in figure 6.6.3).

The 0.38 per cent fall in the *Housing* sector's capital stock in year 2 (which is the same as the percentage fall in its output) is achieved by a 6.22 per cent decrease in investment in year 1. The decrease in the *Housing* sector's investment explains most of the change in aggregate investment (i.e., it accounts for about 1.18 percentage points of the 1.13 per cent decrease in aggregate investment). The export oriented sectors *Rural* and *Mining* benefit from the expansion in exports in the pre-shock years. They expand their capital stocks over this period.

In year 1 the economy's productive capacity cannot change. Aggregate employment, agricultural land and sectoral capital stocks are fixed. Thus, the decrease in investment in year 1 must be accommodated by an increase in some other component of GNE and/or by an improvement in the trade balance. Since real government expenditure is fixed, aggregate real consumption is the only component of GNE that can increase to absorb the fall in investment. However, the consumption-smoothing behaviour of households limits the scope for aggregate real consumption to rise. Figure 6.6.1 shows that aggregate real consumption falls in all years. However, the fall in aggregate real consumption in year 1 is small relative to subsequent years. Households skew their consumption in favour of year 1 because consumer prices, as measured by the consumption deflator, are low in that year relative to subsequent years.

The main reason for the fall in the consumption deflator in year 1 is the fall in the price of *Housing* services which has a large weight in the consumption basket (about 17 per cent). The other major contributors to the fall in the consumption deflator in year 1 are the *Manufacturing* and *W&R trade* commodities. The prices

---

18 *Housing* services are not imported. Thus, the total supply of these services is equal to the *Housing* sector's output.

of these two commodities, which also account for large shares of the consumption basket (i.e., 24 and 19 per cent respectively), fall sharply in year 1. The reductions in the prices of the *Manufacturing* and *W&R trade* commodities can be traced to the fall in investment by the *Housing* sector. The *Construction* sector supplies about 94 per cent of the inputs to *Housing* sector's capital creation process. The 1.94 per cent decrease in the *Construction* sector's activity level in year 1 is driven largely by the reduction in the *Housing* sector's investment. In year 1 the *Construction* sector can contract only by shedding labour. The *Construction* sector is relatively labour intensive and the labour that it sheds must be absorbed by the other sectors. This is achieved by a reduction in wages. The *Manufacturing* and *W&R trade* sectors benefit from the reduction in wages because they are relatively labour intensive. This allows the price of their outputs to fall.

The fall in wages in year 1 allows domestic costs to fall. This is reflected by the 0.62 per cent real devaluation of the exchange rate in year 1. The improvement in competitiveness stimulates the traded-goods sectors (*Rural*, *Mining* and *Manufacturing*). The improvement in the trade balance required to accommodate the fall in investment in year 1 is achieved by a 1.53 per cent increase in exports and by a 0.47 decrease in imports.

In the pre-shock years there is very little change in real GDP. Over this period the trade balance improves to accommodate the reductions in real GNE caused by the reductions in aggregate real consumption and aggregate real investment. Consistent with the constraint on net foreign liabilities the trade account is balanced beyond year 9. Thus, when the economy converge to its new steady state in year 10 the ratio of net foreign liabilities to GDP is stable but below control.

6.7 The Full Intertemporal Experiment

In the *full intertemporal* experiment households and investors are forward-looking. It differs from the *benchmark* experiment in the following ways: the forward-looking investors respond to capital gains/losses; aggregate real consumption is endogenous in all periods; and, in the last two years of the simulation horizon the ratio of net foreign liabilities to GDP is constrained to be identical. A selection of results obtained in this experiment is depicted in figures 6.7.1 — 6.7.3.

The explanation of these results is brief as we can appeal to the explanations of the *investment* and *consumption* experiments in sections 6.5 and 6.6. This is possible because the results of the full intertemporal experiment exhibit two important characteristics. First, with the exception of the interval between years 1 and 2, the *shapes* of the paths obtained in the *full intertemporal* experiment are very similar to those obtained in the *investment* experiment. The second characteristic is that the year 30 results obtained in the *full intertemporal* experiment are almost identical to the year 30 results obtained in the *consumption* experiment. These two characteristics allow us to use the explanations of the results of the *investment* and *consumption* experiments to explain, respectively, the shapes and the positions of the paths obtained in the full intertemporal experiment.

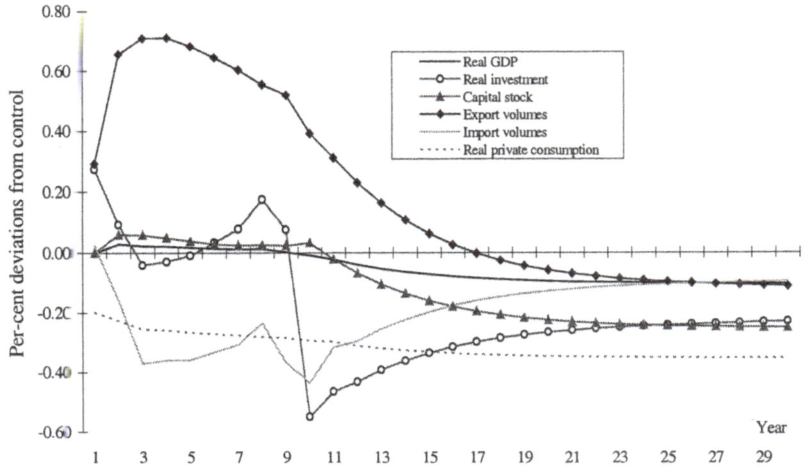

Figure 6.7.1: *Full Intertemporal* Simulation Projections for Selected Real Macro Variables

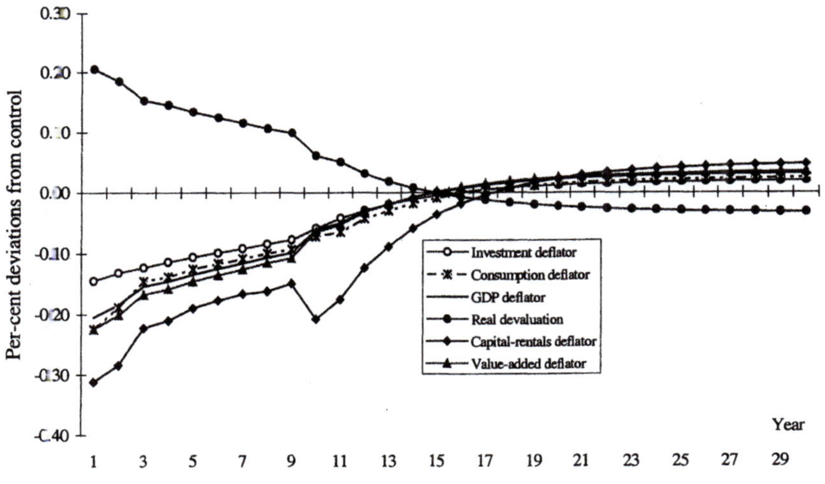

Figure 6.7.2: *Full Intertemporal* Simulation Projections for Selected Deflators

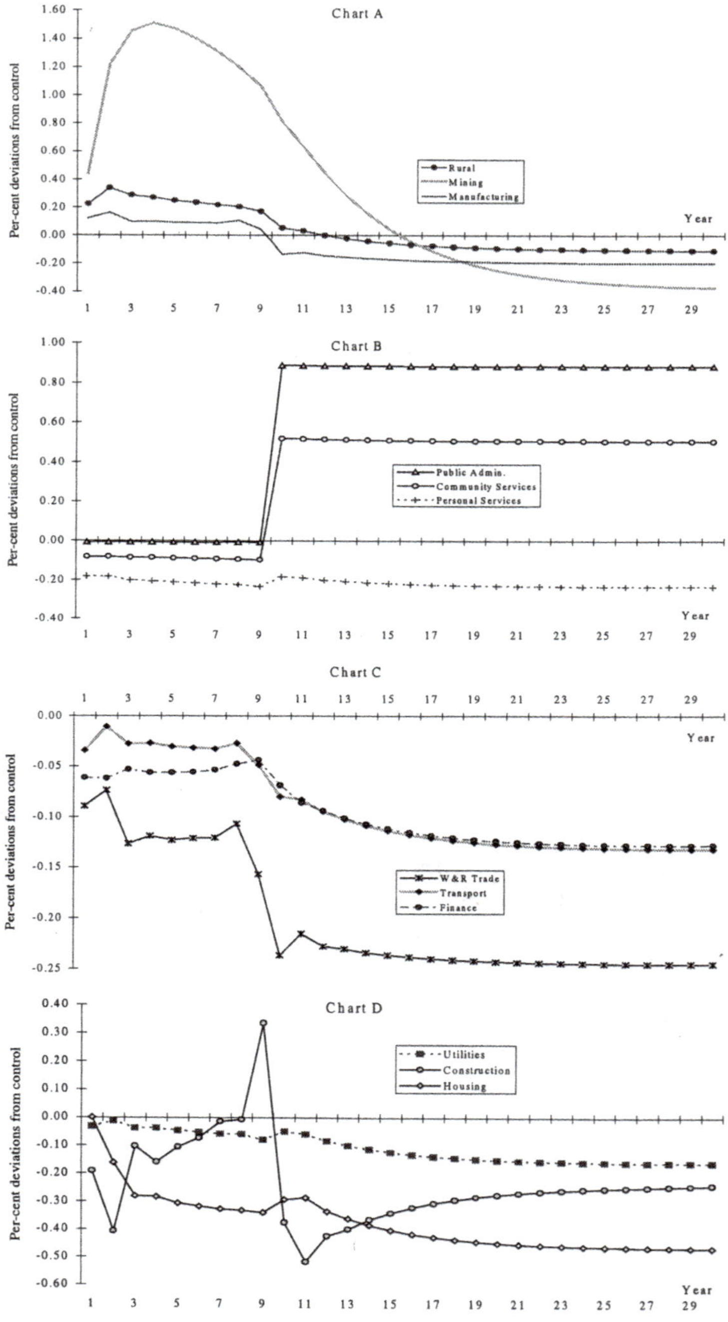

Figure 6.7.3: *Full Intertemporal* Simulation Projections for Sectoral Activity

The long-run results of the *consumption* and *full intertemporal* experiments are almost the same because the effects of capital gains (which affect behaviour in the latter experiment only) become negligible as the economy converges to its new long-run equilibrium growth path. The reason that the shapes of the paths obtained in the *investment* and the *full intertemporal* experiments are similar is that there is little difference between the *rate of growth* of consumption in the two experiments. In the *investment* experiment real consumption is not allowed to deviate from its control path. In the *full intertemporal* experiment the deviations of real consumption from its control path are fairly uniform over time. Thus, except between years 1 and 2, the rate of growth of real consumption does not deviate significantly from control.

The *full intertemporal* experiment can be loosely thought of as version of the *investment* experiment in which real consumption is shocked to 0.3 per cent below control in each year. Beyond year 2 the path of investment in the *full intertemporal* experiment lies below its counterpart in the *investment* experiment. The capital paths are similarly ordered beyond year 5. Relative to the *investment* experiment the reduction in real consumption in the *full intertemporal* experiment has two effects relevant to the capital path. First, it allows for less appreciation (or more depreciation) of the real exchange rate in all years.[19] Second, it increases the bias of the government expenditure shock in favour of labour intensive sectors. As explained previously, both of these effects tend to reduce the demand for capital. The path of exports is higher in the *full intertemporal* experiment than it is in the *investment* experiment (vice versa for imports). This is consistent with the relative movements of the real exchange rate in the two experiments.

The path of real consumption falls more uniformly in the *full intertemporal* experiment than in the *consumption* experiment. This is most obvious in the results for the first year in the two simulations. In both experiments real consumption falls 0.35 per cent below control in the long run. However, in year 1 real consumption falls by 0.04 per cent in the *consumption* experiment compared with 0.20 in the *full intertemporal* experiment. There is less incentive for households to bias their consumption path away from the first year in the latter experiment. This is because the growth in prices between years 1 and 2 is more modest in the *full intertemporal* experiment. Because investors respond to capital gains in the *full intertemporal* experiment the adjustments to the capital stock are more gradual. This smooths out the investment responses, which in turn smooths out the price responses.

In the *consumption* experiment the sharp fall in consumption between years 1 and 2 causes a sharp fall in investment in year 1. With the economy's productive capacity unable to change in that year the fall in investment was accommodated by an improvement in the trade balance. In the *full intertemporal* experiment the fall in consumption between years 1 and 2 is modest. Aggregate investment rises above control in year 1 mainly because the contraction in investment by the

[19] Real GNE falls below control in all years in the *full intertemporal* experiment but rises above control in all years in the *investment* experiment. Because the scarcity of domestic resources is relatively greater in the latter experiment, domestic prices tend to be higher.

Housing sector is more than offset by the expansion in investment by the *Mining* sector. The capital-intensive *Housing* sector sells all of its output to households. The decrease in consumption induces this sector to contract by reducing its capital stock. Favourable relative price and activity effects induce the *Mining* sector to expand its capital stock. This sector is capital-intensive and the fall in the cost of capital relative to labour induces an increase its capital-labour ratio. The *Mining* sector also increases its capital stock to accommodate the increase in demand for its output. The reduction in domestic costs improves the competitiveness of the trade-oriented *Mining* sector. Thus, the *Mining* sector benefits from an expansion in export sales and in domestic sales (through import replacement).

6.8 The Surprise Experiment

The *surprise* experiment is identical to the *full intertemporal* experiment except that agents do not anticipate the increase in government expenditure. A selection of results obtained from the *surprise* experiment is presented in figures 6.8.1 — 6.8.3. Note that the results reported in these figures are for a 30-year period starting in year 10 (i.e., the year in which the policy shock is implemented).[20] Since the shock is unanticipated the economy does not deviate from the control path over the first 9 years. The long run results obtained in the *surprise* and *full intertemporal* experiments are almost identical. The mechanisms underlying the long run results in these two experiments are the same. A key difference between the two sets of results is that the economy reaches its new long-run equilibrium with a higher net-foreign-liabilities-to-GDP ratio in the *surprise* experiment (i.e., relative to control this ratio falls by 0.54 percentage points in the *surprise* experiment compared to 1.77 percentage points in the *full intertemporal* experiment). In the long run the increase in GDP is the same in the two experiments. However, net foreign liabilities decrease by less in the *surprise* experiment. While this result has no implications for any other variable in the long run, it does summarise the different savings paths taken when agents anticipate the policy change.

The decrease in net foreign liabilities is less in the *surprise* experiment relative to the *full intertemporal* experiment because the trade surpluses accumulated over the 30-year simulation period are smaller in the former experiment. Trade surpluses reflect the excess of savings by domestic households over investment and the budget deficit. The larger trade surpluses generated in the *full intertemporal* experiment relative to the *surprise* experiment can be traced to the combined effects of the consumption-smoothing behaviour of households and the length of the anticipation period.

---

[20] We have introduced the surprise shock in the first year of a 30-year horizon. Since we are using a balanced growth control scenario we can pretend that the first year of this 30-year horizon is year 10.

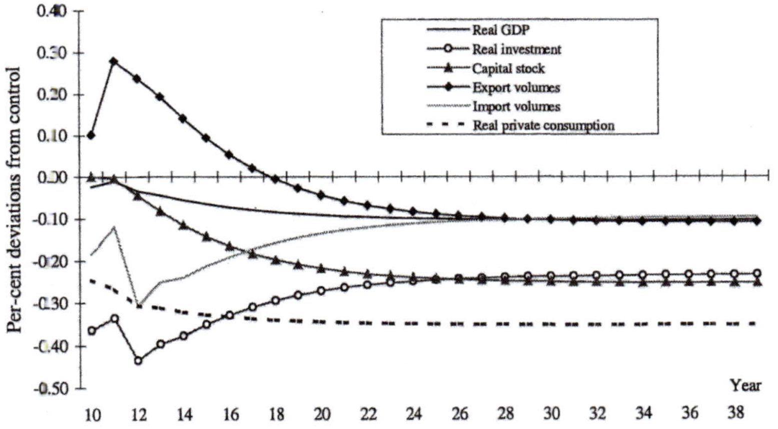

Figure 6.3.1: *Surprise* Simulation Projections for Selected Real Macro Variables

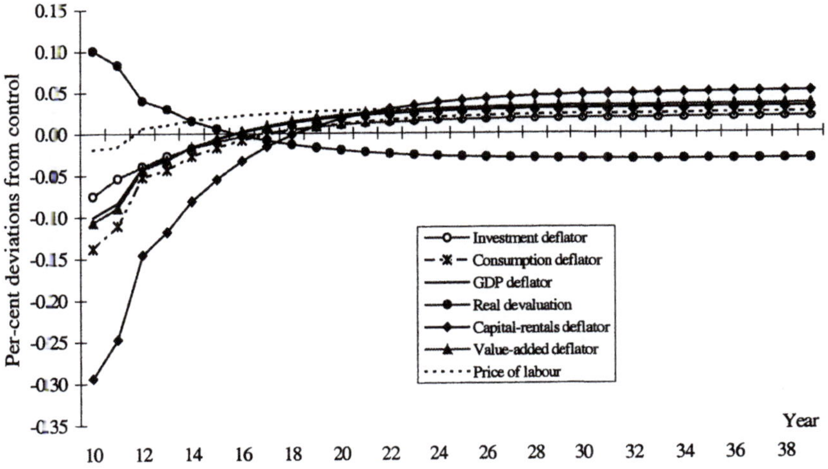

Figure 6.8.2: *Surprise* Simulation Projections for Selected Deflators

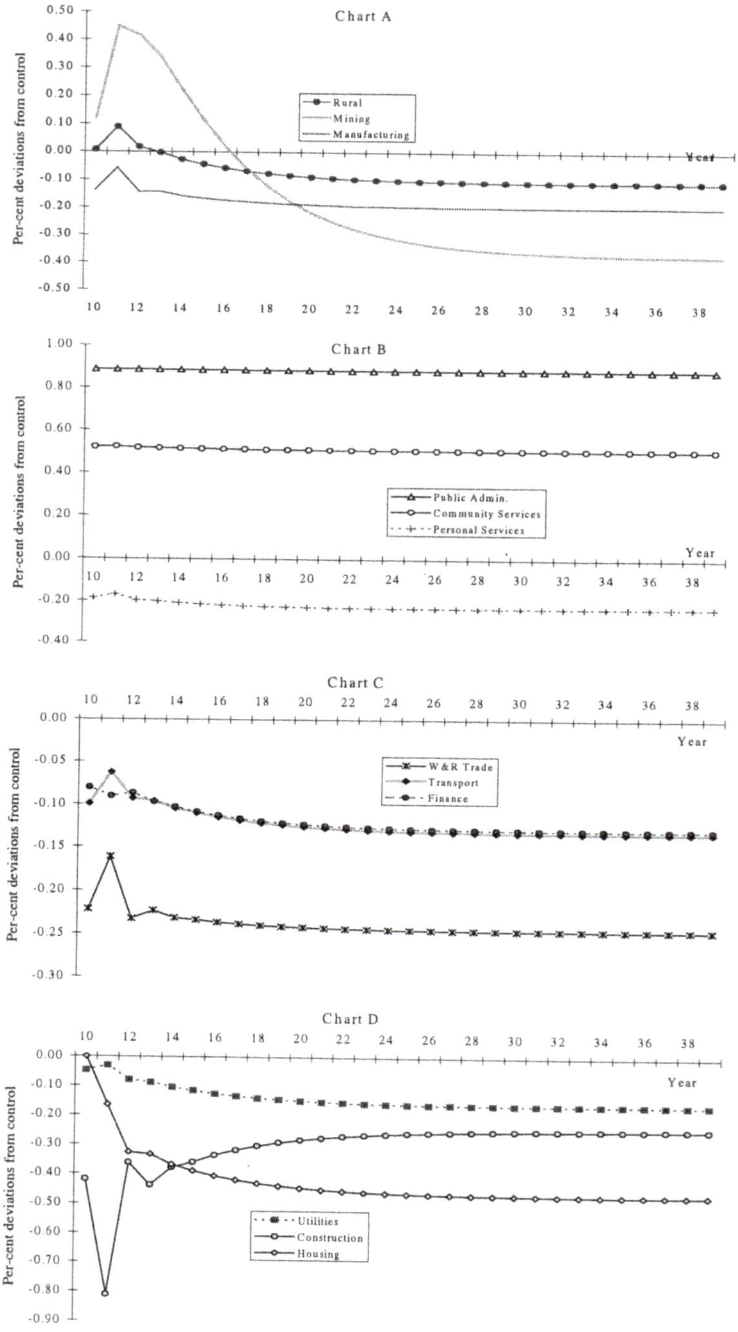

Figure 6.8.3: *Surprise* Simulation Projections for Sectoral Activity

As explained previously, the increase in government expenditure crowds-out consumption. In combination, the intertemporal consumption specification in ORANI-INT and the closure of the model adopted for these experiments imply that households will behave in a consumption-smoothing manner. A shock that reduces the household's stream of disposable income will cause the entire path of consumption to fall. Thus, even though the policy shock is not implemented until year 10 in the *full intertemporal* experiment, the forward-looking households anticipate the increase in government expenditure and reduce their consumption immediately. The fall in consumption has quite different implications for savings in the *surprise* and *full intertemporal* experiments. In the former experiment agents do not anticipate the increase in government spending hence they do not alter their behaviour until year 10, the year in which the policy is implemented. In that year and beyond agents in the *surprise* experiment decrease their consumption but this is offset by the increase in government spending. In the *full intertemporal* experiment, however, the decrease in consumption is not offset by the increase in government spending until year 10. Thus, over the first 9 years savings are greater in the *full intertemporal* experiment than in the *surprise* experiment. The savings achieved in the *full intertemporal* experiment over the first 9 years are used to reduce net foreign liabilities. The resources released from the private sector and re-directed to the foreign sector through trade surpluses.[21]

Beyond year 11 the paths obtained in the *surprise* experiment are qualitatively and quantitatively similar to their counterparts in the *full intertemporal* experiment. The results for year 10 in the *surprise* experiment are heavily conditioned by the assumption that the economy's factor endowments cannot be changed. These supply constraints are similar to those applying in year 1 of the other four simulations. In the *surprise* experiment the investors are caught unawares by the government expenditure shock in year 10. This means that sectoral capital stocks do not respond in that year. As in the other experiments aggregate employment and agricultural land are assumed to be unaffected by the policy shock in all years. With the economy's productive capacity constrained in year 10 the increase in government expenditure in that year can be accommodated by a decrease in some other component of domestic expenditure (i.e., consumption or investment) and/or by a deterioration of the trade balance. The results in figure 6.8.1 show that the trade balance actually improves. This indicates that the decreases in investment and consumption more than offset the increase in government spending.

The increase in government expenditure favours labour intensive sectors (e.g., *Public administration* and *Community services*). Conversely, the decrease in consumption is biased towards capital intensive sectors (e.g., *Housing*, *Finance* and *Utilities*). These changes in the composition of demand tend to reduce the demand for capital and, therefore, investment. Given that the supply of capital is fixed in year 10, the decrease in the demand for capital in that year must be accommodated by a fall in the cost of capital (see figure 6.8.2). The fall in the cost

---

[21] Over the first 9 years of the *full intertemporal* experiment there is also a flow of resources from households to investors. This flow is small relative to the flow of resources from households to foreigners.

of capital improves the economy's competitiveness leading to an improvement of the trade balance. This mechanism is evident in the output path of the capital-intensive *Mining* sector (see chart A in figure 6.8.3). The trade-exposed *Mining* sector benefits from the fall in the cost of capital by gaining export sales and by replacing imports.

The fall in aggregate investment in year 10 is accounted for entirely by the reductions in investment by the *Construction* and *Housing* sectors. The other sectors tend to expand their capital stocks slightly in year 11 in line with the fall in the cost of using capital. The *Construction* sector, which supplies a large proportion of the inputs used by capital creators in other sectors, reduces its investment in anticipation of further reductions in aggregate investment. Despite the fact that aggregate investment falls by less in year 11 than in year 10 the *Construction* sector's output contracts sharply in year 11 relative to year 10. This is because the *Construction* sector's main customers, particularly *Utiltites*, *Transport* and *Finance*, reduce their investment in year 11. These three sectors gradually reduce their capital stocks after year 11 as the cost of capital rises and the demand for their output falls. Beyond year 11 the output paths of these three sectors fall in line with the path of aggregate consumption. The *Housing* sector's output also falls in line with the path of consumption after year 10.

6.9 Chapter Summary

In this chapter we have explored the key properties of ORANI-INT by analysing the model's projections for a series of five illustrative experiments. We can draw four main conclusions from this analysis. First, ORANI-INT provides significantly more information about the effects of a policy change than would a single-period CGE model or a multi-period macroeconomic model. Second, even though the theoretical structure of ORANI-INT is relatively simple, the model generates complicated and interesting dynamics. Third, forward-looking expectations produce outcomes that are significantly different to static expectations. Fourth, announcement effects are potentially significant and, to examine these, it is necessary to assume that expectations are forward looking.

The detailed reconciliation of the results produced by ORANI-INT with its theoretical structure and database was often laborious. However, doing so generates three important payoffs. First, it demonstrates that there are no excuses for treating models such as ORANI-INT as "black boxes". Second, it provides some evidence that the intended computations have in fact been performed correctly. Third, it brings to the fore critical assumptions and critical elements of the database. This last payoff is particularly important because the insights derived from a critical analysis can be used to guide future model developments.

Chapter 7 Should Tariff Reductions be Announced?[1]

7.1 Introduction

In this chapter we use ORANI-INT to examine three different approaches to reducing tariffs that have, in recent history, been adopted in Australia. Under the first approach, which is similar to that adopted in Australia in 1973, the tariff cut is implemented without warning. The second approach is consistent with that adopted in the mid 1980s of phasing reforms in gradually and on giving industries several years advance notice of planned reductions in protection. Under the third approach the tariff cut is implemented several years after it is announced. This approach to reducing tariffs was adopted by the Australian government in its recent policy on protection to the passenger motor vehicle industry.

There have been many studies of the effects of protection on the Australian economy. Surveys of this literature can be found in Lloyd (1978), Anderson and Garnaut (1987) and Powell and Snape (1993). The first CGE analysis of Australia's protection policies was by Evans (1972). Since the late 1970s ORANI, a static CGE model of the Australian economy (see Dixon, Parmenter, Sutton and Vincent, 1982), has become the dominant tool for assessing Australia's protection policies.[2] ORANI has been used to analyse protection issues by government agencies, academics, lobby groups and businesses (see Powell and Snape, 1993).

Previous studies have contributed to the debate about industry protection by providing estimates of how changes in protection affect the fortunes of regions, industries and occupations in either the short or long run. However, because the models used in these studies are static, the timing issues associated with changes to industry protection have not been adequately addressed. Very little attention has been given to the likely adjustment path that the economy would take following a change in protection. Similarly, the previous studies have contributed little to the debate about whether changes in protection should be implemented without warning, as was done in 1973, or pre-announced and implemented gradually, as

---

[1] An abridged version of this chapter entitled "*Should Tariff Reductions be Announced? An Intertemporal Computable General Equilibrium Analysis*" appears in *The Economic Record*, volume 74, number 225, June 1998.

[2] In part, the dominance of ORANI in industry protection analysis reflects the adoption of the model by the Industries Assistance Commission (succeeded in 1990 by the Industry Commission).

has been recent practice. While the Australian government's current approach to reducing industry protection might be justified on political grounds, the economic benefits of such an approach are not obvious.

The Jackson Report (1975), which contains the recommendations of a Committee established to advise the government on policies for the development of the manufacturing industry, favoured tariff reductions that were pre-announced and implemented in a series of small steps. A similar view was taken in The Crawford Report (1979), that contained the recommendations of the Committee established to advise the government on structural adjustment issues. In a review of The Jackson Report, Gregory (1976) argued that the recommended strategy for reducing tariffs 'is not supported by in-depth analysis or evidence'. Gregory suggests that the strategy of pre-announcing tariff reductions might be justified on adjustment assistance grounds. However, he argues that pre-announced reforms might be less successful than unannounced reforms because the latter are more difficult to lobby against and reverse. Gregory also challenges the Jackson Report's recommendation that tariff reductions should be implemented in a series of small steps on the grounds that such a strategy might simply prolong the reform process. Gregory claims that 'tariff reform can proceed reasonably quickly with a tolerable level of adjustment costs'. This claim is based on back-of-the-envelope calculations which show that the variations in the exchange rate experienced in the early 1970s placed greater pressure on industries to adjust than did the 25 percent across-the-board tariff cut in 1973.[3]

Intertemporal CGE models like ORANI-INT are well suited to analysing the implications of alternative strategies for reducing industry protection. In contrast to static multisectoral models, ORANI-INT is able to provide information about how a reduction in industry protection will change the structure of the economy over time. In addition, because ORANI-INT allows consumers and investors to be forward-looking, the implications of announcing policy changes in advance of their implementation can be assessed.

The remainder of this chapter is organised as follows. In section 7.2 we describe how the alternative tariff reduction strategies are modelled. Simulation results are presented and explained in section 7.3. Concluding remarks are offered in section 7.4.

7.2 Simulating the Tariff Reduction Strategies

In Australia industry protection is largely confined to the *Manufacturing* sector (particularly textiles, clothing, footwear and passenger motor vehicles). ORANI-INT is used to simulate three alternative strategies for reducing assistance to the *Manufacturing* sector. The reductions in assistance are implemented as reductions

---

[3] These calculations are supported by Gruen's (1975) estimates that the 25 percent tariff cut in 1973 had a relatively small effect on the fortunes of industries when compared with the effects of the exchange rate revaluation and wage increases experienced in the early 1970s.

in the tariff on the *Manufacturing* commodity. For each experiment ORANI-INT is solved over a thirty year time horizon and results are reported as per-cent deviations from a control scenario. In setting up the experiments we had to choose the following: a control scenario; a closure for the model; and a set of shocks for the exogenous variables. These choices are detailed below.

7.2.1 Control Scenario

For the three experiments we use the CBG control scenario described in chapter 5. In the CBG scenario the economy converges to balanced 3 per cent annual growth asymptotically. There is no economic justification for choosing the CBG scenario over the BG scenario as both are hypothetical characterisations of the economy. We use the CBG scenario simply to demonstrate the ease with which ORANI-INT can accommodate alternative control scenarios.[4]

7.2.2 Choice of Exogenous Variables

The standard closure described in section 5.3.1 of chapter 5 is used in all three tariff-reduction simulations.

7.2.3 Description of the Tariff Shocks

In the three experiments the tariff rate on the *Manufacturing* commodity is the only variable shocked. The size of the tariff reductions modelled is based on the Industry Commission's (1995) estimates of the nominal rate of assistance to *Manufacturing*. According to these estimates, when the program of phased reductions in industry assistance was introduced in 1985-86 the nominal rate of assistance to *Manufacturing* was 12 percent. When the government's current schedule of reductions in assistance is completed in the year 2000-01 the nominal rate of assistance to the *Manufacturing* sector is projected to be 3 percent. Whilst the Industry Commission's estimates of assistance include contributions by tariff and non-tariff measures, the latter account for a very small proportion of the measured assistance to the *Manufacturing* sector.[5] For example, in 1992-93 tariffs accounted for over 95 percent of measured assistance to the *Manufacturing* sector.

The change in assistance to *Manufacturing* between 1985-86 and 2000-01 is modelled as a tariff movement that reduces the price of the imported

---

[4] The results reported in this chapter are not overly sensitive to our decision to use the CBG scenario rather than the BG scenario. This can be deduced by comparing the results with those in Malakellis (1998), an analogous study in which the BG scenario is used.

[5] The Industry Commission's measure of nominal protection is broad but not exhaustive. It includes: tariffs, quantitative import restrictions, domestic pricing arrangements, production subsidies, export subsidies, local contents schemes and export facilitation arrangements.

Manufacturing commodity by 8 per cent (i.e., [1.03 - 1.12]/1.12 = -0.08).[6] In the first experiment the tariff cut is implemented fully in the first year of the planning horizon and is therefore unanticipated. In the second experiment the tariff cut is implemented in the 12th year of the planning horizon (notionally 1996-97) but is announced at the start of the planning horizon (notionally 1985-86). In the third experiment the tariff cut is phased in gradually over 12 years (notionally 1985-86 to 1996-97).[7] The effects that the alternative tariff-cutting strategies have on the path of the domestic currency price of the imported *Manufacturing* commodity are shown in figure 7.2.1.[8] The acronyms STR, ATR and PTR are used to describe the *S*urprise *T*ariff *R*eduction, *A*nticipated *T*ariff *R*eduction and *P*hased *T*ariff *R*eduction experiments.

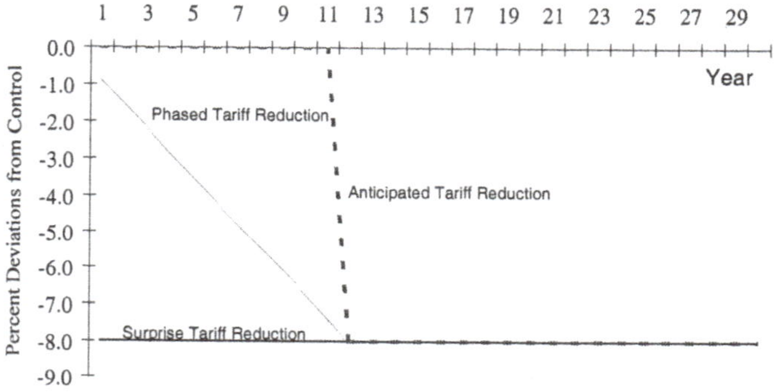

Figure 7.2.1: Price of the Imported Manufacturing Commodity

7.3. Simulation Results

The simulation results are presented in a series of figures. Figures 7.3.M1 – 7.3.M6 show the paths of selected real macroeconomic variables. The paths of a range of price deflators are presented in figures 7.3.P1 – 7.3.P8. The paths of the main

---

6 In the CBG control scenario the tariff rate on the *Manufacturing* commodity is 0.084. Thus, to achieve the 8 per cent fall in the price of the imported *Manufacturing* commodity the tariff rate in ORANI-INT is reduced from 0.084 to -0.003 (a slight subsidy).

7 While the current schedule of tariff reductions extends to the year 2000-01, the cuts planned beyond 1996-97 are small (e.g., the nominal rate of assistance to the *Manufacturing* sector goes from 4 per cent in 1996-97 to 3 per cent in 2000-01). For convenience, we assume that the tariff reductions are completed by 1996-97.

8 As will be explained in section 7.3, the paths of the foreign currency price of imports and the path of the nominal exchange rate are assumed to be exogenous. In combination, these assumptions imply that the 8 per cent fall in the price of the imported *Manufacturing* commodity shown in figure 7.1 emanates directly from the tariff cut.

export and import commodities are depicted in figures 7.3.E1 – 7.3.E3 and 7.3.I1 – 7.3.I2 respectively. Finally, figures 7.3.S1 – 7.3.S10 show the sectoral output paths. In all figures the values on the horizontal axis denote years while the values on the vertical axis denote per-cent deviations from the control scenario. Each figure shows three paths, corresponding to the three alternative tariff-reduction strategies, for a particular variable. The paths depicted as solid black lines are projections from the STR experiment. The grey lines represent projections from the PTR experiment. Dashed lines are used to depict the paths produced by the ATR experiment.

While the long-run effects of the alternative tariff reduction strategies are similar, the adjustment paths are not. Gains in real GDP and real aggregate consumption are greatest under the STR strategy and smallest under the ATR strategy. The tariff on the *Manufacturing* commodity distorts the allocation of resources. The sooner the distortion is reduced the sooner the benefits of improved resource allocation are realised.[9]

The tariff cut causes structural change. Structural adjustment problems will occur if the rate at which sectors must expand or contract exceeds their ability to do so. In ORANI-INT the mobility of sectoral capital is constrained,[10] limiting the ability of sectors to expand or contract. Labour, however, is assumed to be homogeneous and perfectly mobile. These assumptions may be critical to the choice of tariff-reduction strategy.

In the following subsections the critical theoretical assumptions and critical elements of ORANI-INT's database are used in explanations of the macro and sectoral results. The long-run (i.e., year 30) results obtained in the three experiments are explained jointly because they are almost identical. The transition paths differ across simulations and, therefore, are explained separately. In subsection 7.3.3 we indicate how much bigger the labour market adjustment costs must be under the ATR and PTR strategies relative to the STR strategy if the three strategies are to be equally preferred.

The explanation of the long-run results is more formal than is the explanation of the transition paths. This reflects the relative difficulty of understanding these results. By the 30th year of the simulation the economy has reached its new steady state and the absence of transitional dynamics, such as capital gains, means that results for this period can be treated as if they were produced by a single-period model. For this reason it is relatively easy to devise back-of-the-envelope (BOTE) calculations that reconcile the long-run results with the model's theory and data. It

---

[9] In these experiments the removal of the distortionary tariff on the *Manufacturing* commodity is almost complete. While this improves real consumption in the long run, we cannot claim that the optimal tariff is zero because Australia is assumed to have some market power in its export markets.

[10] Capital mobility is constrained by the explicit modelling of non-negativity constraints on sectoral investment and by gestation lags rather than by adjustment costs of the type described by Lucas (1967) and others.

Figure 7.3.M1: Real GDP

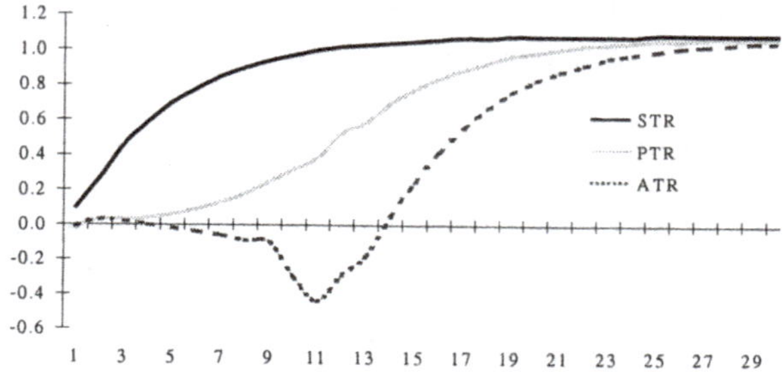

Figure 7.3.M2: Real Consumption

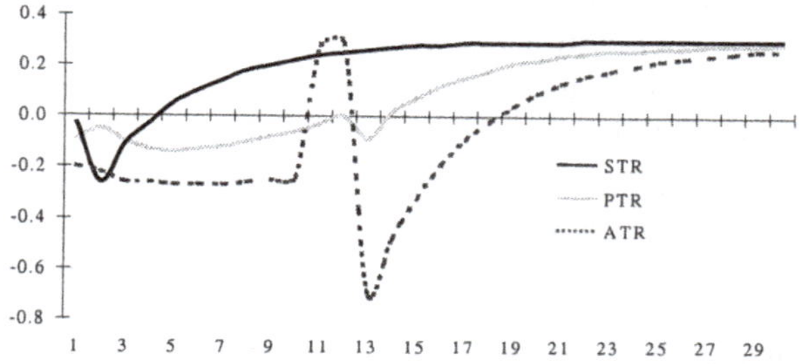

Figure 7.3.M3: Real Aggregate Investment

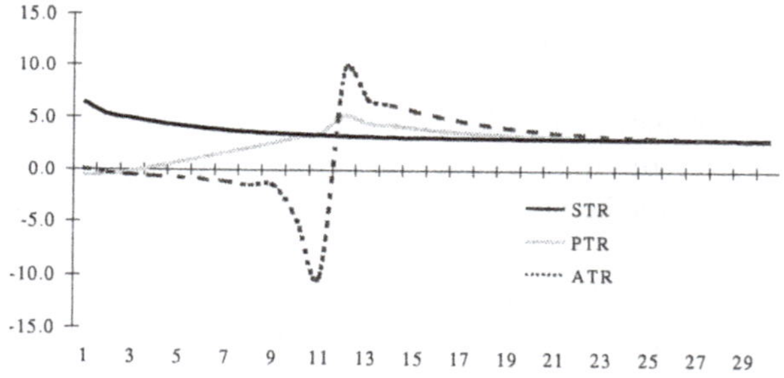

Figure 7.3.M4: Real Aggregate Capital Stock

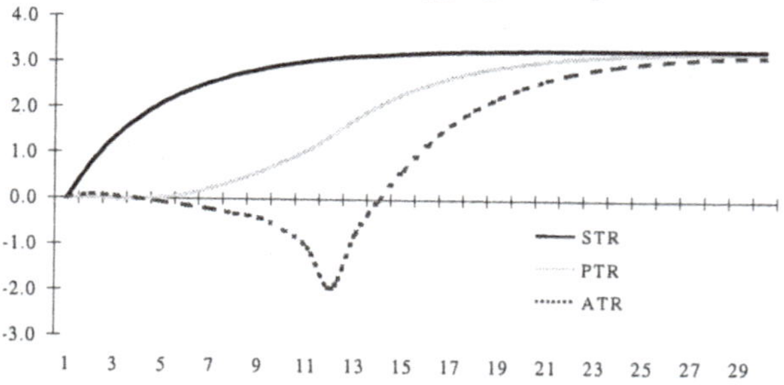

Figure 7.3.M5: Aggregate Export Volumes

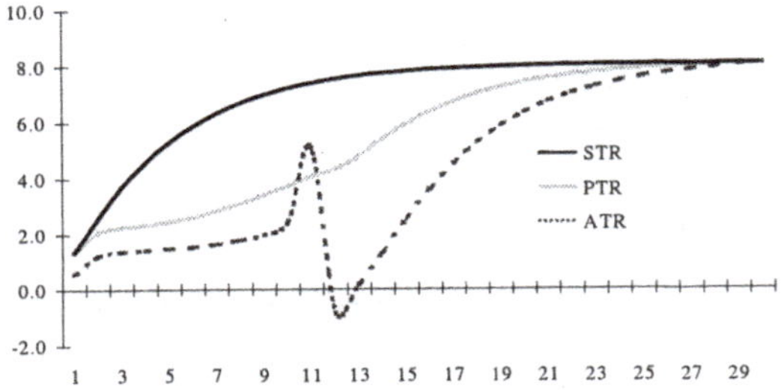

Figure 7.3.M6: Aggregate Import Volumes

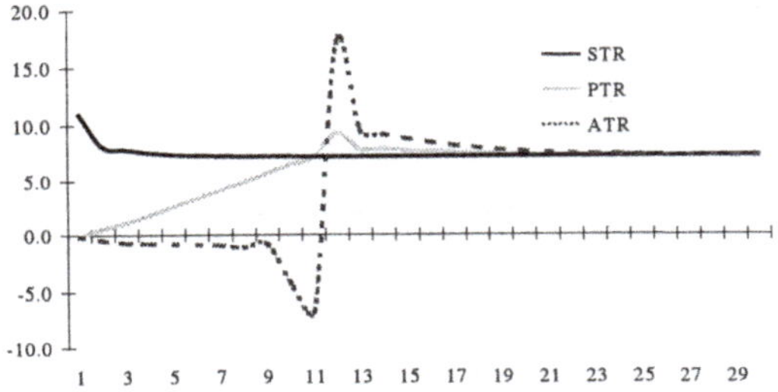

Figure 7.3.P1: GDP Deflator

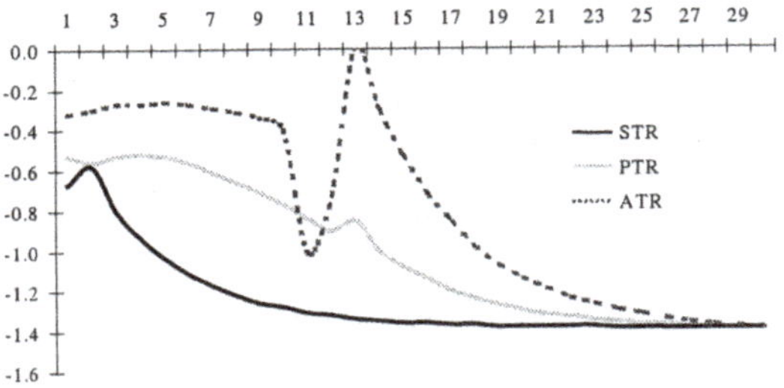

Figure 7.3.P2: Investment Price Deflator

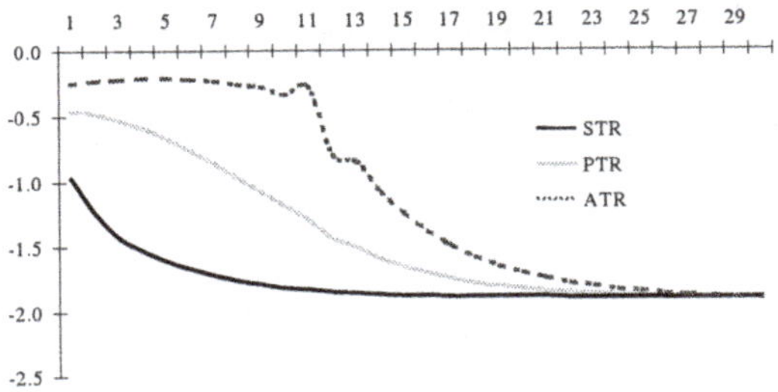

Figure 7.3.P3: Export Price Deflator

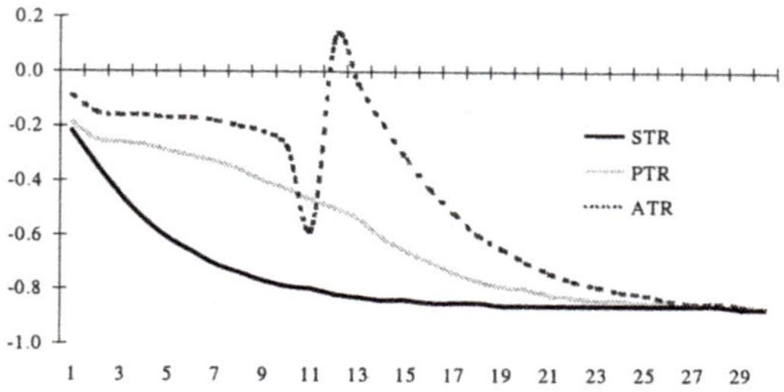

Figure 7.3.P4: Factor Cost Deflator

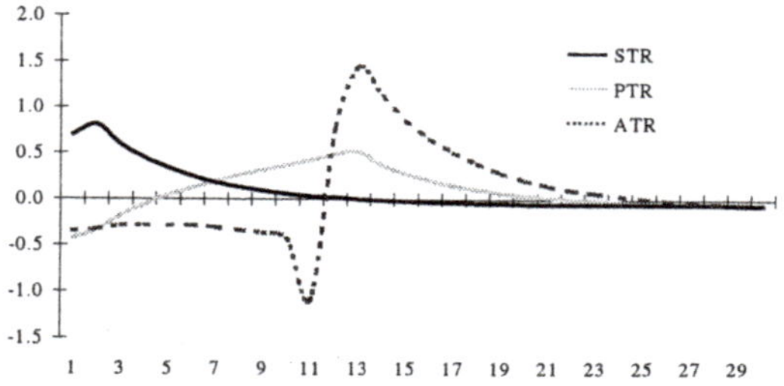

Figure 7.3.P5: Rental Price of Capital Deflatc

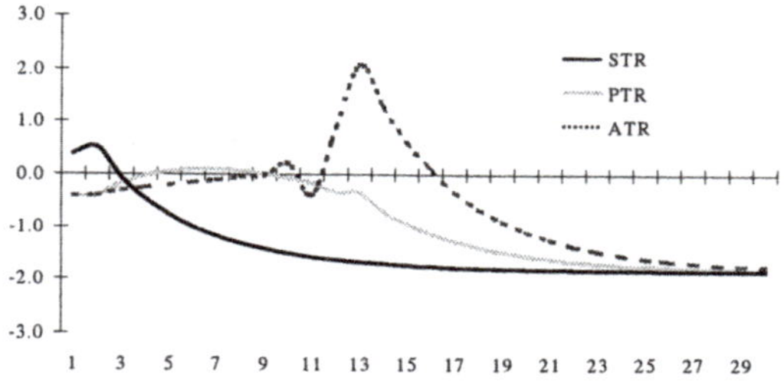

Figure 7.3.P6: Price of Labour

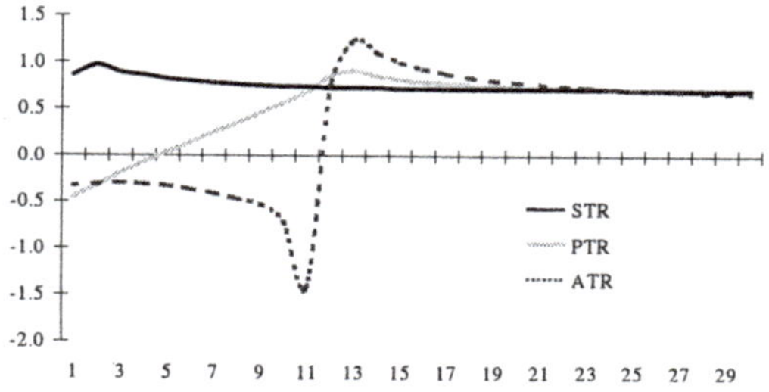

Figure 7.3.P7: Above-subsistence Consumption Deflator

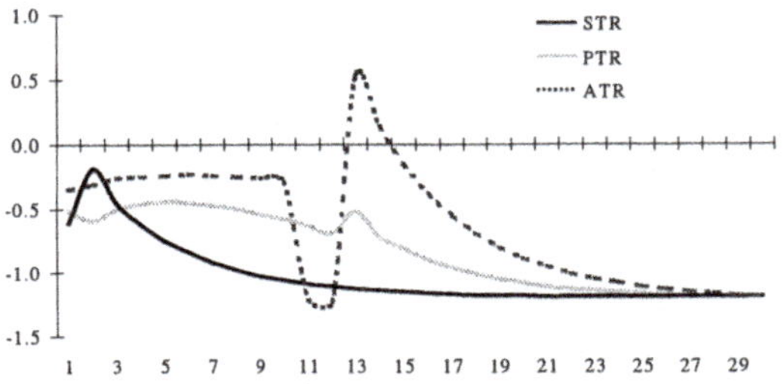

Figure 7.3.P8: Consumption Deflator

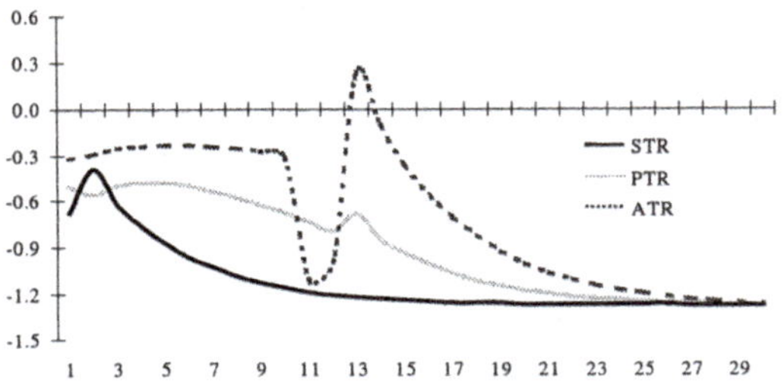

Figure 7.3.E1: Rural Exports

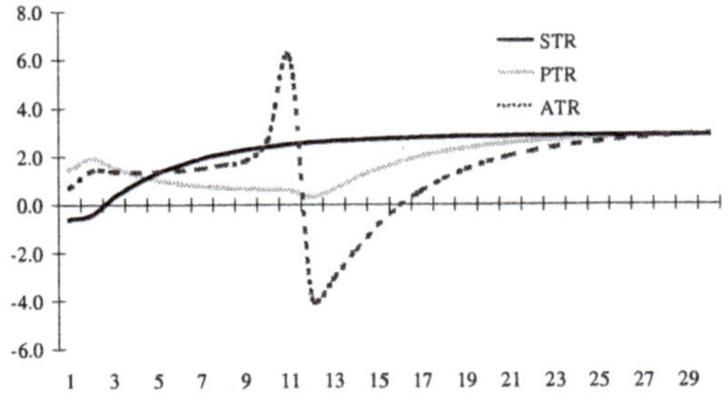

Figure 7.3.E2: Mining Exports

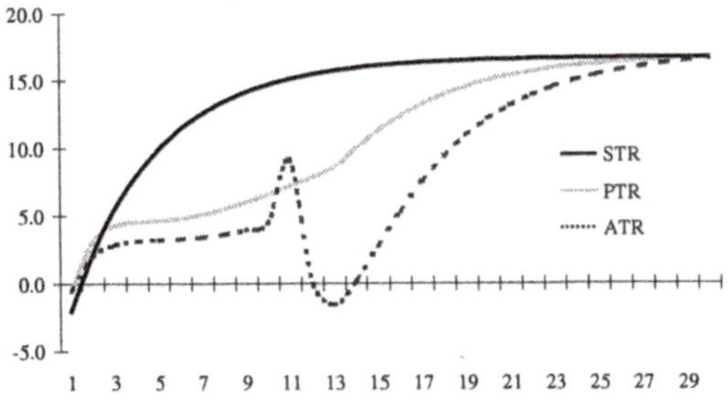

Figure 7.3.E3: Manufacturing Exports

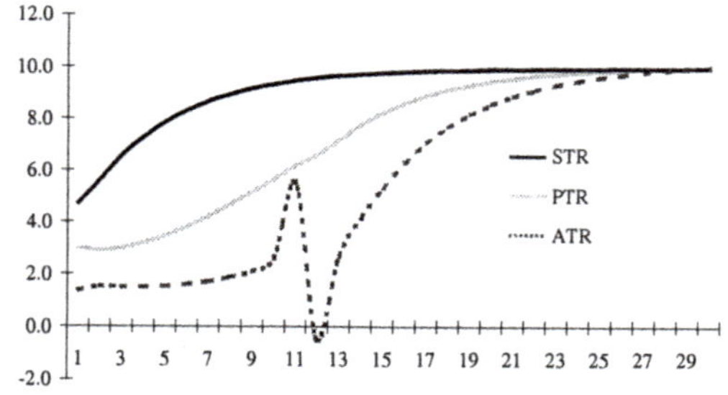

Figure 7.3.I1: Manufacturing Imports

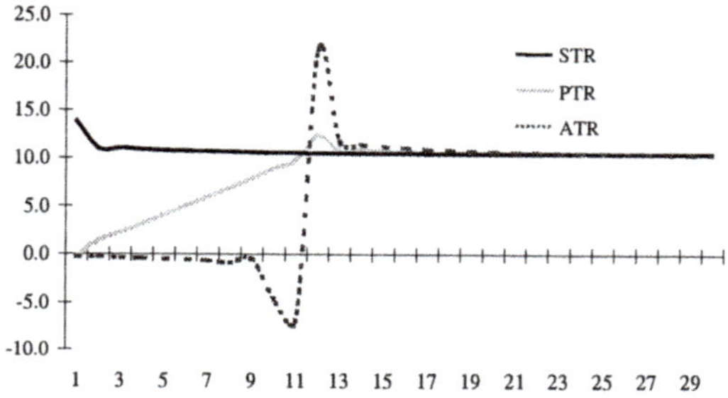

Figure 7.3.I2: Mining Imports

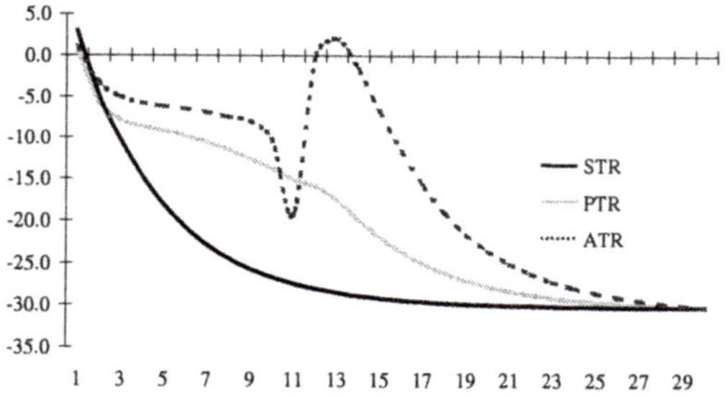

Figure 7.3.S1: Rural Output

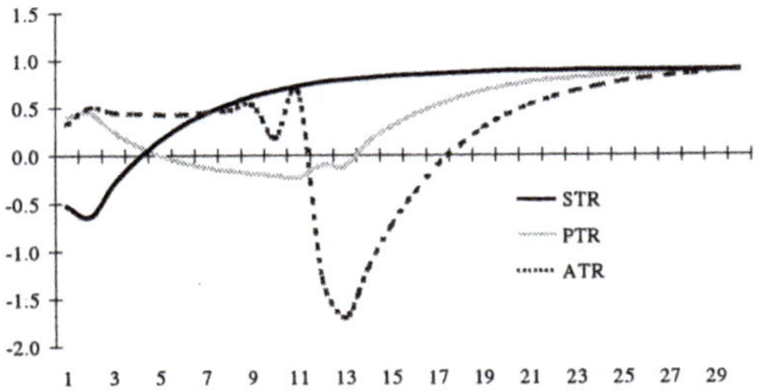

Figure 7.3.S2: Mining Output

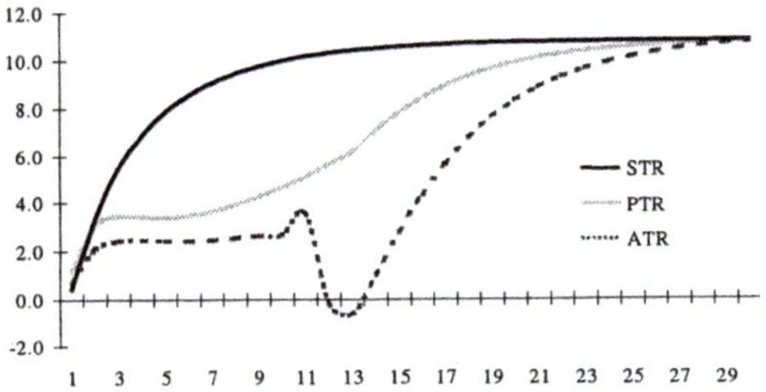

Figure 7.3.S3: Manufacturing Output

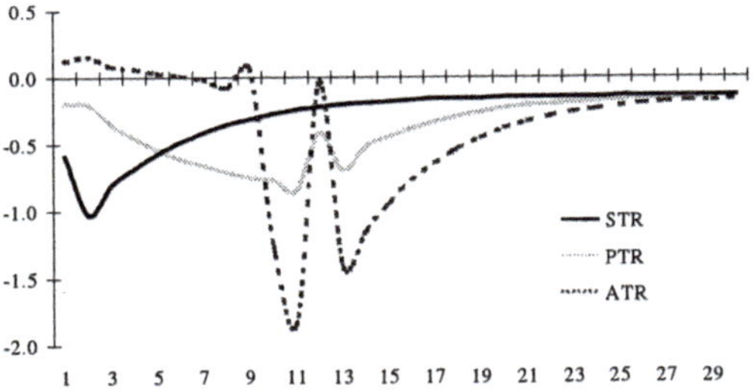

Figure 7.3.S4: Utilities Output

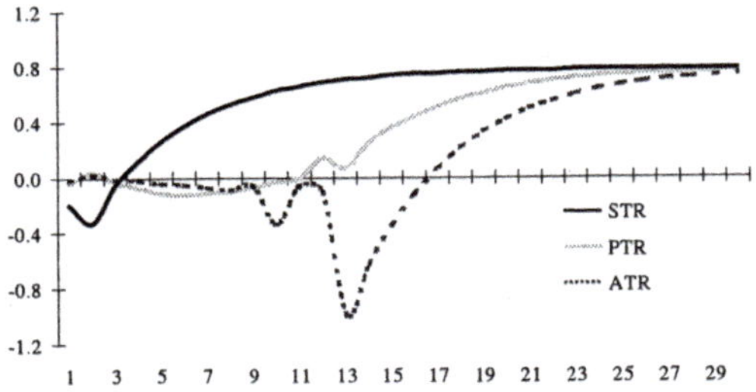

Figure 7.3.S5: Construction Output

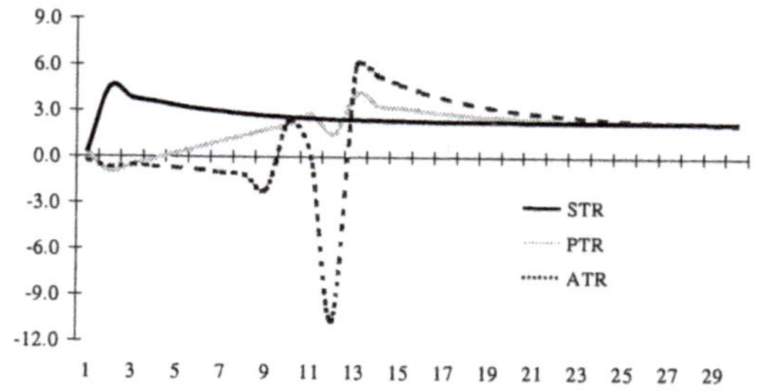

Figure 7.3.S6: Wholesale & Retail Trade Output

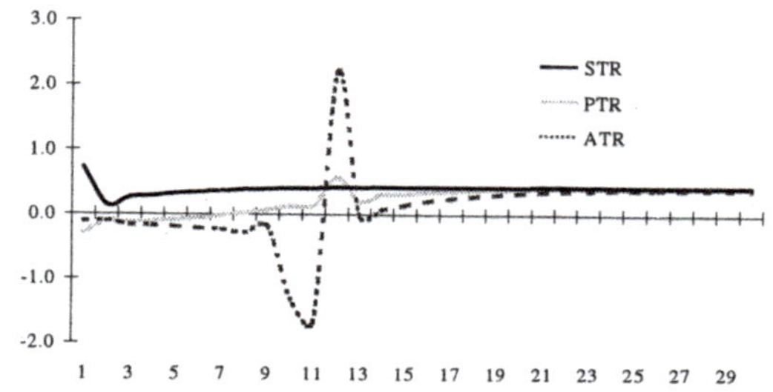

Figure 7.3.S7: Transport Output

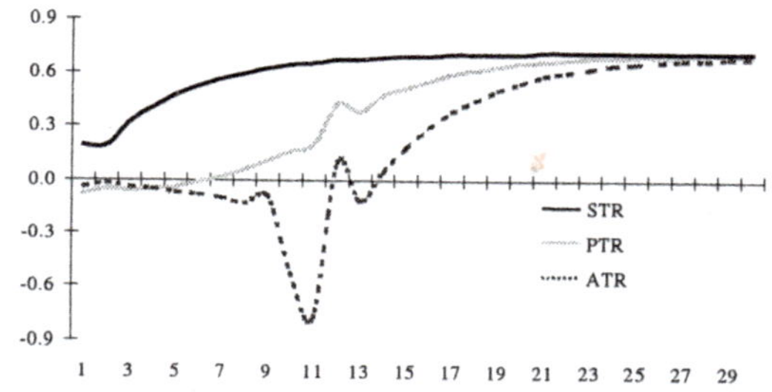

Figure 7.3.S8: Finance Output

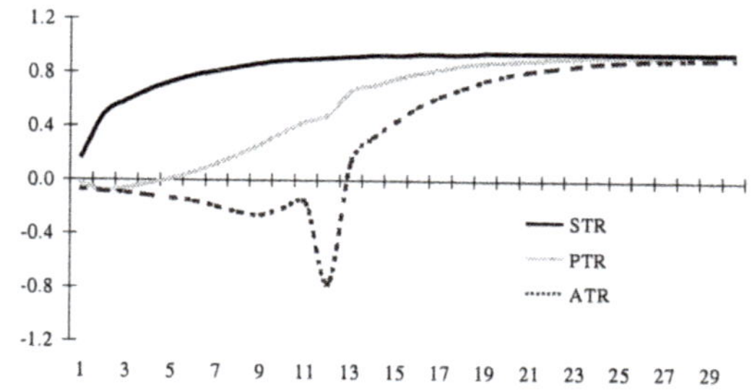

Figure 7.3.S9: Housing Output

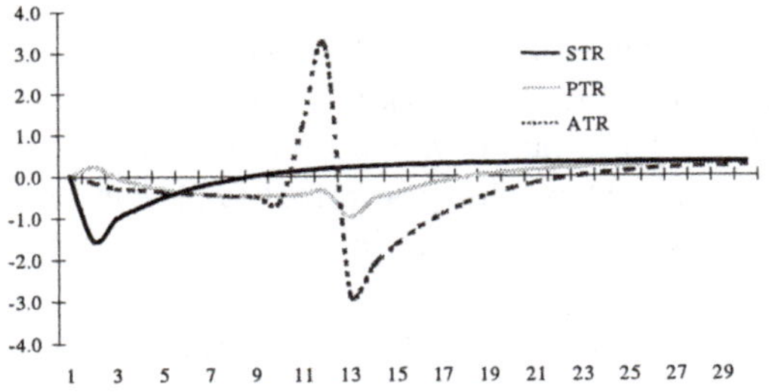

Figure 7.3.S10: Personal Services Output

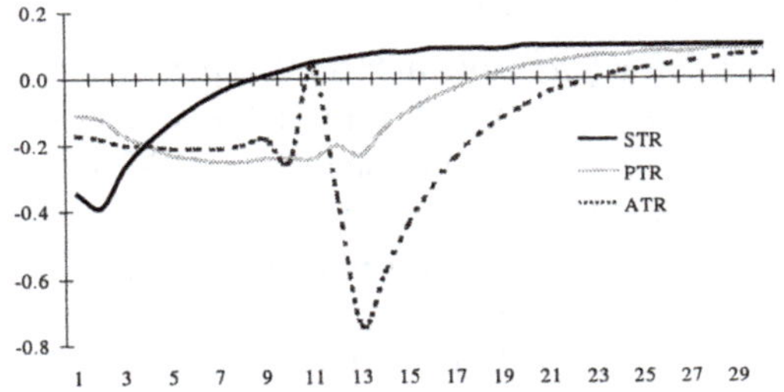

is more difficult to devise convincing BOTE calculations for the transition paths because the speed with which the economy adjusts to its new long run equilibrium is a complicated function of the model's parameters and the manner in which the tariff is reduced. Accordingly, the explanation of the transition paths and the reconciliation of these results with the model's theory and data is less formal.

7.3.1 Long-run Results

The long-run results of the three experiments are almost identical. This is because in all experiments the tariff has been cut to the same level after year 12 and the 30-year time horizon is sufficiently long for the economy to converge to its new long-run equilibrium. While the long-run results offer no basis for discriminating between the alternative tariff reduction strategies, an understanding of the mechanisms underlying these results is a prerequisite for understanding the adjustment paths. Investors and consumers are forward looking and the long-run results will influence the transitional dynamics.

We draw attention to the main mechanisms underlying the long-run results by explaining the following key results: the increase in real GDP; the increase in the economy's capital-labour ratio; the small (relative to GDP) increase in real consumption; and the economy's increased trade orientation. Having set the scene at the macro level we then turn to the sectoral results and explain why some sectors gain from the tariff cut while others lose.

Why Does Real GDP Expand?

In the results reported GDP is measured at market prices. From the income side of the National Accounts GDP is the sum of GDP at factor cost (value-added) and net indirect taxes. Indirect taxes put a wedge between the resource cost and market value of a unit of output. Thus, changes in real GDP can be traced to changes in the usage of resources and/or to changes in the efficiency with which resources are used.

The percentage change in real GDP ($gdpi^{(R)}$) is defined by equation (A3.6.57) in table A3.1.1, appendix A3.1. For convenience we repeat this equation below:

$$gdpi_t^{(R)} = \frac{\mathrm{GDPFC_t}}{\mathrm{GDPI_t}} gdpfc_t^{(R)} + \frac{\mathrm{NIT_t}}{\mathrm{GDPI_t}} nit_t^{(R)}. \qquad t = 1, \ldots, T \qquad (7.3.1)$$

We remind the reader that $gdpfc^{(R)}$ and $nit^{(R)}$ are the percentage changes in real GDP at factor cost (real value added) and real indirect tax revenues and that the coefficients in equation (7.3.1) are the shares in GDP of value added and net indirect taxes. Figure 7.3.M1 shows that in year 30 real GDP increases by about 1.1 per cent. In year 30 the CBG control scenario values of the shares in GDP of value added and net indirect taxes are 0.86 and 0.14 respectively. Using these values as our estimates of the coefficients in equation (7.3.1) and using the year-30 simulation results for $gdpfc^{(R)}$ and $nit^{(R)}$ we can decompose $gdpi^{(R)}$ as follows:

$$gdp_{30}^{(R)} = 1.1 \approx 0.86 \times (0.98) + 0.14 \times (1.73) = 1.1.$$

Thus, about three-quarters of the increase in real GDP emanates from the increase in real value added with the remainder being accounted for by the increase in real indirect tax revenues.

The percentage change in real value added is defined by equation (A3.6.59) in table A3.1.1, appendix A3.1, as follows:

$$gdpfc_t^{(R)} = \frac{\mathrm{W_t}}{\mathrm{GDPFC_t}} w_t^{(R)} + \frac{\mathrm{K_t}}{\mathrm{GDPFC_t}} k_t^{(R)} + \frac{\mathrm{N_t}}{\mathrm{GDPFC_t}} n_t^{(R)}. \qquad t = 1, \ldots, T \qquad (7.3.2)$$

In equation (7.3.2) the coefficients are shares in value added of capital rentals (K), payments to labour (L) and returns to agricultural land (N). The variables $w^{(R)}$, $k^{(R)}$, and $n^{(R)}$ are the percentage changes in aggregate employment, aggregate capital stocks and agricultural land. In the simulations $w^{(R)}$ and $n^{(R)}$ are assumed to be unaffected by the tariff cut. That is, $w^{(R)}$ and $n^{(R)}$ are exogenous and not shocked. Under these assumptions equation (7.3.2) reduces to:

$$gdpfc_t^{(R)} = \frac{\mathrm{K_t}}{\mathrm{GDPFC_t}} k_t^{(R)}. \qquad t = 1, \ldots, T \qquad (7.3.3)$$

We can estimate the value of $gdpfc_{30}^{(R)}$ using the CBG scenario value of the share in value added of capital rentals and the model's projection for $k_{30}^{(R)}$ as follows:

$$gdpfc_{30}^{(R)} = 0.3(3.3) = 0.99.$$

To two decimal places, our estimate of $gdpfc_{30}^{(R)}$ concords with the model's projection.

In chapter 6 we explained that $nit^{(R)}$ is that part of the percentage change in net indirect taxes that is due to changes in the tax bases caused by changes in quantities of goods and services produced and sold. This was formally represented by equation (6.4.3) in sub-section 6.4.1. We also noted that in the absence of any changes in the composition of sectoral outputs and sales $nit^{(R)}$ and, therefore, $gdpi^{(R)}$ will be equal to $gdpfc^{(R)}$. The tariff shock induces a change in the economy's production and sales structures in favour of commodities that are relatively highly taxed. This compositional change causes $nit^{(R)}$ and, therefore, $gdpi^{(R)}$ to increase relative to $gdpfc^{(R)}$. The excess of $gdpi^{(R)}$over $nit^{(R)}$ represents the allocative efficiency gains from changing the composition of the economy in favour of activities that were discouraged (relative to optimum) in the pre-shock tax regime.

Most of the excess of $nit^{(R)}$ over $gdpfc^{(R)}$ can be attributed to: an 11 per cent expansion in the *Mining* sector's output, which is heavily taxed; a 10.5 per cent increase in sales of the imported *Manufacturing* commodity, which attract a relatively high rate of tax; and a 10.5 per cent increase in the volume of the imported *Manufacturing* commodity, which attracts the highest tariff. Although it is tedious to evaluate equation (6.4.3) completely, a partial evaluation verifies that most of the change in real net indirect taxes can be attributed to the above-mentioned changes in the economy's production and sales structures. We further simplify the evaluation of equation (6.4.3) by assuming that sales tax rates do not differ across users. Thus, our partial evaluation of equation (6.4.3) accounts for the following contributions to $nit^{(R)}$ only: the increase in the *Mining* sector's output; the increase in sales of the imported *Manufacturing* commodity (undifferentiated by user); and the increase in the volume of the imported *Manufacturing* commodity. Under these assumptions equation (6.4.3) reduces to:

$$nit_{30}^{(R)} \approx \frac{1}{\mathrm{NIT}_{30}} \left[\mathrm{P}_{j,30}^{(O)} \mathrm{X}_{j,30}^{(O)} x_{j,30}^{(O)} + \mathrm{P}_{i,f,30}^{(Z)} \mathrm{X}_{i,30}^{(M)} \tau_{i,30}^{(\bullet)} x_{i,30}^{(M)} + \mathrm{P}_{i,30}^{(M)} \mathrm{X}_{i,30}^{(M)} \Phi_{30} [\mathrm{T}_{i,30}^{(6)} - 1] \, x_{i,30}^{(M)} \right].$$

$$j \in \text{Mining}; \; i \in \text{Manufacturing} \qquad (7.3.4)$$

The only new notation introduced in approximation (7.3.4) is $\tau_{i,30}^{(\bullet)}$, the average rate of tax on sales of the *Manufacturing* to all users. In order of appearance, the coefficients in approximation (7.3.4) are shares in net indirect tax revenue of: 'other cost' tickets (mainly production taxes) paid by the *Mining* sector; sales taxes collected from sales of the foreign *Manufacturing* commodity; and tariff revenue collected from imports of the *Manufacturing* commodity.

To evaluate equation (7.3.4) we use the year-30 CBG scenario shares and the model's projections of the xs for year 30. The percentage change in real net indirect taxes is estimated as follows:

$$nit_{30}^{(R)} \approx 0.07(11) + 0.03(10.5) + 0.07(10.5) = 1.86$$

Our estimate of $nit^{(R)}$ is about 0.1 percentage points higher than the model's projection.[11]

Why Does the Economy Become More Capital Intensive?

The economy's capital stock expands because the average real cost of using capital falls. That is, on average, the rental price of capital falls relative to the prices of the other factors of production. In combination, the closure of the model and the configuration of the exogenous variables adopted for these experiments imply that sectoral rates of return are equal to the world rate of interest which is assumed not to respond to the tariff cut. Hence, the supply of capital is perfectly elastic at the world rate of interest and the amount of capital used is demand-determined. The sectoral input demand functions have the nested Leontief/CES form where sector j's demand for capital is a function of an industry-specific activity variable and of relative factor prices. At the economy-wide level the percentage change in the demand for capital can be approximated by the following aggregate Leontief/CES input demand function:

$$k_t^{(R)} \approx gdpfc_t^{(R)} - \sigma(k_t^{(\Pi)} - gdpfc_t^{(\Pi)}) . \qquad t = 1, ..., T \qquad (7.3.5)$$

We remind the reader that the superscript (Π) is used to indicate a price deflator. Thus, in approximation (7.3.5) $k^{(\Pi)}$ is the percentage change in the rental price of capital deflator and $gdpfc^{(\Pi)}$ is the percentage change in the value-added deflator. The coefficient σ is the elasticity of substitution between the factors of production. Using equation (7.3.3) to substitute $gdpfc^{(R)}$ out of equation (7.3.5) we can approximate aggregate demand for capital as a function of relative prices only. That is:

$$k_t^{(R)} \approx -\sigma \left[\frac{\mathrm{GDPFC}_t}{\mathrm{GDPFC}_t - \mathrm{K}_t} \right] (k_t^{(\Pi)} - gdpfc_t^{(\Pi)}) . \qquad t = 1, ..., T \qquad (7.3.6)$$

The value of $k_{30}^{(R)}$ is estimated from (7.3.6) using simulation results for year 30 and data from the CBG scenario as follows:

$$k_{30}^{(R)} \approx -1.28\ [1.43]\ ((-1.83) - (-0.06)) = 3.2.$$

The estimate of $k_{30}^{(R)}$ derived from (7.3.6) is very close to the model's projection.

---

11 This small divergence between the model's projection and our back-of-the-envelope calculation can be traced to two sources: first, to the omission in our calculation of the effects on $nit^{(R)}$ of changes in the production and sale of commodities other than *Mining* and *Manufacturing*; and second, to our estimates of the shares in equation (7.3.4), particularly of the share in aggregate net indirect tax revenues of the tariffs collected from imports of the *Manufacturing* commodity. Whilst the value of this share in the CBG scenario is 0.07, its post-simulation value is very close to zero. Therefore, using the CBG value of this share introduces an approximation error in the evaluation of equation (7.3.4).

Approximation (7.3.6) confirms that most of the increase in the economy's capital stock is accounted for by the fall in the rental price of capital relative to the price of other factors (i.e., the cost of using capital). By year 30 the economy has converged to its new steady state and capital gains/losses have been eliminated. This means that the rental price of capital and the construction cost of capital will move together. In year 30 the cost-reducing effect of the tariff cut allows the average construction cost of capital, measured by the investment deflator, to fall by about 1.9 percent (see figure 7.3.P2) and this translates into a 1.83 percent fall in the average rental price of capital (see figure 7.3.P5).[12] In contrast, the value-added deflator, which indicates the average cost of all primary factors, falls by about 0.06 percent (see figure 7.3.P4).

The investment deflator falls by more than the GNE deflator (1.9 per cent compared with 1.2 per cent) because the capital creation process is relatively intensive in the use of the imported *Manufacturing* commodity whose price falls by 8 per cent. In turn, the GNE deflator falls relative to the value-added deflator, which is the GDP deflator net of the deflator for indirect taxes. In these experiments there are two counteracting mechanisms that allow the value-added deflator to move out of line with the GNE deflator. The tariff cut tends to reduce the real cost of using capital by allowing the value-added deflator to rise relative to the GNE deflator. However, the tariff cut also improves Australia's competitiveness. The consequent expansion in exports induces a deterioration in the terms of trade that tends to increase the cost of using capital by allowing the value-added deflator to fall relative to the GNE deflator. The results indicate that the terms of trade deterioration only partially offsets the fall in the user cost of capital induced by the tariff cut.

To highlight the above mechanisms we use the percentage change in the GNE deflator and two measures of the percentage change in the GDP deflator. These three deflators are defined in table A3.1.1 of appendix A3.1. The percentage change in the GDP deflator from the income side of the national accounts, $gdpi^{(\Pi)}$, is given by equation (A3.6.58) as:

$$gdpi_t^{(\Pi)} = \frac{\mathrm{GDPFC}_t}{\mathrm{GDPI}_t}\, gdpfc_t^{(\Pi)} + \frac{\mathrm{NIT}_t}{\mathrm{GDPI}_t}\, nit_t^{(\Pi)} . \qquad t = 1, \ldots, T \qquad (7.3.7)$$

The coefficients in equation (7.3.7) are identical to those in equation (7.3.1). Combining equations (A3.6.54) and (A3.6.56) we can derive the following expression for $gdpe^{(\Pi)}$, the percentage change in the GDP deflator from the expenditure side of the national accounts:

[12] Although not reported, the simulation results for year 30 confirm that for each sector the percentage change in the rental price of capital is equal to the percentage change in the construction cost of capital. The discrepancy in year 30 between the percentage change in the average rental price of capital and the percentage change in the average construction cost of capital is accounted for by aggregation effects. The weights used to construct the two price indexes are different.

$$gdpe_t^{(\Pi)} = \frac{\mathrm{GNE}_t}{\mathrm{GDP}_t} gne_t^{(\Pi)} + \frac{\mathrm{E}_t}{\mathrm{GDP}_t} e_t^{(\Pi)} - \frac{\mathrm{M}_t}{\mathrm{GDP}_t} m_t^{(\Pi)} . \qquad t = 1, ..., T \qquad (7.3.8)$$

The coefficients in equation (7.3.8) are shares in GDP of, in order of appearance, GNE, exports and imports. Since $gdpe^{(\Pi)} = gdpi^{(\Pi)}$, we can obtain the following expression for the percentage change in the value-added deflator:

$$gdpfc_t^{(\Pi)} = \frac{\mathrm{GNE}_t}{\mathrm{GDPFC}_t} gne_t^{(\Pi)} + \frac{\mathrm{E}_t}{\mathrm{GDPFC}_t} e_t^{(\Pi)} - \frac{\mathrm{M}_t}{\mathrm{GDPFC}_t} m_t^{(\Pi)} - \frac{\mathrm{NIT}_t}{\mathrm{GDPFC}_t} nit_t^{(\Pi)} .$$

$$t = 1, ..., T \qquad (7.3.9)$$

In year 30 of the CBG scenario the coefficient on $gne^{(\Pi)}$ in equation (7.3.9) is close to 1 and trade is balanced (i.e., $\mathrm{E}_{30} = \mathrm{M}_{30}$). Thus, for year 30 equation (7.3.9) implies that the value-added deflator will rise relative to the GNE deflator if the terms of trade improve and/or the deflator for indirect taxes falls. As explained above, the tariff cut causes the deflator for indirect taxes to fall and the terms of trade to deteriorate. The results for year 30 indicate that the decrease in the real cost of capital flowing from the reduction in $nit^{(\Pi)}$ dominates the increase in the real cost of capital flowing from the deterioration in the terms of trade. An indication of the relative magnitudes of these competing price effects can be obtained by evaluating equation (7.3.9). Using values for the shares obtained from the CBG scenario and values for the percentage change variables from the simulation results for year 30 we get:

$$gdpfc_t^{(\Pi)} \approx 1.16(-1.2) + 0.19(-0.87) - 0.19(0) - 0.16(-9.3) = -0.07,$$

which is close to the model's projection of $gdpfc_{30}^{(\Pi)}$. The above calculation confirms that the fall in $nit_{30}^{(\Pi)}$ accounts for most of the increase in $gdpfc_{30}^{(\Pi)}$ relative to $gne_{30}^{(\Pi)}$.

Most of the decrease in $nit_{30}^{(\Pi)}$ can be traced to the direct effect of the tariff cut. To show this we use the following definition of $nit^{(\Pi)}$, derived from equations in table A3.1.1 of appendix A3.1:[13]

[13] In chapter 6 we explained that $nit^{(R)}$ is that part of the percentage change in net indirect taxes that is due to changes in the tax bases caused by changes in quantities [see equation (6.4.3) in section 6.4.1]. As defined in equation (7.3.10), $nit^{(\Pi)}$ is that part of the percentage change in net indirect taxes that is not accounted for by $nit^{(R)}$. That is, $nit^{(\Pi)}$ is that part of the percentage change in nominal net indirect taxes that is due to changes in the tax rates and to changes in the tax base caused by price changes. Equation (7.3.10) is derived from equations listed in table A3.1.1 in appendix A3.1 by substituting equations (A3.6.47) – (A3.6.52) into equation (A3.6.46) then substituting the resultant expression, and equation (A3.6.45), into equation (A3.6.62).

$$nit_t^{(\Pi)} = \frac{1}{\mathrm{NIT}_t}\Bigg\{\sum_{j=1}^{13} \mathrm{P}_{j,t}^{(O)}\mathrm{X}_{j,t}^{(O)} p_{j,t}^{(O)}$$

$$+ \sum_{i=1}^{13}\sum_{s=1}^{2}\sum_{j=1}^{13}\mathrm{P}_{i,s,t}^{(Z)}\mathrm{X}_{i,s,j,t}^{(1)}[\mathrm{T}_{i,s,j,t}^{(1)} - 1]\,[p_{i,s,t}^{(Z)} + \mathrm{T}_{i,s,j,t}^{(1)}[\mathrm{T}_{i,s,j,t}^{(1)} - 1]^{-1}\, t_{i,s,j,t}^{(1)}]$$

$$+ \sum_{i=1}^{13}\sum_{s=1}^{2}\sum_{j=1}^{13}\mathrm{P}_{i,s,t}^{(Z)}\mathrm{X}_{i,s,j,t}^{(2)}[\mathrm{T}_{i,s,j,t}^{(2)} - 1]\,[p_{i,s,t}^{(Z)} + \mathrm{T}_{i,s,j,t}^{(2)}[\mathrm{T}_{i,s,j,t}^{(2)} - 1]^{-1}\, t_{i,s,j,t}^{(2)}]$$

$$+ \sum_{i=1}^{13}\sum_{s=1}^{2}\mathrm{P}_{i,s,t}^{(Z)}\mathrm{X}_{i,s,t}^{(3)}[\mathrm{T}_{i,s,t}^{(3)} - 1]\,[p_{i,s,t}^{(Z)} + \mathrm{T}_{i,s,t}^{(3)}[\mathrm{T}_{i,s,t}^{(3)} - 1]^{-1}\, t_{i,s,t}^{(3)}]$$

$$+ \sum_{i=1}^{13}\mathrm{P}_{i,d,t}^{(Z)}\mathrm{X}_{i,t}^{(4)}[\mathrm{T}_{i,t}^{(4)} - 1]\,[p_{i,d,t}^{(Z)} + \mathrm{T}_{i,t}^{(4)}[\mathrm{T}_{i,t}^{(4)} - 1]^{-1}\, t_{i,t}^{(4)}]$$

$$+ \sum_{i=1}^{13}\sum_{s=1}^{2}\mathrm{P}_{i,s,t}^{(Z)}\mathrm{X}_{i,s,t}^{(5)}[\mathrm{T}_{i,s,t}^{(5)} - 1]\,[p_{i,s,t}^{(Z)} + \mathrm{T}_{i,s,t}^{(5)}[\mathrm{T}_{i,s,t}^{(5)} - 1]^{-1}\, t_{i,s,t}^{(5)}]$$

$$+ \sum_{i=1}^{13}\mathrm{P}_{i,t}^{(M)}\mathrm{X}_{i,t}^{(M)}\Phi_t[\mathrm{T}_{i,t}^{(6)} - 1]\,[p_{i,t}^{(M)} + \varphi_t + \mathrm{T}_{i,t}^{(6)}[\mathrm{T}_{i,t}^{(6)} - 1]^{-1}\, t_{i,t}^{(6)}]\Bigg\}.$$

$$t = 1, \ldots, \mathrm{T} \qquad (7.3.10)$$

Equation (7.3.10) is similar to equation (6.4.3) in chapter 6, which defined the percentage change in real net indirect taxes. The coefficients in equations (6.4.3) and (7.3.10) are identical. The key difference between the two equations is that the percentage change variables in equation (7.3.10) relate to prices and tax rates rather than to quantities. Note that the ts are the percentage changes in the corresponding Ts, which are the *powers* of taxes (i.e., one plus the tax rate). The variable φ in equation (7.3.10) is the percentage change in the exchange rate.

To evaluate equation (7.3.10) we make the simplifying assumption that all domestic commodity prices move in line with the value-added deflator. In the simulations we have assumed that: (a) the tariff on the *Manufacturing* commodity is the only tax rate that changes; (b) the exchange rate and the foreign currency c.i.f. prices of imported goods are not affected by the tariff cut; and (c) the price of 'other cost' tickets is indexed to the consumption deflator. Under these conditions equation (7.3.10) reduces to:

$$nit_t^{(\Pi)} \approx \frac{1}{\mathrm{NIT}_t}\left\{\sum_{j=1}^{13} \mathrm{P}_{j,t}^{(O)}\mathrm{X}_{j,t}^{(O)} c_t^{(\Pi)} + \mathrm{VD}_t\, gdpfc_t^{(\Pi)} + \mathrm{VF}_{k,t}\, p_{k,f,t}^{(Z)} + \mathrm{P}_{k,t}^{(M)}\mathrm{X}_{k,t}^{(M)}\Phi_t\mathrm{T}_{k,t}^{(6)}\, t_{k,t}^{(6)}\right\}$$

$$k = \textit{Manufacturing},\ t = 1, \ldots, \mathrm{T} \qquad (7.3.11)$$

where,

$$\mathrm{VD}_t = \sum_{i=1}^{13}\sum_{j=1}^{13}\mathrm{P}_{i,d,t}^{(Z)}\mathrm{X}_{i,d,j,t}^{(1)}[\mathrm{T}_{i,d,j,t}^{(1)} - 1] + \sum_{i=1}^{13}\sum_{j=1}^{13}\mathrm{P}_{i,d,t}^{(Z)}\mathrm{X}_{i,d,j,t}^{(2)}[\mathrm{T}_{i,d,j,t}^{(2)} - 1]$$

$$+ \sum_{i=1}^{13}\mathrm{P}_{i,d,t}^{(Z)}\mathrm{X}_{i,d,t}^{(3)}[\mathrm{T}_{i,d,t}^{(3)} - 1] + \sum_{i=1}^{13}\mathrm{P}_{i,d,t}^{(Z)}\mathrm{X}_{i,t}^{(4)}[\mathrm{T}_{i,t}^{(4)} - 1] + \sum_{i=1}^{13}\mathrm{P}_{i,d,t}^{(Z)}\mathrm{X}_{i,d,t}^{(5)}[\mathrm{T}_{i,d,t}^{(5)} - 1]$$

$$t = 1, \ldots, \mathrm{T} \qquad (7.3.12)$$

and

$$VF_{k,t} = \sum_{j=1}^{13} P^{(Z)}_{k,f,t} X^{(1)}_{k,f,j,t}[T^{(1)}_{k,f,j,t} - 1] + \sum_{j=1}^{13} P^{(Z)}_{k,f,t} X^{(2)}_{k,f,j,t}[T^{(2)}_{k,f,j,t} - 1]$$

$$+ P^{(Z)}_{k,f,t} X^{(3)}_{k,f,t}[T^{(3)}_{k,f,t} - 1] + P^{(Z)}_{k,f,t} X^{(5)}_{k,f,t}[T^{(5)}_{k,f,t} - 1]$$

$k = \textit{manufacturing},\ t = 1, \ldots, T$ (7.3.13)

In order of appearance, the coefficients in equation (7.3.11) are shares in net indirect tax revenue of: 'other cost' tickets; taxes collected from sales of domestic goods; taxes collected from sales of the imported *Manufacturing* commodity; and the duty-inclusive value of imports of the *Manufacturing* commodity. Using values for the shares taken from the CBG scenario and simulation results for year 30 we can estimate $nit^{(\Pi)}_{30}$ as follows:

$$nit^{(\Pi)}_{30} \approx 0.49(-1.28) + 0.36(-0.06) + 0.05(-8) + 0.95(-8) = -8.6$$

While equation (7.3.11) under-estimates the fall in $nit^{(\Pi)}_{30}$ projected by the model[14] it does highlight the big contribution made to this fall by the reduction in the tariff rate on the *Manufacturing* commodity.

Why Does the Economy Become More Trade Oriented?

As explained in chapter 5 (section 5.3.3), the CBG scenario is configured so that in the steady state net foreign liabilities (valued in foreign currency) accumulate passively[15] at 3 percent and GDP grows at 3 percent. We showed that under these assumptions the economy enters year 30 with a stable net-foreign-liabilities-to-GDP ratio only if there is no active accumulation of net foreign liabilities in year 30. That is, only if the trade deficit net of unrequited transfers (both valued in foreign currency) in year 30 is zero. In the three experiments we have assumed that net unrequited transfers are unaffected by the tariff shock (i.e., they are exogenous and not shocked). Thus, in year 30 the stimulus given to imports by the tariff reduction must be completely offset by an expansion in exports.

In the three simulations, the nominal exchange rate and the foreign currency price of imports are assumed to remain at their CBG scenario values in all years. Therefore, in year 30 the percentage increase in the foreign currency value of exports is the same as the 7.2 per cent increase in the volume of imports shown in

---

14 As is the case in the evaluation of $nit^{(R)}$ via equation (7.3.4), the discrepancy between our estimate of $nit^{(\Pi)}$ and the model's projection can be traced to two sources. First, for simplicity we have ignored many compositional effects. Secondly, the share in net indirect taxes of the duty-inclusive value of imports of the *manufacturing* commodity [i.e., the coefficient on $t^{(6)}_{k,t}$ in equation (7.3.11)] that we have used in our computation is an approximation only (see footnote 11).

15 By passive accumulation of foreign liabilities we mean additions to net foreign liabilities emanating from interest charges on existing liabilities.

figure 7.3.M6.[16] In year 30 of the CBG scenario the *Manufacturing* commodity accounts for about 81 per cent of total imports. Thus, the 10.5 percent increase in imports of the *Manufacturing* commodity (figure 7.3.I1) contributes about 8.5 percentage points to aggregate imports (i.e., 0.81×10.5). This is offset by the 30 per cent decrease in imports of the *Mining* commodity (figure 7.3.I2). Imports of the *Mining* commodity account for about 0.04 percent of total imports, hence the contribution of this commodity to aggregate import volumes is about −1.3 [i.e., 0.043×(-30)].

The tariff reduction decreases the price, thus stimulating the volume, of the imported *Manufacturing* commodity. As explained in chapter 3 the treatment of imports in ORANI-INT follows the Armington (1969, 1970) specification with imported commodities modelled as imperfect substitutes for their domestic counterparts. At the economy-wide level the percentage change in the demand for the imported *Manufacturing* commodity, $x_{k,t}^{(M)}$ (k ∈ *Manufacturing*), can be approximated by the following aggregate Leontief/CES import demand function:[17]

$$x_{k,t}^{(M)} \approx gne_t^{(R)} - \sigma_k^{(A)}\, \mathrm{SDOM}_{k,t}\left\{p_{k,t}^{(M)} - p_{k,d,t}^{(Z)}\right\}.$$

$$k = \textit{Manufacturing},\ t = 1, \ldots, T \qquad (7.3.14)$$

The only new notation introduced by approximation (7.3.14) is $\mathrm{SDOM}_{k,t}$, the share in total sales of the *Manufacturing* commodity accounted for by the domestically produced variety. The remaining notation is as follows: $gne^{(R)}$ is the percentage change in real GNE; $\sigma_k^{(A)}$ is the elasticity of substitution between domestic and foreign sources of the *Manufacturing* commodity (i.e., the Armington elasticity); and the *p*s are the percentage changes in the prices of the foreign and domestic *Manufacturing* commodities.[18]

Evaluating approximation (7.3.14) for year 30 using data from the CBG scenario and the simulation results we obtain:

---

[16] Given that the nominal exchange rate is assumed to remain at its CBG scenario values, the increase in the foreign currency value of exports can be deduced by adding the fall in the export price deflator (shown in figure 7.3.P3) to the increase in the volume of exports (shown in figure 7.3.M6).

[17] For each commodity in ORANI-INT there is a separate Leontief/CES import demand function for households, producers and capital creators. In these experiments the demand for imported good i by the government is assumed to be a fixed proportion of total real government spending. For further details see section 3.2.3 in chapter 3.

[18] Conceptually, the relative price term in equation (7.4.14) [i.e., the term in curly brackets] should relate purchasers' prices rather than basic prices. However, because purchasers' prices can vary across users (e.g., consumers, investors, governments, and producers) it is difficult to derive an aggregate measure of the purchasers' price of the *Manufacturing* commodity. Fortunately, in the simulations reported here there is no difference between the basic price and the purchasers' price of the *Manufacturing* commodity because the sales tax rates remain unchanged.

$$x^{(M)}_{k,30} \approx 0.94 - 1.65 \times 0.8 \times \left\{ -8 - (-1.4) \right\} = 9.7 . \qquad \text{k} = \textit{Manufacturing}$$

This back-of-the-envelope calculation provides a reasonable approximation of the model's projection. We can also use the evaluation of approximation (7.3.14) to estimate the direct and indirect effects of the tariff cut on the demand for the imported *Manufacturing* commodity. The impact effect of the tariff cut is to reduce the price of the imported *Manufacturing* commodity by 8 per cent. Other things constant (e.g., $gne^{(R)} = 0$ and $p^{(Z)}_{k,d,t} = 0$), approximation (7.3.14) suggests that the demand for the imported *Manufacturing* commodity will increase by about 11 per cent [i.e., $-1.65\times0.8\times(-8) = 11$]. On balance, the indirect effects of the tariff cut mitigate the impact effect. The imported *Manufacturing* commodity is an important input into capital creation and current production (it accounts for about 10 percent of total intermediate usage and about 11 percent of total inputs into capital creation). The fall in the price of the imported *Manufacturing* commodity tends to reduce domestic costs, thereby improving the economy's competitiveness. This induces competing effects on the demand for the imported *Manufacturing* commodity. The general improvement in the economy's competitiveness leads to an increase in economic activity, which stimulates the demand for both the imported and domestic *Manufacturing* commodities. This positive activity effect is captured by the increase in real GNE in approximation (7.3.14). However, the fall in domestic costs also allows the *Manufacturing* sector's costs to fall. The consequent fall in the price of the domestic *Manufacturing* commodity tends to mitigate the substitution effect in favour of the foreign *Manufacturing* commodity.

The fall in the price of the imported *Manufacturing* commodity relative to the price of the domestic *Manufacturing* commodity induces competing effects on the trade balance. The expansion in imports of the *Manufacturing* commodity tends to worsen the trade balance but this is counteracted by the improvement in competitiveness, which encourages import replacement as well as export sales. The purchasers' prices of imports other than the *Manufacturing* commodity remain unchanged and the fall in domestic costs tends to reduce the demand for these imports. For example, the fall in domestic costs is particularly harmful to *Mining* imports because the domestic and foreign *Mining* commodities are assumed to be very close substitutes (the Armington elasticity for this commodity is 36 reflecting mainly the tradeability of Oil). The demands by foreigners for the *Rural*, *Mining* and *Manufacturing* commodities are cost-sensitive and, as figures 7.3.E1–7.3.E3 show, exports of these commodities increase.

Why is the Increase in Real Consumption Small Relative to the Increase in Real GDP?

The expansion in the economy's capital stock and the allocative efficiency gains induced by the tariff cut allow real GDP to expand by 1.1 per cent. However, not all of this increase is available to Australian households. The contribution made to real GDP by the expansion in capital stocks will be offset by the investment expenditure required to maintain the capital stock at its new higher level. In addition, because the tariff cut induces a deterioration in Australia's terms of trade some of the increase in real GDP accrues to foreigners.

Given that the trade account must be balanced in year 30, the deterioration in the terms of trade means that any increase in the volume of imports must be more than offset by an increase in export volumes. In year 30 of the CBG scenario the shares of exports and imports in GDP are 0.16. In year 30 export volumes increase by 8.1 per cent (figure 7.3.M6) but, because the terms of trade deteriorate, balanced trade is maintained with an increase in imports of 7.2 per cent only. To see how the increase in real GDP is divided among foreigners and among the various domestic agents we use the definition of the percentage change in real GDP from the expenditure side, $gdp^{(R)}$. This definition appears in table A3.1.1 in appendix A3.1 as equation (A3.6.53). We repeat it below for convenience:

$$gdp_t^{(R)} = \frac{C_t}{GDPE_t} c_t^{(R)} + \frac{I_t}{GDPE_t} i_t^{(R)} + \frac{G_t}{GDPE_t} g_t^{(R)} + \frac{E_t}{GDPE_t} e_t^{(R)} - \frac{M_t}{GDPE_t} m_t^{(R)} . \qquad t = 1, \ldots, T \qquad (7.3.15)$$

In this equation the variables $c^{(R)}$, $i^{(R)}$, $g^{(R)}$, $e^{(R)}$ and $m^{(R)}$ are the percentage changes in real: consumption; investment; government spending; exports; and imports. The coefficients are shares in GDP of, in order of appearance, consumption, investment, government spending, exports and imports.

Evaluating equation (7.3.15) using the CBG scenario values of the shares and the simulation results for year 30 we obtain:

$$gdpe_{30}^{(R)} \approx 0.59(0.3) + 0.25(3.1) + 0.16(0) + 0.16(8.1) - 0.16(7.2) = 1.1.$$

We can deduce from the evaluation of equation (7.3.15) that about 0.14 percentage points [i.e., 0.16× (8.1) − 0.16× (7.2)] of the 1.1 per cent increase in real GDP in year 30 is not available for domestic absorption. (i.e., for private and public consumption and for investment). Since government expenditure is assumed to remain at its control scenario level [i.e., $g_{30}^{(R)} = 0$], the deterioration in the terms of trade is absorbed by the private sector. In year 30 real investment increases by 3.1 per cent to accommodate the increase in the demand for capital. As explained previously, the deterioration in the terms of trade damps the fall in the real cost of using capital. This mitigates the increase in the demand for capital and, therefore, the increase in investment. The increase in real investment accounts for about 0.77 percentage points [i.e., 0.25(3.1)] of the increase in real GDP. The residual increase in real GDP goes to private consumption.

Sectoral Results

Other things constant, the tariff cut favours capital intensive industries by allowing the price of labour to rise relative to the price of capital (compare figures 7.3.P5 and 7.3.P6). Since the profitability of supplying capital is exogenous, the gains from the tariff cut (i.e., the allocative efficiency gains less the terms of trade losses) accrue to labour, which is the fixed factor.

The biggest winner from the tariff cut is *Mining* which records an 11 per cent increase in output (figure 7.3.S1). The performance of *Mining* is dependent on the competitiveness of its highly tradeable product. Payments to capital account for about 24 per cent of the sector's total costs and its international competitiveness is improved by the fall in the price of capital. The *Mining* sector gets an additional cost advantage from the fall in the price of the *Manufacturing* commodity, which accounts for about 28 per cent of its intermediate inputs. This improvement in competitiveness allows the *Mining* sector to expand its exports by almost 17 per cent (figure 7.3.E2) as well as to gain market share from the imported *Mining* commodity (figure 7.3.I2).

Compared to *Mining* the improvement in the *Rural* sector's competitiveness is modest. This is reflected by the smaller expansion in its export sales (figure 7.3.E1). The *Rural* sector is an intensive user of the *Manufacturing* commodity (both domestic and foreign) and benefits from the fall in the price of this input. This is mitigated by increases in the prices of labour and agricultural land which account for over half of the *Rural* sector's total costs (i.e., 34 and 17 per cent respectively). The supply of agricultural land is fixed and its price rises as the *Rural* sector expands. The increase in the sector's output is modest because the increase in its export sales is relatively small (about 2.9 per cent) and because it's main domestic customer, the *Manufacturing* sector, contracts.

The *Manufacturing* sector contracts because the tariff cut improves the competitiveness of the foreign *Manufacturing* commodity. This sector is relatively labour intensive and its international competitiveness is reduced further by the increase in wages. The loss of competitiveness is partially offset by the 8 per cent fall in the price of the imported *Manufacturing* commodity, which accounts for about 12 per cent of the sector's intermediate inputs, and by the fall in the cost of capital. While *Manufacturing* is not very capital intensive, the 2.7 per cent fall in the price of its capital is the largest recorded for any sector. This is because *Manufacturing's* capital creation process is the most intensive user of the imported *Manufacturing* commodity. The cost reductions in the *Manufacturing* sector are reflected by the 9.9 per cent expansion in its export sales. However, its output falls by about 0.14 per cent because the expansion in exports is more than offset by the loss of domestic sales to the cheaper imported *Manufacturing* commodity (figure 7.3.I1).

The increase in real consumption is small and is of little benefit to most industries. The allocation of the household budget depends on the relative prices of consumer goods. The fall in the price of the imported *Manufacturing* commodity induces households to reallocate their budget in its favour. Two domestic commodities, *Utilities* and *Housing*, also capture a slightly larger share of the household budget. These sectors are relatively capital intensive and the fall in the cost of capital allows the price of their output to fall relative to the prices of other consumer goods. While the *Utilities* sector benefits from the increase in sales to households, most of the 0.78 per cent increase in its output is accounted for by the increase in sales to intermediate users, in particular to the *Finance* and *Housing* sectors.

The *Personal services* sector sells about 73 per cent of its output to households. Although not reported, sales by this sector to households actually fall slightly despite the increase in aggregate consumption. This is because its production structure is labour intensive and the fall in its costs relatively small. However, the *Personal services* sector records a small increase in output (see figure 7.3.S10) because the loss of sales to households is more than offset by the increase in sales to other industries, particularly *Mining* and *Finance*. The results for the *Wholesale and Retail Trade* (*WRT*) sector are similar to those of the *Personal services* sector. The *WRT* sector is relatively labour intensive and the fall in its costs are not sufficient to prevent a small loss in sales to households.[19] The *WRT* sector records a modest increase in output because the loss of sales to households is outweighed by the increase in sales to intermediate users, particularly to *Mining* and *Construction*.

The *Construction* sector's fortunes are closely related to investment activity, which increases. The expansion in the *Housing* sector is important because it purchases about 27 per cent of *Construction*'s output for the purpose of creating capital. Capital is the only factor of production used by *Housing*. This implies that the *Housing* sector's capital and output change by the same proportion.[20] The domestic *Construction* commodity accounts for almost all of the inputs to *Housing's* capital creation process. The *Housing* sector owns about 30 per cent of the economy's capital stock hence the small increase in its output generates a significant increase in the demand for the *Construction* commodity.

The expansion in the *Transport* and *Finance* sectors is related mainly to the increase in the demand for their outputs by the *Mining* and *Construction* sectors.

7.3.2 The Transition Paths

Since the long-run results obtained in the three experiments are almost identical, the assessment of the relative merits of the alternative tariff reduction strategies must be based on differences in the transition paths. The adjustment to the long-run equilibrium is slowest in the ATR experiment and fastest in the STR experiment. For example, in the STR experiment real GDP completes about 70 per cent of the

---

19 This is an unrealistic result. The *wholesale and retail trade* sector supplies services that facilitate the flow of goods and services from suppliers to users. The demands for such services (margins) are probably best modelled as proportional to the demand for the goods or services that they are being used to transfer from supplier to user (e.g., this is the approach taken in ORANI). As explained in chapter 2, a key simplification adopted in ORANI-INT is that margin services are treated just like any other good or service. The undesirable implications of this simplification is that the demands for margins, such as *wholesale and retail trade* and *transport*, are price sensitive.

20 Recall that primary factors and produced inputs are combined in fixed proportions in the Leontief/CES production technology that we have specified.

adjustment to its long-run value in 5 years. The same adjustment takes about 20 years in the ATR experiment and 15 years in the PTR experiment.

Below we explain why the economy adjusts more slowly in the PTR and ATR experiments than in the STR experiment. We also point out that the volatility evident in the adjustment paths is related to the behaviour of investors rather than consumers.

Speed of Adjustment in Real GDP

In the explanation of the long-run results we related changes in real GDP to changes in capital stocks and to changes in allocative efficiency. This relationship applies in all years. Capital accounts for about 30 per cent of GDP and it is evident from figures 7.3.M1 and 7.3.M4 that in most years the change in capital stocks explains most of the change in real GDP.[21]

In the three experiments capital stocks are unable to adjust in the first year. Thereafter, changes in capital stocks are related to changes in the real cost of using capital. Other things constant, the cut in the tariff on the *Manufacturing* commodity allows the real cost of using capital to fall. Beyond year 1 rates of return on all assets are assumed to be equal. In maintaining this asset market equilibrium, agents investing in fixed capital trade off increases/decreases in rentals with capital losses/gains. It is cheaper for producers to expand their capital stocks gradually, rather than abruptly, because rapid expansion in investment in year t generates capital losses in that year which are traded off for higher rentals in year t+1. However, the higher rentals in year t+1 discourage the use of capital by producers in that year tending to dampen the investment response in year t.

In the STR experiment the tariff cut is implemented fully in year 1 and hence has the same direct effect on the cost of capital (i.e., from the availability of cheaper imports) in all years. However, the reductions in the cost of capital emanating indirectly from the tariff cut become progressively more pronounced after year 1 as the economy's supply constraints become progressively less severe. Accordingly, producers delay their investment decisions because they anticipate (correctly) that investment costs will fall in the future.

---

21 The residual change in real GDP can be traced to changes in allocative efficiency stemming mainly from changes in the structure of sales in favour of or against the highly taxed imported *Manufacturing* commodity. This commodity is used intensively in the capital creation process and demand for it is closely related to investment activity. For example, in year 1 of the STR experiment capital stocks are unable to change but the 6.3 per cent increase in aggregate investment stimulates sales of the imported *Manufacturing* commodity by almost 14 per cent. The resulting allocative efficiency gains generate a small (0.1 per cent) increase in real GDP. Similarly, the ATR results for year 12 (when the announced tariff cut is implemented) indicate that the fall in real GDP is modest (about 0.3 per cent) given that the economy's capital stock falls by around 2 per cent. Again this result is due mainly to the allocative efficiency gains flowing from the 21 per cent increase in imports of the *Manufacturing* commodity.

In the PTR experiment agents do not anticipate the tariff cut implemented in year 1, but anticipate the subsequent tariff cuts. Despite knowing about the impending tariff cuts they react more slowly than in the STR experiment. Forward-looking investors delay their investments in anticipation of further falls in the cost of creating capital. The direct effect of the tariff cut on the cost of capital gets bigger in line with the phasing in of the tariff cut whereas in the STR experiment the direct effect is the same in all years.

The distinguishing feature of the capital path obtained in the ATR experiment is that it falls below control in the lead up to the tariff cut in year 12. The reason for this is that producers allow their capital stocks to fall (by delaying their investments) to avoid anticipated capital losses in year 12. The reduction in capital stocks between years 2 and 12 is gradual because it is cheaper to reduce capital stocks gradually rather than abruptly. Over this period capital losses get progressively bigger and the rental price of capital rises. Beyond year 12 the capital losses get smaller and the rental price of capital falls gradually. This is reflected in the gradual increase in capital stocks after year 12. The capital losses fade away after year 12 because there are no further reductions in the cost of capital emanating directly from the tariff cut and because the economy's supply constraints become progressively less severe.

Behaviour of Consumers

The Klein-Rubin utility function used in ORANI-INT distinguishes between subsistence and discretionary consumption. Since real subsistence consumption (per-capita) is assumed to remain unchanged over time, it is possible to explain the path of real aggregate consumption with reference to the path of real discretionary expenditure only.

The consumption specification in ORANI-INT and the closure adopted for these experiments implies that the proportional change in *nominal* discretionary expenditure will be the same in all years.[22] Moreover, because the results obtained in the three experiments converge in the long run, the path of nominal discretionary expenditure will be the same in the three experiments. However, because the proportional deviations in consumer prices may be different over time, the proportional deviations in *real* discretionary expenditure need not be the same in all years. Households will bias their discretionary consumption in favour of the years in which prices are relatively low (and vice versa).

---

22 This can be deduced from equation (3.3.17) in chapter 3. In the closure adopted for these experiments the nominal rate of interest remains at its control scenario values in all years (because the foreign rate of interest and the nominal exchange rate are held at their control scenario values) as does the number of households. The time preference rate is treated as a parameter, hence, the rate of growth of nominal discretionary expenditure is unaffected by the tariff cut.

The consumption paths depicted in figure 7.3.M2 mirror the CPI paths shown in figure 7.3.P8.[23] In all three experiments households tend to bias their consumption in favour of the later years because consumer prices are lower in the later years relative to the early years. In all experiments the cost reductions emanating directly and indirectly from the tariff cut become progressively more pronounced as the economy's supply constraints become less severe. In the STR experiment the direct cost reductions are the same in all years and the economy's productive capacity is expanded gradually after year 2. In the PTR experiment the direct cost reductions increase gradually with the phasing in of the tariff cut. This delays the expansion of the economy's productive capacity. The cost-reducing effects of the tariff cut are delayed further in the ATR experiment because the policy is not implemented until year 12.

The non-monotonicity of the CPI paths, and consequently the consumption paths, can be traced mainly to the volatility of the price of *Housing*, which has a large weight in the consumption basket (about 18 per cent). A special feature of the *Housing* sector is that capital is the only primary-factor input that it uses. Since capital accounts for over 70 per cent of *Housing's* total costs, the price of *Housing* services is closely related to the cost of its capital stock.

In the first year of the simulations sectoral capital stocks are assumed to be unaffected by the tariff shock and the rental price of capital adjusts to clear the capital markets. In subsequent years capital stocks are free to vary but the rental price of capital is constrained by equilibrium condition (3.3.33), which is presented in chapter 3. The implication of this equilibrium condition is that, beyond year 1, the rental price of the *Housing* sector's capital is constrained to reflect investment costs and capital gains/losses.

The effect on real consumption of holding *Housing's* capital stock at its control scenario level in year 1 is most evident in the STR experiment where the tariff cut is fully implemented in year 1. Contrary to our priors the path of prices does not fall gradually over time as the economy adjusts its productive capacity to the new long-run equilibrium level. Figure 7.3.P7 shows that the CPI falls sharply in year 1 relative to year 2 and this is reflected in figure 7.3.M2 by the modest fall in real consumption in year 1 relative to year 2. The sharp fall in the CPI in year 1 is caused by the fall in the price of *Housing* in that year.

The expenditure elasticity for *Housing* services is high (about 1.4). Hence, the 0.7 per cent reduction in nominal discretionary expenditure causes the demand for these services to fall relatively strongly. Since the supply of *Housing* services cannot change in year 1, the price of these services falls to accommodate the fall in demand. In year 1 the decrease in the price of *Housing* is absorbed by a fall in the rental price of the *Housing* sector's capital stock.

Beyond year 1 the rental cost of the *Housing's* capital depends on investment costs and on the rate of change in investment costs (i.e., capital gains/losses). The *Construction* sector supplies about 95 per cent of the inputs to *Housing's* capital

---

23 Since the discretionary CPI paths and the corresponding CPI paths have the same shapes we can focus on the latter to explain the consumption paths.

creation process. Thus, the rental price of *Housing's* capital stock will reflect the price of the *Construction* commodity and its rate of change over time. The *Construction* sector is an intensive user of the *Manufacturing* commodity (domestic and imported) and sells most of its output to capital creators. Therefore, the price of the *Construction* commodity, and its rate of change over time, depends on the size and timing of the tariff cuts and on the size and timing of the aggregate investment response.

The link between the price of the *Construction* commodity, the cost of *Housing's* capital and real aggregate consumption is most evident in the ATR experiment for the three years centred around year 12 — the year in which the tariff cut is implemented. Although not reported, the rate of growth in price of the *Construction* commodity between years 11 and 12 is positive (i.e., the price of the *Construction* commodity falls by 0.1 per cent in year 11 and rises by 0.5 per cent in year 12). Over this period there are two counteracting impacts on the rate of growth of the price of the *Construction* commodity. The price of the *Manufacturing* commodity falls in year 12 relative to year 11 because the tariff cut is implemented in year 12. Given that the *Manufacturing* commodity is a key input for the *Construction* sector, the direct impact of the tariff cut is to reduce the rate of growth in the price of the *Construction* commodity. However, this direct impact is more than offset by the increase in the rate of growth in the price of the *Construction* commodity caused by the turn-around in aggregate investment between years 11 and 12 (see figure 7.3.M3). In year 11 the sharp decrease in aggregate investment tends, other things constant, to push the price of the *Construction* commodity below control while the sharp increase in aggregate investment in year 12 tends to have the opposite effect. This pattern in the price of the *Construction* commodity generates capital gains for the *Housing* sector in year 12. These gains allow the rental cost of the *Housing* sector's capital stock, and consequently the price of the *Housing* commodity, to fall below control in year 12. In year 12 the fall in the price of *Housing* causes the CPI to fall and real consumption to rise.

Note that the increase in real consumption in year 11 is similar to that in year 12 because the fall in the CPI in those two years is similar. Despite the fact that rate of growth in aggregate investment between years 10 and 11 is declining, the rate of growth of investment by the *Construction* sector increases sharply over this period. This is because the *Construction* sector expands its capacity in anticipation of the aggregate investment surge in year 12. The price of the *Housing* commodity falls in year 11 because the capital gains generated by the growth in investment by the *Construction* sector allow *Housing's* capital costs to fall.

In year 13 the CPI rises above control causing real consumption to fall below control. This is largely due to the capital losses generated by the fall in the rate of growth of aggregate investment between years 12 and 13. Beyond year 13 the rate of growth of aggregate investment falls at a decreasing rate. Thus the capital losses get progressively weaker over time and, as shown in figure 7.3.M2, the path of real consumption rises gradually after year 13.

7.3.3 Structural Adjustment

Over the 30 year simulation horizon[24] the present value of the consumption stream increases by 0.206 per cent in the STR experiment, by 0.084 per cent in the PTR experiment and falls by 0.049 per cent in the ATR experiment. Year 1 of the simulation is assumed to represent 1985-86. Nominal consumption in that year was \$143,791 million. Thus, relative to the control scenario the change in the present value of consumption, in millions of 1985-86 dollars, is \$8886 (i.e., 30×0.00206× \$143,791) in the STR experiment, \$3623 in the PTR experiment, and -\$2114 in the ATR experiment.

Before drawing policy conclusions from the above results, the implications that the alternative tariff reduction strategies have for labour market adjustment costs must be considered. The costs of moving workers have not been explicitly modelled. Labour is assumed to be homogeneous and perfectly mobile between sectors and real wages are assumed to adjust to ensure that aggregate employment is unaffected by the tariff cut. Labour market adjustment costs are likely to be greater when structural change is rapid. Since the STR strategy causes the economy to adjust more rapidly than do the PTR and ATR strategies, it is possible that the former strategy gives rise to greater labour market adjustment costs.

An indication of how sensitive our conclusions are to the labour market assumptions can be obtained by estimating the extent to which labour market adjustment costs might differ in the three experiments and relating these differences to the corresponding consumption gains/losses. We assume that labour market adjustment costs are related to the number of workers that must change occupation. For each experiment the employment results for the 13 ORANI-INT sectors are mapped to the 52 ASCO minor group occupational categories.[25] From the occupational employment results we infer the number of workers who must change occupation in each of the three experiments.

To estimate the number of workers who must change their occupation we make two simplifying assumptions: first, workers change occupation only if there is a decline in employment in occupation o between years t and t+1; and, second, all workers that change occupation obtain another job[26]. Under these assumptions, the number of workers that move from occupation o in year t to some other occupation in year t+1 is equal to the bigger of the following two numbers: zero and the difference between employment in occupation o in years t and t+1 (i.e., $L_{o,t} - L_{o,t+1}$). By summing over occupations and time we obtain the total number of workers that change occupation over the simulation horizon, ΔOCC, as follows:

---

[24] Since the economy has converged to the same long-run equilibrium in the three experiments, there is no need to go beyond the year 30 results to evaluate the alternative tariff reduction strategies.

[25] To do this mapping we use shares derived from 1994-95 industry-by-occupation employment data.

[26] A more detailed analysis of labour market adjustment costs would allow for retrenched workers to move into unemployment (permanently or temporarily) and for some of the new jobs generated by the tariff shock to go to persons that were previously unemployed.

$$\Delta OCC = \sum_{t=1}^{29}\sum_{o=1}^{52} MAX\left\{(L_{o,t} - L_{o,t+1}), 0\right\} \qquad (7.3.16)$$

Applying (7.3.16) to the occupational results we find that the number of workers that must change occupation is greatest in the ATR experiment and least in the STR experiment. The number of workers that must change occupation in the ATR simulation is equivalent to 0.58 per cent of the control scenario level of employment in year 1. The corresponding figures for the PTR and STR experiments are 0.22 percent and 0.17 per cent [27] The tentative conclusion that can be drawn from the occupational results is that there is little evidence of substantial labour market adjustment costs arising from the tariff cuts examined. Our analysis suggests that, whether the objective is maximising real consumption or minimising worker displacement, the STR strategy dominates (or is equivalent to) the PTR strategy which, in turn, dominates the ATR strategy.

Although our assessment of labour market adjustment costs is instructive, it has several limitations and the results should be interpreted with caution. One problem is that we use an unrealistic control scenario. Of particular relevance to the issue of labour market adjustment costs is the assumption in the control scenario that the shares used to disaggregate sectoral employment into the 52 occupational categories are constant over time. Thus, employment in occupation o in sector j grows at the same rate as total employment is sector j. The rate of growth of total employment in occupation o is equal to a share-weighted average of sectoral employment growth rates.

In the three experiments aggregate employment is assumed to be unaffected by the tariff shock. However, the tariff shock is allowed to impact on the distribution of employment across industries and, therefore, on the distribution of employment across occupations. Our results show that there is a redistribution of employment opportunities away from those occupations heavily exposed to industries adversely affected by the tariff cuts (e.g., *trades assistants and factory hands*, about 66 per cent of which are employed in the *Manufacturing* sector) towards occupations exposed to industries that benefit from the policy change (e.g., *construction and mining labourers*, about 53 per cent of which are employed in the *Construction* sector). Our estimates of the number of workers that must change occupation in the three experiments indicate that the changes in the structure of the economy induced by the tariff shocks are rarely big enough to cause employment growth in the 52 occupations to be negative. However, these estimates of labour market adjustment costs are sensitive to the growth rates of employment in the 52 occupations assumed in the CBG scenario. For example, our estimates of the number of workers that change occupation in response to the tariff cuts will be understated if we have overstated the employment prospects of *trades assistants and factory hands* in the CBG scenario.

---

[27] In 1985-86 6.86 million people were employed. Using 1985-86 as the base year we estimate that the number of workers that must change occupation in the three experiments is: 38,788 (i.e., 0.0058×6.86 million) in the ATR experiment; 15,092 (0.0022×6.86 million) in the PTR experiment; and 11,662 (0.0017×6.86 million) in the STR experiment.

Our measure of labour market adjustment costs is also sensitive to the level of aggregation. We have identified 52 occupational groups and movements of workers within these groups are ignored. Moreover, our calculations ignore a range of potentially important adjustment costs. For example, we do not take into account the costs of moving workers between industries and regions. Potentially, the most significant adjustment costs not captured in the simulations are those associated with unemployment. We have assumed that real wages adjust to ensure that aggregate employment is unaffected by the tariff shocks. At least in the short run, it is probable that real wage rigidities exist for some occupations. Under such conditions the tariff shocks may induce changes in the rate of unemployment in particular occupational categories and in aggregate.[28]

7.4. Summary and Conclusions

The results presented in this chapter suggest that the long-run effects of a tariff cut are independent of the way in which the policy is implemented. The three tariff reduction strategies considered generate similar increases in real GDP and real consumption in the long run. The long-run increase in real GDP is related mainly to the expansion of the capital stock. The capital creation process is intensive in the use of the imported *Manufacturing* commodity and the cut in the tariff on this commodity allows the real cost of using capital to fall. The NFL-to-GDP ratio is assumed to stabilise in the long run and this means that the trade balance cannot be affected by the tariff shock in the long run. In the long run, therefore, the expansion in imports that is induced by the tariff cut must be matched by an expansion in exports. Since Australia is assumed to have some market power in its export markets, the increase in exports is accompanied by a decline in the terms of trade. The decline in the terms of trade is borne mainly by private consumers and as a result the increase in real consumption is modest.

The effects of the tariff cut in the short and medium run are sensitive to the way in which the shock is implemented. On the basis of the path of either real GDP or real consumption, the results indicate that an unannounced tariff reduction is preferable to an announced, gradual tariff cut which in turn is preferable to an anticipated tariff reduction. Real GDP is higher in all periods in the case where the tariff cut is implemented without warning. Over the 30-year simulation horizon the present value of the consumption stream increases by 0.065 per cent under the STR strategy and falls by 0.032 and 0.128 per cent under the PTR and ATR strategies. Under the latter two strategies Australians forego some of the benefits that can be derived from the availability of cheaper imports.

---

28 It is difficult to tell a priori whether the economy-wide unemployment rate will fall or increase. The direction of change will depend on two factors: first, the relative shares in aggregate employment of employment in occupations stimulated by the tariff cut and employment in occupations that contract; and, second, the degree of wage rigidity in occupations stimulated by the tariff cut relative to those that contract.

The movement of workers between occupations, industries and regions is costly and must be taken into account in any assessment of alternative tariff reduction strategies. In the PTR experiment the economy adjusts less rapidly than in the STR experiment. Hence it is possible that labour market adjustment problems will be greater under the latter implementation strategy. We found little evidence of significant labour market adjustment problems in any of the three simulations. Moreover, our results suggest that labour market adjustment costs would have to be implausibly large under the STR strategy relative to the PTR and ATR strategies if the latter two implementation strategies are to be preferred. However, before drawing strong policy implications from our results the issue of labour market adjustment costs needs further consideration. As indicated, our assessment of labour market adjustment costs has several important limitations. Further research is required to model both the demand and supply sides of the labour market at a disaggregate level. In addition, more effort is required to generate a control scenario for occupational employment that is more plausible than the CBG scenario used in this paper.

Chapter 8 Summary and Conclusions

8.1 Introduction

The broad objective in this monograph was to formulate and implement an intertemporal CGE model of the Australian economy. We argued that an intertemporal CGE model inherits the strengths of static CGE models for dealing with compositional issues while overcoming their shortcomings for dealing with issues concerning the allocation of resources over time.

Our main contributions can be partitioned into two categories; namely, model development and model application. In the model-development category the formulation and implementation of ORANI-INT provided challenges in the following three key areas:

i. The specification of the model's theoretical structure;

ii. The development of a solution algorithm capable of solving the model accurately and quickly; and

iii. The construction of a suitable database.

In the model application category we demonstrated that:

iv. The model's projections could be reconciled with its theoretical structure and database; and

v. The model can provide insights on topical policy issues.

In sections 8.2 and 8.3 we reflect on our main achievements in developing and applying ORANI-INT. In section 8.4 we outline an agenda for future research. In section 8.5 we provide some final comments.

8.2 Model Development

The Theoretical Structure of ORANI-INT

A novel feature of ORANI-INT is that its theoretical structure is based on ORANI, an existing static CGE model of the Australian economy. ORANI is widely used for policy analysis and the enormous amount of human capital that it embodies is currently being maintained, and broadened, by several institutions. The model and its data files are very well documented and publicly available. These features made it natural for us to base our intertemporal model on ORANI rather than to build it from scratch. The design principles underlying ORANI-INT are generic. The approach used in this monograph can be used to easily embed any conventional static CGE model into an intertemporal framework.

ORANI-INT can be characterised as a modified version of ORANI in which investors and consumers are forward-looking. Our model of forward-looking consumption behaviour is based on the ELES. An economy-wide budget constraint is imposed by constraining the growth of net foreign liabilities in the long run. Investors in ORANI-INT are also intertemporal optimisers and their investment decisions are driven by forward-looking rates of return. In the context of CGE modelling, three aspects of our investment specification are innovative: first, we use a time-to-build approach, rather than an adjustment-cost approach to the capital-creation process; second, the technology for producing capital goods is allowed to differ across sectors; and finally, we explicitly assume that investment decisions are irreversible.

The Solution Algorithm

One of the main challenges of constructing ORANI-INT was to keep it computationally tractable without compromising significantly on the type and degree of economic detail modelled. The ORANI-INT solution algorithm solves for the values of all endogenous variables in a single computational process. We simplify the problem of solving ORANI-INT by converting it from a two-point-boundary-value problem into an initial-value problem. This is done by temporarily modifying the ORANI-INT equation system so that it is satisfied by an easily constructed database. By design, this database is a solution of the modified form of the model. Having converted the problem into an initial-value problem, our algorithm exploits the ability of the GEMPACK software to solve large systems of simultaneous equations using Euler's method. The algorithm does not attach any special significance to the fact that variables have a time dimension. A variable that has a time dimension is treated in the same way as a variable with an industry dimension.

The ORANI-INT solution algorithm is generic. It has the potential to handle very large and complex models efficiently. Moreover, because the algorithm is independent of the model's structure the modeller is provided with maximum scope for model modifications (e.g., altering or adding equations, changing the data, and the partitioning of variables between the endogenous and exogenous categories). This flexibility is a desirable feature for applied economic analysis as the specification of a model is constrained by economic theory or data rather than by computational considerations. For example, there is no special need to constrain the number of costate variables (e.g., by assuming that capital stocks are homogeneous) nor is there is any special need to assume interior solutions. Corner constraints suggested by economic theory (e.g., quotas, inventories, and some investments) can be incorporated explicitly.

Another key feature of the ORANI-INT solution algorithm is that it is readily accessible to other modellers. The algorithm can be easily implemented in

GEMPACK, a commercially available software package, by modellers with no source-code programming skills.

The Database

A database (or control scenario) for ORANI-INT consists of time-series values for all the variables in the model. Variable values in the first year of this database are obtained from a slightly modified 13-sector aggregation of the 1980-81 ORANI database. Using these single-period data, the model is then employed to generate the remaining data requirements.

The flexibility and efficiency of our solution procedure means that economic, rather than computational, considerations limit the type of database that we build. In particular, there is no need to resort to constructing a synthetic database that assumes that the economy is on a steady state or balanced-growth path in all periods. We constructed two control scenarios. The first was characterised by balanced growth in all periods. In the second control scenario the economy converges to a balanced growth path but does not start on one.

In generating the control scenarios we identified several difficulties that must be confronted before models like ORANI-INT can be used to produce realistic control scenarios (forecasts). In common with other CGE modellers, we found that it is difficult to generate plausible sectoral investment responses without resorting to *ad hoc* theoretical specifications and/or data manipulation. We also highlighted the difficulties faced by the modeller in assigning values to the paths of the exogenous variables. Judgements must be made about what is contained in the agents' information set at all points in time.

8.3 Applications

Interpretation of Results

In the applications of ORANI-INT, significant emphasis was placed on interpreting the model's projections. We believe that there are three important reasons for carefully scrutinising the model's projections. First, it demonstrates that models such as ORANI-INT need not be treated as "black boxes". Second, it provides some evidence that the intended computations have been performed correctly. Third, it brings to the fore critical assumptions and critical elements of the database. This last benefit is particularly important because the insights derived from a critical analysis can be used to guide future model developments.

Policy Insights

Three sets of simulations are reported in the monograph. The control-scenario simulations established that ORANI-INT possessed the convergence properties expected of a neoclassical intertemporal model.

The second set of simulations examined the implications of increasing government spending under different expectations hypotheses. The main purpose of these government-spending simulations was to investigate the key properties of ORANI-INT. Four main insights were obtained from these illustrative experiments. First, ORANI-INT provides significantly more information about the effects of a policy change than does a single-period CGE model or a multi-period macroeconomic model. Second, even though the theoretical structure of ORANI-INT is relatively simple, the model generates complicated and plausible dynamics. Third, forward-looking expectations produce outcomes that are significantly different to those produced when expectations are assumed to be static. Fourth, announcement effects are potentially significant and, to examine these, it is necessary to assume that expectations are forward looking.

The third set of simulations was designed to shed light on a topical policy issue. We analysed three different approaches to reducing tariffs that have, in recent history, been adopted in Australia. We found that the three tariff reduction strategies considered generate similar increases in real GDP and real consumption in the long run. However, the effects of the tariff cut in the short and medium run are sensitive to the way in which the shock is implemented. On the basis of the path of either real GDP or real consumption, ORANI-INT's projections indicate that an unannounced tariff reduction is preferable to an announced gradual tariff cut, which in turn is preferable to an anticipated one-step tariff reduction. We noted that the movement of workers between occupations, industries and regions is costly and must be taken into account in any assessment of alternative tariff reduction strategies. We found little evidence of significant labour market adjustment problems in any of the three simulations. However, we acknowledged that our assessment of labour market adjustment costs has important limitations. Mindful of these limitations we cautioned against drawing strong policy conclusions from our analysis of alternative tariff-reduction schemes without further consideration of labour-market adjustment costs.

8.4 An Agenda for Future Research

As with any economic model ORANI-INT can always be improved. The directions for future research suggested below are by no means intended to be exhaustive. Rather, they are an agenda that is motivated by the desire to build an intertemporal CGE model that is both practical and capable of addressing a wide range of issues in a plausible manner. This goal places priority on research in the following areas.

8.4.1 Data and Parameters

To generate a control scenario for ORANI-INT we used an aggregated ORANI database developed by Parmenter, Meagher and Higgs (1984). This database is based on the 1980-81 input-output data. For comparative-dynamic experiments, like those reported in chapters 6 and 7, the use of out-dated data may be justifiable but it is not optimal. Ideally, the ORANI-INT control scenario should be our best forecast of the future path of the economy. These forecasts should contain the latest available information about the state of the economy. We do not anticipate that the Australian Bureau of Statistics will produce up-to-date input-output data. A more promising source for such data is emerging from the ongoing work of Dixon and McDonald (1993). Their strategy is to update the most recently published input-output tables by an ORANI simulation. For example, using the 1986-87 input-output tables as a base they have produced an input-output database for 1993-94 that is consistent with all relevant data from reliable sources for the period 1987-88 to 1993-94.

The generation of a more up-to-date database for ORANI-INT is clearly desirable. However, the existing database should be exploited further in future work. In particular, 1980-81 database is probably ideal for conducting historical validation exercises with ORANI-INT.

Apart from the time preference rate the parameters in ORANI-INT are taken from the ORANI parameter files. Many of these parameters, such as the trade and household demand elasticities, were econometrically estimated in the 1970s. Other parameters, including the primary factor substitution elasticities, could not be estimated econometrically and were derived from literature surveys.

Several authors have recently provided new econometric estimates of many of the parameters in ORANI. For example, Rimmer (1990) has estimated primary factor substitution elasticities; Rimmer and Powell (1992) have estimated household demand elasticities; and Menon (1993) has estimated some of the trade parameters. This work may provide the basis for updating the ORANI-INT parameter file.

8.4.2 Treatment of Expectations

In ORANI-INT investors and consumers are assumed to have perfect foresight. That is, their expectations are model-consistent and held with certainty. This assumption, which is common to CGE models that allow for forward-looking expectations, is extremely strong and stems from the need to maintain computational tractability. In the near future, at least, we anticipate that computational considerations will continue to limit the feasibility of dealing explicitly with uncertainty in intertemporal CGE models.

While the empirical evidence about how agents form their expectations is scant, several studies have found evidence that agents are not very forward looking when making decisions (for investment see McKibbin and Siegloff (1988) and for consumption Campbell and Mankiw (1989) and Poterba (1988)). Ballard and Goulder (1985) argued, correctly, that in reality the degree of foresight that agents have is somewhere between none and perfect. Without attempting to provide theoretical justifications, Ballard and Goulder used a model to demonstrate that endowing agents with varying lengths of *perfect* foresight (i.e., the number of years into the future that agents can forecast prices correctly) makes significant differences to the results obtained.

McKibbin and Sachs (1991) and McKibbin and Wilcoxen (1995) use a different approach to limiting the degree to which investment and consumption decisions are forward looking. They assume that some part of agents' decisions is based on expectations about the future and some other part is based on current variables. While the micro-foundations of such an assumption are not made clear they claim that it increases the 'empirical realism' of the model.

The ad hoc approaches offered by Ballard and Goulder and McKibbin and Sachs are practical alternatives to the all-or-nothing approach implied by commonly adopted expectations hypotheses. Typically, agents are assumed to have either no foresight or perfect foresight. Further study is required to provide more solid micro-foundations for the way agents form expectations. The literature on bounded rationality (see Conlisk, 1996 for a recent survey) contains many insights that can be explored in models like ORANI-INT.

8.4.3 Investment Technology

Much of the recent literature on investment behaviour attributes observed lags in the capital creation process to the presence of adjustment costs. The economic justifications of such costs are often vague. More work is required in identifying the exact sources and magnitudes of such costs before they can be convincingly incorporated into the CGE framework.

In ORANI-INT the sources of observed lags in the capital creation process are made explicit. However, in the absence of empirical evidence we made some arbitrary assumptions about the length of gestation lags in the capital creation process and the reversibility of investment decisions. Future research could be directed at providing empirical evidence on the length of gestation lags in different sectors and the degree of mobility of physical capital between sectors. This research may also provide evidence about the lumpiness (i.e., physical indivisibility) of capital in various sectors and the existence of delivery lags for certain capital goods.

8.4.4 Greater Disaggregation

The quest for a more disaggregated model of the economy is endless and costly. A very natural extension to ORANI-INT is to use ORANI rather than ORANI-13 as its atemporal core. Several other aspects of the model can also be readily extended by borrowing infrastructure from special-purpose versions of ORANI, including: (i) a dissagregation of the household sector into different household types (see Meagher, 1996); (ii) a disaggregation of the labour market into different occupational categories (see Meagher, 1996); (iii) a disaggregation of the government accounts (see Dee, 1989); and (iv) a regional disaggregation of the economy (see Naqvi and Peter, 1996). Each alteration to the model's theory and/or database requires a new computation. For development purposes, therefore, a less cumbersome model was desirable.

Our experience is that once the theoretical structure of ORANI-INT becomes settled the main computing costs are associated with the generation of a control scenario. For the current configuration of ORANI-INT (13 sectors and 30 periods) each step of a multi-step calculation takes about 35 seconds of CPU time on a standard PC (32-bit Pentium Pro with 32 mb RAM).[1] To generate a control scenario large shocks to the exogenous variables are often required. Under these circumstances many steps may be necessary to obtain an accurate solution. We obtained an accurate control path solution by extrapolating results obtained from 4-, 8- and 16-step calculations.

The number of periods modelled makes a significant difference to the solution time. For example, a single-step solution of a 20 period version of ORANI-INT takes about a quarter of the time necessary to solve the 30 period version. This suggests that the computational burden can be reduced by exploiting time aggregation procedures which reduce the number of periods necessary to model a given time horizon. The gains in computational ease need not be at the expense of numerical accuracy. As foreshadowed in chapter 2, time aggregation errors can be minimised by allowing for variable period lengths. In addition, recent work by Mercenier and Michel (1994b) demonstrates that time aggregation errors can be minimised by ensuring that a model's long-run equilibrium is invariant to the degree of time aggregation.

8.5 Final Comments

The main contribution of this monograph is that we have demonstrated how a comparative static CGE model can be readily embedded into an intertemporal framework without compromising on the type and degree of economic detail incorporated. Of course, the worthiness of a model such as ORANI-INT must, ultimately, be measured by the quality of its input to the analysis of policy issues.

The illustrative experiments showed how ORANI-INT overcomes a key limitation of static models by providing information about how the economy evolves over time. In addition, our analysis of these experiments demonstrated that the results produced by ORANI-INT could be reconciled with its theory and data. Because the robustness of ORANI-INT cannot be tested by traditional statistical techniques this is an important prerequisite for sound policy analysis.

---

[1] Note that in 1993, when ORANI-INT was being developed, it took far longer to solve the model. At that stage ORANI-INT was solved on Monash University's VAX 6520 mainframe computer. Each step of a multi-step calculation took about 4 minutes of CPU time.

References

Anderson, K. and R.G. Garnaut (1987) *Australian Protectionism: Extent, Causes and Effects*, Sydney: Allen and Unwin.

Arrow, K.J. (1968) "Optimal Capital Policy with Irreversible Investment", pp. 1-19 in: J.N. Woolfe, ed., *Value, capital and growth. Papers in honour of Sir John Hicks*, Edinburgh: Edinburgh University Press.

Auerbach, A.J. and L.J. Kotlikoff (1983) "National Savings, Economic Welfare, and the Structure of Taxation", pp. 459-493 in: M. Feldstein, ed., *Behavioural Simulation Methods in Tax Policy Analysis*, Chicago: University of Chicago Press.

Auerbach, A.J. and L.J. Kotlikoff (1987) *Dynamic Fiscal Policy,* Cambridge, MA: Cambridge University Press.

Auerbach, A.J., L.J. Kotlikoff and J. Skinner (1983) "Efficiency Gains from Tax Reform", *International Economic Review,* Vol. 245, February, pp. 81-100.

Australian Bureau of Statistics (1990) *Australian National Accounts: Capital Stock,* ABS Catalogue No. 5221.0.

Ballard, C.L., D. Fullerton, J.B. Shoven and J. Whalley (1985) *A General Equilibrium Model for Tax Policy Evaluation*, Chicago: University of Chicago Press for the National Bureau of Economic Research.

Ballard, C.L. and L.H. Goulder (1985) "Consumption Taxes, Foresight, and Welfare:A Computable General Equilibrium Analysis," pp. 253-282 in: J. Piggott and J. Whalley eds., *New Developments in Applied General Equilibrium Analysis*, Cambridge, England: Cambridge University Press.

Bergman,L. (1990) "The Development of Computable General Equilibrium Modeling", pp. 3-32 in: L. Bergman, D.W. Jorgenson and E. Zalai, eds., *General Equilibrium Modeling and Economic Policy Analysis*, Oxford: Basil Blackwell.

Blanchard, O.J. and S. Fischer (1989) *Lectures on Macroeconomics,* Cambridge, Massachusetts: The MIT Press.

Blitzer, C.R. and R. Eckhaus (1986) "Energy-Economy Interactions in Mexico:A Multiperiod General Equilibrium Model", *Journal of Development Economics,* No. 21, pp. 259-282.

Blitzer, C.R., R.S. Eckhaus, S. Lahiri and A. Meeraus (1994) "A General Equilibrium Analysis of the Effects of Carbon Emissions Restrictions on Economic Growth in a Developing Country", pp. 255-278 in: J. Mercenier and T.N. Srinivasan, eds., *Applied General Equilibrium and Economic Development*, Ann Arbor: University of Michigan Press.

Blitzer, C.R., H. Cetin and A.S. Manne (1970) "A Dynamic Five-Sector Model for Turkey, 1967-1982", *Papers and Proceedings of the Eighty-second Annual Meeting of the American Economic Association,* New York, New York, December, 1969, Vol. 60, pp.70-75.

Bovenberg, A.L. (1985) "Dynamic General Equilibrium Tax Models with Adjustment Costs", pp. 40-55 in: A. Manne, ed., "Economic Equilibrium:Model Formulations and Solution", *Mathematical Programming Study* 23, Amsterdam: North-Holland.

Bovenberg, A.L. (1988) "The Corporate Income Tax in an Intertemporal Equilibrium Model with Imperfectly Mobile Capital", *International Economic Review,* No. 29, May, pp. 321-340.

Bovenberg, A.L. and L.H. Goulder (1991) "Introducing Intertemporal and Open Economy Features in Applied General Equilibrium Models", pp. 47-64 in: H. Don, Theo van de Klundert and J. van Sinderen, eds., *Applied General Equilibrium Modelling,*Dordrecht: Kluwer Academic Publishers.

Brechling, F. (1975) *Investment and Employment Decisions,* Manchester: Manchester University Press.

Campbell, J.Y. and N.G. Mankiw (1989) "Consumption, Income, and Interest Rates:Reinterpreting the Time Series Evidence", *NBER Macroeconomics Annual*, Vol. 4, pp. 185-216.

Chirinko, R.S. (1993) "Business Fixed Investment Spending: A Critical Survey of Modeling Strategies, Empirical Results, and Policy Implications", *Journal of Economic Literature,* Vol. XXXI, No. 4, December, pp. 1875-1911.

Codsi, G., M. Horridge and K.R. Pearson (1988) "An Implementation of ORANI Using the GEMPACK Program TABLO", *Impact Project Computing Document* No. C8-01, 76 pp. September, University of Melbourne.

Codsi, G., K.R. Pearson and P.J. Wilcoxen (1991) "General-Purpose Software for Intertemporal Modelling", *Impact Project Preliminary Working Paper* No. IP-51, 39 pp. May, University of Melbourne.

Commonwealth Treasury (1996) "Documentation of the Treasury Macroeconomic (TRYM) Model of the Australian Economy", Canberra: AGPS

Conlisk, J. (1996) "Why Bounded Rationality?", *Journal of Economic Literature,* Vol. XXXIV, No. 2, June, pp. 669-700.

Dee, P.S. (1989) "FH-ORANI: A Fiscal ORANI with Horridge Extension", *Impact Project Preliminary Working Paper* No. OP-66, 359 pp. March, University of Melbourne.

Dervis, K. (1975) "Planning Capital-Labour Substitution and Intertemporal Equilibrium with a Non Linear Multi-Sector Growth Model", *European Economic Review,* Vol. 6, pp. 77-96.

Dixit, A. (1992) "Investment and Hysteresis", *Journal of Economic Perspectives,* Vol. 6, No. 1, pp. 107-132.

Dixon, P.B. (1975) *The Theory of Joint Maximization*, Amsterdam: North-Holland.

Dixon, P.B. (1989) "A General Equilibrium Approach to Public Utility Pricing: Determining Prices for a Water Authority", *IAESR Working Paper* No. 8/1989, 35 pp. July, University of Melbourne.

Dixon, P.B. (1990) "A General Equilibrium Approach to Public Utility Pricing: Determining Prices for a Water Authority", *Journal of Policy Modeling,* Vol. 12, No. 4, pp. 745-767.

Dixon, P.B.and D.J. Baker (1992) "Optimal Prices for Urban Water:A General Equilibrium Model Applied to Melbourne", *Research Report,* No. 43, 128 pp. June, Urban Water Research Association of Australia.

Dixon, P.B. and D. McDonald (1993) "Creating 1990-91 Input-Output Tables for Australia by ORANI Simulations", paper presented at *The Economic Society of Australia 22nd Conference of Economists,* Murdoch University, Perth, 40 pp.

Dixon, P.B. and B.R. Parmenter (1979) "Advances in Input-Output Modeling: A Review Article", *Journal of Policy Modeling*, Vol. 1, No. 2, pp. 271-285.

Dixon, P.B. and B.R. Parmenter (1990) "Dynamics in ORANI, A Large Scale General Equilibrium Model", *IAESR Working Paper* No. 1/1990, 31 pp. February, University of Melbourne.

Dixon, P.B. and B.R. Parmenter (1996) "Computable General Equilibrium Modelling for Policy Analysis and Forecasting", pp. 3-85 in H. Amman, D. Kendrick and J. Rust (eds), *Handbook in Computational Economics*, Volume 1, Amsterdam: North Holland.

Dixon, P.B. and M. Malakellis (1996) "Investment Behaviour in the MONASH Model of the Australian Economy", in Lj. Vlacic, T. Nguyen and D. Cecez-Kecemanovic, editors, *Modelling and Control of National and Regional Economies 1995*, Pergamon, Great Britain.

Dixon, P.B., M. Malakellis, D. McDonald, and G.A. Meagher (1996) "Cuts in Public Expenditure: Some Implications for the Australian Economy in 1996-97 and 1997-98", *Australian Bulletin of Labour*, Vol. 22, No. 2, June, pp.83-108.

Dixon, P.B., B.R. Parmenter and M. Horridge (1986) "Forecasting Versus Policy Analysis with the ORANI Model", *IAESR Working Paper* No. 4/1986, 27 pp. June, University of Melbourne.

Dixon, P.B., B.R. Parmenter, A.A. Powell and P.J. Wilcoxen (1992) *Notes and Problems in Applied Equilibrium Economics,* Amsterdam: North-Holland.

Dixon P.B., B. R. Parmenter, J. Sutton and D.P. Vincent (1982) *ORANI:A Multisectoral Model of the Australian Economy,* Amsterdam: North-Holland.

Dixon, P.B. and M.T. Rimmer (1998a) *MONASH: A Disaggregated, Dynamic Model of the Australian Economy.* (Partial draft of a book, available from the Centre of Policy Studies and IMPACT Project, Monash University).

Dixon, P.B. and M.T. Rimmer (1998b) "The levels representation of price and quantity indexes in MONASH", *section 47 in MONASH: A Disaggregated, Dynamic Model of the Australian Economy.* (Partial draft of a book, available from the Centre of Policy Studies and IMPACT Project, Monash University).

Duff, I.S. (1977) "MA28– A Set of FORTRAN Subroutines for Sparse Unsymmetric Linear Equations", *Harwell Report*, R8730, London: HMSO.

Eckhaus, R.S. and K.S. Parikh (1968) *Planning for Growth: Multisectoral, Intertemporal Models Applied to India,* Cambridge: MIT Press.

Eichengreen, B. and L.H. Goulder (1991) "The Impact of Permanent and Temporary Import Surcharges on the U.S. Trade Deficit", in: R. Baldwin ed., *Empirical Studies of Commercial Policy,* Chicago: University of Chicago Press.

Eisner, R. and R.H. Strotz (1963) "Determinants of Business Investment", in *Commission on Money and Credit,* Englewood Cliffs, New Jersey: Prentice-Hall, pp. 59-233.

Evans, H.D. (1972) A General Equilibrium Analysis of Protection: The Effects of Protection in Australia, North-Holland, Amsterdam.

Fair, R.C. and J.B Taylor (1983) "Solution and Maximum Likelihood Estimation of Dynamic Nonlinear Rational Expectations Models", *Econometrica,* Vol. 51, No. 4, pp. 1169-1185.

Fischer, S. (1977) "Long-Term Contracts, Rational Expectations, and the Optimal Money Supply Rule", *Journal of Political Economy,* Vol. 85, No. 1, pp. 191-205.

Gould, J.P. (1968) "Adjustment Costs in the Theory of Investment of the Firm", *Review of Economic Studies,* Vol. 83, No. 4, pp. 47-55.

Goulder, L.H. and B. Eichengreen (1989) "Savings Promotion, Investment Promotion and International Competitiveness", pp. 5-44, in: R. Feenstra ed., *Trade Policies for International Competitiveness,* Chicago: University of Chicago Press.

Goulder, L.H. and B. Eichengreen (1992) "Trade Liberalization in General Equilibrium: Intertemporal and Inter-Industry Effects", *Canadian Journal of Economics,* Vol. XXV, No. 2, May, pp. 253-280.

Goulder, L.H. and L.H. Summers (1989) "Tax Policy, Asset Prices, and Growth:A General Equilibrium Analysis", *Journal of Public Economics,* No. 38, October, pp. 265-296.

Gregory, R.G., (1976) "The Green Paper on Policies for Manufacturing Industry: A Review", Australian Journal of Management, Vol. 1, pp. 51-75.

Gruen, F.H., (1975) "The 25% Tariff Cut, was it a mistake?", *The Australian Quarterly,* 47(2), pp. 7-20.

Hall, S.G. (1985) "On the Solution of Large Economic Models", *Bulletin of Economic Research,* Vol. 37, May, pp. 157-161.

Hanoch, G. (1971) "CRESH Production Functions", *Econometrica,* Vol. 39, September, pp. 695-712.

Horridge, M. (1992) "Augmented Dam Management Problem", Mimeo, Centre of Policy Studies, Monash University.

Horridge, M., B.R. Parmenter and K.R. Pearson (1993) "ORANI-F: A General Equilibrium Model of the Australian Economy", *Economic and Financial Computing*, Vol. 3, No. 2, European Economics and Financial Centre: London.

Hudson, E.A. and D.W. Jorgenson (1974) "U.S. Energy Policy and Economic Growth, 1975-2000", *Bell Journal of Economics and Management Science,* Vol. 5, No. 2, Autumn, pp. 461-514.

Industry Commission (1995) Assistance to Agricultural and Manufacturing Industries, *Information Paper*, March, Australian Government Publishing Service, Canberra.

Johansen, L. (1960) *A Multisectoral Study of Economic Growth,* Amsterdam: North-Holland.

Jorgenson, D.W. (1993) "Econometric Studies of Investment Behaviour: A Survey", *Journal of Economic Literature,* Vol. IX, No. 4, December, pp. 1111-11147.

Jorgenson, D.W. and P.J. Wilcoxen (1990) "Intertemporal General Equilibrium Modeling of U.S. Environmental Regulation", *Journal of Policy Modeling,* Vol. 12, No. 4, pp. 715-744.

Jorgenson, D.W. and P.J. Wilcoxen (1993) "Energy, the Environment and Economic Growth", Mimeo, pp. 1-87 in: A.V. Kneese and J.L. Sweeney, eds., *Handbook of Natural Resource and Energy Economics,* Volume III. Amsterdam: North-Holland.

Jorgenson, D.W. and K.Y. Yun (1986) "Efficiency of Capital Allocation", *Scandinavian Journal of Economics,* No. 28, pp. 85-107.

Kydland, F.E. and E.C. Prescott (1982) "Time to Build and Aggregate Fluctuations", *Econometrica,* Vol. 50, No. 6, November, pp. 1345-1370.

Leontief, W.W. (1937) "Interrelation of Prices, Output, Savings and Investments", *Review of Economics and Statistics,* Vol. 19, pp. 109-132.

Lipton, D., J. Poterba, J. Sachs and L. Summers (1982) "Multiple Shooting in Rational Expectations Models", *Econometrica,* Vol. 50, No. 2, pp. 1329-1333.

Lloyd, P.J., (1978) "Protection Policy", chpt 5 in F.H. Gruen (ed.) *Surveys of Australian Economics*, Vol. 1, Sydney: George Allen and Unwin.

Lluch, C. (1973) "The Extended Linear Expenditure System", *European Economic Review,* Vol. 4, pp.21-32.

Longva, S., L. Lorentsen and Ø. Olsen (1985) "The Multi-Sectoral Growth Model MSG-4. Formal Structure and Empirical Characteristics", pp. 187-240 in: F.R. Førsund, M. Hoel and S. Longva eds., *Production, Multi-Sectoral Growth and Planning,* Amsterdam: North-Holland.

Lucas, R.E., (1967) "Adjustment Costs and the Theory of Supply", *Journal of Political Economy*, Vol. 75, No. 4, pp. 321-334.

Lucas, R.E., (1972) "Expectations and the Neutrality of Money", *Journal of Economic Theory*, Vol. 4, No. 2, pp. 103-124.

Lucas, R.E., (1976) "Econometric Policy Evaluation: A Critique", pp. 19-46 in *Carnegie-Rochester Conference Series on Public Policy* No. 1, Supplement to the *Journal of Monetary Economics*.

Malakellis, M. (1998) "Should Tariff Reductions be Announced? An Intertemporal Computable General Equilibrium Analysis", *The Economic Record*, Vol. 74, No. 225, pp. 121-138.

Malakellis, M. and P.B. Dixon (1994) "The Economic Implications of an Improvement in Labour Productivity: Comparative Dynamic Results from the *MONASH* Model" pp. 161-190 in C. Hargreaves, editor, *A Comparison of Economy-wide Models of Australia,* Economic Planning Advisory Commission, Commission Paper No.2, Australian Government Publishing Service, Canberra.

Mankiw, N.G. (1990) "A Quick Refresher Course in Macroeconomics", *Journal of Economic Literature,* Vol. XXVIII, No. 4, December, pp. 1645-1660.

Manne, A.S. (1973) "DINAMICO, A Dynamic Multi-Sectoral, Multi-Skill Model", in: L.M. Goreaux and A.S. Manne eds., *Multi-Level Planning: Case Studies in Mexico,* Amsterdam: North-Holland.

Manne, A.S. (1977) "ETA-Macro:A Model of Energy Economy Interactions", in: C. Hitch ed., *Modeling Energy-Economy Interactions: Five Approaches,* Washington D.C: Resources for the Future.

Manne, A.S. (1985) "On the Formulation and Solution of Economic Equilibrium Models", pp. 1-22 in: A. Manne, ed., "Economic Equilibrium:Model Formulations and Solution", *Mathematical Programming Study* 23, Amsterdam: North-Holland.

Manne, A.S. (1991) "Global 2100:An Almost Consistent Model of CO_2 Emission Limits", *Swiss Journal of Economics and Statistics,* Vol. 127, No. 2, pp. 181-197.

Manne, A.S. and T.E. Weisskopf (1970) "A Dynamic Multi-Sectoral Model for India, 1967-1975", in: A. Carter and A. Brody eds., *Applications of Input-Output Analysis,* Amsterdam:North-Holland.

McKibbin W.J. and J.D. Sachs (1991) *Global Linkages: Macroeconomic Interdependence and Cooperation in the World Economy,* The Brooking's Institution, Washington, D.C.

McKibbin, W.J. and E.S. Siegloff (1988) "A Note on Aggregate Investment in Australia", *Economic Record,* Vol. 64, pp. 209-215.

McKibbin, W.J. and P.J. Wilcoxen (1992) "G-Cubed: A Dynamic Multi-Sector General Equilibrium Growth Model of the Global Economy. (Quantifying the costs of Curbing

CO_2 Emissions)", Mimeo, 47 pp. September, The Brookings Institution and University of Texas at Austin.

McKibbin, W.J. and P.J. Wilcoxen (1995) "The Theoretical and Empirical Structure of G-Cubed", *Brookings Discussion Paper in International Economics*, No. 118, 59 pp. Washington DC: The Brookings Institution.

McKibbin, W.J. and P.J. Wilcoxen (1998) "The Theoretical and Empirical Structure of the G-Cubed Model", *Economic Modelling* (forthcoming).

Meagher, G.A. (1978) "A Multiperiod Multisector General Equilibrium Model of the Australian Economy", unpublished Ph.D dissertation, Monash University.

Meagher, G.A. (1996) "Forecasting Changes in the Distribution of Income: An Applied General Equilibrium Approach" in A. Harding (ed.) *Microsimulation and Public Policy*, North-Holland, Amsterdam.

Menon, J. (1993) "Import Price and Activity Elasticities for the Monash Model: Johansen FIML Estimation of Cointegration Vectors", *Centre of Policy Studies/Impact Project Preliminary Working Paper* No IP-58, 35 pp. July, Monash University.

Mercenier, J. and P. Michel (1994a) "A Criterion for Time Aggregation in Intertemporal Dynamic Models", *Mathematical Programming*, Vol.64, No. 2, pp. 179-199.

Mercenier, J. and P. Michel (1994b) "Discrete-Time Finite Horizon Approximation of Infinite Horizon Optimization Problems With Steady-State Invariance", *Econometrica*, Vol. 62, No. 3, pp.635-656.

Mercenier, J. and M. Sampaio de Souza (1994) "Structural Adjustment and Growth in a Highly Indebted Market Economy: Brazil", pp. 281-310 in: J. Mercenier and T.N. Srinivasan, eds., *Applied General Equilibrium and Economic Development,* Ann Arbor: University of Michigan Press.

Mussa, M.L. (1977) "External and Internal Adjustment Costs and the Theory of Aggregate and Firm Investment", *Economica,* Vol. 44, No. 174, pp. 163-178.

Mussa, M.L. (1978) "Dynamic Adjustment in a Hecksher-Ohlin-Samuelson Model", *Journal of Political Economy,* Vol. 86, pp. 775-791.

Naqvi, F. and M.W. Peter (1996), "A Multiregional, Multisectoral Model of the Australian Economy with an Illustrative Application", *Australian Economic Papers*, Vol. 35, No. 66, pp.94-113.Nickell, S.J. (1978) *The Investment Decisions of Firms,* Cambridge: Cambridge University Press.

Parmenter, B.R. (1982) "Inter-Industry Analysis", pp. 69-110 in: L.R. Webb and R.H. Allan eds.,*Industrial Economics, Australian Studies,* George Allen and Unwin, Sydney.

Parmenter, B.R. (1988) "ORANI-F: User's Manual", *IAESR Working Paper* No. 7/1988, University of Melbourne.

Parmenter, B.R., G.A. Meagher and P.J. Higgs (1994) "Technical Change in Australia During the 1980's: Simulations with a Computable General Equilibrium Model", *Economic and Financial Modelling*, Vol. 1, No. 1, pp. 61-80.

Pearson, K.R. (1988) "Automating the Computation of Solutions of Large Economic Models", *Economic Modelling*, Vol. 5, pp. 385-395.

Pearson, K.R. (1991) "Solving Nonlinear Economic Models Accurately Via a Linear Representation", *Impact Project Preliminary Working Paper* No. IP-55, 39 pp. July, University of Melbourne.

Pereira, A.M. and J.B. Shoven (1988) "Survey of Dynamic Computable General Equilibrium Models for Tax Policy Evaluation", *Journal of Policy Modeling,* Vol. 10, No. 3, pp. 401-436.

Poterba, J.M. (1988) "Are Consumers Forward Looking? Evidence from Fiscal Experiments", *Papers and Proceedings of the One-Hundredth Annual Meeting of the American Economic Association,* Chicago, Illinois, Dec., 28-30, 1987, .pp. 413-418. Vol. 78.

Powell, A.A. (1974) *Empirical Analytics of Demand Systems,* Lexington Books, D.C. Heath and Company, Lexington, Mass.

Powell, A.A. and C.W. Murphy (1997) *Inside a Modern Macroeconometric Model: A Guide to the Murphy Model,* 2nd Edition, Springer-Verlag, Berlin, Heidelberg and New York.

Powell, A.A. and R.H. Snape (1993) "The Contribution of Applied General Equilibrium Analysis to Policy Reform in Australia", *Journal of Policy Modeling,* Vol. 15, No. 4, pp. 393-414.

Press, W., B. Flannery, S. Teukolsky and W. Vetterling (1986) *Numerical Recipes*, New York: Cambridge University Press.

Pindyck, R.S. (1991) "Irreversibility, Uncertainty, and Investment", *Journal of Economic Literature,* Vol. XXIX, No. 3, pp. 1110-1148.

Rimmer, M.T. (1990) Primary Factor Substitution and the Real Wage Explosions", *Impact Project Working Paper* No. O-69, 28 pp. October, University of Melbourne.

Rimmer, M.T. and A.A. Powell (1992) "An Implicitly Directly Additive Demand System: Estimates for Australia", *Impact Project Preliminary Working Paper* No. OP-73, 38 pp. October, Monash University.

Robinson, S. (1989) "Multisectoral Models", pp. 885-939 in: H. Chenery and T.N. Srinivasan, eds., *Handbook of Development Economics,*Vol. II. Amsterdam: North-Holland.

Robinson, S. (1991) "Macroeconomics, Financial Variables and Computable General Equilibrium Models", *World Development,* Vol. 19, No. 11, pp. 1509-1525.

Samuelson, P.A. and S. Swamy (1974) "Invariant Economic Index Numbers and Canonical Duality: Survey and Synthesis", *American Economic Review,* Vol. 64, No. 3, pp. 566-593.

Sargent, T.J. and N. Wallace (1975) "Rational Expectations, the Optimal Monetary Instrument, and the Optimal Money Supply Rule", *Journal of Political Economy,* Vol. 83, No. 2, pp. 241-254.

Shoven, J.B. and J. Whalley (1984) "Applied General Equilibrium Models of Taxation and International Trade", *Journal of Economic Literature,* Vol. XXII, No. 3, pp. 1007-1051.

Summers, L.H. (1981) "Capital Taxation and Accumulation in a Life Cycle Growth Model", *American Economic Review,* No. 71, pp. 533-544.

Taylor, L. (1975) "Theoretical Foundations and Technical Implications", in: C.R. Blitzer, P.B. Clark and L. Taylor eds., *Economy Wide Models and Development Planning,* London:Oxford University Press.

The Crawford Report (1979) Commonwealth of Australia, *Study Group on Structural Adjustment Report*, Australian Government Publishing Service, Canberra.

The Jackson Report (1975) Committee to Advise on Policies for Manufacturing Industries, *Policies for Development of Manufacturing Industry*, Australian Government Publishing Service, Canberra.

Treadway, A.B. (1969) "On Rational Entrepreneurial Behaviour and the Demand for Investment", *Review of Economic Studies,* Vol. 36, No. 5, pp. 227-239.

Turnovsky, S.J. (1989) "The Intertemporal Optimizing Approach to International Macroeconomics: An Overview", Handout for *Presentation to Australian Meeting of the Econometric Society July 13-15,* University of New England, Armidale, 27 pp.

Uzawa, H. (1969) "Time Preference and the Penrose Effect in a Two Class Model of Economic Growth", *Journal of Political Economy,* Vol. 77, pp. 628-652.

Vincent, D.P., P.B. Dixon and A.A. Powell (1980) "The Estimation of Supply Response in Australian Agriculture: The CRESH/CRETH Production System", *International Economic Review,* Vol. 21, February, pp. 221-242.

Vogt, A. (1978) "Divisia Indices on Different Paths", pp. 297-305 in Eichhorn, W., R. Henn, O. Opitz and R.W. Shephard, eds., *Theory and Applications of Economic Indicies,* Proceedings of an International Symposium held at the University of Karlsruhe, April-June 1976, Physica-Verlag, Wurzburg.

Wilcoxen, P.J. (1985) "Numerical Methods for Investment Models with Foresight", *Impact Project Preliminary Working Paper,* No. IP-23, 47 pp. October, University of Melbourne.

Zangwill, W.I. and C.B. Garcia (1981) *Pathways to Solutions, Fixed Points, and Equilibria.* Englewood Cliffs: Prentice Hall.

Author Index

Allan, R.H. 266
Amman, H. 263
Anderson, K 221, 261
Arrow, K.J. 110, 111, 261
Auerbach, A.J. 6, 261
Australian Bureau of Statistics 164, 197, 258, 261

Baldwin, R. 263
Ballard, C.L. 4, 7, 258, 259, 261
Baker, D.J. 143, 262
Bergman, L. 3, 261
Blanchard, O.J. 97, 261
Blitzer, C.R. 5, 6, 261, 267
Bovenberg, A.L. 6, 8, 9, 17, 106, 126, 261, 262
Brechling, F. 105, 108, 262
Brody, A. 265

Campbell, J.Y. 258, 262
Carter, A. 258
Cecez-Kecemanovic, D. 263
Cetin, H. 5, 261
Chenery, H. 267
Chirinko, R.S. 104, 108, 110, 262
Codsi, G.
Conlisk, J. 259, 262
Commonwealth Treasury 5, 262

Dee, P.S. 259, 262
Dervis, K. 6, 262
Dixit, A. 109, 262
Dixon, P.B. 3, 4, 5, 6, 9, 24, 27, 28, 43, 107, 110, 118, 124–126, 128, 129, 133, 143, 149, 221, 258, 262, 263, 265, 268
Don, H. 262
Duff, I.S. 263

Eckhaus, R.S. 5, 6, 261, 263
Eichengreen, B. 8, 263, 264
Eisner, R. 105, 263
Evans, H.D. 221, 263

Fair, R.C. 127, 263
Feenstra, M. 264
Feldstein, M. 261
Fischer, S. 19, 97, 261, 263
Flannery, B. 267
Førsund, F.R. 265
Fullerton, D. 4, 261

Garcia, C.B. 134, 268
Garnaut, R.G. 221, 261
Goreaux, L.M. 265
Gould, J.P. 105, 263
Goulder, L.H. 7, 8, 9, 17, 106, 258, 259, 261, 262, 263, 264
Gregory, R.G. 222, 264
Gruen, F.H. 222, 264

Hall, S.G. 126, 264, 268
Hanoch, G. 264
Higgs, P.J. 167, 257, 266
Hitch, C. 265
Hoel, M. 265
Horridge, M. 4, 24, 27, 28, 143, 149, 262, 263, 264
Hudson, E.A. 4, 264

Industry Commission, 221, 223, 264

Johansen, L. 3–6, 130, 132, 144, 264, 266
Jorgenson, D.W. 4, 7, 9, 17, 104, 107, 261, 264

Kendrick, D. 263
Kneese, A.V. 264
Kotlikoff, L.J. 6, 261
Kydland, F.E. 43, 264

Lahiri, S. 261
Leontief, W.W. 3, 10, 11, 12, 14, 30, 32, 34, 47, 236, 241, 245, 264
Lipton, D. 127, 264
Lloyd, P.J 221, 264
Lluch, C. 35, 265
Longva, S. 4, 265
Lorentsen, L. 265
Lucas, R.E. 1, 18, 105, 165, 225, 265

Malakellis, M. 5, 110, 223, 263, 265
Mankiw, N.G. 1, 258, 262, 265
Manne, A.S. 5, 18, 124, 261, 265
McDonald, D. 5, 258, 262, 263

McKibbin, W.J. 8, 9, 17, 105, 110, 165, 258, 259, 265, 266
Meagher, G.A. 5, 6, 167, 257, 259, 263, 266
Meeraus, A. 261
Menon, J. 258, 266
Mercenier, J. 7, 9, 17, 22, 107, 260, 261, 266
Michel, P. 22, 260, 266
Murphy, C.W. 5, 8, 127, 267
Mussa, M.L. 105, 266

Naqvi, F. 259, 266
Nickell, S.J. 105, 266
Nguyen, T. 263

Olsen, Ø. 265

Parikh, K.S. 5, 263
Parmenter, B.R. 2, 3, 4, 9, 24, 27, 28, 107, 133, 149, 167, 221, 257, 262, 263, 264, 266
Pearson, K.R. 24, 27, 28, 118, 128, 129, 133, 262, 264, 266
Pereira, A.M. 3, 6, 266
Peter, M.W. 259, 266
Piggott, J. 261
Pindyck, R.S. 109, 267
Poterba, J.M. 258, 264, 267
Powell, A.A. 5, 8, 23, 107, 127, 221, 258, 263, 267, 268
Prescott, E.C. 43, 264
Press, W. 126, 128, 267

Rimmer, M.T. 5, 118, 258, 263, 267
Robinson, S. 3, 267
Rust, J. 263

Sachs, J. 8, 110, 165, 259, 264, 265
Sampaio de Souza, M. 7, 9, 17, 266
Samuelson, P.A. 54, 267
Sargent, T.J. 19, 267
Siegloff, E.S. 258, 265
Shoven, J.B. 3, 4, 6, 261, 266, 267
Skinner, J. 6, 261
Snape, R.H. 23, 221, 267
Srinivasan, T.N. 261, 266, 267
Strotz, R.H. 105, 263
Summers, L.H. 6, 7, 264, 267
Sutton, J. 4, 24, 27, 28, 133, 221, 263
Swamy, S. 54, 267
Sweeney, J.L. 264

Taylor, J.B. 127, 263
Taylor, L. 6, 267
Teukolsky, S. 267
The Crawford Report, 222, 267
The Jackson Report, 222, 267
Treadway, A.B. 105, 165, 267
Turnovsky, S.J. 1, 268

Uzawa, H. 105, 268

van de Klundert, Theo. 262
van Sinderen, J. 262
Vetterling, W. 267
Vincent, D.P. 4, 24, 28, 133, 221, 263, 268
Vlacic, Lj. 263
Vogt, A. 54, 268

Wallace, N. 19, 267
Webb, L.R. 266
Weisskopf, T.E. 265
Whalley, J. 3, 4, 261, 267
Wilcoxen, P.J. 7, 8, 9, 17, 22, 105, 107, 110, 126, 128, 129, 259, 262, 263, 264, 265, 266, 268
Woolfe, J.N. 261

Yun, K.Y. 7, 264

Zalai, E. 261
Zangwill, W.I. 134, 268

Subject Index

accumulation of stocks and flows 4, 5, 11, 12, 13, 14, 25, 40, 43, 91, 96, 101, 151–152, 162, 184
  see also capital accumulation, foreign liabilities
adjustment costs 6, 7, 8, 9, 11–13, 16, 43, 104–109, 165, 259
  and inertia in capital-creation 104, 106–107, 165, 259
  convexity of 105
  empirical support for 108, 165, 259
  in a multisectoral model 107
  types of 106–107
  see also investment
agricultural land 27, 29, 31–34, 52–54, 59, 153–155, 186, 189, 194, 207, 211, 219, 234, 244
  aggregate payments to 53–54, 234
  as input to production 31
  cost of 32
  demand for effective units of 33
  effective units of 32
  market clearing 52
  supply of 153, 189, 194
algorithm, solution 18, 127–129, 148, 164, 255
  see also solution method
allocative efficiency 190, 246
  impact of government expenditure on 189–191
  impact of tariff shocks on 234, 246, 244
anticipation effects 184
  of government expenditure shocks 196, 203, 209, 216, 220
  of tariff shocks
arbitrage 15, 16, 41
  condition, enforcement of 42, 153
  see also rate of return, investment
Australian economy 6, 8, 10, 19
  and tariff reform 19, 221–222
  CGE models of 6, 10
  macro models of 8

balanced growth 9, 17, 20, 149–152, 157, 162, 164, 166, 256
  convergence to 152, 166
  path, neo-classical 9
  see also control scenario
balance of trade, *see* trade balance
basic prices 27, 49–51
  defined 27
  relationship with purchasers' prices 50–52
  uniformity across agents 49
  see also prices
bond rate 39, 153, 156, 163
  and rates of return on other assets 42, 160, 163
  domestic 39, 193
  domestic and foreign, relationship 51
  foreign 40, 153, 160, 162, 193
  impact on consumption path 40
  value of 171
boundary conditions 25, 126, 128
  see also initial conditions, terminal conditions
budget constraint 7–10, 12, 15, 38–40, 91–103
  economy-wide 40, 91, 97, 255
  household 38–39, 91
  in state-of-the-art CGE models 10–12, 15
  public 91
  see also government, households, stylised model

calibration technique 7, 16, 17
  versus econometric technique 7, 17
capital 4–9, 11–16, 18, 27, 29–34, 41–54, 153, 189, 191
  aggregate payments to 54
  aggregation of 54, 56
  as input to production 30–31
  demand for effective units of 34
  effective units of 32
  fixity of in producers short-run profit maximisation decision 31, 32
  impact of shock to government spending on the stock of 189, 191–194
  impact of tariff reduction on the stock of 234–237
  lumpiness of 110

market clearing 52
price of 33, 193
real user cost of193–194, 200, 202, 207, 236
sector specificity of 25, 41, 153
substitutability of 31–34
supply of 153, 160
capital accumulation 25, 43, 151, 195, 202, 208
implications of 195–196, 202
capital gains 183, 185, 197, 202, 203
capital creation 41-48, 104–110
cost of 47, 193
gestation lags in 43, 108, 196
import intensity of 161, 193, 201
optimal path of 41–46
process, optimal level of inputs to 41
technology 47–48, 105–106
zero pure profits in 49, 50
capital price deflator, *see* investment deflator
capital stock, aggregate 189, 195, 200, 203, 209
CES 10–14, 29, 31–33, 35–38, 47, 131
commodity aggregation 10, 36, 47
function, notation for 32
production function 31, 35
unit cost function 33, 35
utility function 10, 37
CGE models 1–9, 17–19, 124–126, 128–130, 148, 254
approach of 2
influence of in Australian policy reform 23, 221, 222
interfaced with macro models 5
intertemporal 5–9, 17–19
key applications 2
recent trends 2–3, 9
reconciliation with macro models 1–2
recursive 4–5
solution of 124–126
static versus dynamic 2–3, 23
closure 41, 46, 136, 144–146, 148, 152–157
choice of 144, 152
flexibility to change 41, 46
key exogenous variables 153
Cobb-Douglas 10, 11, 92
commodity aggregation 10, 92
production function 92
utility function 10
competitiveness 194–195, 196, 212, 216, 219–220, 237, 242, 244
and the real exchange rate 194–195
impact of government spending on 219–220
impact of tariff cuts on 237, 242, 244
composite commodity 10–14, 29, 32, 34–39, 47
demand for by capital creators 47
demand for by households 36–38
demand for by producers 34
inputs to production 35
notation for 29
computable general equilibrium 1
programming approach to 4–5
see also CGE
constant returns to scale 30, 50
see also production technology
consumption deflator 55, 211
defined 55
impact of tariff cut on 247–249
consumer price index 52
see also consumption deflator
consumption, *see* household expenditure
control scenario 17, 149–152, 156–157, 162–166, 223, 256, 260
balanced growth 149–152
construction of 150–162
realism of 162–166, 256
cost minimisation 35, 47
by capital creators 47
by producers 35

data 149–151, 163–167, 170
historical 149, 163
input-output 149–151, 167
listing of 170–181
problems with 164
timeliness of 257–258
depreciation of capital 43, 112, 151, 163
listing of sectoral rates 171
differential equations 107, 128, 130, 139, 141
solution of 128
see also solution method
Divisia indexes 54–60, 118–123
and Laspeyres indexes 55, 118, 122–123
and Paasche indexes 55, 118, 122–123
defined 55, 119
properties of 55, 120–121
use of 54–55, 122–123
elasticities 171, 258
sources of 258
values of 171
elasticity of foreign demand 38, 49
employment 5, 9, 56, 189, 196
aggregate 56
growth of in the control scenario 161
see also labour
Euler method 17, 19, 124–125, 128–130, 132–141, 255
convergence properties of 133
description of 130–138
use of to solve ORANI 124–125
see also solution method, initial value problem
exchange rate 8, 40, 51, 154, 156, 162

defined 40
role of as numeraire 156
see also uncovered interest parity, numeraire
exogenous variables 149–157, 160, 162–164, 166
implications of 152–156
list of 154
see also closure
expectations 3–5, 10–14, 18, 27, 36, 40, 46, 105–106, 108, 126–128, 163–164, 185, 193, 220, 257–259
and estimation difficulties 108, 258
backward-looking 126
boundedly rational 259
explicit treatment of 104
forward-looking 25, 126, 257
implications of for computations 126
perfect foresight 3, 109, 258
rational, model consistent 15–16, 36, 40, 163, 258
static 46, 126, 185, 193, 257
exports 49, 156
demand for 49
elasticity of demand for 49
impact of government expenditure on 194
prices of 194
traditional versus non-traditional 49, 156

Fair-Taylor algorithm 17, 127
see also solution method
financial markets 9, 41
competitiveness of 41
in state-of-the-art CGE models 15–16
foreign liabilities 25, 40, 41, 91, 97, 162, 170, 171, 185, 204, 216, 219, 240, 255
accumulation of 40
and the trade balance 40, 162, 204, 207, 209
constraint on the growth of 40–41, 204
denomination of 40
impact of the bond rate on 40, 162
in the steady state 97, 212, 216

G-Cubed model 8
GEMTAP model 4, 7
GEMPACK software 118–119, 122–123, 128, 144, 145, 148, 255, 256
accessibility of 148, 255–256
flexibility of 144, 255
symbolic differentiation routines 119
government 15, 27–29, 35, 42, 48, 51–54, 56, 57
as source of final demand 35
budget deficit 216
demands 35
expenditure 20, 41, 53, 98
in state-of-the-art CGE models 15
see also government expenditure, government expenditure simulations
government expenditure 182–220
impact on net foreign liabilities 209, 212, 216, 219
sectoral bias of 191
sectoral impacts of 194–195, 196, 211
government expenditure simulations 182–220
description of 182–184
main findings 257
long run results 186–195, 197–200, 207, 212, 216
short run results 196, 203, 209

homogeniety 131, 156, 157
properties 156, 157
homotopy 134–135, 150
households 4, 6, 7, 9, 11, 13–16, 29, 35–40, 183, 209
behaviour of 35–40, 183, 209
constraints faced 38, 39
demands for composite commodities by 36
number of 36, 156, 157
see also household expenditure
household expenditure 10–12
aggregate 53
impact of budget constraint on 97–98, 101–103
impact of government spending on 204, 207–211, 215–216, 219
impact of tariff cuts on 242–243, 247–249
in state-of-the-art CGE models 10–12
optimal allocation across goods 36–38
optimal allocation across time 40, 209
treatment of in static models 23

imports 153, 162, 186
competitiveness of 162
demand for 241
foreign currency price of 153, 193
impact of government expenditure on 186, 194, 196
impact of tariff cuts on 241–242
non-competing 153
substitutability of 162, 241
inflation 156
indexes 54–60, 118–123
see also Divisia indexes, Paasche indexes, Laspeyres indexes
indirect taxes 53–54, 59
deflator for 59
see also sales taxes
information set 3, 5, 21, 163–166, 256

constancy over time 163
used by backward-looking agents
used by forward-looking agents 164, 165
initial conditions 25, 127
for capital stock 26, 43
for stock of debt 26
initial solution 125, 136
derived from input-output data 130
for intertemporal models 125, 133
for static model 133
initial-value problem 124, 126, 128, 255
solution of 128
see also solution method
input demands 31–32, 35, 47
by capital creators 47
by producers 31–32, 35
input-output models 3
input-output data 5, 17, 20, 130–131, 149–151, 167, 257
adjustments made to 177–181
conventions 177
disequilibrium in 150
timeliness of 257–258
use of in control scenario 149–151, 166
interest rate 8, 15, 16, 153, 156, 160, 163
see also bond rate
intertemporal base solution 150
see also control scenario
intertemporal equilibrium 165
intertemporal optimisation 1–2, 42, 43
by households 36, 39
by investors 30, 42, 105
in CGE models 5–17
in macro models 1–2
investment 4–9, 12–16, 19, 42, 111–117, 160–162
aggregate 53
and the role of uncertainty 109, 163, 258
by government-dominated sectors 42, 153
cost of adjustment 43, 104–109
financing of 110
impact of government expenditure shock on 195–196, 200, 201, 202, 203, 204, 210–211, 215–216
in state-of-the-art CGE models 12–16
intertemporal nature of 23, 41,104
nonnegativity of 42, 45, 111–117
sectoral 160–162
treatment of in static models 23
see also capital creation
investment-capital ratios 157, 160
adjustment of 160–161
in equilibrium 157
investment deflator 56, 194, 237
composition of 194
impact of tariff cuts on 237
investment responses, plausibility of 163–166, 256
investment technology 43, 105–106, 259
cost-of-adjustment 105, 259
sector specificity of 108
time-to-build 43, 108, 259
see also capital creation

labour 4, 6–9, 11–14, 32, 33, 52, 153, 196
cost of adjusting 250
homogeneity of 52
price of 32, 52, 192, 196, 212
real cost of using 192
sectoral mobility of 52, 250
supply of 153
labour-capital ratio 192
Laspeyres index 55, 118, 122–123
Leontief 3, 10–12, 14
commodity aggregation 10, 12, 14
production function 11, 12

linear expenditure system 38
extended 35
macroeconomic aggregates 53–59
margins 24
distinguished from direct demands 24
market clearing conditions 52
microeconomic 1, 104
foundations of CGE models 1-2
foundations for investment 104
foundations of macro models 1
models, focus of 1-2
MM2 model 8
mobility of factors 8
and characterisation of length of run 2
sectoral capital 8
MONASH model 4, 5
relationship with ORANI 5
special purpose versions 5
MSG2 model 8
MSG-4 model 4, 6
multiple shooting algorithm 127
see also solution method

non-negativity constraint on investment 9, 19, 41–45, 111–117, 144, 146
implications of 111–117
see also solution method, investment
Newton-Raphson method 124, 129, 138–143
efficiency of 139
see also solution method
numeraire 97, 96, 156
and the absolute level of prices 156

'other cost' tickets 27, 28, 31
defined 27

demand for 34
optimal tariffs 225
optimisation 1, 3, 11, 13, 23
in CGE models 1, 11, 13, 23
in macro models 1
intertemporal 3
static versus intertemporal 23
see also intertemporal optimisation
ORANI model 4, 5, 6, 9, 19, 20, 27,124, 130, 254–259
database 20, 38, 167, 256, 257
dimensions of 24, 259
relationship to ORANI-INT 19, 27, 254
solution of 124, 130

Paasche index 55, 118, 122–123
payments to capital, aggregate 54, 56, 57
deflator for 57
real 56
payments to labour, aggregate 54, 56, 57
deflator for 57
real 56
perfect foresight 3, 7, 9, 109, 258
see also expectations
production technology 12–14, 30–32
for output 30–32
in state-of-the-art CGE models 12–14
see also CES, Leontief, Cobb-Douglas
prices 27, 32–34, 49–52, 149
basic and purchasers' 51–52
growth of in steady state 149–151
of commodities for households 36–38
of exports 49
of imports 49, 153
of inputs to capital creation 51
of intermediate inputs 35
of primary factors 32–34
unit, relationship to unit costs 50–51
primary factors 27, 31
composite of 31
demands for 32–34
prices of 32–34
substitutability of 31
see also agricultural land, capital, labour
private consumption
see household expenditure
pure time preference rate 39, 170, 171

rate of return 4, 15, 25, 41–42, 153, 160–161, 163–165, 177, 180, 181
equalisation of across assets 15, 153, 163
forward-looking 25
historical values 160, 181
risk adjusted 41, 160
sector specific 42
rental price of capital 33, 45, 112–117
and the marginal product of capital 45
and the nonnegativity constraint 112–117
deflator 57, 194
resource allocation 2, 23
static versus intertemporal 2, 23
Ricardian equivalence 9
risk premia 15, 16, 41–42, 153
exogeneity of 153
in state-of-the-art CGE models 15–16
sector specificity of 42
values assigned to 179
sale taxes 49, 51, 59
aggregate revenues from 53–54
and purchasers' prices 49
exogeneity of rates 153
types 54
shooting algorithm 127
see also solution method
simulations 182, 221
see also government expenditure simulations, tariff reduction strategies
solution method 19, 20, 128, 130, 139–140, 143
allowing for corner constraints 143–148
and forward-looking expectations 126
comparison of alternatives 125–128
efficiency of 22, 133, 139, 164
flexibility of 127, 148
hybrid 129, 139
tailor-made versus general purpose 148
structural adjustment 222
induced by tariff reductions 222, 225
stylised model 91–103
closure of 96
equation list 93–94
parameter list 94
role of the budget constraint 97
theoretical structure of 92, 96
variable list 95
substitution 22, 35, 91, 241, 242
between assets 91
between domestic and foreign goods 35, 241
between primary factors 22, 236
between private and public savings 91

tariffs 1, 19, 20, 51, 115
history of in Australia 221–222
optimal 225
see also tariff cuts, tariff reduction strategies
tariff cuts 221–253
announcement effects 246–247
anticipated 224
dynamic adjustment effects 245–252

efficiency gains from 235
impact on competitiveness 241–242
impact on the real cost of capital 237–238
long run effects of 233–245
phased 224
sectoral implications 243–245
unanticipated 224
see also tariff reduction strategies
tariff reduction strategies 221–253
description of 221, 223–224
implications for structural adjustment 250–252
long run implications of 233–245
main results 257
modelling of 223–224
taxes 4, 6, 7, 15, 17, 27–29, 51, 54, 56–58, 153
see also sales taxes
taste change 24
technical change 24, 32–33
agricultural-land-saving 32–33
capital-saving 32–33
labour-saving 32–33
terminal conditions 25–26, 40, 46, 91, 96, 126
for foreign liabilities 40–41, 96
for sectoral capital stocks 46, 153
terms of trade 101, 103
and the budget constraint 103
and the foreign demand elasticity 101
impact of government spending on
impact of tariff cuts on 237, 238, 243, 252
time-to-build 43, 104, 108
see also capital creation, investment technology
trade balance 41, 53, 186, 200, 204, 207, 208
and the real exchange rate 186, 201, 212
impact of debt constraint on 41
impact of government spending on 186, 196, 200, 207, 211
impact of tariff cuts 242
transversality condition 106
see also terminal condition
two-point boundary value problem 126, 128
solution of 126
see also solution method

uncertainty 109, 163, 258
see also investment
uncovered interest parity 51, 96, 186, 208
unit costs 33, 35, 38, 49, 50, 51
see also zero pure profits
utility function 10, 11, 12, 36, 38–39, 247
aggregation across households 35–36
homotheticity of 156
Stone-Geary 36
utility maximisation 9, 14, 35–40
intertemporal 39–40
static 35–38

wages 5, 56, 252, 244, 250
see also labour, prices

zero pure profts 27, 33, 49–52
in capital creation 50
in exporting 50–51
in importing 51
in production 50

List of Tables

1.1:	Comparison of ORANI-INT with Four State-Of-The-Art Models	10
2.1:	Notational Conventions	22
A3.1.1:	A Log-Linear Representation of the ORANI-INT Equation System	62
A3.1.2:	The Variables in ORANI-INT	82
A3.1.3:	The Parameters in ORANI-INT	90
A3.2.1:	The Stylised Model's Equations	93
A3.2.2:	The Stylised Model's Parameters	94
A3.2.3:	The Stylised Model's Variables	95
A3.2.4:	The Stylised Model's Exogenous Variables	96
A3.2.5:	The Steady-state Form of the Stylised Model	99
A3.2.6:	The Log-linear Form of the Stylised Model's Steady State	100
A3.2.7:	Plausible Values for the Stylised Model's Parameters	103
A3.2.8:	Elasticities of Selected Variables with Respect to the Exogenous Variables	103
5.3.1:	The Standard Closure of ORANI-INT	154
5.3.2:	Sectoral Investment-capital Ratios and Rates of Return	160
A5.1.1:	A Description of the Flows in Figure A5.1.1.	169
A5.1.2:	Sectors, Commodities and their Identifiers	171
A5.1.3:	Sundry Data Items (not in the PMH Database)	171
A5.1.4:	Parameter Values	171
A5.1.5:	Flows of Domestic Commodities into Current Production (BAS1D*)	172
A5.1.6:	Flows of Imported Commodities into Current Production (BAS1M*)	172
A5.1.7:	Flows of Domestic Commodities into Capital Creation (BAS2D*)	173
A5.1.8:	Flows of Imported Commodities into Capital Creation (BAS2M*)	173
A5.1.9:	Taxes on Flows of Domestic Commodities into Current Production (TAX1D)	174
A5.1.10:	Taxes on Flows of Imported Commodities into Current Production (TAX1M)	174
A5.1.11:	Taxes on Flows of Domestic Commodities into Capital Creation (TAX2D)	175
A5.1.12:	Taxes on Flows of Imported Commodities into Capital Creation (TAX2M)	175
A5.1.13:	Sundry Commodity Flows and Indirect Taxes	176
A5.1.14:	Flows of Primary Factors, 'Other Costs' and the Asset Value of Capital Stocks	176
A5.1.15:	Changes to Commodity Flows	178
A5.1.16:	Changes to Industry Flows	179
A5.1.17:	Changes to Sectoral Variables	180
A5.1.18:	Sundry Adjustments to Database	181
A5.1.19:	Sectoral Investment-Capital Ratios and Rates of Return	181
6.2.1:	Key Feature of the Five Illustrative Simulations	183

List of Figures

2.1:	Schematic Representation of ORANI-INT	26
3.1:	Specification of Production Technology	31
3.2:	Specification of Household Utility	37
3.3:	Technology for Creating Capital	48
A3.4.1:	A Hypothetical Investment Plan	113
A3.4.2:	The Construction Sector's Capital and Investment Paths	116
A3.4.3:	The Asset Value and Cost of the Construction Sector's Capital	116
A3.4.4:	The Rental Value and Cost of the Construction Sector's Capital	116
4.1:	The Johansen or 1-Step Euler Method	132
4.2:	Euler Multi-step Method	134
4.3:	Euler Method: A Pathological Case	135
4.4:	Three Step Euler Method Where the Initial Solution is Unknown and Exogenous Variable X is Held Constant	137
4.5:	Three Step Euler Method: Initial Solution Unknown and Exogenous Variables X set to Forecast Values	138
4.6:	Three Iteration Standard Newton-Raphson Method	140
4.7:	Hybrid Method	142
4.8:	Sign Constraints	147
5.1:	CBG Scenario Projections for Selected Real Macro Variables	158
5.2:	CBG Scenario Projections for Selected Deflators	158
5.3:	CBG Scenario Projections for Sectoral Activity Levels	159
A5.1.1:	A Schematic Representation of the PMH Database	168
6.3.1:	Division of the 30 Year Horizon into Four Sub-intervals	185
6.4.2:	Benchmark Simulation Projections for Selected Real Macro Variables	187
6.4.3:	Benchmark Simulation Projections for Selected Deflators	187
6.4.4:	Benchmark Simulation Projections for Sectoral Activity Levels	188
6.5.1:	Investment Simulation Projections for Selected Real Macro Variables	198
6.5.2:	Investment Simulation Projections for Selected Deflators	198
6.5.3:	Investment Simulation Projections for Sectoral Activity Levels	199
6.6.1:	Consumption Simulation Projections for Selected Real Macro Variables	205
6.6.2:	Consumption Simulation Projections for Selected Deflators	205
6.6.3:	Consumption Simulation Projections for Sectoral Activity Levels	206
6.7.1:	Full Intertemporal Simulation Projections for Selected Real Macro Variables	213
6.7.2:	Full Intertemporal Simulation Projections for Selected Deflators	213
6.7.3:	Full Intertemporal Simulation Projections for Sectoral Activity	214
6.8.1:	Surprise Simulation Projections for Selected Real Macro Variables	217
6.8.2:	Surprise Simulation Projections for Selected Deflators	217
6.8.3:	Surprise Simulation Projections for Sectoral Activity	218

7.2.1: Price of the Imported Manufacturing Commodity 224
7.3.M1: Real GDP 226
7.3.M2: Real Consumption 226
7.3.M3: Real Aggregate Investment 226
7.3.M4: Real Aggregate Capital Stock 226
7.3.M5: Aggregate Export Volumes 227
7.3.M6: Aggregate Import Volumes 227
7.3.P1: GDP Deflator 227
7.3.P2: Investment Price Deflator 227
7.3.P3: Export Price Deflator 228
7.3.P4: Factor Cost Deflator 228
7.3.P5: Rental Price of Capital Deflator 228
7.3.P6: Price of Labour 228
7.3.P7: Above-subsistence Consumption Deflator 229
7.3.P8: Consumption Deflator 229
7.3.E1: Rural Exports 229
7.3.E2: Mining Exports 229
7.3.E3: Manufacturing Exports 230
7.3.I1: Manufacturing Imports 230
7.3.I2: Mining Imports 230
7.3.S1: Rural Output 231
7.3.S2: Mining Output 231
7.3.S3: Manufacturing Output 231
7.3.S4: Utilities Output 231
7.3.S5: Construction Output 232
7.3.S6 Wholesale & Retail Trade Output 232
7.3.S7: Transport Output 232
7.3.S8: Finance Output 232
7.3.S9: Housing Output 233
7.3.S10: Personal Services Output 233

Contributions to Economics

Sabine Spangenberg
The Institutionalised Transformation of the East German Economy
1998. ISBN 3-7908-1103-3

Hagen Bobzin
Indivisibilities
1998. ISBN 3-7908-1123-8

Helmut Wagner (Ed.)
Current Issues in Monetary Economics
1998. ISBN 3-7908-1127-0

Peter Michaelis/Frank Stähler (Eds.)
Recent Policy Issues in Environmental and Resource Economics
1998. ISBN 3-7908-1137-8

Jessica de Wolff
The Political Economy of Fiscal Decisions
1998. ISBN 3-7908-1130-0

Georg Bol/Gholamreza Nakhaeizadeh/ Karl-Heinz Vollmer (Eds.)
Risk Measurements, Econometrics and Neural Networks
1998. ISBN 3-7908-1152-1

Joachim Winter
Investment and Exit Decisions at the Plant Level
1998. ISBN 3-7908-1154-8

Bernd Meyer
Intertemporal Asset Pricing
1999. ISBN 3-7908-1159-9

Uwe Walz
Dynamics of Regional Integration
1999. ISBN 3-7908-1185-8

Michael Carlberg
European Monetary Union
1999. ISBN 3-7908-1191-2

Giovanni Galizzi/ Luciano Venturini (Eds.)
Vertical Relationships and Coordination in the Food System
1999. ISBN 3-7908-1192-0

Gustav A. Horn/Wolfgang Scheremet/ Rudolf Zwiener
Wages and the Euro
1999. ISBN 3-7908-1199-8

Dirk Willer
The Development of Equity Capital Markets in Transition Economies
1999. ISBN 3-7908-1198-X

Karl Matthias Weber
Innovation Diffusion and Political Control of Energy Technologies
1999. ISBN 3-7908-1205-6

Heike Link et al.
The Costs of Road Infrastructure and Congestion in Europe
1999. ISBN 3-7908-1201-3

Simon Duindam
Military Conscription
1999. ISBN 3-7908-1203-X

Bruno Jeitziner
Political Economy of the Swiss National Bank
1999. ISBN 3-7908-1209-9

Irene Ring et al. (Eds.)
Regional Sustainability
1999. ISBN 3-7908-1233-1

Katharina Müller/Andreas Ryll/ Hans-Jürgen Wagener (Eds.)
Transformation of Social Security: Pensions in Central-Eastern Europe
1999. ISBN 3-7908-1210-2

Stefan Traub
Framing Effects in Taxation
1999. ISBN 3-7908-1240-4

Pablo Coto-Millán
Utility and Production
1999. 3-7908-1153-X

Frank Riedel
Imperfect Information and Investor Heterogeneity in the Bond Market
2000. ISBN 3-7908-1247-1

Kirsten Ralf
Business Cycles
2000. ISBN 3-7908-1245-5

Michele Bagella/Leonardo Becchetti (Eds.)
The Competitive Advantage of Industrial Districts
2000. ISBN 3-7908-1254-4

Frank Bohn
Monetary Union and Fiscal Stability
2000. ISBN 3-7908-1266-8